STUDIES
IN
MEANING
3

Also available from Pace University Press

Studies in Meaning:
Exploring Constructivist Psychology
(2002)

Studies in Meaning 2:
Bridging the Personal and Social
in Constructivist Psychology
(2004)

www.pace.edu/press

STUDIES IN MEANING 3: CONSTRUCTIVIST PSYCHOTHERAPY IN THE REAL WORLD

Edited by
Jonathan D. Raskin
State University of New York at New Paltz

and

Sara K. Bridges
The University of Memphis

Pace University Press
2008

Copyright © 2008 by
Pace University Press
One Pace Plaza
New York NY 10038

ISBN 0-944473-86-5

Table of Contents

Contributors   viii

Preface   xi

PART I
CONSTRUCTIVIST PSYCHOTHERAPY:
AN INTRODUCTION

1. Constructivist Psychotherapy in the Real World   3
   Sara K. Bridges and Jonathan D. Raskin

2. Epistemological Commitments Among Seasoned   31
   Psychotherapists: Some Practical Implications
   of Being a Constructivist
   *Greg J. Neimeyer, Jocelyn Lee, Gizem Aksoy-Toska, and
   Daniel Phillip*

PART II
APPLYING CONSTRUCTIVIST THERAPY
IN EVERYDAY PRACTICE

3. Coherence Therapy: Swift Change at the Roots of   57
   Symptom Production
   Bruce Ecker and Laurel Hulley

4. Mind and Self in Context-Centered Psychotherapy   85
   Jay S. Efran and José Soler-Baillo

5. Embodiment in Experiential Personal Construct   107
   Psychotherapy: Theoretical and Technical Concerns
   Larry M. Leitner and April J. Faidley

PART III
CONSTRUCTIVIST THERAPY FOR SPECIFIC ISSUES

6. Meaning and Change with Domestic Abusers   127
    James Horley and Amy Johnson

7. A Constructivist Approach to Child-Centered   145
    Play Therapy
    Richard E. Watts and Yvonne Garza

8. Talking Back to Stuttering: Constructivist   165
    Contributions to Stuttering Treatment
    Anthony DiLollo and Robert A. Neimeyer

9. Methods of Reconstruction with Adolescent   183
    Substance Abusers: Combining REBT and
    Constructivism
    Robert Adelman

10. Constructivist Treatment of Divorce   201
    Donald K. Granvold

PART IV
PROFESSIONAL ISSUES IN CONSTRUCTIVIST THERAPY

11. Personal Construct Psychotherapy in a National   229
    Health Service Setting: Does Survival Mean
    Selling Out?
    David A. Winter

12. Counseling Multiracial Clients in Context: 253
    A Constructivist Approach
    Ronnie Priest and Nancy Nishimura

13. When Constructs Collide: Constructivist   273
    Research on When and How to Challenge Clients
    Daniel C. Williams and Heidi M. Levitt

PART V
CONSTRUING CONSTRUCTIVIST
THERAPY IN EVERYDAY LIFE

14. Everyday Constructivism   295
    Michael F. Hoyt

15. Looking for the Context: Therapy as Social Critique   329
    Mark Eliot Paris

About the Editors   361
Appendix   362
Index of Proper Names   364
Subject Index   373

Contributors

Robert Adelman, Independent Practice and Sundown Ranch, Canton, Texas, USA

Gizem Aksoy-Toska, Department of Psychology, University of Florida, Gainesville, Florida, USA

Sara K. Bridges, Department of Counseling, Educational Psychology and Research, The University of Memphis, Tennessee, USA

Anthony DiLollo, Department of Communication Sciences and Disorders, Wichita State University, Wichita, Kansas, USA

Bruce Ecker, Independent Practice, Oakland, California, USA

Jay S. Efran, Department of Psychology, Temple University, Philadelphia, Pennsylvania, USA

April J. Faidley, Meridian Psychological Associates, Indianapolis, Indiana, USA

Yvonne Garza, Department of Educational Leadership and Counseling, Sam Houston State University, Huntsville, Texas, USA

Donald Granvold, School of Social Work, The University of Texas at Arlington, USA

James Horley, Department of Psychology, Augustana University College, Camrose, Alberta, Canada

Michael Hoyt, Kaiser Permanente Medical Center, San Rafael, California, USA

Laurel Hulley, Independent Practice, Oakland, California, USA

Amy Johnson, Wetaskiwin Regional Public Schools, Wetaskiwin, Alberta, Canada

Jocelyn Lee, Department of Psychology, University of Florida, Gainesville, Florida, USA

Larry M. Leitner, Department of Psychology, Miami University, Oxford, Ohio, USA

Heidi M. Levitt, Department of Psychology, The University of Memphis, Tennessee, USA

Greg J. Neimeyer, Department of Psychology, University of Florida, Gainesville, Florida, USA

Robert A. Neimeyer, Department of Psychology, The University of Memphis, Tennessee, USA

Nancy Nishimura, Department of Counseling, Educational Psychology and Research, The University of Memphis, Tennessee, USA

Mark Eliot Paris, Department of Counselor Education, University of Florida, Gainesville, Florida, USA

Daniel Phillip, Department of Psychology, University of Florida, Gainesville, Florida, USA

Ronnie Priest, Department of Counseling, Educational Psychology and Research, The University of Memphis, Tennessee, USA

Jonathan D. Raskin, Department of Psychology, State University of New York at New Paltz, New York, USA

José Soler-Baillo, Department of Psychology, Temple University, Philadelphia, Pennsylvania, USA

Richard E. Watts, Department of Educational Leadership and Counseling, Sam Houston State University, Huntsville, Texas, USA

Daniel C. Williams, Addictive Disorders Treatment Program, G.V. (Sonny) Montgomery VAMC, Mississippi, USA

David A. Winter, Department of Psychology, University of Hertfordshire and Barnet, Enfield and Haringey Mental Health Trust, Hertfordshire, UK

Preface

Constructivist psychotherapy endeavors to help people change the frameworks of meaning by which they conceptualize themselves, others, and life in general. Despite offering a variety of very innovative and practical therapeutic approaches and techniques, constructivist therapy remains somewhat unfamiliar to many clinicians. Perhaps this is due to constructivism often being perceived (unfairly in our view) as overly philosophical—and thus as not something readily translated into practice. This is unfortunate because constructivist therapists, with their pragmatic emphasis on assisting people to develop more effective ways of understanding and maneuvering through problems in living, are very much invested in practical interventions.

In this volume, we proudly present contributions by constructivist therapists who share our conviction that constructivist therapy is well-suited to the expediencies of everyday clinical practice. All the contributors were invited to write chapters that present practical applications of constructivist therapy. The volume's playful subtitle, "Constructivist Psychotherapy in the Real World," challenges the idea that constructivists refuse to concern themselves with the real world. It also reflects our desire to share with readers the versatile ways constructivist approaches to therapy can be utilized in everyday life. Constructivist therapy often gets labeled as too theoretical and lacking in clinical specificity. Yet here is a volume that counters that with chapters that succinctly and understandably explicate basic theoretical concepts and then demonstrate them with vivid case examples taken from applied experience in the field.

Part I of the volume presents two initial chapters. The first (Bridges & Raskin) introduces basic approaches to and issues in constructivist psychotherapy, while the second (G. J. Neimeyer et al.)

reviews how an epistemological commitment to constructivism has important implications for the consulting room. Part II expands on this, outlining in detail three different types of constructivist therapy: coherence therapy (Ecker & Hulley), context-centered therapy (Efran & Soler-Baillo), and experiential personal construct therapy (Leitner & Faidely). Part III shifts from types of constructivist therapy to how a constructivist approach informs work with particular clinical problems, including domestic abuse (Horley & Johnson), play therapy with children (Watts & Garza), stuttering (DiLollo & R. A. Neimeyer), adolescent substance abuse (Adelman), and divorce (Granvold). Part IV tackles a number of commonly encountered professional issues: practicing within the constraints of a large health care system (Winter), working with multiracial clients (Priest & Nishimura), and knowing when and how to challenge clients (Williams & Levitt). Finally, Part V wraps up the volume by examining the presence of constructivism in everyday life (Hoyt) and exploring the powerful implications for thinking about constructivist therapy as a form of social critique (Paris).

We wish to acknowledge Mark Hussey at Pace University Press for his continued support and patience. Special thanks go to those who helped with page proofing: Stephen Walko, Elise Grant, Melanie Harasym, and Samantha Daniel. We also are grateful to our respective spouses (Shay and Eric) and children (Ari, Noa, and Jacob) for their patience as we worked on this volume. We also thank readers and hope they find herein an exciting portrayal of constructivist psychotherapy in the real world.

Finally, the constructivist community has lost several seminal figures since the last *Studies in Meaning* volume appeared. We would like to dedicate this volume to the memories of the following colleagues whose contributions to constructivist and narrative psychotherapy have been immeasurable: Michael J. Mahoney, James C. Mancuso, María Laura Nuzzo, Tom Ravenette, Phillida Salmon, and Theodore R. Sarbin. They will be missed, but their work lives on in our constructions of it.

Jonathan D. Raskin   Sara K. Bridges
New Paltz, New York   *Memphis, Tennessee*

September, 2007

PART I

CONSTRUCTIVIST PSYCHOTHERAPY: AN INTRODUCTION

⒈ 1 ⒊

Constructivist Psychotherapy
in the Real World

Sara K. Bridges and Jonathan D. Raskin

Constructivist psychology, in its broadest contours, focuses on how people create ways to understand and conceptualize themselves, their relationships, and their surroundings. It emphasizes the personal and social meanings that people develop to organize their experience and guide their lives (Gergen, 1985, 1994; Kelly, 1955/1991a, 1955/1991b; Mahoney, 1991; Maturana & Poerksen, 2004; Maturana & Varela, 1992; von Glaserfeld, 1995). When these meanings cease being helpful and generative in daily life, problems in living arise. Constructivist psychotherapy, then, focuses on helping people examine and reconsider their constructed understandings, with a view towards encouraging the development of alternative understandings that potentially open up new life possibilities (Ecker & Hulley, 1996; Efran, Lukens, & Lukens, 1990; Eron & Lund, 1996; Mahoney, 2003; McNamee & Gergen, 1992; R. A. Neimeyer & Mahoney, 1995; R. A. Neimeyer & Raskin, 2000b; Sexton & Griffin, 1997; White & Epston, 1990; Winter & Viney, 2005). That is, constructivist psychotherapy has very practical ends, namely helping clients devise new solutions to life difficulties by encouraging them to examine their current ways of understanding themselves and their problems and, in turn, experimenting with alternatives.

Yet constructivist psychotherapy has a reputation for being somewhat abstract and difficult to grasp (R. A. Neimeyer, 1997). The philosophical underpinnings of constructivist theory, emphasizing epistemological arguments about truth and reality, sometimes act as a barrier to therapists interested in exploring new avenues to working more effectively with their clients. This is not surprising. After all, most psychotherapists have pressing concerns that make debates over how people know or understand reality seem far removed from the necessities of everyday clinical practice. Consequently, constructivist psychotherapy has sometimes been dismissed for its perceived lack of coherence and relevance to everyday practice (Held, 1995). Yet dismissing any approach to therapy outright because of the perceived complexity of its theoretical foundations is unfortunate. Constructivist therapy has a great deal to offer both in its rich theoretical foundations and also in its coherent approaches to the process of psychotherapy. While the implications of constructivist theory for psychotherapy have been outlined more comprehensively elsewhere (e.g. Ecker & Hulley, 1996; Epting, 1984; Hoyt, 1994, 1996; Mahoney, 2003; McNamee, 1996; R. A. Neimeyer & Mahoney, 1995; R. A. Neimeyer & Raskin, 2000b; Sexton & Griffin, 1997; White & Epston, 1990; Winter & Viney, 2005), this chapter marks an attempt to highlight five specific constructivist clinical strategies therapists can adopt, along with four constructivist-influenced suggestions for everyday practice. The goal is to present theories in their broadest contours, with attention primarily paid to their practical implications.

CONSTRUCTIVIST PSYCHOTHERAPY IN THE REAL WORLD: MEANING-BASED PRACTICE

Dealing with the Real World

Constructivist psychology studies how people psychologically construe the world (Chiari & Nuzzo, 1996; Kelly, 1955/1991a, 1955/1991b; Mahoney, 1991; Raskin & Bridges, 2002; Sexton & Griffin, 1997). It assumes that the number of possible ways to construe things is unlimited and that very different constructions can often be viable for different people (Kelly, 1955/1991a, 1955/1991b). This has very practical and relevant implications for everyday clinical practice, hence our use of the phrase *constructivist psychotherapy in the real world*. Of course, we are well aware that many people do not think constructivist psychologists believe in a real world (Held, 1995). That is, constructivist critics lament constructivism's supposed rejection of reality—in other words, its alleged antirealism (Held, 1995). However, we do not consider constructivism as necessarily antirealist, nor do we accept the claim that any approach suggesting that people only know the world from an embedded perspective is unable to assert a theory of how things are. To the contrary, when constructivists assert something as true, they simply pay more explicit attention to the foundational postulates from which their truth claims spring (Butt, 2000; Edwards, Ashmore, & Potter, 1995; R. A. Neimeyer, 1997; Raskin, 2001). Yes, some constructivist theorists question whether what people know can ever reproduce the real world verbatim; others even go so far as to endorse the idealist view that what we experience as reality is all in our heads (Chiari & Nuzzo, 1996). However, what critics often overlook is that constructivist psychotherapists are generally not too interested in epistemological debates intended to pin down the nature of reality in some sort of final way. Rather, constructivist therapists, in keeping with their practical aims, are generally much more interested in the *experiential realities* of their clients—people's ever-changing, deeply personal and unique meanings. Thus, from a therapeutic perspective, settling on what is really real is a lot less important than the constructivist assertion that each of us believes quite strongly in our own experiential reality. It is working with each client's distinctive experiential reality that forms the nucleus of constructivist psychotherapy.

Meaning-Based Practice

Constructivist psychotherapy constitutes a form of *meaning-based practice* (Raskin, 2007). Put simply, meaning-based practice (MBP) focuses on helping clients change the meanings they use to guide their lives. It is not driven by a particular technique or singular theory of client change. Regardless of the therapeutic strategies used, MBP practitioners emphasize the transformation of client meanings because they assume that how clients make sense of empirical experience is as (or more) important than events in and of themselves. This is in contrast with the medical model, which tends to see client problems as discrete disorders with common underlying meanings that produce them or, even worse, little to no rhyme or reason to them at all. In the latter instance, symptom reduction becomes the focus of treatment and client meanings are minimized or ignored completely (Raskin, 2007).

Constructivist therapy is an excellent example of meaning-based practice because it assumes that how clients meaningfully construe events is central to their psychological functioning (Raskin, 2007). After all, how people construe things frames, organizes, and

5

structures their experience. When, for whatever reason, people construe things in new ways, their experience necessarily changes, too. Therefore, constructivist psychotherapy stresses how personal and social meanings psychologically shape and guide clients. When clients seek therapy, they are unhappy with their current ways of meaningfully construing life. This is not to say that life events themselves are irrelevant. Surely someone living in poverty has reason to construe the situation negatively. However, constructivist therapy emphasizes how clients might unlock new possibilities by entertaining novel ways of construing events; it is when we construe in fresh ways that new prospects for understanding and action often reveal themselves to us. Further, for many practitioners constructivist therapy also involves working with clients to understand the origins of personal constructs or ways of making meaning, with the idea that this kind of insight often leads to therapeutic change. The five constructivist therapies presented below, along with their associated clinical strategies, make meaning transformation the center of therapeutic work.

FIVE CLINICAL STRATEGIES FOR CONSTRUCTIVIST PSYCHOTHERAPISTS

Strategy #1: Have the Client Adopt a Fixed-Role (Personal Construct Psychotherapy)

Personal construct psychotherapy grows out of George Kelly's (1955/1991a; 1955/1991b) seminal *personal construct theory*. Kelly was one of the first psychotherapists to develop a full-fledged personality theory rooted in the assumption that it is how people make sense of things, not things themselves, that structures psychological experience. What people know is constituted in their construing rather than in events themselves. Along these lines, Kelly posited that experience is not a window on the world-as-it-is, but rather something that gets shaped, pruned, filtered, and organized by the person. People do this by devising sets of interrelated *personal constructs*, which are bipolar dimensions of meaning, each divided into an idea and its perceived opposite. Kelly saw constructs as bipolar because he believed that in order to define what something is, one needs to define what it is not. Each person devises a unique set of personal constructs to organize and make sense of lived experience. Importantly for

6

Kelly, there are an unlimited number of ways one can construe events. Thus, what makes a construct effective is its workability in everyday life. Different people under different circumstances may develop very different, but nevertheless equally effective, constructs for dealing with similar circumstances. From a therapeutic point of view, therefore, what matters most is not whether constructs best "match" an external state of affairs, but whether they are proving satisfactory and effective in helping a client get by in daily life. Personal construct psychotherapy focuses, then, on helping clients to (1) gain understanding of the rational, affective, and bodily ways in which they construe themselves, their relationships, and their lives; and (2) experiment with new and more personally rewarding and effective ways to construe things.

Personal construct psychotherapists are clinically rather eclectic, seeing all counseling theories and their resulting therapy techniques as potentially generative construct systems that therapists apply in meaningfully comprehending and addressing their clients' problems. If a particular theoretical conceptualization or clinical strategy seems like it might prove helpful with a client, personal construct therapists have no qualms using it and encourage other therapists to do the same. However, this does not imply an unreflective eclecticism; in the spirit of assimilative integration (Lampropoulos, 2001; Messer, 2001), personal construct therapists make clear that any technique imported from another theoretical vantage point must be conceptualized as a momentarily useful clinical construction rather than a universal clinical truth (Raskin, 2007). In this way, PCP therapy is not technique-driven because every technique is simply one constructive alternative a therapist is free to try.

The one specific clinical procedure unique to personal construct therapy is *fixed-role therapy*. In fixed-role therapy, the client is asked to write a "character sketch" describing him or herself in the third person. Then, the therapist (sometimes alone, sometimes in conjunction with the client), subtly alters the sketch in an important way and assigns it a new name. The client is then instructed to "play" the part of this new "character" across a set period of time (usually a week or two). This kind of behavioral experiment, known as a *fixed-role enactment*, allows clients to test out new ways of being without the guilt of violating their core sense of self. After all, they are only acting! By behaving in new ways, clients come to have different experiences in the world. They often incorporate into their everyday lives the new ways of construing that accompany these new behaviors. Echoes of fixed-role therapy are heard in many of the more recent solution-focused therapies, which actively encourage clients to "do one thing different" (O'Hanlon, 1999). Such therapies institute fixed-role principles much more informally, but still owe a great debt to George Kelly and personal construct psychotherapy.

For example, consider the case of Nina, a 35-year old married mother of a one-year old daughter. Nina presented feeling stressed about caring for her daughter and getting along with her husband; when she would fight with her husband over childcare issues, she felt their marriage was in jeopardy. Across the first few sessions, it became apparent that Nina's childhood was riddled with abuse from her father, which was regularly enabled by her mother. Because her parents regularly told Nina that she was the reason her father often became angry, Nina came to construe herself as blameworthy and responsible when others seemed unhappy. Disagreeing with others was, justifiably, construed as extremely dangerous.

Fixed-role therapy was undertaken. Nina's fixed-role enactment required her to "play" the part of "Ruth," a woman much more confident in herself and her beliefs than Nina. Unlike Nina, "Ruth" did not construe disagreement as dangerous or as indicating a relationship was no good. Nina played the part of "Ruth" during a week in which her parents came to visit. Now elderly, her father had not been physical with Nina in many years. However, both he and Nina's mother continued to strongly dissuade Nina from diverging from their opinions about things. Nina was worried because, during their visit, her parents would see her new rock climbing equipment. Rock climbing was an activity towards which her parents had voiced strong opposition; after all, everyone knew it was simply too dangerous for their daughter! In the past, Nina would have repudiated her love of rock climbing to pacify her parents and keep the peace. However, while enacting the part of "Ruth," Nina experimented with behaving differently. When her mother commented on the foolishness of rock climbing, Nina (as Ruth) simply acknowledged her mother's comment and stated that they should "agree to disagree." To her utmost surprise, rather than getting angry or pressing their point, Nina's parents dropped the subject, never mentioning rock climbing or Nina's new equipment again the rest of their visit.

As a result of her fixed-role enactment, Nina began experiencing disagreement with her parents quite differently. Rather than being a dangerous relationship breaker to be avoided, it gave her influence. Her parents backed off whenever she stood up for her point of view. Further, Nina began generalizing this strategy beyond her relationship with her parents. Negotiating child rearing issues with her husband became a lot easier once it was okay for them to disagree over things. Rather than seeing these disagreements as indicating the impending collapse of the marriage, Nina began to see them as opportunities to talk more freely with her husband—thus strengthening their partnership. For more on fixed-role therapy, see Kelly (1955/1991b, Chp. 8), G. J. Neimeyer (1995, pp. 119–122), and Winter (1992, pp. 268–275).

Strategy #2: Make Unconscious Knowings Conscious (Coherence Therapy)

Coherence therapy, formerly known as depth oriented brief therapy (DOBT; Ecker & Hulley, 1996), is a process of therapy that aims for the unconscious, compelling, coherent reasons for the maintenance of problematic moods, thoughts or behaviors. Similar to PCP in its attention to personal meanings and constructions of reality, coherence therapy emphasizes how these personal, symptom-generating meanings or knowings often constitute unconscious "emotional truths" rather than conscious constructions of reality. Coherence therapists assume an *active, experiential stance* in order to help elicit those aspects of the client's unconscious ways of understanding the world that necessitate the existence of the presenting problem. In other words, the presenting problem is viewed as a form of protection from some other, worse suffering. For example, a client who presents with difficulties establishing a trusting long-term relationship may, through carefully crafted experiential exercises, come to re-experience the painful abandonment he suffered following the break-up with a first love and the emotional truth that was created at that time: "If I let anyone really know me and get close to me, then I am opening myself up yet again to horrible pain that I will not be able to survive."

Coherence therapists are careful not to make interpretations of the underlying emotional truth or meanings that necessitate a client's current trouble. Rather, they experientially help clients to

9

uncover and encounter directly how their troubles are coherently necessary. In this way, coherence therapists look for the client's *pro-symptom position(s)* by directing attention to the personal constructs that support the presence of the symptom, rather than by attending to the many possible ways of counteracting the identified problem, as many therapies recommend.

Once the underlying constructions or emotional truths that support the symptom are identified, coherence therapists help clients to integrate these previously unconscious constructs, meanings, knowings, or feelings into their current conscious constructs. In the above mentioned example of the client who is having difficulty forming intimate relationships, integration experiences could be arranged by writing the following statement on an index card for the client to read twice daily: "The enormous pain of ending a romantic relationship feels unbearable to me. Getting into a trusting romantic relationship and being abandoned again is a risk I can't afford to take. I hate to admit it, but I feel it's better to be alone forever than to suffer that ever again." The index card is designed to help the client stay in touch with and integrate the emotional truth that is necessitating the current system without attempting to counteract it at all.

A fundamental shift or transformation occurs for the client as a result of holding the previously hidden emotional truth maintaining the problem in juxtaposition with some other, quite different knowing that is equally real to the client. In experiencing this juxtaposition, the client is confronted with a dilemma: the symptom-requiring emotional truth and the other, contradictory knowledge of the world cannot both be true. As a result, one of those knowings gets disconfirmed and naturally falls away— typically the unconscious, former emotional truth. In our example, the hidden emotional truth that the pain of a breakup is not survivable might be juxtaposed with current knowledge of the lived experience that he did actually survive a breakup, did not suffer horribly, and is intact. It is likely that through the juxtaposition of these two contradictory knowings, the construct that a breakup is not survivable would not hold up to scrutiny, would no longer feel real, and would dissolve. A revisiting of earlier disconnections or experiences of abandonment could be important in the process. With the disappearance of the emotional truth that made the symptom necessary to have, the symptom ceases to occur.

If a juxtaposition experience does not arise spontaneously following integration of the symptom-requiring emotional truth, coherence therapists help to create it for the client through experiential exercises. It is a tenet of coherence therapy that it is not for the therapist to indicate which of the two juxtaposing knowledges is more true or preferred. The therapist empathizes with both realities and guides the client to find which is experienced as decisively real.

A caveat offered by coherence therapy theorists and practitioners is that often there is more than one unconscious theme or knowing sustaining an unwanted symptom and that the discovery of all the "feeders" for a symptom is a necessary and multifaceted process.

Recent developments in neuroscience and advances in brain imaging have led to an account of the process of coherence therapy in terms of brain functioning. Because emotional implicit knowledge is known to be stored in the limbic system, experiential discovery of emotional truths is believed to access knowings held in neural circuits in that region (Ecker & Toomey, in press; Toomey & Ecker, 2007, in press). Through the integration process described above, the limbic knowledge is brought into conscious, cortical awareness, which produces neural integration of the two brain systems for the knowledge structures involved. Once that is accomplished, it has been proposed that the juxtaposition experience then de-potentiates the subcortical, previously ruling neural pathways through a recently discovered neural process of *reconsolidation*, which can erase neural circuits of emotional conditioning previously thought indelible. The evidence indicating that coherence therapy produces reconsolidation is significant but circumstantial, and direct neural evidence is needed for confirmation. For a more thorough discussion of this topic see Ecker and Hulley (this volume) and a series of three articles published in the *Journal of Constructivist Psychology* (Toomey & Ecker, 2007; Ecker & Toomey, in press; Toomey & Ecker, in press). For more on coherence therapy in general, see Ecker and Hulley (1996, 2000).

*Strategy #3: Help Clients Retell their Stories
(Narrative Therapy)*

Narrative therapy views clients as both the authors and the principal characters in ongoing life stories or narratives that guide how meaning is made. It conceptualizes each person as writing his or her own personal reality or life story. Therefore, narrative therapists build the therapeutic relationship around deconstructing and *restorying* dominant cultural and social narratives that clients have internalized as unassailable truths. As such, narrative therapy strikes us as a clear exemplar of constructivism (White & Epston, 1990).

People create and maintain narratives that are the basis for understanding and making sense of their everyday lives. For example, consider the case of April, a client whose dominant narrative casts her in the role of someone with "low self worth." In April's personal narrative, she portrays herself as emotionally weak, believing that "I am not strong enough to handle crisis or real challenges in life and I must depend on others to do so for me." This becomes the core element of all her narratives, so she often is unaware of times when she does not necessarily succumb to the effects of "low self worth." In situations such as April's, the dominant, albeit problematic, life narrative is viewed as a static, unchanging, and fundamentally true quality of the person. Further, because these dominant life narratives are the lenses through which daily life is experienced, difficulties in life situations become seen as core parts of one's identity rather than as problems emanating from currently accepted self-narratives.

Viewed as part of one's identity, these dominant life narratives are not seen as open to alteration when a client first presents for therapy. Narrative therapists focus on helping clients to explore their problem-saturated stories more fully and to identify the ways in which they actually have agency in re-authoring their dominant life narratives. Often this is done by separating the internal identity of the person from the problem by *externalizing the problem*, a common strategy in narrative therapy.

Externalizing the problem helps a client to know that the "problem is the problem" rather than "I am the problem." For example, consider Jonah and Simone, a married couple who continually fight over financial concerns. A narrative therapist might help Jonah and Simone to see "money" as the problem rather than internalizing the financial stress or placing blame on one another for the financial situation. By consistently using externalizing language, searching for the real effects of money on the couples' life situation, and generating an "allied front" against the negative influences of money, Jonah and Simone are able to author a narrative that places them on the same side against money's negative influence and allows them to resist the blame and shame that had accompanied their conflicts over financial concerns.

As in most constructivist therapy, narrative therapists are careful not to impose their views, instead respecting the unique experience and subjective understandings of each client. Towards this end, narrative therapists inquire about the *relative influence of the problem* (i.e. "How have money problems separated you as a couple?" "How does money act like it's working for you, when it is actually working against you?" "When are you least susceptible to money's negative influence on your relationship?"). At the same time, they also look for *unique outcomes*, times when clients resisted the negative influence of the problem. By taking a collaborative and empathetic position, narrative therapists help clients identify times when they were strong or resourceful in counteracting the dominant problem-saturated narrative while also clearly expressing their understanding of the real effects of the problem.

Often when clients are dominated by problem-saturated stories, small successes and victories are obscured. Therefore, narrative therapists ask questions like, "When was a time when money problems tried to take over but you did not let them?" or "When you have withstood the pressure of money, who in your life has appreciated the enormity of that accomplishment?" in order to start the process of identifying times when the problem did not control them as completely as their dominant narrative might indicate. These *sparkling moments* are amplified by narrative therapists as a starting point for re-authoring life narratives.

In the re-authoring of life narratives, it is important to note that narrative therapists are not simply looking to remove the problem from the client. Instead the goal is for a fundamental shift in dominant life narratives. Continuing the case of Jonah and Simone's money troubles, a therapist might ask questions like, "What does it say about you as a couple that you were able to defeat money's negative influence on those occasions?" or "What else can you tell me about your past to help me understand how you were able to handle money trouble so well?" These questions help the couple to counteract the dominant narrative and replace it with a narrative that better fits with their hopes, desires and potential as a couple.

Once a new narrative is created, narrative therapists are careful to reinforce the new story by helping clients create an "audience" for their new narratives by telling and retelling their new stories, asking about their ability to resist the influence of the problematic narrative between sessions, and providing anchors for the new narrative through letter writing, summarizations and collaborative attempts to celebrate the existence of the new narrative. For further elaboration of this approach to narrative therapy, see Drewery, Winslade, and Monk (2000), Monk, Winslade, Crocket, and Epston (1997), Payne (2006), and White and Epston (1990).

Strategy #4: Narrow the Gap between Client Stories and Behavior (Narrative Solutions Therapy)

Narrative solutions therapy combines aspects of strategic, solution-focused, and narrative therapies with a constructivist emphasis on personal meaning (Eron & Lund, 1996, 2002). In this form of therapy, attention is paid to a client's *preferred view*, which is the way the client ideally wishes to be seen by self and others. Problems often develop when there is a *gap* between a client's preferred view and behavior. Unless a therapist understands a client's preferred view, knowing what constitutes a successful therapeutic outcome is difficult; after all, understanding how a client prefers to be provides a vivid sense of what kinds of things the client needs to do differently. Importantly, narrative solutions therapists assume that clients, unbeknownst to themselves, often have their own solutions to problems. That is, there had to be times in the past when the client was able to behave in ways more (if not wholly) consistent with his or her preferred view. Consequently, therapist questioning typically pushes clients to explore times in the past when they were more successful in living according to their preferred views of self. Such instances are contrasted with times when clients were less able to sustain their preferred view. By discussing the differences between these times, clients begin to (1) become aware of the effective solutions they have sometimes used previously and (2) to incorporate these solutions more extensively into their daily lives.

For example, consider the case of Maureen, a twenty-five year old woman who sought therapy to help her with obesity issues. Maureen was exceedingly overweight and despite dieting and working out at a gym regularly, she found herself unable to shed pounds. As she became more comfortable sharing her feelings in therapy, Maureen's preferred view of herself slowly came into focus. Apparently, Maureen had been sexually assaulted at age thirteen. Not surprisingly, this had been a very traumatic and difficult experience for her. She coped with the experience by not sharing what had happened with anyone; she had borne the burden of this awful experience for all the intervening years. It became clear during therapy that Maureen preferred to see herself as a strong and self-sufficient person who took every step she could to make herself safe. She learned karate and other means of self-defense, avoided intimate relationships of any kind, shared personal details of her life with no one, and made herself physically uninteresting to men by dressing plainly, keeping her hair extremely short, and gaining weight. Thus, although Maureen outwardly stated a desire to lose weight, to do so violated her preferred view of herself as someone who played it safe by being invisible to others—especially men. Though she had sought a great deal of help over the years from many people with expertise in weight loss, none of these people understood how Maureen's weight tied into her preferred view of self. Consequently their interventions, which focused on diet and exercise, repeatedly failed. Almost as bad, Maureen came across as less than motivated to lose weight.

In sessions, Maureen's therapist often wondered aloud how someone who clearly stated that she wanted to lose weight kept doing so many things that undermined the task. This led to many conversations about how Maureen saw herself and—ultimately—led her to disclosing the sexual assault. As Maureen began to process the sexual assault and its impact on her, she began to understand that the preferred view she had long maintained was actually more in line with the overweight person she had become than the thinner one she thought she wished to be. However, as Maureen came to understand how her preferred view of self was intimately related to her maintenance of extra weight, she gained new insight into the situation and could approach it differently. She began to question what it would psychologically mean for her to lose weight and to realize that she either needed to alter her preferred view of self or to give up on losing weight. While Maureen did not immediately begin losing weight, her understanding of her reasons for maintaining it allowed her to cope more effectively with her frustration about it. For more on narrative solutions therapy, see Eron and Lund (1996, 2002).

Strategy #5: Adopt a Not-Knowing Approach
(Social Constructionist Therapy)

As a theory that construes constructs as created through social interactions and language, social constructionist therapy views the therapist's constructions or conceptualizations of a client's problem situation as no more but not less valid or valuable than the client's view. In social constructionist therapy, the language that is used in the session and the language that is used to describe the problem situation are the keys to both how problems are understood and also how problem-saturated narratives are created or co-created.

With a main focus on both the use of language and the influence of social and cultural factors, social constructionist therapy shares a great deal of similarity with multicultural and feminist therapies. These therapies propose that it is impossible to separate the individual from their environments. Therefore, to treat clients as though they do not exist in an environment filled with prejudice, bias, and sociocultural pressure is to treat clients unjustly.

Further, social constructionist therapy tends to focus minimally on the individual self and instead examines the blending of individuals in the social milieu (Martin & Sugarman, 1997). Although truly self-less psychotherapy and practice is somewhat rare, constructionist therapy focuses on interpersonal interactions and social conversation as a means to altering personal theories or constructs and achieving goals. For instance, often role plays, experiential exercises, journal writing and sharing, and systemic observations are used to highlight client theories about the problems that have brought them to therapy. This contrasts with approaches expecting clients to fit into the therapists' theories of problematic situations or diagnostic categories (Gonzalez, Biever, & Gardner, 1994).

In addition to being an approach to therapy that focuses on the social construction of problems and difficulties, social constructionist therapy tends to be a strength based approach (Wong, 2006). In this way, a social constructionist therapist focuses on utilizing the client's strengths rather than simply alleviating client difficulties. This is not to say that underlying biological or psychological difficulties are ignored; rather, by attending to strengths and acknowledging the pervasive negative impact that terminology such as "disorder" and "illness" can have on clients and the views of their potential, social constructionist therapists consider life contexts and the enduring impact diagnosis can have on clients' overall wellbeing (Wong, 2006).

Moreover, by not imposing a preconceived conceptualization of the client's difficulty on the client, the therapeutic process is seen as co-constructed and the therapist is seen as inseparable from the client. Because therapy is seen as co-constructed, great attention is paid to language and how it impacts the socially structured roles derived from the therapeutic process (Anderson & Goolishian, 1988). Additionally, social constructionists posit that all language is created and thus no clear, precise understanding of what is said can be assumed. All statements are open to further interpretation and hidden meanings.

An example of therapy from this perspective comes from a couple's simple description of their roles in their relationship. Harry and Jenny presented for therapy saying that they were constantly in conflict over the parenting of their two young children. Jenny stated that she was "just a housewife" and that it was her role in the family to ensure "the safety and wellbeing of the family." Harry stated that he was the "breadwinner for the family" and that it was also his role in the family to ensure "the safety and wellbeing of the family." Taking a not-knowing approach the therapist helped Harry and Jenny to explore what safety, wellbeing and parenting meant for both of them and how their meanings were influenced by the roles they each played in the family and in a social context.

Jenny's description of being "*just* a housewife" and Harry's description of being the "breadwinner" could have been overlooked from some perspectives by instead privileging the presenting issue of conflicts regarding parenting. It would have been fairly simple to take a straightforward approach to their difficulties by initiating discussions of parenting styles and expectations and to provide didactic information about parenting. However, from a social constructionist perspective, the personal and shared meanings about working either in or outside of the home would be explored—in addition to exploring the meanings surrounding parenting—to see the role these meanings play in the couple's conflict over parenting. For Jenny and Harry the constructions of "worker" versus "staying at home" were not as shared as they had thought when starting therapy.

Harry was finding his way between two worlds. The first was one in which having a "mom" at home was favored over having "someone else raise your kids." It was important to work and make as much money as possible to allow Jenny to be at home while the children were young. Yet Harry also existed in a second world where he valued being an active and involved parent and absolutely did not want to be an absent father, as his own father had been.

17

At the same time, Jenny truly understood how fortunate she was to not "have to work" and while she did not take this for granted, she had formed an understanding of women in the world through her undergraduate degree in psychology and women's studies and through her own mother's success as a CEO of a large corporation. While she believed that it was both parents' role to raise children, she personally could not justify letting Harry dictate how she parented during the day when it was her "job" to take care of the household while he worked. Although the couple had agreed on the role of work while the children were young, taking a not-knowing approach allowed the therapist to help the couple to elaborate their shared and personal meanings about work and family and thereby unearth a multifaceted power struggle between the couple. Once the struggle was brought into the open, it was then possible to explore revisions of their shared meanings and move forward from their stuck positions. For more information on social constructionist therapy see Gergen (1994), Gergen and McNamee (2000), McNamee (1996), McNamee and Gergen (1992), and Wong (2006).

FOUR CONSTRUCTIVIST-INFLUENCED SUGGESTIONS

Rationality is in the Eye of the Construer

Most constructivist therapists reject the idea that any one person or therapist has an unfaltering grasp of what is or is not rational for another person. Constructivist therapists honor the experiences and rationality of clients whether or not the client's rationality happens to match the therapist's. Does this mean that constructivists must believe that all clients' ways of making sense of their difficulties or life experiences are rational? Not at all—and yet constructivist therapists do endeavor to understand the idiographic rationality that is held by the client, and to see the world through the "eyes of the construer" even if only for the 50-minute therapy hour. Further, constructivist therapists—even when they challenge client constructions—always help clients to explore their own constructions of rationality and to decide for themselves whether their ways of understanding life situations continue to work for them (e.g. are rational) or perhaps have lost their utility and merit revision. The key here is that it is not for the therapist to decide for clients, but rather for clients to decide for themselves, with the therapist working as a collaborator.

Often clients present for therapy so deeply entrenched in their difficulties and "rational" way of viewing their life situations that not only are they isolated from any possible alternatives, but also they often are unaware that their view of the difficulties is itself a construction. In these situations, a constructivist therapist might help the client to consider possible alternatives by offering a variety of possibilities or ways of understanding the difficulties. Of course, when alternatives are overtly offered, it is done with the clear caveat that the choice of alternatives or even keeping the personally nonpreferred way of viewing the difficulties remains firmly within the client's purview. Further, often clients loosen their hold on their construction of what is rational simply as a result of exploring possible alternatives. This is particularly evident in the case of Mark, a somewhat forlorn man in his early thirties who came to therapy for issues related to his job choice and the ongoing care of his invalid father.

In the course of therapy, Mark revealed that he believed it was his "lot in life" to live with his father and never form an intimate meaningful relationship. To Mark, it was completely rational to believe that no partner could ever be happy living with him and his father, nor could he ever expect a partner to accommodate to his unusual living arrangement. Thus, Mark would go out with women a few times, and then suddenly become "unavailable" when things started to look like they might get more serious. For Mark, opening himself up to the possibility of a meaningful relationship meant also opening himself up to rejection and abandonment once the potential partner discovered his situation with his father. Thus, he never risked disclosing his living arrangement to his dates, inviting women to his home, or breaking his personal pledge to be very private and as vague as possible about his past. Instead he would constantly keep the focus of conversations on "light" topics or on his date rather than himself.

As the therapist began to understand Mark's assertion that rejection and abandonment were rational expectations, she was able to gently offer possible alternatives to help Mark extend the range of possibilities available to him. Additionally, as an indirect consequence of the interactions with the therapist, Mark's rigid constructions concerning the risk associated with disclosure subtly loosened and what had previously seemed rational to Mark began to look somewhat different than it had before. Mark's view of rationality was never overtly questioned. Instead, by seeing rationality through Mark's eyes while keeping a firm hold of her own personal view of rationality, the therapist was able to envision some alternatives that Mark had not yet been able to consider. By offering these alternatives as mere possibilities, Mark was able to make choices that fit his way of understanding the world. Mark shifted his constructions of rationality without surrendering to those held by his therapist.

Diagnoses are Just Constructs

Because constructivist therapy places idiographic meaning at the center of psychological realities, it is not surprising that constructivist therapists are often uncomfortable with (and sometimes downright hostile to) traditional psychiatric diagnosis as exemplified in the American Psychiatric Association's (2000) *Diagnostic and Statistical Manual of Mental Disorders* (DSM) (Duffy, Gillig, Tureern, & Ybarra, 2002; Gaines, 1992; Gergen & McNamee, 2000; Honos-Webb & Leitner, 2001; Leitner & Faidley, 2002; Perez-Alvarez & Garcia-Montes, 2007; Raskin & Epting, 1993; Raskin & Lewandowski, 2000). The DSM's authors tend to see mental disorders as universal disease entities that are discovered rather than constructed. By contrast, constructivist therapists usually see mental disorders as socially constructed categories used to make sense of confusing clients. Further, constructivist therapists are quick to stress that different people with similar symptoms (and therefore the same DSM diagnosis) often hold very different underlying psychological constructions. Thus, once constructivist therapists shift from symptoms to meaning, the utility of DSM diagnoses declines markedly for them.

This does not mean that constructivist therapists never use diagnostic labels such as those found in the DSM. In the course of everyday practice, constructivist clinicians are similar to many clinicians. However reluctantly, they often find themselves needing to use DSM language when communicating with insurance companies, the legal system, and more medical-model oriented colleagues (R. A. Neimeyer & Raskin, 2000a). Though constructivist therapists remain aware of the stigmatizing aspects of psychiatric diagnosis and understand the long term implications of applying a diagnosis to an individual, they do use the DSM. Yet constructivist therapists remember that (1) diagnoses (even those in the DSM!) are just constructs, and (2) others often overlook the constructed nature of DSM categories and in so doing sometimes lock people into reified and unhelpful views of themselves and others. That is, rather than seeing the DSM as containing universally valid, once-and-for-all categories of disorder that correspond in some kind of one-to-one way with the world itself, constructivists see the DSM as a complex professional construct system that is helpful at times and harmful at others. Constructivist therapists remain attentive to the idea that DSM categories are a professional creation. As a result, when necessary they are able to help their clients see the diagnoses that follow them as constructs rather than essential and immutable aspects of their personhood. After all, it is usually through the hardening of the DSM categories that problems arise. When clients, professionals, and the lay public take DSM labels too literally by forgetting that they are constructions, difficulties inevitably emerge. In a constructivist therapist's ideal world, DSM would simply be one of many competing construct systems used to understand therapy clients. Unfortunately, DSM often becomes the only accepted meaning-framework utilized and when this happens, alternative frameworks are stifled (Raskin & Lewandowski, 2000). Constructivist therapists urge clients and clinicians alike to remain attuned to the constructed nature of our diagnostic systems so that alternative understandings that move beyond a DSM framework are never foreclosed.

Doing is Construing

A common concern about psychotherapy is that what occurs within the consulting room does not always generalize beyond it. That is, clients talk about things with their therapists, but do not do anything differently in their lives. Constructivist therapists are aware of this pitfall. They realize that changing people's constructions involves getting them to behave in new ways in order to see how things turn out. This harkens back to Kelly's (1969) assertion that behavior is an experiment. In other words, people make predictions about life and then by acting in accord with those predictions, they see what happens. Behavior becomes critical in the evolution of people's constructs. Put colloquially, "doing is construing." A great deal of human meaning making occurs though our behavior. Thus, counter to those who see constructivism as obscure, philosophical, and full of too much "epistobabble" (R. A. Neimeyer, 1997), we see constructivist therapy as quite pragmatic and rooted in everyday goings-on. To this end, constructivist therapists often encourage clients to "do something different" in order to see how this changes things for them (Epting, 1984; O'Hanlon, 1999; Viney, 1996; Winter, 1992). We previously discussed fixed-role therapy along these lines, but any intervention that results in clients using their therapeutic conversations to generate new behaviors and (concomitantly) new constructions in the course of daily living are encouraged.

For example, consider the case of Eduardo, a twenty-eight year old Wall Street financier who presents with anxiety over wanting to change careers. Eduardo regularly discusses his desire to pursue law school, an idea he has grappled with but avoided doing anything about for seven or eight years. He is ambivalent about what law school entails and what applying might mean for him economically, academically, and personally. Economically, he worries about the loss of income that would accompany going from full time Wall Street financier to law student. Academically, he is concerned about whether he can handle law school. Personally, he is cognizant of his wife's skepticism about his changing careers. He is aware of his feelings on the issue but somehow has remained "stuck," unable to figure out how to move forward in figuring out whether to pursue law school or not.

During the first few sessions of therapy, Eduardo discusses each of his long-held concerns. However, his therapist realizes that these are conversations Eduardo has had many times over, both in his own head and with his wife. Very little changes and both the therapist and client feel "stuck" churning over Eduardo's career-related constructions and his associated ambivalence over how to proceed. In the fourth or fifth session, Eduardo once again reiterates how stuck he is about whether to pursue law school or not. The therapist asks Eduardo rather directly what he has done to learn more about law school. Eduardo, for all his many years of pondering the issue, has never done anything concrete about it. Amazingly, he does not know anything about the law schools in the area or what is involved in the admissions process. Nor does he know anything at all about what law school classes are like.

In other words, all Eduardo's thinking on the issue has been abstract and general. Very little behavior (actually, none!) has been directed at testing out Eduardo's long-held hypothesis that law school might be path for him. The therapist asks Eduardo what he would counsel someone considering law school to do. Eduardo readily generates a list of three specific things such a person could do: (1) surf the Internet to learn about what the application requirements for law school are; (2) contact one or two local law school admissions offices to discuss the application process; and (3) sit in on one or two classes at a local law school to see what they are like. The therapist then asks Eduardo to do these three things in between sessions. Eduardo hesitantly agrees in order to see what he might learn.

In many ways, this is a much more directive approach than what occurs in some constructivist therapy. Yet it is also very focused on the notion of "doing as construing." By asking Eduardo to generate things someone interested in law school could do to help decide whether to apply, the therapist gets Eduardo to generate possibilities. Then by asking Eduardo to behaviorally enact these possibilities as a between sessions homework assignment, the therapist transforms Eduardo's struggle from an abstract debate that occurs in the therapy room to one that involves doing new things as a way to see how they turn out and—most importantly—get Eduardo to revise and expand his constructs related to attending law school. Eduardo returns the next week with concrete knowledge of the local law school's admissions process and application deadlines. He also has set up a time to sit in on a law school class. As he does these things, he has new experiences that give him much more concrete information upon which to base his decision. He even goes so far as to inquire with his employer about working part time should he return to school. Eventually, Eduardo decides to apply to law school. However, only by doing new things (in this case, very concrete things geared towards learning more about law school) does Eduardo have experiences that enable him to revise his constructs, which in turn opens new behavioral possibilities.

Just Say "No" to Manuals

Constructivist psychotherapists are generally skeptical about therapy treatment manuals and their attempt to structure therapeutic change in a carefully delineated set of concrete steps. The impetus behind manuals is understandable, namely using research data to break therapy into manageable and operationalized behavioral units that any therapist could ostensibly follow. However, it strikes us as inconsistent with the meaning-based practice perspective of constructivist therapy. From a constructivist perspective, client problems are tied to idiographic meanings which must be addressed on their own terms. The same set of procedures or actions is unlikely to work in every case because one size does not fit all when it comes to changing clients' experiential realities. Stated succinctly, "psychotherapy is not a specific set of procedures—it is a form of education" (Efran & Clarfield, 1992, p. 211).

Here again we see some divergence between a constructivist conception of dysfunction and that of more medically based models. If clients suffer from etiologically discrete disorders, then a one-size-fits-all treatment for a given configuration of symptoms makes intuitive sense. But when we adopt the more humanistic, idiographic constructivist perspective—in which, regardless of observable symptoms, it is assumed each client develops a unique set of personal meanings within a unique social context—then rote steps to remedy standard symptoms no longer seem appropriate. More explicitly, if we accept the radical constructivist assertion that each client is a closed system that reorganizes itself to reestablish its equilibrium upon being disrupted by external events, then a treatment manual's assumption that all or most people should respond identically to each step within the manual is called into question. That is, it becomes impossible to know for sure exactly how a given step of a therapy manual may impact the person because it is the internal processes of the person more than the intervention itself that determines the client's response. We can have a general sense of techniques or relational factors that often trigger client change, but must do so within a larger framework that acknowledges the amazing variability that exists within human change processes (Mahoney, 1991).

For example, consider the case of Bob, a 24-year old computer technician seeking therapy for depression. Bob presented feeling quite dissatisfied with his life, though he had no idea why because—as he was quick to point out—he had a good job, a spacious apartment, and enough money to buy all the things he wanted. Interestingly, Bob had no close friends and he rarely referred to other people during therapy sessions. Instead he regaled his therapist with detailed accounts of his regular house chores and shared a journal in which he had, for the past ten years, meticulously recorded each day's weather. His only social activity was playing softball on an intramural team. However, it never occurred to him to speak to his teammates before or after games; once the game ended, he immediately would go home and play computer games or watch TV.

Not surprisingly, Bob's therapist struggled to connect with him. She tried a variety of clinical interventions—first some person-centered empathy, then some object relations work, and finally some rational-emotive behavior therapy techniques. But nothing seemed to help and little progress was made until, at the end of a session several months into therapy, the therapist was showing Bob to the door at the end of a session. As Bob exited, the therapist placed her hand on his back as she said goodbye. This unplanned action ended up being the event that "triggered" change in Bob. When Bob returned the next session, he wanted to discuss the therapist placing her hand on his back. The therapist initially did not even recall doing so, but quickly realized it had constituted a highly meaningful communication to Bob. He had experienced it as a deep and important connection with another person, something unfamiliar to him. While he did not know exactly how to go about it, Bob had come to see "connecting with others" as his goal for therapy. From that point onward, Bob and his therapist worked extremely well together, with Bob steadily expanding his social horizons across the next year. He developed a number of friendships with members of his softball team and with people at work. No manual could have predicted that the therapist's "intervention" of placing her hand on Bob's back would be the thing that set off change in him, but by hanging in there long enough and trying a number of different things, the therapist eventually stumbled upon something that broke the therapeutic log jam. Luckily not all therapeutic interventions are so accidental. The techniques in a therapist's toolkit are there because they seem to trigger internal changes in people reasonably often. However, to assume that a highly structured manual can improve therapeutic effectiveness in highly predictable ways is to overlook not only the therapist-client relationship, but the vast variability and infinite uniqueness of client meaning systems. That is, with each client a therapist needs to try different things until hitting upon a way of communicating that the client responds to. Even so, therapists can never know precisely how their clients will change as a result because client change is dictated not by the therapeutic intervention, but by the client's structural response to it. Therapists engage clients hoping that something they say or do provokes internal processes that set clients down a new path. In this way, therapy is as much an unpredictable art form as a scientific set of standardized techniques.

CONCLUSION

Clearly constructivist psychotherapy takes many forms and is carried out in many different ways in everyday practice. Yet however different the particular forms of therapy may be, the stance of the therapist remains consistent; clients are the experts on their own experiences and a therapist's particular view of reality is not favored over a client's. This stance does not make constructivist psychotherapists endorse an "anything goes" or "willy-nilly" stance in their therapeutic interventions. Quite the contrary! Through being clear about their own personal constructs and ways of making meaning, constructivist psychotherapists are able to delineate the boundaries of their own meaning systems and have a clear idea about what constitutes legitimate therapeutic strategies. In doing so, they reduce the risk of imposing their meanings on clients. This does not make constructivist psychotherapists incoherent, but rather cognizant of the difference between what is true for them and what is true for others. As such, they take a firm stance against imposing their own notions of what is good, right, or best for clients.

Constructivist psychotherapists are also aware of the inevitable interaction between client and therapist meaning systems and do not turn a blind eye to the power differential inherent in therapeutic relationships nor to the influence they have on clients' ways of meaning making. By being aware of one's own constructions of rationality/reality, the interplay of meanings between therapist and client, and the client's own ways of consciously and unconsciously understanding and making meaning in the world, constructivist psychotherapists are well situated to understand their clients and to co-create interventions that are well suited to client needs.

REFERENCES

American Psychiatric Association. (2000). *Diagnostic and Statistical Manual of Mental Disorders* (4th ed., Text Revision). Washington, DC: Author.

Anderson, H., & Goolishian, H. A. (1988). Human systems as linguistic systems: Preliminary and evolving ideas about the implications for clinical theory. *Family Process, 27*(4), 371–393.

Butt, T. (2000). Pragmatism, constructivism, and ethics. *Journal of Constructivist Psychology, 13,* 85–101.

Chiari, G., & Nuzzo, M. L. (1996). Psychological constructivisms: A metatheoretical differentiation. *Journal of Constructivist Psychology, 9,* 163–184.

Drewery, W., Winslade, J., & Monk, G. (2000). Resisting the dominating story: Toward a deeper understanding of narrative therapy. In R. A. Neimeyer & J. D. Raskin (Eds.), *Constructions of disorder: Meaning-making frameworks for psychotherapy* (pp. 243–263). Washington, DC: American Psychological Association.

Duffy, M., Gillig, S. E., Tureern, R. M., & Ybarra, M. A. (2002). A critical look at the DSM–IV. *The Journal of Individual Psychology, 58,* 363–373.

Ecker, B., & Hulley, L. (1996). *Depth-oriented brief therapy.* San Francisco: Jossey-Bass.

Ecker, B., & Hulley, L. (2000). The order in clinical "disorder": Symptom coherence in depth-oriented brief therapy. In R. A. Neimeyer & J. D. Raskin (Eds.), *Constructions of disorder: Meaning-making frameworks for psychotherapy* (pp. 63–89). Washington, DC: American Psychological Association Press.

Ecker, B., & Toomey, B. (in press). Of neurons and knowings: Depotentiation of symptom-producing implicit memory in coherence therapy. *Journal of Constructivist Psychology.*

Edwards, D., Ashmore, M., & Potter, J. (1995). Death and furniture: The rhetoric, politics and theology of bottom line arguments against relativism. *History of the Human Sciences, 8,* 25–49.

Efran, J. S., & Clarfield, L. E. (1992). Constructionist therapy: Sense and nonsense. In S. McNamee & K. J. Gergen (Eds.), *Therapy as social construction* (pp. 200–217). London: Sage.

Efran, J. S., Lukens, M. D., & Lukens, R. J. (1990). *Language, structure, and change: Frameworks of meaning in psychotherapy.* New York: Norton.

Epting, F. R. (1984). *Personal construct counseling and psychotherapy.* New York: John Wiley.

Eron, J. B., & Lund, T. W. (1996). *Narrative solutions in brief therapy.* New York: Guilford.

Eron, J. B., & Lund, T. W. (2002). Narrative solutions: Toward understanding the art of helpful conversation. In J. D. Raskin & S. K. Bridges (Eds.), *Studies in meaning: Exploring constructivist psychology* (pp. 63–97). New York: Pace University Press.

Gaines, A. D. (1992). Ethnopsychiatry: The cultural construction of psychiatries. In A. D. Gaines (Ed.), *Ethnopsychiatry: The cultural construction of professional and folk psychiatries* (pp. 3–49). Albany: State University of New York Press.

Gergen, K. J. (1985). The social constructionist movement in modern psychology. *American Psychologist, 40,* 266–275.

Gergen, K. J. (1994). *Realities and relationships.* Cambridge, MA: Harvard University Press.

Gergen, K. J., & McNamee, S. (2000). From disordering discourse to transformative dialogue. In R. A. Neimeyer & J. D. Raskin (Eds.), *Constructions of disorder: Meaning-making frameworks for psychotherapy* (pp. 333–349). Washington, DC: American Psychological Association.

Gonzalez, R. C., Biever, J. L., & Gardner, G. T. (1994). The multicultural perspective in therapy: A social constructionist approach. *Psychotherapy, 31*(3), 515–524.

Held, B. S. (1995). *Back to reality: A critique of postmodern theory in psychotherapy.* New York: Norton.

Honos-Webb, L., & Leitner, L. M. (2001). How using the DSM causes damage: A client's report. *Journal of Humanistic Psychology, 41*(4), 36–56.

Hoyt, M. F. (Ed.). (1994). *Constructive therapies (Vol. 1).* New York: Guilford.

Hoyt, M. F. (Ed.). (1996). *Constructive therapies (Vol. 2).* New York: Guilford.

Kelly, G. A. (1991a). *The psychology of personal constructs: Vol. 1. A theory of personality.* London: Routledge. (Original work published 1955)

Kelly, G. A. (1991b). *The psychology of personal constructs: Vol. 2. Clinical diagnosis and psychotherapy.* London: Routledge. (Original work published 1955)

Kelly, G. A. (1969). Ontological acceleration. In B. Maher (Ed.), *Clinical psychology and personality: The selected papers of George Kelly* (pp. 7–45). New York: John Wiley.

Lampropoulos, G., K. (2001). Bridging technical eclecticism and theoretical integration: Assimilative integration. *Journal of Psychotherapy Integration, 11,* 5–19.

Leitner, L. M., & Faidley, A. F. (2002). Disorder, diagnoses, and the struggles of humanness. In J. D. Raskin & S. K. Bridges (Eds.), *Studies in meaning: Exploring constructivist psychology* (pp. 99–121). New York: Pace University Press.

Mahoney, M. J. (1991). *Human change processes.* New York: Basic Books.

Mahoney, M. J. (2003). *Constructive psychotherapy.* New York: Guilford.

Martin, J., & Sugarman, J. (1997). The social-cognitive construction of psychotherapeutic change: Bridging social constructionism and cognitive constructivism. *Review of General Psychology, 1*(4), 375–388.

Maturana, H. R., & Poerksen, B. (2004). *From being to doing: The origins of the biology of cognition* (W. K. Koek & A. R. Koek, Trans.). Heidelberg, Germany: Carl-Auer.

Maturana, H. R., & Varela, F. J. (1992). *The tree of knowledge: The biological roots of human understanding* (R. Paolucci, Trans. rev. ed.). Boston: Shambhala.

McNamee, S. (1996). Psychotherapy as social construction. In H. Rosen & K. T. Kuehlwein (Eds.), *Constructing reality: Meaning-making perspectives for psychotherapists* (pp. 115–137). San Francisco: Jossey-Bass.

McNamee, S., & Gergen, K. J. (Eds.). (1992). *Therapy as social construction.* London: Sage.

Messer, S. B. (2001). Introduction to the special issue of assimilative integration. *Journal of Psychotherapy Integration, 11,* 1–4.

Monk, G., Winslade, J., Crocket, K., & Epston, D. (Eds.). (1997). *Narrative therapy in practice: The archaeology of hope.* San Francisco: Jossey-Bass.

Neimeyer, G. J. (1995). The challenge of change. In R. A. Neimeyer & M. J. Mahoney (Eds.), *Constructivism in psychotherapy* (pp. 111–126). Washington, DC: American Psychological Association Press.

Neimeyer, R. A. (1997). Problems and prospects in constructivist psychotherapy. *Journal of Constructivist Psychology, 10,* 51–74.

Neimeyer, R. A., & Mahoney, M. J. (Eds.). (1995). *Constructivism in psychotherapy.* Washington, DC: American Psychological Association.

Neimeyer, R. A., & Raskin, J. D. (2000a). On practicing postmodern therapy in modern times. In R. A. Neimeyer & J. D. Raskin (Eds.), *Constructions of disorder: Meaning-making frameworks for psychotherapy* (pp. 1-14). Washington, DC: American Psychological Association.

Neimeyer, R. A., & Raskin, J. D. (Eds.). (2000b). *Constructions of disorder: Meaning-making frameworks for psychotherapy.* Washington, DC: American Psychological Association.

O'Hanlon, B. (1999). *Do one thing different: Ten simple ways to change your life.* New York: William Morrow and Company.

Payne, M. (2006). *Narrative therapy: An introduction for counsellors* (2nd ed.). Thousand Oaks, CA: Sage.

Perez-Alvarez, M., & Garcia-Montes, J. M. (2007). The Charcot Effect: The invention of mental illnesses. *Journal of Constructivist Psychology, 20,* 309–336.

Raskin, J. D. (2001). On relativism in constructivist psychology. *Journal of Constructivist Psychology, 14,* 285–313.

Raskin, J. D. (2007). Assimilative integration in constructivist psychotherapy. *Journal of Psychotherapy Integration, 17*(1), 50–69.

Raskin, J. D., & Bridges, S. K. (Eds.). (2002). *Studies in meaning: Exploring constructivist psychology.* New York: Pace University Press.

Raskin, J. D., & Epting, F. R. (1993). Personal construct theory and the argument against mental illness. *International Journal of Personal Construct Psychology, 6,* 351–369.

Raskin, J. D., & Lewandowski, A. M. (2000). The construction of disorder as human enterprise. In R. A. Neimeyer & J. D. Raskin (Eds.), *Constructions of disorder: Meaning-making frameworks for psychotherapy* (pp. 15–40). Washington, DC: American Psychological Association.

Sexton, T. L., & Griffin, B. L. (1997). *Constructivist thinking in counseling practice, research, and training.* New York: Teachers College Press.

Toomey, B., & Ecker, B. (2007). Constructivism, coherence psychology, and their neurodynamic substrates. *Journal of Constructivist Psychology, 20,* 201–245.

Toomey, B., & Ecker, B. (in press). Competing visions of the implications of neuroscience for psychotherapy. *Journal of Constructivist Psychology.*

Viney, L. L. (1996). *Personal construct therapy: A handbook.* Norwood, NJ: Ablex.

von Glaserfeld, E. (1995). *Radical constructivism: A way of knowing and learning.* London: The Falmer Press.

White, M., & Epston, D. (1990). *Narrative means to therapeutic ends.* New York: Norton.

Winter, D. A. (1992). *Personal construct psychology in clinical practice: Theory, research and applications.* London: Routledge.

Winter, D. A., & Viney, L. L. (Eds.). (2005). *Personal construct psychotherapy: Advances in theory, practice and research.* London: Whurr.

Wong, Y. J. (2006). Strength-centered therapy: A social constructionist, virtues-based psychotherapy. *Psychotherapy: Theory, Research, Practice, Training, 43*(2), 133–146.

⟪ 2 ⟫

Epistemological Commitments Among Seasoned Psychotherapists: Some Practical Implications of Being a Constructivist

Greg J. Neimeyer, Jocelyn Lee,
Gizem Aksoy-Toska, and Daniel Phillip

The rapid proliferation of different forms of psychotherapy has occurred against the backdrop of some significant, consolidating shifts within the field. While the sheer number of distinctive psychotherapies has grown at a meteoric rate (Gutsch, Sisemore & Williams, 1984; Mahoney, 1991), the trajectory of this growth has been shaped by a range of forces that has constrained and directed its course of development. The development of brief therapies, for example, has dramatically outpaced the development of new long-term forms of intervention (Safran & Muran, 1998), highlighting the role of broader social and cultural factors in the growth of the field.

Another of these regulating influences concerns significant epistemological shifts within otherwise diverse forms of clinical practice. Epistemology refers to theories of knowledge, and the field of psychotherapy has experienced a decided shift from realist to constructivist traditions in this regard. At the broadest level, for example, Mahoney and Albert (1996) have looked to the field's published vocabulary as a reflection of its shifting epistemological leanings. Across a two-decade period of time, Mahoney and Albert (1996) documented a significant decline in the field's use of mechanistic metaphors, for instance, and a corresponding increase in terms reflecting personal agency, meaning, and interpretation. The use of terms such as "reinforcement," "contingency," and "operant," have waned across time in the professional literature, while terms such as "constructivism," and "systems" have waxed correspondingly. This "war of the words," as Mahoney and Albert

31

(1996, p. 22) have dubbed it, provides a glimpse into the shifting allegiances of contemporary psychotherapies.

A closer inspection of these shifting tides supports the conclusion that the field of psychotherapy is experiencing a sea change in its epistemological commitments. Noting the rapid growth of cognitive-behavioral therapies in recent years, for example, R. A. Neimeyer and Raskin (2001) have identified significant qualitative features that distinguish the profusion of newer therapies from those more traditional therapies that formed the foundation of the field. "Cognitively oriented therapies have 'deepened' across time by refining their approaches to less easily accessed core features of personal knowledge, and by reaching toward models more adequate to the complexity of human meaning systems and their social embeddedness" (R. A. Neimeyer & Raskin, 2001, p. 394). As Mahoney (1991) has noted, constructivist therapies are particularly well suited to accommodate this sort of shift, and the rapid development of constructivist therapies across the broad terrain of different psychotherapies supports this position. Recent developments within psychodynamic, systems, narrative, social constructionist, and cognitive-behavioral therapies, for example, attest to the increasing emphasis placed by modern psychotherapies on aspects of human meaning, languaging, and coordinated social action in negotiating the construction and deconstruction of psychological development and disorder. In short, the field of psychotherapy has taken a decidedly constructivist turn.

This chapter addresses a set of questions central to these developments. In particular, it assesses the translation of these epistemological leanings into practical therapeutic features, and explores whether differential epistemological commitments are linked in any predictable ways to therapists' personal qualities, to their therapeutic styles, or to the intervention methods that they choose to use. Following from Mahoney (1991), we assume that "our assumptions and assertions about human nature and psychological development are necessarily reflected in how we approach and 'conduct' psychotherapy" (p. 267), and our aim is to understand better the relationship between epistemological orientations and therapeutic practices (Lyddon, 1991). If an epistemological orientation can be understood as an overarching world view, the question is whether these differing world views might translate into theoretically consistent differences in (a) the characteristics of those practitioners, (b) the styles of the therapeutic enactment that characterize their practice, and (c) the specific interventions that they use in support of the clients they serve.

RATIONALIST AND CONSTRUCTIVIST THERAPY

The distinction between rationalist and constructivist epistemologies has been developed in a number of contexts. Mahoney and Lyddon (1988) trace the implications of these divergent epistemologies at meta-theoretical, theoretical, and technical levels. These levels have received further attention in subsequent work by a range of other scholars and practitioners, as well (Granvold, 1996; Lyddon, 1991; Mahoney, 1991, R. A. Neimeyer, 1993, 1995a, 1995b). Mahoney (1991) has noted that rationalist psychotherapists

> tend to operate from an authority-based (justificational) perspective.... Such a perspective essentially 'authorizes' or 'justifies' their practices, which tend to be ('rationally') 'interventional' (corrective, instrumental, manipulative, therapeutic). More often than not, psychotherapies based in a rationalist-interventionalist tradition are also teleological (goal-directed), ahistorical, and homeostatic (that is, they pursue a return to a static, rather than dynamic, equilibrium). (pp. 239-240)

But constructivists, as Meichenbaum (1992) has noted, regard it as both "presumptuous and pejorative to characterize someone's beliefs as 'irrational,' as if one holds the axiomatic system of rationality" (p. 127-128). By contrast, constructivists are "only vaguely interested in the ontological question of whether a real world exists in any meaningful way beyond our construction of it" and instead are "far more interested in what psychotherapy might look like if it were liberated from the quest to judge a client's personal reality by extraspective criteria of rationality or objectivity" (R. A. Neimeyer, 1995a, pp. 341-342).

These fundamental differences in orientation lead rationalist and constructivist therapists in substantially different directions—the former towards effecting a greater correspondence between their clients' presumably faulty or dysfunctional cognitions and an external reality that does not fully support them, and the latter towards a broadening of the field, an exploration of the constructions, and a fuller understanding of the personal and social processes that inform and support them. So, for example, "as a rationalist model, REBT encourages therapists to actively identify and label thoughts that cause clients distress and misery as irrational thoughts. In this model, therapists are thought to have the objectivity to examine clients' thoughts and accurately judge those thoughts as rational or irrational" (Sommers-Flanagan & Sommers-Flanagan, 2004). As Beck and Wieshaar (1995) have observed, therapy then represents an attempt "to improve reality testing through continuous evaluation of personal conclusions" (p. 230). That is, "cognitive therapy and rational emotive behavior therapy (REBT) share emphases on the primary importance of cognition in psychological dysfunction, seeing the task of the therapy as changing maladaptive assumptions and the stance of the therapist as active and directive" (Beck & Wieshaar, 1995, p. 231).

The translation of this position into therapeutic practice naturally leads the rationalist therapist towards structuring a therapeutic relationship that facilitates this process and privileges these particular mechanisms of change. As noted elsewhere (Mahoney & Lyddon, 1988; G. J. Neimeyer, Saferstein, and Arnold, 2005; R. A. Neimeyer, 1995a, 1995b), this translates into a therapeutic relationship that is oriented more towards the delivery of guidance, technical instruction, and behavioral rehearsal regarding the role of cognitions in the development and maintenance of emotional distress. The use of therapist-directed exercises, structured interventions, and directed homework assignments illustrates the relative emphasis placed on the development of technical skills as a means of generating change.

In contrast to a position that draws its force from facilitating the correspondence between perceptions and reality, constructivism is animated by the recognition of a plurality of realities. By relinquishing the pursuit of objectivity as the central goal of psychotherapy, constructivists work instead to understand, support, and extend extant systems of meaning that are understood as contextually dependent ways of knowing. "The therapist is not the guru leading the client to health," observe Faidley and Leitner (1993, pp. 6-7). Instead, "both the client and therapist embark on an uncharted journey that will require them to enter unknown territory, to struggle, to bear fear and pain, and hopefully, to grow" (Faidley & Leitner, 1993, p. 6-7).

This characterization highlights the essential indeterminacy of human growth and development from a constructivist perspective, echoing the distinction between what Mahoney (1991) referred to as "teleonomic" versus "teleological" processes. Whereas teleological approaches target known destinations at the outset, teleonomic processes, like evolution, generally scaffold an approach to development without preordaining the precise direction, nature, or outcomes associated with change. "The two best examples of teleonomy are perhaps biological evolution and human personality development," notes Mahoney (1991), because "there is an apparent directionality to both (at least in historical hindsight), yet neither can be said to be seeking a specific final form or destination" (p. 410). Indeed, the primacy placed on exploratory behavior and on the systematic introduction of novelty into the therapeutic experience is a hallmark of constructivist therapy. Mahoney (1991, p. 19) noted "the importance of active exploratory behavior on the part of the changing individual," emphasizing that "there can be no real learning without novelty—that is, without a challenge to or elaboration of what has become familiar." Exploration into the unknown becomes central to psychotherapy (see Leitner, 1995), and these forays into uncharted territory can be fraught with powerful emotional experiences that are engaged and embraced, rather than disengaged or disputed, within constructivist forms of therapy.

Moreover, because constructivists recognize the essential "embeddedness" of the subject into the object, and that no knowledge is "context free," they are burdened by the need for the continuous pursuit of self-awareness. Recognizing that they are both author and reader of the accounts they forge in therapy, they view the process of negotiating new meaning as a fundamentally emergent process that involves multiple players and multiple layers. Psychotherapy becomes understood less as the therapist's utilization of change-generating techniques to modify the client's constructions, and more as the mutual exploration and negotiation of new meanings between the client and therapist within broader interpersonal, familial, and social processes. These processes themselves are both informed and bounded by still broader cultural and historical contexts.

Overall, constructivism places distinctive burdens on its practitioners that may be reflected in the characteristics of those practitioners and the way(s) in which they conduct their work.

Mahoney (1988) has aptly summarized the special challenges associated with constructivism by noting that:

> The psychological demands of constructive metatheory are unsurpassed by those of any other contemporary perspective. No other family of modern theories asks its adherents to maintain such a degree of self-examining openness, to so painstakingly tolerate and harvest (rather than eliminate) ambiguity, or to so thoroughly question both the answers and the questions by which they inquire. It is not easy to be a constructivist. (p. 312)

If the adherence to a constructivist epistemology poses such special challenges, then it is worth determining whether these burdens carry distinctive implications regarding the qualities of therapists who practice within this tradition, the styles of interaction that characterize their practice, and the methods they utilize in conducting their trade. To address these questions, we recruited a large sample of seasoned psychotherapists, assessed their epistemological leanings, and compared them along a range of variables discussed within the literature as distinguishing between constructivist and rationalist therapists.

SAMPLING SEASONED PSYCHOTHERAPISTS

In order to explore the relationship between epistemic commitments and therapist characteristics, therapeutic styles, and the utilization of therapeutic techniques, we wanted to assess a broad range of seasoned psychotherapists. Our goal was to recruit a substantial sample of practicing professionals with considerable psychotherapeutic experience and a range of epistemological commitments and then explore whether their epistemological commitments were related to their therapeutic practices.

To develop this sample we conducted an Internet survey of practicing psychotherapists who were listed in a variety of professional associations and organizations. Participants were therapists recruited via online listservs of various professional organizations. The therapists were primarily recruited from the online practitioner directory (www.apapractice.org) of the American Psychological Association's Practice Organization (approximately 15,057 members). Additionally, solicitation emails were sent to APA's Division 17 (Counseling Psychology, approximately 355 members), Division 32 (Humanistic Psychology, approximately 130 members), and Division 29 (Psychotherapy, approximately 224 members) listservs. They were also sent the Personal Construct Psychology e-mail list (an open-interest listserv), the Albert Ellis Institute e-mail list (approximately 57 members), and a number of APA-approved counseling centers. The solicitation e-mail encouraged participants to forward the e-mail survey to other eligible practitioners, as well; thus, calculating an accurate response rate was not possible.

The sample consisted of approximately 1,000 therapists (64% female, 35% male) with a mean age of 45.09 (SD = 12.54). The sample was primarily Caucasian (88.8%), followed by Multiracial (2.9%), Hispanic (2.7%), African American (2.4%), Asian American (2.1%), and other (1.1%). Most participants had Ph.D. degrees (60.1%), followed by M.A./M.S. (18.6%), Psy.D.(11.0%), BA/BS (3%), Ed.D.(1.7%), MSW (1.4%), and other (2.9%). Additionally, the average total number of years spent in clinical practice was 14.01 years (SD = 11.03), reflecting a fairly seasoned sample of practicing psychotherapists.

MEASURING DIFFERENCES

Personal Epistemologies

To assess epistemological differences within the sample of therapists, we used the Therapist Attitudes Questionnaire-Short Form (TAQ-SF). The TAQ-SF is a revision of the Therapist Attitudes Questionnaire (TAQ) developed by DisGiuseppe and Linscott (1993). The TAQ-SF measures philosophical, theoretical, and technical dimensions of rationalist and constructivist therapies (G. J. Neimeyer & Morton, 1997). The self-administered instrument contains 16 items, eight pertaining to a rationalist commitment (e.g. "Reality is singular, stable and external to human experience") and eight items pertaining to a constructivist commitment (e.g. "Reality is relative. Realities reflect individual or collective constructions of order to one's experiences"). Respondents are asked to rate the degree to which they agree or disagree with each item on a 5-point Likert scale ranging from 1 (strongly disagree) to 5 (strongly agree).

The TAQ-SF yields subscale scores that reflect each psychotherapist's commitment to a rationalist epistemology (possible scores of 8 - 40) and a constructivist epistemology (possible scores of 8 - 40), with higher scores indicating greater epistemological commitment. To distinguish groups of therapists that were primarily committed to a constructivist epistemology from those primarily committed to a rationalist epistemology, a median split was performed on the distribution of the difference scores between rationalist and constructivist subscale ratings. This resulted in two groups of therapists that were substantially different in their epistemological commitments; those who were more strongly committed to rationalist epistemic beliefs were designated as *rationalists*, whereas those who were more strongly committed to constructivist epistemic beliefs were designated as *constructivists*.

In order to explore the possible implications of these epistemic differences, we identified three sets of variables that focused on the personal qualities of the therapists, their distinctive styles of conducting psychotherapy, and the nature of the interventions they utilized within the psychotherapeutic context.

Epistemology and Therapist Characteristics

The first set of variables concerned personal characteristics of the therapists. Based on a review of the literature characterizing the distinctive qualities associated with constructivist and rationalist therapies, we identified five qualities that we expected would distinguish between constructivist and rationalist therapists. These variables concerned their levels of self-awareness, attention to emotions, tolerance for ambiguity, tolerance for overall social diversity, and openness to experience.

Self-awareness. Constructivist epistemology imposes particularly strong demands for self-awareness on the part of the therapist. Unlike rationalism, which orients the therapist towards assessing the correspondence between a client's perspective and an independent, knowable reality, a constructivist position obligates therapists to recognize their important role in the process of knowing. As Mahoney (1991, p. 113) has observed, "we are, in fact, both subject and object of our own personal knowing, and aware of only a few of the processes that underlie our efforts." Awareness of these efforts, and a fundamental recognition of the necessarily limited positions that we can occupy, are fundamental to a constructivist position. As a consequence, the ongoing quest for self-reflection and awareness is integral to constructivist practice.

With the boundary blurred between the knower and the known, constructivists cannot reach beyond themselves in an effort to locate the validity of their perspectives in an objective reality external to themselves and the social contexts in which they operate.

In our study, self-awareness was measured with the Private Self-Consciousness scale (Scheier & Carver, 1985), which assesses the tendency to attend to more covert and personal aspects of the self such as personal beliefs, aspirations, values and feelings. The Private Self-Consciousness scale is a 9-item self-administered measure in which participants are asked to indicate the extent to which each statement is like them on a 4-point Likert scale ranging from 0 (not at all like me) to 3 (a lot like me).

Results of an ANOVA test of differences between means found that constructivists showed significantly higher levels of self-awareness (M = 19.79; SD = 4.43) than rationalists (M = 18.29; SD = 4.00), $F(1, 1004)$ = 30.95, p < .0001. This difference is consistent with the greater premium placed on self-awareness by constructivist positions.

Attending to emotions. A number of authors have identified differences between the roles that emotional processes play within constructivist and rationalist perspectives (Mahoney & Lyddon, 1988; R. A. Neimeyer, 1995a; 1995b). One dimension of difference concerns emotional control versus exploration. Rationalist therapies, for example, generally promote processes of emotional control and regulation, with methods of intervention that are directed at emotional containment and diminution, often through the application of logical reasoning, rational disputation, or emotional distancing. Constructivists, by contrast, tend to regard emotions as primitive knowing systems and deliberately attend to, explore or amplify emotional processes in the interest of better understanding and more effectively transforming, painful patterns of perturbance.

In our work we measured this quality by using the Attending to Emotions (Goldberg, 1999) subscale from the International Personality Item Pool (IPIP) scales. Respondents rate how accurately each item (e.g. "I think about the causes of my emotions"; "I am not in touch with my feelings") describes themselves on a five-point scale ranging from 1 (very inaccurate) to 5 (very accurate), with higher scores reflecting higher levels of emotional awareness.

Results of the ANOVA were again significant, with constructivists reporting greater attention to emotions ($M = 44.52$; $SD = 4.83$) than rationalists ($M = 42.61$; $SD = 6.02$), $F(1, 1004) = 30.43$, $p < .0001$. This difference is consistent with the differential role that emotion plays within rationalist and constructivist forms of therapy.

Tolerance for ambiguity. Mahoney (1995) has noted that, "besides the emotional demands of optimal psychotherapy, there are limits to what any individual counselor can understand or fathom" (p. 388). Constructivists recognize the limits of their knowing and the essential ambiguity associated with human knowing, experience, and change. Unlike rationalist therapists, "the constructive counselor cannot fall back on the collected works of a chosen leader as a bedrock of reassurance or authorization for what she or he is doing," nor can he or she "naively trust that his or her own perceptions or experiences are unbiased (or less biased) efforts at knowledge" (Mahoney, 1995, p. 837). The consequence is that constructivists must tolerate considerable uncertainty and navigate capably within contexts of ambiguity that are endemic to processes of human knowing and experience.

In our work we used the Multiple Stimulus Types Ambiguity Tolerance (MSTAT) measure to assess therapists' overall tolerance for ambiguity. McLain (1993) designed the MSTAT to assess individual's reactions to ambiguous situations and stimuli. The MSTAT is a 22-item self-administered measure. Respondents rate how accurately each item describes themselves on a seven-point scale ranging from 1 (strongly disagree) to 7 (strongly agree). Sample items include "I'm drawn to situations that can be interpreted in more than one way," with higher scores reflecting higher tolerance for ambiguity.

Results of the ANOVA along this measure of Ambiguity Tolerance were significant. Constructivists showed higher levels of tolerance for ambiguity ($M = 114.04$; $SD = 15.16$) than rationalists ($M = 109.11$; $SD = 14.91$), $F(1, 1004) = 26.14$, $p < .0001$. This result is again consistent with differences between the teleonomic processes associated with constructivist therapy and the more teleological processes associated with rationalist therapy.

Tolerance of diversity. Constructivism has been linked to multiculturalism in that both traditions acknowledge and respect cultural differences in the development of knowledge. As a constructivist therapist, Mahoney (1995) has reported that his own experience has "rendered a greater personal appreciation and respect for the diversity of belief systems" (p. 394), a quality that may extend more broadly to therapists who share an appreciation for diverse ways of knowing while resisting the temptation to privilege one over another. Mahoney (1995) suggested that constructivist therapies entail bi-directional learning during the therapy process, and that therapists come to realize the uniqueness of each of their clients.

In our work we used the Tolerance subscale of the International Personality Item Pool (IPIP). The Tolerance subscale is among the IPIP scales measuring constructs similar to those in Cloninger's Temperament and Character Inventory (TCI), and it corresponds to the TCI's Social Acceptance subscale. The Tolerance subscale is a 12-item self-administered measure. Sample items include, "I accept people as they are" and respondents rate how accurately each item describes them on a five-point scale ranging from 1 (very inaccurate) to 5 (very accurate), with higher scores reflecting greater tolerance.

Results of the ANOVA again supported differences between constructivists (M = 48.15; SD = 5.34) and rationalists (M = 46.98; SD = 5.46) in relation to their Tolerance for Social Diversity, $F(1, 1004)$ = 11.32, $p < .001$. Consistent with expectations, compared to rationalists, constructivists showed significantly greater tolerance for diverse perspectives.

Openness to experience. A constructivist epistemology may be linked to greater openness to experience for a number of reasons. Openness to experience is defined as one's openness to fantasy, aesthetics, feelings, actions, ideas, and values. It reflects imagination, aesthetic sensitivity, receptivity of inner feelings, preference for variety, intellectual curiosity, and independence of judgment (McCrae & Costa, 2003). Higher levels of openness to experience imply flexibility and tolerance for ambiguity and novelty, whereas lower levels of openness imply rigidity and intolerance for ambiguity and complexity (McCrae & Costa, 2003). A constructivist epistemology places a premium on the introduction of novelty and exploration in support of human growth and development. Berzonsky (1994), for example, found that constructivist beliefs were associated with a more "information-oriented" style of personal knowing that reflected greater openness to varied ideas, values, and actions (Berzonsky, 1994). Similarly, related work has shown that individuals with

41

constructivist commitments tended to be more open and active in their identity-construction processes (Berzonsky, 1994). These findings are broadly consistent with what Mahoney (1995) has underscored as the explicit connection between constructivism and openness to experience that follows from the belief that humans construct their own reality, and that human values cannot be justified or authorized on bases external to the personal and social processes that support and sustain them.

In our work we used the Openness to Experience subscale of the International Personality Item Pool (IPIP) to measure this quality. Sample items include, "I enjoy hearing new ideas," with higher scores reflecting higher levels of openness to experience. Respondents rate how accurately each item describes them on a five-point scale ranging from 1 (very inaccurate) to 5 (very accurate).

Results of the ANOVA using the Openness to Experience scores indicated significant differences between constructivists (M = 44.25; SD = 4.36) and rationalists (M = 42.40; SD = 4.87), $F(1,1004)$ = 39.10, $p < .01$. Consistent with earlier work, constructivists showed greater openness to experience in a way that underscores the premium they place on novelty in support of human development.

Epistemology and Therapist Styles

Personal style refers to "the set of characteristics that each therapist applies in every psychotherapeutic situation, thus shaping the main attributes of the therapeutic act" (Fernandez-Alvarez Garcia, Bianco, & Santoma, 2003, p. 117). The Personal Style of the Therapist Questionnaire (PST-Q) was developed by Fernandez-Alvarez et al. (2003), and designed to assess five dimensions of therapeutic style: an instructional dimension (flexibility–rigidity), expressive dimension (less expressive–more expressive), engagement dimension distance–closeness), attentional dimension (broad focus–narrow focus), and operative dimension (spontaneous–planned). The PST-Q is a 36-item self-report measure that asks therapists to evaluate their therapeutic styles along a series of questions using a Likert-type rating scale ranging from 1 to 7, where 1 represents total disagreement and 7 represents total agreement with each statement, with higher scores indicating higher levels of the dimension being measured.

42

The conceptual translation of these dimensions into expected differences between constructivist and rationalist therapists can be gleaned from existing literature characterizing the stylistic tendencies of these orientations. Mahoney and Lyddon (1988), for example, point out that rationalists conceptualize the therapeutic relationship as involving "the service or delivery of direct guidance and technical instruction" (p. 221). The use of therapist-directed exercises, structured interventions, and homework assignments illustrates the relative emphasis placed on the development of technical skills over exploratory or relational processes as active agents of change in rationalist psychotherapy (G. J. Neimeyer et al., 2005).

By contrast, Mahoney and Lyddon (1988) depict constructivist therapists as viewing the human component of the therapeutic relationship as a crucial component of therapeutic change that "functions as a safe and supportive home base from which the client can explore and develop relationship with self and world" (p. 222). Granvold (1996) underscores this point by noting "the development of a quality therapeutic relationship with such characteristics as acceptance, understanding, trust and caring is a prime objective of constructivists" (p. 350).

Together with the differences outlined earlier in relation to constructivist and rationalist epistemologies, the greater emphasis on relational processes over technical outcomes suggests that constructivists would more likely be marked by higher levels of flexibility (instructional dimension), expressiveness (expressive dimension), broad focus (attentional dimension), closeness (engagement dimension), and spontaneity (operative dimension) in comparison to rationalist therapists.

Results supported these predictions. A MANOVA was conducted and found to be significant, $F(5, 1006) = 52.55$, $p < .01$. Pairwise comparisons revealed significant differences at the $p < .05$ level for each of the therapy style subscales. Rationalists revealed more rigidity (instructional dimension; mean difference = .85), more narrowness of focus (attentional dimension; mean difference = 3.64), and more planfullness (operative dimension; mean difference = 4.60) in their personal styles compared to constructivists. By comparison, constructivists showed higher levels of emotional expression (expressive dimension; mean difference = 3.64) and closeness (engagement dimension; mean difference = 2.38) in their personal styles. These findings converge to support the characterization of constructivist therapy as being less directive and instructional, and more oriented instead towards broader personal themes, more intimate emotional engagement, and greater therapeutic spontaneity (See Table 1).

TABLE 1. MEANS AND STANDARD DEVIATIONS FOR
EPISTEMOLOGY BY THERAPY STYLE.

	TAQ	MEAN	SD	N
INSTRUCTIONAL	Constructivist	30.43	6.64	491
	Rationalist	31.67	5.57	515
EXPRESSIVE	Constructivist	42.81	5.82	491
	Rationalist	39.56	5.91	515
ENGAGEMENT	Constructivist	30.24	4.94	491
	Rationalist	27.99	4.96	515
ATTENTIONAL	Constructivist	20.71	3.99	491
	Rationalist	21.75	3.68	515
OPERATIVE	Constructivist	19.52	5.14	491
	Rationalist	24.01	5.77	515

Epistemology and Intervention Techniques

In addition to differences in personal qualities and styles, constructivist and rationalist therapists might be expected to utilize different intervention techniques in the course of their work (Lyddon, 1991; Mahoney & Lyddon, 1988; G. J. Neimeyer et al., 2005; R. A. Neimeyer, 1995a; 1995b). Depictions of specific rationalist and constructivist therapies underscore possible differences in this regard. For example, in characterizing cognitive therapy, Beck, Rush, Shaw, and Emery (1979) provide the following description:

> Cognitive therapy consists of highly specific learning experiences designed to teach patients (1) to monitor their negative, automatic thoughts (cognitions), (2) to recognize the connections between cognitions, affect, and behavior, (3) to examine the evidence for and against distorted automatic thoughts, (4) to substitute more reality-oriented interpretations for these biased cognitions, and (5) to learn to identify and alter the beliefs that predispose them to distort their experiences. (p. 250)

In contrast to this depiction, consider the following characterization of constructivist therapy provided by R. A. Neimeyer (1995b, p. 18).

> As a process-oriented approach to therapy, constructivism encourages a delicate attunement to the often-inarticulate questions implicit in the client's behavior . . . and attempts to help the client weave through his or her experience threads of significance that lead either to provisional answers or toward better, more incisive questions . . . Ultimately, the aim of therapy is to create a personal and interpersonal atmosphere in which presenting problems can be reformulated and resolved in language . . . and in which clients can recruit social validation for new, less 'problem-saturated' identities.

Overall, Mahoney and Lyddon (1988) characterize rationalist interventions as tending to focus on the "control of the current problems and their symptomatology" (p. 217) in contrast to constructivist interventions, which tend to focus on "developmental history and current developmental challenges" (p. 217). Key differences between these two approaches can be understood broadly as their differential focus on problems versus processes. Therefore, they tend to utilize different methods in the service of different ends. For example, given that "the goals of cognitive therapy are to correct faulty information processing and to help patients modify assumptions that maintain maladaptive behaviors and emotions," it follows that "methods are used to challenge dysfunctional beliefs and to promote more realistic adaptive thinking" (Beck & Weishaar, 1995, p. 236). By contrast, because the goals of constructivist therapy are fundamentally developmental, greater inflection is placed on processes of exploration, experimentation, and elaboration. One consequence of this difference concerns the range of different procedures that may characteristically be utilized by practitioners within these two traditions. Whereas cognitive-behavioral theories have promoted the systematic development of an identifiable set of intervention techniques tailored to their objectives, constructivists' commitment to plurality denies them a specific technology of change and predisposes them instead towards the creative integration of a vast range of methods that can support their efforts to facilitate constructive meaning making among the clients they serve. As R. A. Neimeyer (1995b) has noted,

> nearly any model of psychotherapy can be a legitimate resource for the postmodern practitioner, as long as it is interpreted as a historically and culturally bounded set of provisional metaphors and guidelines rather than as an applied science that compels only a certain conceptualization of the problem and only a single approved from of intervention. (p. 16)

Although the conceptual distinctions between the techniques used by constructivist and rationalist traditions have received considerable attention in the literature, research has only recently turned towards documenting these differences in clinical practice. Vasco's (1994) work represents one effort to identify the distinctive features of constructivist psychotherapy. His findings indicated that stronger constructivist commitments among the psychotherapists he studied were inversely related to the degree of therapeutic structure and direction, to a focus on current problems, and to the use of therapeutic confrontation in response to resistance. Work by Winter and Watson (1999) provided an additional glimpse into procedural features that distinguish different epistemological traditions. Studying the work of four personal construct therapists and six rationalist therapists, Winter and Watson (1999) found that the former demonstrated greater regard for their clients and favored interventions that facilitated more loose, rather than tight, construing.

Our interests were to explore further the ways in which epistemological leanings may be associated with the use of different therapeutic interventions. In particular, we were interested in determining whether epistemological preferences predicted the greater utilization of techniques that were "epistemologically consistent" with the therapists' own epistemic orientation, rather than methods from outside that tradition. Additionally, we were interested in exploring the differential range of methods utilized by constructivist and rationalist therapists.

To explore these issues, we adapted a measure from an extensive list of 108 different counseling and psychotherapy techniques gleaned from the literature. In order to distill from this list those techniques that best represented rationalist and constructivist traditions, we recruited 16 graduate students in psychology to rate the extent to which each technique is used by cognitive-behavioral therapists and by constructivist therapists), using a 5-point Likert type scale (1 = Never or Almost Never; 5 = Always or Almost Always). Results of a paired-differences analysis for all 108 items indicated that there were 77 techniques that were rated as being used with significantly different frequency by the two types of therapists. We then selected the 20 techniques that were most illustrative of cognitive behavioral therapy (e.g. instruction and guidance) and the 20 that were most illustrative of constructivist techniques (e.g. emotional processing).

These 40 intervention techniques were listed alphabetically for our sample of seasoned psychotherapists, who were asked to rate the extent to which they use each therapy technique in their practice of therapy, using the same 5-point scale. The ratings of the 20 cognitive-behavioral items were summed and a mean was calculated to reflect the average likelihood of using cognitive-behavioral interventions (possible range = 1 - 5), and the same was done using constructivist interventions (possible range = 1 - 5).

To examine the match between epistemological orientation therapeutic interventions, a mixed factorial 2 X 2 ANOVA was conducted. The first factor was a between subject's factor that reflected epistemological orientation (Constructivist or Rationalist) and the second factor was a within subject's factor that reflected the type of the technique (cognitive-behavioral or constructivist). As expected, there was a significant interaction between these two factors, $F(1, 883) = 81.64$, $p < .0001$. Overall, rationalists reported utilizing the cognitive-behavioral techniques significantly more ($M = 65.10$; $SD = 10.54$) than the constructivist techniques ($M = 51.00$; $SD = 10.20$), whereas the constructivists did not report significant differences in the frequency with which they drew upon cognitive-behavioral ($M = 58.2$; $SD = 11.93$) and constructivist ($M = 56.50$; $SD = 9.91$) techniques. These findings suggest that rationalists were more selective in their utilization of techniques consistent with their epistemic framework. Constructivists, by contrast, utilized techniques across epistemological domains in a way that is consistent with the technical eclecticism that has been associated with this epistemological position (R. A. Neimeyer, 1995; Vasco, 1994).

DOES EPISTEMOLOGY MATTER?

As constructivist perspectives continue to direct the course of developments within psychotherapy, it is reasonable to ask what practical consequences might follow from these epistemological shifts (Lyddon, 1991). Will the postmodern practitioner intervene in any characteristically distinctive ways? Will his or her epistemological commitments translate into discernibly different psychotherapeutic patterns, processes, or procedures?

The present work suggests the likelihood that practical procedures may in fact follow epistemological preferences, at least in relation to select qualities of the therapist, personal styles of interaction, and the methods that are utilized in the service of psychotherapy. Constructivist epistemologies were generally linked to therapists who were more dedicated to self-awareness, more attuned to emotion, more tolerant of ambiguity, and more open to social diversity and novel experience. Stylistically, their practice was characterized by greater flexibility and spontaneity, higher levels of emotional expression and personal engagement, and an attention to broader therapeutic issues and themes. Moreover, they seemed to employ a broader range of intervention techniques in a way that supports previous descriptions of their greater technical eclecticism (R. A. Neimeyer & Raskin, 2001; Vasco, 1994).

The overall image resonates well with conceptual characterizations of constructivist therapy, as well as the available empirical findings that document its distinctive strategic practices. For example, Winter and Watson (1999) found that the clients in personal construct therapy experienced greater personal involvement in therapy, suggesting the primacy of relational features in this form of constructivist therapy. From her study of the transcripts of psychotherapy sessions, Viney (1994) found that personal construct therapy was characterized by greater acknowledgement of the client's distress and, as a consequence, fuller expressions of that distress on the part of their clients. And Vasco's (1994) work underscored the relationship between stronger constructivist commitments and technical eclecticism, emotional expression, and less directive and confrontational styles of therapy. Each of these findings supports the vision of the constructivist practitioner as open to diverse perspectives and novel experience, respectful and attuned to the client's expression of emotion, and willing to intervene with a variety of strategies in support of forging a constructive growth and development.

But this picture is best regarded as only an impressionist blur at the present time, an image that emerges as we gain some distance from the sparse particulars that currently form its central features. Closer inspection reveals significant gaps, and highlights the likelihood that the present image remains a joint product of our current findings and our ongoing anticipations. Two qualifications sharpen this concern and clarify important directions that future work might take in this regard. The first involves the increasing recognition that rationalism and constructivism may serve less as divisions among various forms of psychotherapy than as dimensions along which various therapies can be situated (DiGiueseppe & Linscott, 1993; R. A. Neimeyer & Raskin, 2001). Within any given school of therapy (e.g. systems theory, cognitive-behavioral therapy, psychoanalytic therapy), specific therapies range widely in their constructivist leanings. In our work we have respected this variation by including in each group (Constructivists and Rationalists) practitioners who designated themselves in a wide variety of different ways, but we nonetheless dichotomized them on the basis of their underlying epistemological leanings, whatever their therapeutic self-designations. Data analytic procedures that respect the continuous nature of these epistemological leanings, such as multiple regression analyses, might be useful mechanisms for augmenting the current findings. Conversely, the comparison of extreme groups, such as "purists" whose epistemological leanings match their theoretical self-designations (e.g. personal construct therapists vs. rational emotive therapists, see Winter & Watson, 1999) may provide alternative ways to clarify further differences owing to epistemological commitments. The critical point, however, is that differences may best be understood as differences in degree, rather than in type, because it is likely that therapists have varying blends of rationalist and constructivist commitments rather than wholesale allegiances to one over the other.

The second qualifying consideration concerns the nature of the differences that we have sought to explore. Because we were interested in exploring the translation of constructivist commitments into practice, we examined features and processes that we expected would characterize constructivist practice. In a sense, the measures we chose could be viewed as favoring constructivism insofar as they were designed to assess dimensions that distinguish psychotherapeutic practice within this tradition. The same could be done in relation to rationalism where, for example, measures of precision, consistency, persuasion, logic, perseverance, self-monitoring, or other characteristics might be found to favor rationalist practitioners over constructivists. Put simply, different epistemological commitments may predispose qualities and practices broadly consistent with those commitments, but these differences do not necessarily imply or represent "better" or "more effective" practices. As Lyddon (1989) has noted, "none of these worldviews provides the 'correct' or 'best' frame of reference. They simply suggest different forms of understanding, inquiry, and theory" (p. 446).

That being said, a better understanding of the practices and processes that are associated with varying epistemological positions could open a window onto further work that directly addresses the coherence of various epistemologies and practices. It may be worth exploring those instances in which epistemological commitments are inconsistent with therapeutic styles or practices, for example, and comparing them with more theoretically and technically coherent practices to determine the differential impact or effectiveness of those approaches. R. A. Neimeyer (1995) has convincingly argued in favor of a form of theoretically progressive integrationism in which therapeutic processes and practices derive from a consistent epistemological base. This contrasts with a technical eclecticism that borrows techniques across epistemological domains without respect to their relationship to a common or coherent theoretical base. Better understanding of the relationship between epistemological commitments on the one hand, and therapists' characteristics, styles and interventions on the other, may allow us gradually to come to identify instances of "coherent" and "incoherent" practices, and to assess the differential impact or effectiveness of these different psychotherapeutic approaches. In any event, the results of the present work do not imply a general preference for one form of therapy over another, nor do they provide any direct assessment of theoretical and practical coherence among the seasoned psychotherapists we sampled. It seems likely that future work will identify a range of distinctive advantages and disadvantages that follow from any given set of epistemological commitments or psychotherapeutic practices. And any given set of epistemological commitments, in turn, is likely to spawn substantial variation in the extent to which its practitioners utilize processes and procedures that are consistent with the underlying epistemology that informs their practice.

And finally, an extension of this work might address the role of epistemological commitments and issues of therapist self-care. Mahoney (1991; 1999) has identified self-care as vital to the effective functioning of psychotherapists in general and, perhaps, of constructivist therapists in particular. Drawing from our current work it seems likely that therapists with different epistemological leanings might well experience psychotherapy in distinctively different ways and, by extension, engage in substantially different forms of self-care. As an example, the expression of powerful emotions is a common experience in psychotherapy, and rationalist and constructivist therapists might vary markedly in relation to their response to this experience. A key method of cognitive therapy, according to Prochaska and Norcross (2003), is the method of distancing, where individuals can "learn to deal with upsetting thoughts objectively, reevaluating them rather than automatically accepting them" (p. 356). When confronted with his or her own powerful emotions in the course of conducting psychotherapy, rationalist commitments may predispose the therapist to use similar efforts to gain perspective, effectively removing themselves from the emotional experience in an effort to analyze it more objectively.

Constructivist commitments, by contrast, may instead translate into more focused attunement to this emotion for the potential meaning that it may contain or convey; a practice that characterizes a number of more depth-oriented constructivist therapies (R. A. Neimeyer & Raskin, 2001). Broadly speaking, therapist self-care strategies might cohere with the epistemological commitments that inform them. Emotional distancing, rational self-talk, and active efforts to effectively problem solve stress-related symptoms may predominate for rationalists, for example, whereas emotional attunement, relational processing, or the use of experiential focusing methods might more commonly characterize constructivist self-care. As with the therapeutic practices themselves, no one set of self-care procedures may be natively superior to others, although different epistemic commitments may minimize or maximize the likelihood of particular types of stress and strain on the therapist. Continuing work in this area might concentrate on the relationship between a therapist's epistemological commitments on the one hand, and the characteristic practices and procedures they employ in the support of themselves, as well as their clients, over the ongoing course of conducting psychotherapy.

REFERENCES

Beck, A. T., Rush, J., Shaw, B., & Emery, G. (1979). *Cognitive therapy of depression.* New York: Guilford Press.

Beck, A. T., & Weishaar, M. E. (1995). Cognitive therapy. In R. J. Corsini & D. Wedding (Eds.) *Current psychotherapies* (pp. 229-261). Itasca, IL: F.E. Peacock Publishers.

Bersonsky, M. D. (1994). Individual differences in self construction: the role of constructivist epistemological assumptions. *Journal of Constructivist Psychology, 7,* 263-281.

DiGiueseppe, R., & Linscott, J. (1993). Philosophical differences among cognitive behavioral therapists: rationalism, constructivism, or both? *Journal of Cognitive Psychotherapy, 7,* 117-130.

Faidley, A. F., & Leitner, L. M. (1993). *Assessing experience in psychotherapy: Personal construct alternatives.* Westport, CT: Praeger.

Fernandez-Alvarez, H., Garcia, F., Bianco, J., & Santoma, S. (2003). Assessment questionnaire on the personal style of the therapist. *Clinical Psychology and Psychotherapy, 10,* 116-25.

Goldberg, L. R. (1999). A broad-bandwidth, public domain, personality inventory measuring the lower-level facets of several five-factor models. In I. Mervielde, I. Deary, F. DeFruyt, and F. Ostendorf (Eds.), *Personality Psychology in Europe* (Vol 7, pp. 7-28). Tilburg: Tilburg University Press.

Granvold, D. K. (1994). Concepts and methods of cognitive treatment. In D. K. Granvold (Ed.) *Cognitive and behavioral treatment: Methods and applications.* Pacific Grove, CA: Brooks/Cole.Gutsch. K. U., Sisemore, D. A., & Williams, R. L. (1984). *Systems of psychotherapy.* Springfield, IL: Charles C. Thomas.

Leitner, L. M. (1995). Optimal therapeutic distance. In R. A. Neimeyer & M. J. Mahoney (Eds.) *Constructivism in psychotherapy* (pp. 357-370). Washington, DC: American Psychological Association.

Lyddon, W. J. (1989). Root metaphor theory: A philosophical framework for counseling and psychotherapy. *Journal of Counseling and Development, 67,* 442-448.

Lyddon, W. J. (1991). Epistemic style: implications for cognitive psychotherapy. *Psychotherapy, 28,* 588-597.

Mahoney, M. J. (1988). Constructive metatheory II: Implications for psychotherapy. *International Journal of Personal Construct psychology, 1,* 299-315.

Mahoney, M. J. (1991). *Human change processes.* New York: Basic Books.

Mahoney, M. J. (1995). The psychological demands of being a constructive psychotherapist. In R. A. Neimeyer & M. J. Mahoney (Eds.), *Constructivism in psychotherapy* (pp. 385-399). Washington, DC: American Psychological Association.

Mahoney, M. J., & Albert, C. J. (1996). Worlds of words: The changing vocabulary of psychology 1974-1994, *Constructivism in the Human Sciences, 3,* 22-26.

Mahoney, M. J., & Lyddon, W. J. (1988). Recent developments in cognitive approaches to counseling and psychotherapy. *The Counseling Psychologist, 16,* 190-234.

McCrae, R. R., & Costa, P. T. (2003). *Personality in adulthood: A five-factor theory perspective.* New York: Guilford Press.

McLain, D. L. (1993). The MSTAT-I: A new measure of an individual's tolerance for ambiguity. *Educational and Psychological Measurement, 53,* 183-189.

Meichenbaum, D. (1992). Evolution of cognitive behavior therapy: Origins, tenets, and clinical examples. In J. K. Zeig (Ed), *The evolution of psychotherapy: The second conference* (pp. 114-128). New York: Brunner/Mazel.

Neimeyer, G. J. & Morton, R. J. (1997). Personal epistemologies and preferences for rationalist versus constructivist psychotherapies. *Journal of Constructivist Psychology, 10,* 109-123.

Neimeyer, G. J, Saferstein, J., & Arnold, W. (2005). Personal construct psychotherapy: Epistemology and practice. In D. Winter & L. Viney (Eds.), *Personal construct psychotherapy: Advances in theory, practice, and research* (pp. 81-95). London: Whurr.

Neimeyer, R. A. (1993). Constructivism and the cognitive psychotherapies: Some conceptual and strategic contrasts. *Journal of Cognitive Psychotherapy, 7,* 159-172.

Neimeyer, R. A. (1995a). Limits and lessons of constructivism: Some critical reflections. *Journal of Constructivist Psychology, 6,* 339-361.

Neimeyer, R. A. (1995b). Constructivist psychotherapies: Features, foundations and future directions. In R. A. Neimeyer & M. J. Mahoney (Eds.) *Constructivism in psychotherapy* (pp. 11-38). Washington, DC: American Psychological Association.

Neimeyer, R. A., & Raskin, J. D. (2001). Varieties of constructivism in psychotherapy. In K. S. Dobson (Ed.) *Handbook of cognitive-behavioral therapies* (2nd ed., pp. 393-430). New York: Guilford.

Prochaska, J. O., & Norcross, J. C. (2003). *Systems of psychotherapy: A transtheoretical approach.* Pacific Grove, CA: Brooks/Cole.

Safran, J., & Muran, C. (1998). *The therapeutic alliance in brief psychotherapy.* Washington, DC American Psychological Association Press.

Scheier, M. F., and Carver, C. S. (1985) The self-consciousness scale: A revised version for use with general populations. *Journal of Applied Social Psychology, 15*, 687-699.

Sommers-Flanagan, J., & Sommers-Flanagan, R. (2004). *Counseling and psychotherapy theories in context and practice: Skills, strategies, and techniques.* Hoboken, NJ: Wiley.

Vasco, A. B. (1994). Correlates of constructivism among Portuguese therapists. *Journal of Constructivist Psychology, 7*, 1-16.

Viney, L. L. (1994). Sequences of emotional distress expressed by clients and acknowledge by therapists: are they associated more with some therapists that others? *British Journal of Clinical Psychology, 33*, 469-81.

Winter, D. A., & Watson, S. (1999). Personal construct theory and the cognitive therapies: Different in theory but can they be differentiated in practice? *Journal of Constructivist Psychology, 12*, 1-22.

PART II

APPLYING CONSTRUCTIVIST THERAPY IN EVERYDAY PRACTICE

○ʒ 3 ဆ

Coherence Therapy:
Swift Change at the Roots of
Symptom Production

Bruce Ecker and Laurel Hulley

Coherence therapy is a methodology for dispelling a wide range of symptoms at their emotional and subcortical roots in far fewer sessions than is expected in conventional in-depth therapies. It is a system of personal construct therapy that shares certain fundamental assumptions with that of Kelly (1955/1991a, 1955/1991b), yet differs significantly in methodology.[1]

Originally developed and described entirely in phenomenological terms (Ecker & Hulley, 1996, 2000a, 2000b), a more neural and neuropsychological view of how coherence therapy works has also been articulated (Toomey & Ecker, in press; Toomey & Ecker, 2007). These two levels of description—the experiential and the neurophysiological—are mutually illuminating, and we combine them in the present article to best indicate how coherence therapy operates as a practical implementation of constructivism.

Basic to the approach is the constructivist understanding that any given thoughts, feelings or behaviors, including those that seem to be irrational, out-of-control clinical symptoms, arise from the activation and enactment of specific personal constructs, conscious and unconscious, held by the individual. In the view of coherence therapy, all personal constructs operate as knowings. The methodology consists of actively guiding the client to access, experience and revise the specific knowings that are the very basis of the existence of the presenting symptom or problem.

The clinical challenge inheres in the fact that (a) the brain forms and holds knowings (constructs) in several different memory

---

[1] The original moniker, depth-oriented brief therapy or DOBT, was used from 1993 through 2005. The change to "coherence therapy" and "coherence psychology" more clearly reflects the central principle of the approach.

systems (Milner, Squire, and Kandel 1998), and (b) the knowings driving symptom production are nearly always held not in the cortex's explicit memory, which is readily conscious and verbalized, but in subcortical systems of implicit memory, which are unconscious and nonverbal.[2] In short, the symptom-generating knowings are not known to the conscious personality, which is why clinical symptoms plague clients and appear to have a life of their own.

The knowings that make up implicit memory are multi-modal, that is, they exist in several different types of representation—a composite of sensory, emotional, interpersonal, kinesthetic, somatic and energic knowings. The specific regions of the subcortical brain that form, store and retrieve these various types of constructs are only partially mapped. Best understood to date is the role of the amygdala in encoding fear-based, aversive learnings in implicit memory circuits (Phelps & LeDoux, 2005).

The individual, of course, has a vast universe of implicit, unconscious knowings or constructs. In order to be swift and accurate in finding the specific few that generate a particular symptom, coherence therapy utilizes what Ecker and Hulley (1996) found to be the unique property of the symptom-producing constructs: they are coherent in relation to the symptom. That is, they define personal reality in a cogent, well-knit way that makes the symptom necessary to have, despite the very real suffering that it entails. For example, a woman's troubling inability to make progress in building her career was found to be necessary because, unconsciously, "working hard on career" equals "abandoning your family," a construction she formed in childhood when Mom divorced Dad and blamed it on his chronic absence for his work. A man with an attention problem that fit the checklist for Attention Deficit Disorder and kept him from learning skills needed at work had parents who often criticized him shamingly for allowing something to go wrong that could have been spotted and prevented. His coherent response was the self-protective tactic of

---

[2] Implicit memory is qualitatively different from the vernacular meaning of the word "memory" as denoting the conscious recall of past personal experiences (episodic, autobiographical memory) or facts (semantic memory), which are stored cortically. In contrast, an implicit memory of the type relevant here is experienced, when activated, as a bodily immersion in a particular emotional tone (such as anxiety, anger or sadness) typically with an urge to carry out a particular behavior, such as avoiding attention, talking incessantly or eating. There is no recall of past incidents in which this state was first experienced, no sense of experiencing a memory at all, and little if any awareness as to why this experience is occurring.

vigilantly covering all bases with a perpetual scanning of attention, but this had never been conscious. According to his subcortical brain, keeping attention steadily in one place was always absolutely the wrong thing to do.

The symptom-necessitating constructs are a complete mystery at the start of therapy, but therapist and client together can zero in on them efficiently by making use of their coherence, as the clinical example below shows. When the client consciously retrieves and directly experiences these specific knowings, he or she discovers a compelling, well-defined, personal theme and purpose with a deep core of emotion and meaning. This symptom-necessitating material is referred to *as the emotional truth of the symptom* and also, more technically, as the person's *pro-symptom position,* denoting an implicit knowing that is *for* having the symptom. A person may have two or more pro-symptom positions maintaining the same symptom.

Of course, the client is initially aware of the symptom only as a cause of great distress, and so construes it consciously as something entirely negative, senseless, defective, involuntary and unwanted. This conscious attribution of meaning is conspicuously *against* having the symptom, and so is termed the client's *anti-symptom position.*

The essence of these ideas is embodied in the principle of *symptom coherence,* coherence therapy's model of symptom production (Ecker & Hulley, 1996, 2000a, 2004): A person produces a particular symptom because it is compellingly necessary to have according to at least one unconscious, nonverbal, emotionally potent schema or construction of reality held in implicit memory. Conversely, the person ceases producing the symptom as soon as there no longer exists any construction of reality in which the symptom is necessary to have, with no need for counteracting the symptom itself.

A major milestone in the methodology of coherence therapy with each client occurs when a discovered pro-symptom position becomes fully experienced and well-integrated into conscious awareness. This has two important effects: (a) The client becomes lucidly aware of the deep sense and coherent necessity of having the symptom and in most cases has a direct experience of agency, that is, of producing the symptom to fulfill an important purpose; and (b) the knowings constituting the pro-symptom position become susceptible to immediate transformation (revision or dissolution), which is now the next stage of the work. Coherence therapy spells out the steps of a built-in process of the brain-mind-body system for a transformation of constructs (Ecker & Hulley, 1996, 2000a, 2004), a process that matches the subsequently discovered neurological process for the depotentiation of conditioned responses in implicit memory (reviewed in Ecker & Toomey, in press). This specificity regarding how constructs change enables the work to achieve deep, lasting effectiveness with enhanced reliability.

Though simple in essence, the symptom coherence model of symptom production has been clinically found to be relevant for a broad range of symptoms.[3] With each client the process of coherence therapy phenomenologically reveals and verifies the presence of powerful, symptom-requiring personal constructs, the depotentiation of which directly yields symptom cessation.

Methods of change that attempt to counteract, override or avoid the symptom and replace it with a desired state follow a clinical strategy antithetical to that of coherence therapy because they increase rather than decrease the dissociated, unconscious status of the constructs causing symptom production. Counteractive methods[4] compete against pro-symptom positions without changing or eliminating them, and so are always vulnerable to relapse. To counteract symptoms is to side with the weaker, anti-symptom, cortical position against the always-more-powerful, pro-symptom, subcortical position of the client. In contrast, the aim in coherence therapy is to embrace, integrate and then transform the symptom-generating constructs, truly eliminating rather than opposing the cause of symptom production. (For a detailed

---

[3] Symptoms that have been dispelled by coherence therapy include depression, anxiety, panic, agoraphobia, low self-worth, attachment problems, sequelae of childhood abuse, sexual problems, food/eating/weight problems, rage, attention deficit, complicated bereavement, codependency, underachievement, procrastination, fidgeting, and a wide range of interpersonal, couple and family problems. For case examples of anxiety and panic, see Ecker (2003); for depression, Ecker and Hulley (2002a). Ecker and Hulley (1996) provide a wide range of examples.

[4] Examples of counteractive methods include some of the most widely used methods in the field, such as teaching a relaxation technique to a client who has anxiety attacks; building up hopefulness in a depressed client; teaching communication skills and tools to an adversarial couple; reframing the meaning of the problem situation; having therapy group members describe what they do to keep themselves from isolating; and getting a client with low self-worth to take in clear evidence of worth (loved by friends, recognized as talented and competent at work, etc.).

neuropsychological account of these points see Toomey & Ecker, in press; Toomey & Ecker, in press.)

The methodology of coherence therapy consists, then, of three therapeutic activities: discovering, integrating and transforming unconscious pro-symptom positions. These activities must be experiential, because subcortical implicit knowings are accessed by subjectively experiencing them, not through having cognitive insights or other thoughts *about* them in the neocortex. Experiences yield cognitive insights in this approach, not the other way around. The therapist creates experiences that discover, experiences that integrate, and experiences that transform the person's pro-symptom constructs. In creating these experiences, the therapist is active and leading as regards process but defers to the client's authority as regards content. (For detailed methodological procedures and techniques, see Ecker & Hulley, 1996, 2000a, 2004.)

A COHERENCE THERAPY SESSION[5]

A 36-year-old married professional woman, whom we will call Susan, phoned one of the authors (B.E.) seeking therapy for "a problem I've had for twenty years." She began her first session in a fast-talking, cerebral, incongruently cheerful manner, describing "basically an overeating issue—a weight issue . . . I've, like, processed it to death in therapy, so I can tell you exactly where it came from, exactly when it started, you know, why I do it, why I'm uncomfortable when I get thin . . . I'm so intellectually aware of every part of it but it's not helping me change, like, one bit. And I also know everything there is to know about dieting. I know exactly what to eat, when to eat . . . But I just decided I'm not going to pay for one more diet 'cause it has nothing to do with the diet. It's in my head. So, I just have, like, an enormous amount of insight but it's not really helping me."

Susan's twenty years of fruitless efforts make her a "poster child" for the ineffectuality of counteractive methods and cognitive insights to produce change. The therapist replied:

---

[5] We recognize that much of what can be learned from case examples is apparent only in seeing and hearing the nuances of the process. A video of the following session will be available for study. Here, due to length constraints, we present excerpts that best illustrate the unfolding of coherence therapy methodology. Every deletion is indicated by an ellipsis (. . .).

Therapist: So, do you have a sense of where amongst the several, or many, different inner emotional causes of your pattern with food we should focus? Or should I just begin my own way of looking?

Client: . . . When I was 16, I started gaining weight and my Mom, my Mom would actually say things to me like, "Nobody's ever going to love you, no one's ever going to marry you if you don't lose weight." You know, I mean she'd really tell me and, like, in a way, in my family's world that's true: that everything has to look perfect, everyone has to be perfect or else you can't be loved . . . But even now I think I'm sort of the black sheep of my family, you know, I'm just, I'm not thin[6] . . . They all live in like mansions and their lives are perfect and I live in this little house and, you know, they just don't, they just can't comprehend me . . . They almost disowned me at the election time because I voted for [a certain candidate] and that's just so not right . . . The whole thing is that I just refuse to get thin because I refuse to acknowledge that they're right about that. You know, like I refuse to get thin and have them look at me and go, "Oh, she's finally fitting in . . . She finally realized that we were right this whole time" . . . So, I know that the, the crux of the problem is in there somewhere. [Laughs.] But knowing all that doesn't seem to—I mean it pisses me off but I still totally overeat, you know, even though it doesn't make sense to me . . . because I want to be thin . . . not because I want to look perfect or I think that's gonna, sort of make my life perfect, but I want, I more want to be fit. Like I want to be healthy, I don't want to get diabetes or, you know, like stomach cancer because I was defying my family, you know, it doesn't make sense to me . . . When I think back on the times when I've gotten thin, I can see that I was uncomfortable with like fitting in with them in some way. I just immediately became uncomfortable even though one side of me was so happy about it, but the other side of me was just uncomfortable that I was somehow, you know, proving them right . . . So, that's kind of where I get stuck. That's as far as I can kind of go but then I don't know how to actually work that into some sort of a change in my behavior.

Therapist: Ok. Well, thanks. You've rapidly put me on the trail with how much you already know about this and, and so I do have some ideas.

Along with her views *against* having the symptom—her anti-symptom position—Susan has expressed some apparently

---

[6] Susan was not slender, but neither was she particularly noticeable as being overweight.

pro-symptom ideas and insights about why her symptoms of over-eating and being overweight are necessary for her, citing an autonomy struggle. The therapist cannot yet know whether these ideas will prove to be an accurate description of deeper emotional truths requiring the symptom. Even correct ideas about pro-symptom positions are only ideas, only a map, not the territory itself. The therapist will use experiential methods to have Susan find and directly feel and inhabit her living pro-symptom material.

Susan has described her ongoing struggle against her parents' *terms of attachment,* the specific rules and roles they demand in exchange for giving acceptance, connection and nurturance. By Susan's convincing account, she has received little if any attuned understanding or acceptance of her authentic self from them, and instead perpetually receives messages of nonacceptance and demands for compliance with their definitions of how she should think and live. What Susan has suffered under these terms of attachment is very likely to be involved in her pro-symptom position(s) maintaining her eating and weight. This too will be brought to light through the creation of experiences that non-speculatively and accurately reveal the operation of these themes.

Picking up on Susan's theory of why she felt uncomfortable being thin, the therapist said, "becoming thin and fit would mean that your family has won that long-standing battle over defining and controlling you . . . It would look to them and feel to you like you admitted they're right . . . And [avoiding] that apparently outweighs your own desires to be thin and fit." Susan confirmed this summation. This initial focus on Susan's experience of the problem has led the therapist to understand that he should regard as a presenting symptom not only her eating and weight, but also her intense need to keep her family from thinking that she admits they are "right" about how she should think and behave.

From various possible ways of proceeding with the discovery work, the therapist chose to guide Susan into an experience of *symptom deprivation.* In this technique, the client samples what she will experience in living without the symptom. Because a given symptom is in some specific, coherent way necessary to have, being without it is likely to bring some form of unwelcome experience, which normally is avoided unconsciously through *having* the symptom. This technique reveals the client's previously unconscious need to avoid that unwelcome experience by having the symptom—

a need that is, by definition, a pro-symptom position. The point of symptom deprivation is *not* the counteractive aim of arranging for the client to be symptom-free. Rather, the technique is used solely to cause the client's symptom-requiring implicit knowings to begin to reveal themselves. Symptom deprivation elicits a response from the subcortical pro-symptom constructs, a response that is noticeable to the conscious personality, submitting those constructs to cortical attention for the first time. In this way symptom deprivation, like other techniques of discovery, selectively finds and draws forth pro-symptom constructs through their unique property of being the constructs that coherently require the symptom to exist.

The therapist guided Susan to get a glimpse of being without both symptoms: her excess weight and also her need to keep her parents and two brothers from thinking that her becoming thin has proven them right. Symptom deprivation can be carried out in a variety of ways with different levels of experiential immersion. Here, it seemed best to match Susan's strongly cognitive style. The therapist began by prompting a somewhat conceptual preview of *not* feeling disturbed by her family thinking she has proven them right by being thin, and of thinness therefore being viable for her. This was put as an invitation to look at "where you would have to get to in yourself in order to lose weight and keep it off . . . You could tolerate what your thinness means to them and how they talk about it, and you could just let it be . . . You would have to tolerate not feeling seen and understood by them."

Susan immediately described a new awareness of an unwelcome result of being without her symptoms:

> *Client:* . . . the thing is, they misunderstand me anyway. I mean they misunderstand me now. I'm overweight and they still misunderstand me. I *still* don't feel seen by them. So what *difference* does it make, you know what I mean? It's not helping that I'm overweight 'cause they *still* don't see me. I mean they don't, they don't . . . They're not seeing me and understanding me anyway, so it's sort of like: so what's it getting me to continue in this behavior 'cause [laughs] it's really not getting me anything.

> *Therapist:* . . . I have a sense it might be really useful here for you to let that sink in, drop down below the neck that, wow, the battle I feel I'm winning by being heavier than they approve of, I'm not winning. And by being thin, I'd hardly lose more than I already don't get from them. What if that really got very real, um, not just as an idea? . . .

Client: Yeah. Yeah, I mean, I'm already tolerating it in some way. I already am, all the time.

Therapist: And so let's look at how much *more* of feeling unseen, treated like a child you would be if they thought you'd come 'round to their view about body and weight and thinness. How much more painful or vexing or futile would it be for you than already? [*This is a further step of symptom deprivation.*]

Client: Um, I think I've been—It's like they already don't see me but now, they still wouldn't really see me or acknowledge me, but in their minds—It's again that "winning" thing. Like, it's not that they would see me or acknowledge me more, it's just that, like, I would sort of feel like, I don't know how to put it, like they could almost think about me *less* because now they're not quite as worried about me as they were before, or something. You know what I mean? Like, they, they would say like, "Ok, she's coming around so now we don't, you know, we can even brush her aside a little bit more, even, 'cause now she's started coming around." You know, like the only attention I get from them is them being worried about me because I'm not measuring up . . .

Therapist: I see. Well, that—You just brought into the picture a whole other major dimension there.

Client: Yeah, and I haven't really thought of that part before. Yeah. Hmm. It's like, I guess, the only attention that I get from them is that I'm not fitting in. So even though it's not [the kind of] attention that I want, at least I know my brother's speaking about me 'cause I voted for [the candidate disapproved by the family], whereas if I voted for [the candidate approved by the family] maybe he wouldn't think about me at all! . . .

A coherence therapist is always listening closely for any spontaneous pro-symptom indication in what is emerging verbally and nonverbally. In conducting symptom deprivation, the therapist does not know what the client will find. Here the exercise consisted of prompting Susan to envision becoming thin, tolerating her family thinking this means she has agreed with them about how to live, and tolerating being neither seen nor understood by them. As a result of sampling this symptom-free state, she has bumped into implicit, pro-symptom knowings, and turned them into explicit, conscious knowings: (a) Not fitting in, such as by being overweight, is how she keeps family members worried about her in order to extract the little attention that she does get from them, which she expects to lose if she fits in. (b) Not fitting in is supposed to result in her family seeing and understanding her. Awareness of these emotional truths in turn led her immediately to recognize that (c) actually "it's not helping," that is, not fitting in is failing utterly to get them to see and understand her, leaving her with all of the costs but none of the hoped-for benefits of being overweight; heavy or thin, they do not see who she is.

A key component of a pro-symptom position is a well-defined, compelling *purpose* that necessitates producing the symptom either as part of how this purpose is carried out or in consequence of how it is thwarted. A specific purpose for being overweight and for other forms of "not measuring up" has just emerged: getting caring attention and personal understanding from family members through keeping them "worried about me," which, according to Susan's implicit knowings, is the only way to get any caring attention from them at all. The therapist now understands that her eating and weight symptoms, which seemed to be the problem, are actually part of Susan's *solution* to the problem of getting her attachment needs met in a family that demands conformity and forbids differentiation and individuation.

Becoming conscious of these knowings and meanings makes sense of her symptoms in an entirely new way. Previously Susan understood her weight only in terms of defying family dictates. Now she is beginning to experience her own agency in resorting to excessive weight as her way of struggling to make her family pay attention to her, negative attention being better than no attention. She has for twenty years felt "stuck" in excessive eating and weight only because of being unconscious of her own coherent purposes for creating this condition. Her distress over being heavy and her desire for healthy thinness are very real, but are no match for the passionate urgency of her desire for caring attention, which she gets for being heavy.

In contrast to her intellectual mode at the start of the session, Susan has now begun attending more directly to her emotional themes, so the therapist, pacing with her, will use more fully experiential work.

> *Therapist*: Ok. Alright. So I'd like to try something at this point, now that we've bumped into this, if you're willing.

> *Client*: Sure.

66

Therapist: It would be to picture, visualize in your mind's eye your whole family: it's your parents and...your two brothers . . . Picture them, as if in the same room with you, and then—do you have them?

Client: Mm-hm.

Therapist: To try out saying to all of them, ah, "Any attention I get from you is for how I *don't* fit in with the family, and your attention is so important to me that I know I'd better *not* fit in, because |if I fit in| I'll be brushed aside."

Client: Do you want me to say that?

Therapist: Yeah.

Client: |Sighs.| Ok. I'll get them in my mind again. |Closes her eyes, then says to family members:| The only attention that I get from you is for not fitting in, and your attention is so important to me that I'd better not fit in because then I won't get any attention from you at all. I'll just get brushed aside. |Pause.| The funny thing is, I already feel brushed aside, though . . . I'll say it like I'm saying to them |closes eyes again|: The only attention I do get from you is, like, minuscule as it may be, is that like if my weight is, you know, up for discussion or, you know, you say you can't come visit me because you don't want to cram butts in our little house or whatever, and so at least like, you know, even if it's disparaging remarks, that's all I get from you but at least I get something, |crying| something. Yeah.

The work has now become fully experiential. In coherence therapy, "experiential" means a subjective immersion in the symptom-requiring themes and purposes. Here the therapist has prompted such an immersion by guiding Susan to make an *overt statement* of her just-discovered emotional truth, a present-tense, highly candid I-statement spoken directly to her family members, visualized. This simple technique is a reliable way to bring about a deepening into the material, so that the person is no longer only talking *about* it and instead directly inhabits the material, feeling and knowing it as her own emotional truth. In this way, an *integration experience* is created—an experience of relating to the problem *from* and *in* her pro-symptom position. The simultaneous feeling-knowing (occurring in the subcortex and right cortex) and verbal-knowing (involving the left neocortex) brings about the experiential and neural integration of the material.

Integration experiences incorporate the pro-symptom position into the client's conscious experiential world. Generally, a series of integration experiences is required, spanning a few days to a few weeks, for stable integration to be achieved, rendering the pro-symptom position open to transformation.

Susan, for the first time in her life, is now aware of being overweight as her own tactic for keeping family members troubled about her and therefore responding to her with what little caring attention is available from them. Her pro-symptom position consists of all of her knowings, tactics and behaviors involved in this. As noted previously, the client's recognition of her personal agency in producing the symptom is an integral aspect of experiencing a pro-symptom position in most cases, and is a key milestone in the methodology.[7] A symptom that previously seemed to be a mysterious affliction with a life of its own now makes deep sense in terms of important personal meanings and purposes. This in itself is a deeply therapeutic relief for many clients who had been regarding themselves as defective or deficient due to having the symptom.

Imaginal methods, such as the visualization of family members used here for the overt statement, can be highly effective for creating both discovery experiences and integration experiences because, as brain research has shown, subcortical brain systems such as the amygdala respond to imagined situations almost as strongly as they respond to actual, externally perceived situations (see for example Kreiman, Koch, & Fried, 2000).

Note that the therapist's role is to guide the client into inhabiting and experiencing her own symptom-necessitating themes, purposes and tactics. Working phenomenologically, the

---

[7] An exception regarding the encounter with agency occurs when the symptom is a mood state, such as depression or anxiety, that arises unconsciously in response to past or present suffering of a loss, violation, or the thwarting of a purpose or need. Common examples are depression that expresses ungrieved losses or unconscious despair over being neglected, and anxiety that expresses an unconscious state of insecure attachment, dread of aloneness, or reactivation of traumatic memory. In such cases the mood symptom is entirely coherent, the symptom coherence model fully applies, and the client awakens to the emotional truth of how the mood makes deep sense to have, but there is no accompanying experience of agency. Agency is involved only in relation to a symptom that has a function, that is, a symptom that is the very means of carrying out an unconscious purpose. It is the discovered pro-symptom material that reveals whether a particular client's mood symptom is a functionless (but coherent) response to suffering or a functional tactic that carries out a purpose (such as depression that keeps oneself well hidden and therefore safe from attack).

therapist has done no interpreting and has not used any methods or words that attempt to change, stop, override, avoid, fix, get away from, or in any way counteract either the client's symptom of compulsive eating or the underlying themes maintaining that symptom.

Susan's sufferings clearly center on emotional wounds of insecure attachment and lack of attunement. This would lead many therapists to assume that her therapy should centrally make use of the client-therapist relationship to create reparative attachment experiences. Reparative attachment work is an option within coherence therapy, but it is appropriate only if the client's attachment pattern is maintained by a pro-symptom position amenable to being discovered, integrated and transformed through working in this way (see Toomey & Ecker, in press, for criteria regarding that clinical discernment). As this session illustrates, coherence therapy provides other experiential methods that are effective with troubled attachment patterns.

The therapist continued to foster Susan's integration experience:

Therapist: So how is it to openly acknowledge that to them like that?

Client: Huh. I guess it's sad. Yeah, I feel sad, because when I acknowledge that I don't get any attention from them, I also have to acknowledge that I probably never will, you know. I don't see any point that I'll ever get from them what I've always wanted. I think, fat or thin, I'm not going to get it.

Therapist: It's not available from them.

Client: No. [Cries.]

Therapist: It's how they are.

Client: Yeah. It's just how they are. Yeah. I guess, I don't think I've ever like acknowledged that to myself before. I keep hoping that, you know, somehow I'm gonna get it.

Therapist: . . . [Get] their attention—what little bit you do get.

Client: Teeny tiny bit.

Therapist: Teeny tiny bit. And I'm inferring that since that teeny tiny bit is all you get, it's precious.

Client: Mm-hm.

Therapist: And, and if you let yourself look like you're fitting in, you feel you'll lose that little bit you get.

Client: Yeah. Yeah, that's it. |Cries.| . . . I guess this is the whole struggle about like separation from your family or whatever. It feels lonely, you know, to think like that if I conquer this problem then they're going to think, "Ok, she's fine, I don't need to worry about her anymore," and then, you know, like what if I never hear from them again? You know, I mean like, what if I never, ever like even hear from my Mom or anybody that they thought about me, you know? . . .

The therapist's accurate empathy toward Susan's pro-symptom position—the *coherence empathy* that is central to this methodology—has made it possible and even natural for her to stay attentively immersed in the material. As a result she has dropped into a still deeper recognition of how she construes her dilemma: she expects her family members to cease contacting her and to have nothing at all to say to her if she appears to be fine and proper. What is at stake is emotional abandonment, which she prevents by keeping them concerned about her weight, her politics, and so on. This is a further discovery experience of the knowings and constructs that make up her attention-seeking pro-symptom position. The deepening encounter with emotional truth continued about two minutes later:

Client: . . . I've always sort of felt like I kind of landed in a family in which I didn't belong . . . You know, even when I was little and, I mean, I just never felt like they got me, you know . . . They have all the nice things, they have all the right cars they've bought, but they don't spend a lot of time thinking about how people might feel or you know, it's just really not important to them. And it's highly important to me so I've never, you know, I've always been struggling to get, um, kind of acknowledged, you know what I mean? To get acknowledgement from them, and I never can.

Therapist: Mm-hm—never can.

Client: Uh-uh . . . They're just not like that.

Therapist: They're not like that . . . They don't have it to give, that kind of attention that you're struggling your whole life to get from them.

Client: Right.

Therapist: . . . And you don't want that to get severed—that little bit you *do* get.

Client: Mm-hm. 'Cause then it's like I'll be an orphan. Ha, I mean, I'll be familyless, you know, like then I'll just—then they'll just expect me to be happy with what *they* get, which is kind of nothing, you know. I'm not happy with that, you know.

Therapist: Well, that's putting it mildly. You're not happy with that but you would feel like you're an orphan. That sounds like it means that to you, the very essence of family attachment or family connection would go down to zero for you.

Client: Yeah. Yeah.

Therapist: It sounds catastrophic.

Client: Hm. I think that's—I don't know. When, when I overeat it's almost like I dissociate, you know, it's almost like I, I'm not present, you know. And I think that's why it's like so traumatic for me to, you know, to even think about that. It's like I can't watch myself doing what I'm doing because I hate that about myself but I can't stop doing it because I hate what I think the result would be, you know.

Therapist: Yes, it's even worse.

Client: So I'm stuck. So, I have to just like not be present, you know, 'cause I can't stand either eventuality.

Therapist: You can't stand knowing either eventuality, but you pick one of those eventualities as the lesser misery.

Client: Right. But in the moment I pretend like I'm not choosing that.

Therapist: Yes. Yes.

Client: [Small laugh.] Yeah.

Early in the session, Susan described how "uncomfortable" she has become over being thin, and she attributed this discomfort to her view that her family members were thinking they were "proven right" by her finally "fitting in with them." That these conscious notions were incomplete is now apparent. She has now brought her awareness and attention to the unconscious emotional truth of why her fitting in warrants such discomfort: she expects that if she fits in, they will no longer worry about her, and if they

71

no longer worry about her, they will have no real interest in her and pay no attention to her at all, leaving her "familyless" and "orphaned."

This is "so traumatic" a jeopardy that she must avoid awareness of it by dissociating through eating compulsively, which is yet another distinct purpose for eating, a second pro-symptom position discovered in this session. Not to overeat would be to feel the raw truth of an unbearable absence of genuine connective tissue in the family, as she experiences it.

The coherent necessity of overeating consists, then, of at least two distinct purposes discovered thus far: to get caring attention by causing worry, and to avoid feeling unbearable, desolate aloneness. Until now these urgent purposes and the implementation of them by overeating were implicit (unconscious) knowings held subcortically. They are now being translated into explicit (conscious) feeling-knowings and verbal-knowings.

In saying, "I can't stand either eventuality," Susan indicated that now, with awareness of her pro-symptom positions, she sees the structure of her dilemma, a terrible choice and tradeoff that is always facing her: She must either overeat, in order to avoid awareness of disconnection and to elicit attention, at the cost of harming her health and hating being an overweight overeater; or, she can eat healthily, at the cost of plunging herself into the crisis of being emotionally familyless and abandoned.

Here we see another distinctive feature of what unfolds in coherence therapy: having the symptom entails a very real suffering, yet the symptom is necessary to have because *not* having it is expected, unconsciously, to bring an even worse suffering (here, feeling "familyless," "orphaned"). The predicament of being caught between *the two sufferings* (the one with, and the one without, the symptom) becomes conscious in the course of the work as a direct awareness of emotional truth, not as an interpretation or rational explanation from the therapist. In bumping into the *greater* misery—the misery encountered by *not* having the symptom—the client awakens to an existential dilemma that has been unconscious. Susan is now facing the reality that the caring attention and personal understanding that she has always been aching for and striving to get from her family members is simply not available from them. She is facing the disconfirmation of her unconsciously construed fantasy and hope that they *could* understand her, a big step of separation and individuation. In other

72

words, she is now in a position to solve the existential dilemma of unavailable attunement and fragile attachment in a new, conscious way.

The therapist will immediately work to create ongoing integration experiences of these key emotional truths by structuring a simple way for Susan to keep having daily experiences of them.

> *Therapist:* Well, right there is perhaps a new path for you in this, especially given the new—the emotional truths that are newly in view now about *attention* being what's really at stake here.
>
> *Client:* Right.
>
> *Therapist:* I'm wondering if it could work for you to have a personal practice of staying present when you eat too much, and in particular staying present to this emotional truth of how come it's really necessary to be doing this right now. I'll write on a card for you these simple words: "I've *got* to eat like this to keep what little attention I get from them from disappearing completely and making me an orphan."
>
> *Client:* Mm-hm. Yeah.
>
> *Therapist:* Is that—I wonder if that's too big a step?

Writing freshly discovered, key material on a small, yellow index card for daily reading is a mainstay method of creating daily integration experiences in coherence therapy. The phrasing again embodies the qualities needed for verbalizing subcortical emotional truths: first-person, present tense, succinct and emotionally vivid in naming what is at stake and what response is necessary. The content stays very close to Susan's own words and meanings; again there is no interpreting or explaining, and no attempt to counteract her overeating or build up healthy eating patterns. The aim at this stage is to gain access to the constructs driving symptom production by integrating them.

In response to being asked if the task is too big—engaging the client in task design is always important—Susan replied, "I don't know," and explained why she was unsure about being able to do the task. She revealed that she heavily overeats secretly at any and every opportunity to do so throughout the day, and that she has no self-awareness while doing so. "I'm just *compelled* because I'm alone and I have this opportunity. It's almost like I don't even wake up until I'm half-way through," she said, indicating that the task as described by the therapist wouldn't work because it required her to be mindful of her actions. The therapist now regarded the incessant quality of the compulsion to eat as a specific symptom in itself and saw in it an opportunity for further coherence-focused discovery.

> *Therapist*: . . . I think maybe you're pointing us to another piece of this, another part of the emotional truth of this, perhaps. Let's see . . . Thinking of what you just described, how continual is that compulsion to eat whenever there's an opportunity . . . The part that might be the emotional basis or truth of the eating at every opportunity is a big part of what you've told me about in connection with *how little attention* you get from your family: . . . you're a person who's *starving* for that, *all* the time . . . You're clearly a person who's been running on empty for a certain major, fundamental kind of emotional food your whole life.

> *Client*: Yeah.

> *Therapist*: Is that an exaggeration for you, to put it like that?

> *Client*: [Much softer, slower, quieter voice than previously.] No, I think it's true. Yeah.

> *Therapist*: Attention, caring attention. *Attuned* attention to who you are and what you're experiencing.

Here the therapist, in introducing the word "starving," was somewhat leading on content, which is to be avoided in coherence therapy. It needs to be the therapist who learns from the client what the symptom-requiring emotional truth is, not the other way around. However, he was transparent about not presuming to know whether his inference is actually the client's emotional truth, and he submitted it to her for verification. Aiming to make explicit the coherence of her *always-present* compulsion to eat, he has named the truer nature of the hunger that she always feels—the hunger for caring attention. (A less leading way to usher Susan into the same emotional truth would be to have asked, "On a feeling level, *what's the connection*, if any, between always, always feeling attention-deprived, and always seizing any chance to eat?")

This recognition of being starved for attention is yet a further step of discovery. It remained the focus of the last fifteen minutes of the session. Susan now began describing various areas of her life that were coming to mind, making new sense of them:

"Most of the guys I dated, when they would break up with me they would say, 'You're just too needy,' you know, like this is the major flaw in my personality." "And my husband . . . [T]he only time when we have arguments is when I can't get his attention . . . It's like our major thing if I feel like I can't get his attention." "It's just so interesting, this connection about attention . . . [M]y best friend just had a baby a couple weeks ago and I've been really emotional the last couple days 'cause, you know, she's like unavailable and my husband's been a little unavailable and I'm like, you know, there's times when it gets so pressing that I actually have to admit it consciously like, 'I need attention,' you know. But I never thought about it being connected to my eating . . . "

The following dialogue about her deprivation of attention occurred in the midst of this focus.

> *Therapist:* . . . [T]hat's a powerful distress to be carrying around all the time . . . And when one is carrying a distress that powerful, one needs continuous doses of something that soothes . . . So I'm wondering if that might be why part of you gets into that urge to eat whenever there's an opportunity.
>
> *Client:* Yeah. I think that's a lot, that has a lot of truth to it . . . And after I eat like that, although I'm like super guilty and feel terrible about myself, there is a certain, like, just very calm, like I'm full, you know?
>
> *Therapist:* Exactly. It works, in other words.
>
> *Client:* Yeah, it does work. Yeah.
>
> *Therapist:* Yes. That deep distress, that deep ache, the desperation is temporarily gone.
>
> *Client:* Yeah. Yeah.

As a result of discovering and for a few minutes integrating (staying in touch with, and speaking *from* and *in*) the emotional truth of feeling always starved and desperate for caring attention, Susan has now recognized that she eats for the purpose of having a respite of "calm" from that specific emotional ache. It was found earlier in the session that eating blocks her intense distress over feeling always on the verge of being "orphaned." These seem to be two related but different facets of what Susan suffers in relation to her family, and suppresses by eating.

Susan's emotional purposes for eating were now clearer still. Five minutes later she said, "I can see that I have this hunger that never got met, so now I have this huge, gaping appetite for it which, yeah—I mean it's not my fault. It's just that I didn't get it." Her voice was now considerably quieter and slower than during the first half of the session, and her eye movements indicated a great deal of internal processing. When, about a minute later, the therapist commented that "eating handles the emotional reality of the ache of getting no attention," Susan replied, "Yeah. I mean it does a really good job of handling that problem."

This session's progression through several layers of alternating discovery and integration is typical of how coherence therapy unfolds, often across several sessions. The session was now nearly out of time, so the therapist again focused on creating a post-session task of reading an index card to produce ongoing integration experiences.

> *Therapist*: . . . Tell me if this fits for you and let's tune it up and revise it if it's off in some way and get it to feel accurate to you, ok? . . . So you would eat, but first you would just insert 30 seconds of tuning into this. "I've *got* to eat because if I don't, I'll feel how much I'm hurting and starving for the attention I never got, and I'd get thin and lose the little bit of attention I do get for not fitting in."

> *Client*: Yeah. I think that's pretty much it. That feels really true to me.

> *Therapist*: . . . Now, it won't be easy to open this space of mindfulness in that trance that powerfully sets in . . . You might want to read this once in the morning just to keep it near awareness, and then carry the card and each time there's the opportunity to eat and you're about to do that, take out the card, look at it, just see if you can give yourself enough seconds of focus on it to feel, to touch into the feeling like you're having right now, the realness of it. And then eat knowing it's true, even if it feels tragic. Even if it feels sad.

> *Client*: . . . Yeah, that feels like a good plan 'cause I think if I could do that then I would like sort of realize after eating that that's not helping. You know, I mean it's not actually feeling, it's not actually doing what I'm trying to do . . .

After the card was written, Susan and the therapist discussed scheduling a second session. Susan felt she had plenty to work with and was uncertain as to how much time it would take for her to be ready for more, so she opted not to schedule and to call as and when needed. She sent a short email to the therapist at one week and again at one month after the session, the latter saying, "I have been doing well since our session. I am still working on this issue every day, but so far haven't hit any blocks."

Five months after the session, the therapist sent Susan an email asking how these matters had developed. Susan replied as follows:

> Thanks for the follow up. Our session was very helpful, but not in the way I expected or necessarily wanted when I went in. I wanted some shift that would help me lose the weight I'd been wanting to lose—to take care of all the baggage. Well, the session was very effective and got me in touch with the core issues in a different and better way. But I also saw that I didn't have to buy into my family's push for me to be thin in order to be acceptable. The decision that I made was to start a daily yoga and meditation practice. I want to be healthy and fit, but not necessarily to buy into the thinness issue. Yoga has helped me to accept myself and my body exactly the way it is, with the nice effect that this acceptance helps me choose healthier foods and lifestyle choices, etc. I am a LOT stronger and more fit. My weight on the scale hasn't really changed and I'm a lot more okay with that than I have ever been. I can't say I'm TOTALLY okay with it, but I practice being okay with it every day as I just do my best to try to make healthy choices and exercise.
>
> So yes, it was very helpful, mostly in releasing me from the MIND games I and my family was playing with me [sic], not in changing my weight. And that's a great result. . . . [W]hen I start giving myself those old messages [I] remind myself of what the cycle is in my family and that accepting myself is the only answer.

DISCUSSION

This kind of outcome, with resolution through changes in areas unexpected by the client, is not uncommon in coherence therapy because the client invariably finds that the presenting symptom, which at first seemed to be the problem, is a surface manifestation of a more central problem that was not conscious. An authentic resolution of that deeper problem may or may not entail the changes originally sought.

In the session Susan became aware of her central, lifelong dilemma of having a family in which she feels so starved for personal understanding, acceptance and caring attention that she feels very nearly familyless and orphaned, and is unbearably distressed over this. Previously her knowledge of that dilemma and those feelings had been almost entirely implicit (unconscious). She had been responding according to three distinct implicit knowledges (pro-symptom positions): (a) eating whenever possible is necessary in order to avoid feeling the unbearable distress; (b) causing worry and consternation by not fitting in, such as by being overweight, is necessary as the only way to get any attention at all from family members; (c) not fitting in with their standards of perfection is necessary for making them come to see and understand her as a distinct individual. Each of those three knowings is a coherent, compelling emotional truth that makes her symptoms of excessive eating and weight more important to have than not to have. Each became conscious experientially in the session.

The loss of the subjective realness of a pro-symptom construct is the main indication that it has been transformed. Susan's email message indicates that a degree of transformation has occurred in the three different pro-symptom positions just enumerated. Her sense of feeling a "release" from the longstanding "mind games" in the family suggests this. She also refers to a positive change in her food habits and is "a lot more okay with [my weight] than I have ever been." The last phrase in the message, "accepting myself is the only answer," more specifically indicates a fundamental shift in the implicit knowings defining how to respond to her dilemma of insecure attachment. Her phrase implies that, having consciously revisited and reassessed how she strives to solve that dilemma, she is arriving at a very different solution in which she accepts rather than struggles against the profound unavailability of attuned understanding and acceptance from her parents and brothers. As a result she has begun to be *self*-accepting and *self*-nurturing, because of seeing that this is the only basis of well-being that actually and always is available to her. This is a liberating step of separation-individuation and emotional health, and Susan recognizes it to be an even bigger prize than the weight loss she initially was seeking.[8]

[8] Ordinarily, a coherence therapist actively seeks a confirmation of transformation, that is, a confirmation of the loss of subjective realness of key pro-symptom constructs. This is best done through applying experiential cues and triggers that have reliably activated the pro-symptom constructs in the past, in order

Integration of pro-symptom positions leads to their spontaneous transformation about half the time, as appears to have occurred for Susan. If, on the other hand, an integrated pro-symptom position does not transform spontaneously and persists in its felt realness, the therapist must deliberately prompt an experience that transforms it.

Coherence therapy delineates a specific methodology for this transformation of constructs. The methodology is designed to utilize the brain-mind-body system's inherent process of construct revision, a process that was identified phenomenologically by Ecker and Hulley (1996, 2000a, 2004) and that receives support through its close correspondences with the recently discovered neural process of *reconsolidation* of implicit memory (detailed in Ecker & Toomey, in press). Conditioned response schemas in emotional implicit memory (such as pro-symptom positions) had been believed indelible and immutable throughout the 20th century, a conceptual pillar that was toppled in the year 2000 by evidence of reconsolidation, a neural mechanism that can alter and even erase implicit memory through a previously unsuspected type of neuroplasticity (synaptic change).

The critical condition for a transformation of pro-symptom constructs consists of a *disconfirming juxtaposition*: the client simultaneously experiences as real both a pro-symptom knowing and some other, contradictory knowing. Experiencing an incompatible construct can disconfirm and dissolve the pro-symptom construct

---

to determine whether those constructs still exist and activate. An overt statement of the original pro-symptom material is one of several suitable methods. For example, Susan would be asked to picture her family members and say out loud, "If I got thin and fit in with your standards, it would be the end of my chances of getting you to see who I am. And then you wouldn't be worried about me and wouldn't pay *any* attention to me any more, and that terrifies me, so *no way* am I willing to get thin—even though I *hate* how being heavy hurts my health and how I feel about myself. But I'd rather endure that than be invisible and orphaned." Overt statements properly facilitated are quite effective in deepening the speaker into the subjective, emotional realness of the constructs being spoken, but only if those constructs still exist in the brain's emotional systems (subcortex and right cortical hemisphere). An overt statement of pro-symptom constructs that no longer exist fails to evoke any felt realness. Rather, the previously dire, vivid material now seems implausible, silly, lifeless, absurd or even laughable. (For an example of that test of transformation in a real session on video, showing the client describe a major, lifelong, newly conscious pro-symptom position as seeming quite funny at the end of one session of therapy, see Ecker and Hulley, 1997.) The work during Susan's one session did not go quite far enough for a confirmation of transformation to be carried out.

if the client experiences both at once, in the same field of awareness, in juxtaposition: both knowings seem real, yet both cannot be true. This produces a recognition of the more archaic and limiting pro-symptom construct as false, which rapidly de-commissions it as a representation of reality. Thereafter the pro-symptom construct no longer has subjective realness and cannot be re-triggered, which is the primary indicator of actual transformation.

Like the rest of coherence therapy, disconfirmation through juxtaposition is a non-counteractive process. The therapist says and does nothing that opposes the pro-symptom position and guides the client to stay in touch with it, not to get away from it, while also attending to some other, contradictory knowledge. The therapist lets the contradiction speak for itself, never tries to indicate how to resolve it or which construct to regard as more valid, and trusts the client's native process to do that and to carry out the depotentiation of the pro-symptom knowings and synapses.

If instead, as occurs with counteractive methods, the client were to focus attention only on experiencing the disconfirming construct, without sustained, *simultaneous* awareness of the pro-symptom construct, then the disconfirming construct is set up separately and merely opposes and competes against the pro-symptom construct.[9] This situation fails to actually transform or dissolve the more powerful pro-symptom construct, which retains its realness and remains re-triggerable, causing relapses. Counterintuitively, it is by *maintaining* awareness of the trouble-making pro-symptom construct alongside the contradictory, disconfirming construct that transformation occurs.

When a pro-symptom position transforms spontaneously following integration, as it did for Susan, the same process is responsible. Upon becoming integrated, a pro-symptom construct is suddenly susceptible to being juxtaposed spontaneously in the same field of awareness with all manner of other knowings held by the individual. For example, one of the pro-symptom constructs transformed by Susan is (in verbalized form), "By visibly *not* fitting in, they will see me and understand me." This emotionally urgent

---

[9] According to mounting neural evidence, the medial pre-frontal cortex (mPFC) is the brain's storage site for knowings that counteract and compete against activation of aversive, fear-based pro-symptom construals and schemas, which are stored in the amygdala, presumably. For details see Ecker and Toomey, in press.

knowing, carried in her subcortical library of nonverbal knowings, became conscious and was disconfirmed by being juxtaposed with a new knowing that Susan formed and articulated fairly early in the session, "They have *no* capacity to see me and understand me in *any* case, heavy or thin." Both of those constructs were real to her, but both cannot be true.

CONCLUSION

Coherence therapy is defined by its methodology of experientially discovering, integrating and transforming pro-symptom positions. Within that methodology, a coherence therapist has a wide latitude for moment-to-moment choices of technique and interactional style. We teach trainees about a dozen specific techniques (Ecker and Hulley, 2004) that are particularly versatile, simple and reliable (such as symptom deprivation, overt statement, what's the connection, and index card techniques illustrated in the case example), but the therapist is free to adapt or invent any experiential methods that can serve this methodology. Our case example of Susan should therefore not be taken as defining the particulars of technique and style, but only as showing how the core methodology was carried out in this instance. The therapist had sessions with other clients on that same day with a quite different quality and rhythm, while carrying out the same methodology. (For a discussion of coherence therapy [depth-oriented brief therapy] in relation to the broader context of constructivist psychotherapies, see Neimeyer and Bridges, 2003 and Neimeyer and Raskin, 2001.)

The principles of change followed in coherence therapy can be summarized in simple terms in this way (Ecker and Hulley, 2004):

- Change of a symptom is blocked when a person tries to make the change from a position that does not actually have control of the symptom—a position merely against having the symptom (an anti-symptom position).

- For a person to achieve rapid change of the symptom, first have him or her experience, inhabit, verbalize and embrace the emotional truth in the symptom-requiring position, because that is the

81

position that does have control over producing the symptom (a pro-symptom position).

- People are able to change a position they experience having, but are not able to change an unconscious position that they do not know they have.

- Counteracting is counterproductive: it fails to transform and only maintains the split-off, unconscious condition of the person's symptom-requiring knowings.

- A person will transform a pro-symptom position when this position is experienced simultaneously and in juxtaposition with other living knowledge that is incompatible with it, so that the two knowledges cannot possibly both be true, yet both are present in the same field of awareness.

Several integral aspects of coherence therapy are not addressed in this short introduction, such as working with resistance; the functions and use of client-therapist relationship; the internal, hierarchical structure of constructs in a pro-symptom position; and coherence-focused work with couples and families. These and other features of the methodology are described in detail elsewhere (Ecker & Hulley, 1996, 1996a, 1997, 1997a, 2000a, 2000b, 2002b, 2004; Ecker & Toomey, in press).

Usually more than one session is needed; a majority of clients require five to ten sessions, and a small minority requires more than twenty. Our experience with coherence therapy tells us that the human capability for swift, accurate, in-depth change is far greater than was recognized during the first century of the psychotherapy field; that surprisingly effective work can happen routinely, in most every session, if the therapist remains coherence-focused continually. In the session detailed here, the significant progress and appearance of easiness and inevitability is due largely to the coherence-mindedness maintained by the therapist. Whether it is easy or difficult for a trainee in coherence therapy to learn to maintain coherence-mindedness moment-to-moment depends on how many *non*-coherence-oriented constructs and commitments he or she has.

REFERENCES

Ecker, B. (2003). The hidden logic of anxiety: Look for the emotional truth behind the symptom. *Psychotherapy Networker, 27* (6), 38-43, 58.

Ecker, B., & Hulley, L. (1996). *Depth oriented brief therapy: How to be brief when you were trained to be deep, and vice versa.* San Francisco: Jossey-Bass.

Ecker, B., & Hulley, L. (Producers). (1996a). *Stuck in depression.* [Video and viewer's manual.] Oakland, CA: Pacific Seminars. Online: www.dobt.com/video.htm

Ecker, B., & Hulley, L. (Producers). (1997). *Compulsive underachieving.* [Video and viewer's manual.] Oakland, CA: Pacific Seminars. Online: www.dobt.com/video.htm

Ecker, B., & Hulley, L. (Producers). (1997a). *Down every year.* [Video and viewer's manual.] Oakland, CA: Pacific Seminars. Online: www.dobt.com/video.htm

Ecker, B., & Hulley, L. (2000a). Depth-oriented brief therapy: Accelerated accessing of the coherent unconscious. In J. Carlson & L. Sperry (Eds.), *Brief therapy with individuals and couples* (pp. 161-190). Phoenix: Zeig, Tucker and Theisen.

Ecker, B., & Hulley, L. (2000b). The order in clinical "disorder": Symptom coherence in depth oriented brief therapy. In R. A. Neimeyer & J. D. Raskin (Eds.), *Constructions of disorder: Meaning-making frameworks for psychotherapy* (pp. 63-89). Washington, DC: American Psychological Association.

Ecker, B., & Hulley, L. (2000c). A new zone of effectiveness for psychotherapy. *New Therapist, 6,* 31-33.

Ecker, B., & Hulley, L. (2002a). Deep from the start: Profound change in brief therapy. *Psychotherapy Networker, 26*(1), 46-51, 64.

Ecker, B., & Hulley, L. (2002b). DOBT toolkit for in-depth effectiveness: Methods and concepts of depth-oriented brief therapy. *New Therapist, 20,* 24-29.

Ecker, B., & Hulley, L. (2004). *Depth-oriented brief therapy practice manual and training guide.* Oakland, CA: Pacific Seminars. Online: www.dobt.com/manual.htm

Ecker, B., & Toomey, B. (in press). Depotentiation of symptom-producing implicit memory in coherence therapy. *Journal of Constructivist Psychology.*

Kelly, G. A. (1991a). *The psychology of personal constructs. Vol. 1: A theory of personality.* New York: Norton. (Original work published 1955)

Kelly, G. A. (1991b). *The psychology of personal constructs. Vol. 2: Clinical diagnosis and psychotherapy.* New York: Norton. (Original work published 1955)

Kreiman, G., Koch, C., & Fried, I. (2000). Imagery neurons in the human brain. *Nature, 408,* 357-361.

Milner, B., Squire, L. R., & Kandel, E. R. (1998). Cognitive neuroscience and the study of memory. *Neuron, 20,* 445-468.

Neimeyer, R.A., & Bridges, S.K. (2003). Postmodern approaches to psychotherapy. In Gurman, A.S. & Messer, S.B. (Eds.), *Essential psychotherapies*, (2nd ed., pp. 272-316). New York: Guilford.

Neimeyer, R.A., & Raskin, J. D. (2001). Varieties of constructivism in psychotherapy. In Dobson, K.S. (Ed.), *Handbook of cognitive-behavioral therapies* (2nd ed., pp. 407-411). New York: Guilford.

Phelps, E.A. & LeDoux, J.E. (2005). Contributions of the amygdala to emotion processing: from animal models to human behavior. *Neuron, 48,* 175-187.

Toomey, B., & Ecker, B. (2007). Of neurons and knowings: Constructivism, coherence psychology and their neurodynamic substrates. *Journal of Constructivist Psychology, 20,* 201-245.

Toomey, B., & Ecker, B. (in press). Competing visions of the implications of neuroscience for psychotherapy. *Journal of Constructivist Psychology.*

∝ 4 ∞

Mind and Self in
Context-Centered Psychotherapy

Jay S. Efran and José Soler-Baillo

In 1990, we described an approach to psychotherapy based in part on Humberto Maturana's theory of structure determinism (Efran, Lukens, & Lukens, 1990). However, we did not give the method a name because the editor felt that therapy "brand names" limit a book's readership. An unfortunate side effect of that decision was that when the book was published, graduate students began to refer to our approach as "Efran's stuff"—hardly an elegant label. Therefore, we now call what we do "context-centered psychotherapy"[1] in recognition of the approach's emphasis on the frameworks of meaning within which events are shaped and experienced. In this chapter, we discuss two core contexts—*mind* and *self*—that form a basic organizing scheme for our work with clients. We describe the implications of those contexts and discuss a series of related clinical principles and interventions.

WHY CONTEXT?

Experience can be described in terms of three levels of abstraction—content, process, and context. Therapeutic interventions can target any of these levels. For example, if a client complains of frequently oversleeping and arriving late for work, a content-oriented therapist might recommend that he invest in a good alarm clock. If setting the alarm doesn't do the trick, the therapist might then suggest that he move the clock further away from the bed so that it is harder to turn off. In our experience, beginning counselors and therapists often make these kinds of

---

[1] We would have preferred the term "contextual psychotherapy," but Ivan Boszormenyi-Nagy (1987) was already using it to describe his version of family therapy.

content-oriented suggestions, responding concretely to the client's complaints with factual information and practical advice.

However, more experienced clinicians generally attend to *process* or relationship factors rather than the specific content. For instance, in our hypothetical example, they might interpret oversleeping as an avoidant strategy aimed at postponing the start of an unpleasant workday. If the client wasn't getting along with his boss, they might interpret his lateness as an act of rebellion or passive-aggression. Psychoanalytically oriented therapists might go a step further, construing the problem as an authority issue with roots in the Oedipal conflict. Such interventions are usually considered more sophisticated and more efficient than content-based responses.

Context-centered therapists move another rung up the ladder of abstraction, focusing on contextual changes that can automatically rearrange processes and generate new content. In our example, the context-oriented therapist might assist the client in clarifying his career goals and reassessing his work-related attitudes. If the client began to see his job as a choice rather than an encumbrance, he might feel less antipathy toward his boss and his passive-aggressive behaviors might cease. Alternatively, he might conclude that he was in the wrong job altogether. In either event, oversleeping and buying alarm clocks would have become non-issues.

WHAT ARE CONTEXTS?

Contexts are sets of presuppositions that shape experience, establish goals, and generate meanings. Because they operate in the background, they typically go unnoticed. We are usually so focused on the painting that we fail to notice that it is the frame that defines these particular blobs of paint as a work of art.

The fact that the frame of a painting happens to have physical dimensions is not what makes it a contextual marker. The essential aspect of a contextual boundary is that it is "made of information" rather than "stuff" (Durkin, 1981, p. 57). For instance, two people are just as married whether or not they wear their wedding rings. Contexts transcend the usual space-time boundaries. For instance, although the traditional marriage vow contains the phrase "till death do us part," the legal, social, and financial implications of a marital context do not necessarily end when the spouses die.

Because contexts are not physical entities, they can shift in the blink of an eye—literally outside of time. Finding a spouse can take years, but saying "I do" takes only an instant. Like all contextual transformations, the shift from "single" to "married" is *digital* rather than *analogic*—either/or rather than gradual. Although the processes they spawn unfold over time, contexts are instantaneously created and dissolved.

We use language to label and describe contexts. There is no other choice. However, the words and symbols that denote a context are not to be confused with the context itself—the map is not the territory (Korzybski, 1941). Contextual designations such as "married" or "divorced," "employed" or "unemployed," "Christian" or "Buddhist" hardly begin to tell the person's story. A context sets a process in motion, but the final outcome remains partly unknowable. No two marriages ever unfold in the same way, and no two years of any particular marriage are ever the same.

The experiential domains created by contexts do not overlap. Playing chess brings a unique world into being, and that world is completely separate from the domain that checkers creates (even though the board design is the same). A person can play both games, but he or she can not transpose the rules of one game to the other. Although contexts do not mix, narrower contexts can be subsumed by more inclusive frameworks. Thus, an individual can play a variety of games—for instance, checkers, chess, and backgammon—under the broader rubric of competitive "gamer."

During the course of a typical day, people move smoothly through many contexts. However, we sometimes find ourselves obliged to play two or more contradictory roles at roughly the same time. This results in what Maturana calls "an emotional contradiction" (Mendez, Coddou, & Maturana, 1988). As journalist Mignon McLaughlin reminds us, it is nearly impossible "to be loyal to your family, your friends, your country, and your principles, all at the same time."[2] Thus, we all live through occasional emotional contradictions. However, if these become chronic, we seek therapy.

One way to resolve such difficulties is to move to a context large enough to encompass otherwise incompatible role demands.

[2] McLaughlin, M. Retrieved January 18, 2007, from http://www.dontquoteme.com/search/search_result.jsp?sid=10082.

As Maturana points out, the "solution to apparent contradictions lies in moving away from the opposition . . . to embrace a broader context" (Maturana & Varela, 1987, p. 135). For example, we saw a client who was upset because her husband wanted to quit dental school and try his luck on Wall Street. She was frightened about the prospect of him sacrificing the family's financial stability to dabble in stocks. The resolution occurred when she realized that no amount of security was worth dooming a spouse to a lifetime of job dissatisfaction and that pressuring him to stay in dentistry would only create long-term resentment. So, she shifted from her narrow preoccupation with security to the larger principle that everyone deserves a chance to pursue his or her vocational dreams, even if doing so entails a certain amount of risk.

In the natural order of events, contexts precede the processes and contents they shape. For example, some concept of education must be in place before you can begin to build classrooms, hire teachers, and select students. The clearer the context, the easier it is to achieve one's goals. Thus, much of the work of context-centered therapy consists of helping clients clarify the assumptions that define the contexts in which they live.

Finally, all meanings are context-dependent. When the chess game ends, the "Queen" loses her royal status and reverts to being just a piece of plastic or wood. Similarly, the senior-class ring that was such a source of pride in high school can quickly become an object of scorn as soon as the individual sets foot on a college campus. The rule of thumb is that every shift in context rearranges meanings, closing off some options and creating others.

PSYCHOTHERAPY AS A CONTEXT

Of course, psychotherapy is itself a context, and a problematic one at that. Although the term was coined in the late 1880s by combining *psyche* (mind or soul) and *therapie* (treatment), it continues to defy precise definition. In fact, many of the 500 or so techniques that have been labeled therapeutic have very little in common. From our perspective, this definitional ambiguity results from the original error of considering psychotherapy a medical procedure. This *category mistake* situated the therapist's activities in an inappropriate conceptual envelope. Therapists do not treat symptoms or cure diseases. They have no salves to apply, no antibiotics to prescribe, and no surgical instruments to wield.

The association with the medical model and disease-entity approach continues to seduce us into analyzing our craft using conceptual tools that are not well suited to the task. As even Freud acknowledged, psychotherapy is not a medical treatment—it is merely a form of dialogue or conversation.

Note that the word conversation is a combination of *vertere* (to turn) and *con* (with). Thus, to converse is to "turn with" someone. This strikes us as a particularly apt metaphor for our work with clients—we "turn" with them and, in the process, help them turn over and examine problems from fresh angles. The goal of context-centered therapy is exactly that—to illuminate the hidden contextual constraints that limit the client's problem-solving options.

THE MIND AND THE SELF

Although clients operate in many specific contexts, *mind* and *self* are useful labels for the broad frameworks with which almost all clients grapple. Psychiatrist Ron Smothermon (1979) defines the *mind* as the totality of a person's defensive postures and survival mechanisms.[3] The mind will do just about anything "to survive and be right" (p. 3). Its main preoccupations are ensuring safety and maintaining control. The mind is risk-averse. The *self*, on the other hand, is the non-defensive recognition that we are all an integral part of our community and are intricately connected to the world at large. As Alan Watts puts it: "Every individual is an expression of the whole realm of nature, a unique action of the total universe" (Watts, 1966, p. 8). The self has little investment in personal survival or selfish pursuits. Love, because it expresses the "fundamental relatedness in the universe" (Smothermon, 1979, p. 124), is a function of the self. Lust and infatuation, on the other hand, have more to do with the mind's desire to possess and control.

Within each of us there is a running mind-self debate. If we lived exclusively in the context of mind, we would stay at home and avoid all risks, selfishly putting our own interests above the welfare of others. If we operated entirely "from self," we might emulate the kind of selfless[4] existence we generally attribute to Gandhi or

---

[3] Note that "mind," as we use the term, does not refer to the brain or the nervous system. It is a psychological context, not a set of physical structures.
[4] Language customs are an obstacle here. We call operating from self being "self-less" when it should be called "being self-ful." Similarly, we call operating from mind

Mother Teresa, subordinating our personal desires to the interests of the community. The mind's operations are fear-driven and survival-oriented; the self's perspective is open and accepting.

Being the larger framework, the self accepts the mind as a legitimate subset of human concerns. However, because the mind's perspective is more limited, it does not return the favor. The mind takes as its mission not only the survival of the individual but also the preservation of the person's property—car, home, clothes, books, and so on. It also defends the individual's psychological "property," such as attitudes, positions, and opinions.

As the individual's self-appointed advocate, the mind always wants to win, dominate, and be right. If those goals are blocked, it works to achieve its secondary objectives: avoiding loss, resisting domination, and refusing to be made wrong. At a press conference, when President George W. Bush was forced to concede that we weren't winning the war in Iraq, he adopted the fallback position that we weren't losing, either. That kind of convoluted logic is typical of the mind's insistence on maintaining the upper hand.

Obviously, the mind's protective strategies have had evolutionary value. The problem is that it tends to go overboard, seeking the kind of absolute safety and protection that simply isn't available in the real world. Thus, in the interest of avoiding danger, it forgoes opportunity. For instance, socially phobic individuals often refuse to meet someone if there is even the slightest risk of rejection. The tyranny of their minds interferes with their taking advantage of the kinds of opportunities that might lead to satisfying relationships. "Taking a chance" is not a strategy the mind endorses.

Consider, for example, the case of a woman who was living in Manhattan at the time of the September 11th attacks. In the following months, she became increasingly hesitant to ride public transit. She also avoided crowds and, despite knowing that it was irrational, felt wary around anyone who looked Arabic. As her discomfort intensified, she quit her job as a department-store buyer and moved into a friend's condo in a nearby city. She took a waitressing job to help make ends meet but soon gave it up because the constant flow of customers made her edgy.

The therapist she saw at a community clinic had her look at computerized photographs of the 9/11 disaster to "desensitize" her

"being selfish" when it would be more consistent to call it "being mindish."

fears. Unfortunately, she found that viewing these pictures had the opposite effect, and she dropped out of treatment. A month later, on the advice of a friend, she consulted another therapist (who happened to be more context-oriented). In their first meeting, he assured her that she would not have to do anything that made her uncomfortable. He began by describing in some detail how the "mind" operates (and why), using examples from her recent and past experiences.[5] She began to understand, for example, why a mind would oppose riding on *any* buses or subways rather than risk being caught in the wrong place at the wrong time. The mind typically errs on the side of caution and has little interest in counterbalancing actual costs and payoffs.

The therapist's main goal was to assist this woman in noticing how her mind operates, but not necessarily combating or silencing it. The context-centered approach is acceptance-based, not deficiency-oriented. Unlike with "eliminative" methods, the objective is not to directly banish troublesome thoughts or extinguish unwanted behaviors. In fact, as many therapists have learned, directly challenging the mind is generally a futile exercise. As they say in the East, *whatever you resist persists; whatever you let be lets you be.* The irony is that the more one tries to dismiss or obliterate a particular thought, the more preoccupying it becomes. This point is well illustrated by what has been called the "Sister Mary Complex."

> Sister Mary was a new nun and, understandably, she really, really wanted to please God. One day she was being such a good nun that she was allowed to bring tea to the Mother Superior—a great, great honor. Everything was going perfectly. The tea service was beautifully arrayed and the sugar and cookies were precisely laid out. Sister Mary took the tray and proudly, devoutly, and gracefully moved into the room. Then, she tripped on the carpet, spilling everything. She automatically cursed: "Oh Christ." Then she swore again: "Oh God, I said Christ!". . . "Oh damn, I said God!". . . "Oh shit, I said damn!" Get the picture? (Gregson & Efran, 2002, p. 43)

Mindful of the Sister Mary effect, context-centered therapists invite clients to observe the mind rather than mount a frontal assault against it. Ironically, even calling the mind "wrong"

[5] As in this case, we typically teach the terms "mind" and "self" to the client. Most clients seem to like the terms and catch on quickly to their meaning. However, with a young child or in other special circumstances we would adjust the vocabulary accordingly.

is self-defeating—as pointless as being angry about being mad or upset about being anxious. The paradox is that name-calling itself is a function of the mind. Therefore, attempts to make it wrong merely increase its power. By contrast, if you simply allow the mind to "do its thing," you ultimately diminish its power.

As clients watch their minds operate, its excesses often bemuse them. For instance, they notice that it relentlessly issues "over the top" warnings, even though its previous doom-and-gloom predictions were not confirmed. It also goes to great lengths to be right, refusing to drop arguments that have long since become moot.

Of course, you cannot observe the mind while you are immersed in it. As they say, "It would hardly be fish who discovered the existence of water." In our model, it is the wider context of self that provides the observational "perch" from which the mind's operations can be clearly seen.

The woman in our example began to improve when she realized that her defensive posture had caused her to surrender much of her life to the terrorists. With the therapist's encouragement, she devised a plan to reassert her "self" by contributing to the war effort. Therefore, over the Christmas holidays, she volunteered at a local church to help assemble care packages for the troops. She realized that her excursions to the church might very well provoke anxiety. However, after having thought the matter through, she committed herself to the project, concluding that its importance warranted taking the risk. As she set out on the first of these trips, she "thanked her mind," as therapist Steven Hayes (in press) says, for issuing the usual warnings but proceeded anyway, prepared to accept the consequences. As it turned out, the commutes were relatively uneventful and she found herself looking forward to socializing with the other volunteers. Moreover, as she proudly reported to her therapist, she was the one others began to rely on to lift their spirits when they worried about their relatives overseas. While working on this project she discovered what many of us already know—committing yourself to a larger cause reduces the urgency of personal concerns. A problem seems smaller when viewed in a larger context. As Gandhi put it, "The best way to find yourself is to lose yourself in the service of others."[6]

6 Gandhi, Mahatma. Retrieved January 20, 2007 from
http://www.worldofquotes.com/author/Mahatma-Gandhi/1/index.html.

This client wondered why she had such strong reactions to 9/11, particularly given that she was not at ground zero when the attacks occurred. Context-centered therapists do not question a person's unique reactions, and they are disinclined to label such responses "inappropriate," "maladaptive," "excessive," or "deficient." All of an organism's reactions are legitimate—shaped by their idiosyncratic genetic and environmental history. Also, context-centered therapists are less interested in the possible links between childhood events and adult personality that seem to fascinate so many other clinicians. For example, a client may fervently believe that her obsessive tendencies are due to having been raised by a controlling mother. However, such hypotheses are of dubious validity. They typically ignore genetic determinants, cannot be substantiated in the absence of a control group, and have received virtually no empirical support (e.g. Dawes, 1994; Efran & Greene, 2000; Harris, 1998; Seligman, 1993). Unfortunately, therapists sometimes endorse these sorts of causal attributions, unwisely lending their authority to the client's false and misleading beliefs.

MIND AND SELF: A GLOSSARY OF DISTINCTIONS

Because context-centered therapists recognize that we all "live and breathe in language" (Varela, 1979), they emphasize using words precisely. Therefore, we have developed an illustrative (but not exhaustive) glossary of contrasting mind-self terms to help therapists understand the sometimes subtle differences between these two contexts (Table 1). In our chart, the first term of each pair is associated with the mind and the second with the self. For example, *agreement* and *alignment* seem nearly synonymous, but we use the first term to represent the mind's insistence on consensus and the second to refer to the larger meshing of goals. The mind strives for continuous agreement, but the self recognizes that dissent is a necessary component of progress. Two individuals who are aligned take differences of opinion in stride.

The therapeutic alliance, which has become increasingly important in the therapy literature (e.g. Hubble, Duncan, & Miller, 1999), is a good example of alignment. We define the therapeutic alliance as the joining of the client's self and the therapist's self for the purpose of "taming" the client's overzealous mind. Despite the enormous heterogeneity of client complaints,

93

successful therapy is almost invariably a matter of shifting the balance from the smaller context of mind to the larger context of self.

TABLE 1. MIND/SELF CONTRASTS

SURVIVING (MIND)	LIVING (SELF)
Agreement	Alignment
Judgments	Considerations
At effect (victim)	At cause (author)
Decisions	Choices
Reasons (excuses)	Results
Blame	Responsibility
Insecurity	Certainty
Insufficiency	Sufficiency
Gratification	Satisfaction
Later	Now
Demands	Invitations
Obligations	Gifts

Because of the importance of a strong alliance, context-centered therapists start negotiating a clear contract almost immediately. They usually begin by asking, "What can I do for you?" rather than "What is the problem?" or "What brings you here?" The first phrasing highlights the issue of mutual goals, putting the project on the right track, even if the client has not yet formulated a complete answer to the question.

Judgment and *consideration*, the second pair of listed terms, are also close in meaning but used differently. Judgments imply that *Zeus has spoken*; considerations are more malleable expressions of the person's point of view. Unlike judgments, considerations include an implicit acknowledgment that the position being taken is just a personal opinion. As Smothermon (1979) says, "positions offered as positions are an absolute contribution . . . Positions offered as the truth are pure venom" (p. 220).

A couple seen by the first author illustrate the distinction: In an early session, he interrupted their latest shouting match by explaining that the two of them evidently had "different considerations." Having never heard the term used that way, they stopped cold in their tracks. In the resulting pause, the author described the difference between "having a consideration" and engaging in a judgmental "conversation of accusation, characterization, and recrimination" (Mendez, Coddou, & Maturana, 1988, p. 158). At their next session, the couple enthusiastically reported that they had avoided many potential fights by playfully reminding each other that everyone is entitled to a few "considerations." To this day, they recount how learning that term helped save their marriage.

In fact, the novel use of terms such as "consideration" often helps break up unproductive patterns and gets clients to think in new directions. For example, the phrases *at effect* and *at cause* (Erhard & Gioscia, 1977) are odd, but they invariably succeed in grabbing the client's attention. People are "at effect" when they operate from mind—evading responsibility, blaming their actions on external factors, and adopting the role of "victim." Individuals can be at the effect of an almost infinite array of factors, from bad weather to unfair labor practices. Unfortunately, all such external attributions shrink the self. In the words of Richard Bach, "Argue for your limitations, and sure enough, they're yours" (1977, p. 100). Being *at cause* is the more powerful position. It signifies the person's willingness to acknowledge ownership of his or her life experience. Therapy invites the person to shift from being at effect to being at cause.

Of all the distinctions we intend to describe, the difference between *decisions* and *choices* is arguably the subtlest. A *choice* is a pure preference. When the waiter arrives, you simply tell him whether you prefer salmon or steak. Such choices do not need to be defended. By contrast, decision-makers deny personal responsibility by portraying their selections as the "right" or "correct" course of action: "I have to order the fish because it's healthier." Smokers, for example, often diminish their personal autonomy by blaming their decisions on job stress, tobacco advertising, nicotine levels, and so on. Some claim they are being "forced" to quit for health reasons. However, health risks do not have the power to make anyone quit, as evidenced by the large numbers of people who continue using cigarettes right up until the bitter end. Ironically, the mind's attempt to portray itself as a hapless victim of circumstance makes quitting (or any other course of action) that much more difficult. In our experience, it is those who quit on their own authority—as a clear choice of the self— who are most likely to succeed. As Smothermon (1979) puts it, "Do what you do in life because you are doing it, not because you believe in it, have a high opinion of it, or have faith in it. Doing what you do out of belief, opinion, or faith takes *you* out of the picture" (p. 52, emphasis added). In our terminology, it weakens the self.

One of the mind's favorite techniques for dodging blame is to use *reasons* to justify a lack of *results*. Almost any fact or circumstance can be pressed into service in the mind's quest to be right and avoid fault. As a colleague recently said, "It is pretty difficult to catch people with their reasons down." If you claim you went off your diet *because* you did not want to be impolite to the hostess, "everything that follows the word 'because' is a reason" (Smothermon, 1979, p. 30). Reasons sidestep responsibility but contribute little to achieving results. It is the self that focuses on solutions rather than excuses.

Whenever possible, the mind constructs its reasons and rationalizations out of bits and pieces of the truth. In our smoking example, rising nicotine levels and health risks are indeed legitimate concerns. However, it is still a detriment to cede personal responsibility to external factors. It is worth noting that once results have been produced, reasons drop out of the picture. When a child brings home an "F," the parents want an explanation— when she brings home an "A," they don't. Desirable results render reasons irrelevant.

Although the terms *blame* and *responsibility* are practically polar opposites, people often use them interchangeably. They say, "You are responsible for my nervous breakdown" when they mean, "You are to blame" for it. Blaming a person makes him or her wrong. True responsibility, on the other hand, is non-evaluative—it is a simple acknowledgment that you own your own life. Although responsibility cannot be imposed from the outside, therapists can help empower their clients by holding them accountable for inconsistencies in their narratives. As the late psychoanalyst Sidney Rubin used to argue, a therapist's main obligation is to keep asking questions until all of the ambiguity has been wrung out of the client's story. From his perspective, the therapist's questions are equivalent to the surgeon's scalpel.

Although the mind works overtime to avoid threat, it never achieves the security it craves. The mind's refusal to accept risk only serves to amplify the salience of threatening themes. For instance, clients who try not to think about death usually wind up ruminating about it more than the rest of us. Richard Schwartz (2004), the originator of Internal Family Systems Therapy, writes that whenever his clients try to rid themselves of their destructive and suicidal impulses, "the more powerful and resistant these feelings [become]" (p. 41). Again, whatever you resist persists.

The mind also worries that resources such as money, power, safety, and love are in short supply. This context of *insufficiency* leads to selfishness, greed, possessiveness, and jealousy. Often the person seems to be following the rule that you can never have too much of what you don't really need. By contrast, the self's stance is *sufficiency*—the point of view that we live in a bountiful universe in which one gains more through sharing and generosity than stinginess and hoarding. In the matter of love, for example, jealousy is a small-minded and self-defeating position. If you truly loved someone, wouldn't you want that person to be happy even if it meant that he or she chose to be with someone else?

The context of sufficiency allows the self to experience *satisfaction* in the *now*. However, the mind never accepts the status quo—it is always angling for a better deal. Again, Smothermon (1979) writes compellingly about the mind's stubborn refusal to live in the present:

> How many times have you dwelled on the relationship you don't have and ignored the ones you do have? How often have you wished for that job you don't have and neglected the one you do have? When was the last time you wished you had different parents and didn't give consideration to the ones you do have? And what about living in another place? That would make life much better, wouldn't it? What about someone just coming along and saving you altogether? (p. 41)

X

Satisfaction is equivalent to the peacefulness described by Eastern mystics. It is a quiet contentment that derives from knowing that the universe is—in each and every moment—whole and complete. From the perspective of the self, satisfaction is *now* or it isn't. It does not require waiting until you get married, earn a degree, receive a promotion, or have children. Each of those life transitions will inevitably bring new challenges, new pleasures, and new frustrations. However, as in Beckett's (1954) play, waiting for Godot is a self-defeating strategy.

The mind, incapable of satisfaction, settles for *gratification*.[7] Frankly, there is much to be said for the enjoyment of a tasty meal, good sex, or a rise in the Dow-Jones average. However, satisfaction is the broader context that elevates the value of those otherwise immediate and fleeting pleasures.

It is the mind that *demands* and the self that *invites*. Invitations issued by the self are free and clear opportunities to participate with others. Unfortunately, the mind often gets into the act, disguising its demands as invitations and making those who decline feel guilty. In other words, if an invitation to the movies is genuine, you should be able to accept or decline without having to apologize or explain your motives.

The mind's demands can also be disguised as questions, such as when a person asks, "Is there a particular reason you left the dishes in the sink?" Gifts, too, can be less than they seem. Several years ago, a client gave a small gift-wrapped statue to her therapist. Later that same session, she suggested that they meet more frequently. When the therapist explained that extra sessions wouldn't be advisable, she pointedly reminded him that she had just given him a present. The therapist replied that he had assumed that the statue was a gift—not a bribe. "Well, if we're not going to have more sessions," she protested, "I'd like the statue back." "Too late," said the therapist, "you already gave it to me, and now it's mine." Although the therapist's reaction may sound harsh, it led to an immensely productive discussion about gifts, obligations, and manipulation. Their interaction also illustrates that whatever you accept as a gift tends to become one, even if that wasn't the donor's original intention.

Genuine gifts do not come with strings attached. They do not require that the recipient reciprocate. Gifts can be given at any

---

[7] Our choice of satisfaction to represent the self and gratification to represent the mind is arbitrary. The terms could have been reversed.

time and can be verbal as well as physical. By the way, verbal gifts can contain criticisms as well as compliments. Last year, an instructor at a nearby college was at first disconcerted by some disparaging comments his students made on his teacher evaluation form. However, rather than lick his wounds, he chose to freely share this negative feedback with his next group, inviting the students to help him improve his course. His openness earned their respect and turned an unpleasant situation into a valuable experience for all.

AVOIDANCE AND MASTERY

Avoidance is the mind's preferred approach to handling problems. It includes sidestepping issues, evading responsibility, making excuses, blaming others, and postponing confrontations. However, these avoidant strategies are usually temporary fixes that shrink the person's experiential world. The more effective solution is mastery. As we have described elsewhere (Efran & Nath, 2004), the path from avoidance to mastery can be conceptualized as a series of fixed steps (Figure 1). At the most primitive level, there is outright avoidance, including the tension-reducing strategies that family therapy pioneer Murray Bowen called "cut-offs" (Kerr & Bowen, 1988). Cut-offs include hanging up on people, refusing to read their letters, and avoiding places where they might show up. Sometimes people are willing to interact superficially with the person as long as they can avoid any truly meaningful conversation. Cut-offs can last just a few hours or a lifetime. In addition to cut-offs, simple avoidance includes withdrawing from college, drinking to excess, or quitting your job.

We call the next step on the way to mastery, "right/wrong." For example, when you are offered frog legs, you don't simply refuse to taste them. You argue that they are gross and might even be dangerous to eat. In other words, you denigrate the avoided object. Right/wrong is a slightly more sophisticated strategy than simple avoidance because at least you actively address the problematic circumstance rather than just ignoring it.

The step above "right/wrong" is "entitlement." This is another step toward mastery, because rather than devaluing the external object—in our example, frog legs—you claim a point of personal privilege: "I've had a long, hard day at the office, so I think I'd better stick to something I know." Although this strategy involves excuse-making, it contains at least a modicum of personal responsibility—that is, you talk about yourself rather than the external object.

FIGURE 1.

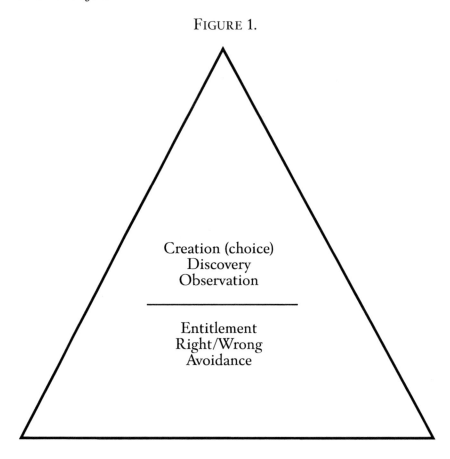

Creation (choice)
Discovery
Observation

Entitlement
Right/Wrong
Avoidance

After entitlement comes "observation," in which you are finally willing to suspend judgment and process new information. Whereas the earlier levels were dominated by mind, the process of observation empowers the self. Observation, in turn, leads to "discovery." Actually tasting the frog legs allows you to notice new flavors and textures and to supplant old stereotypes with more accurate perceptions. You may discover, for instance, that the flavor is milder and less gamey than you had anticipated. Out of such discoveries, new choices emerge. For instance, you realize how the addition of frog legs as an ingredient can enhance your cooking. Note that as you move up the mastery chart, you progress from defensiveness to openness.

Some ask what happens after you reach the top of the chart, having achieved mastery in a particular domain. The answer is that as soon as a new threat comes along—perhaps Mexican agave worms this time—you revert to simple avoidance and begin the mastery process all over again. Hopefully, with experience, the excursion from bottom to top picks up speed, and mastery is achieved more easily. Sometimes people seem to linger more at one step than another, or appear to skip steps altogether. However, in the interest of theoretical purity, we prefer to assume that mastery always requires making the complete journey, even if some steps take only a moment. A therapist helps clients move to the next step by inviting them to notice where, in the chart, they are stuck.

DOES LIFE MEAN ANYTHING?

Too much overlap between the therapist's life assumptions and those of the client are a therapeutic liability—it is apt to lead to both client and therapist finding themselves trapped in the same conceptual ditch. Couples therapists, for instance, learned a long time ago that an investment in preserving the couple's marriage interfered with their ability to work effectively. Similarly, context-centered therapists have learned to guard against subscribing to any of the client's basic suppositions. Furthermore, the best protection against this occupational hazard is to adopt a very broad interpretation of self, akin to the radical constructivist proposition that life is essentially a purposeless drift (Maturana & Varela, 1987). In Sartre's (1956) words, "It is meaningless that we are born; it is meaningless that we die" (p. 547).

Moral philosopher Richard Taylor (1984) describes deep caves in New Zealand in which the ceilings are covered by thousands of dots of light. The light is created by the luminous tails of blind, ugly worms that attach themselves to the upper surfaces of the cave. Their tails attract small insects that the worms then proceed to trap and eat. Eventually, these larval creatures are transformed into tiny winged insects that live only a day or two—never leaving the cave or seeing the light of day. In their brief existence, they mate, lay eggs, and are then consumed by other worms of the same species. This cycle has been going on for

101

millions of years, "and to no end other than that the same meaningless cycle may continue for another millions of years" (p. 261). As Taylor suggests, our own lives do not differ from the existence of these worms as much as we would like to believe. We rush hither and thither, going about our daily chores, mainly so that our children (and our children's children) can follow in our footsteps. In other words, when boiled down to essentials, "the point of any living thing's life is, evidently, nothing but life itself" (p. 262). Therefore, as we sometimes tell our clients, the overarching truth is that "it doesn't matter, and it doesn't matter that it doesn't matter" (Efran, 1999, p. 56).

When you first say that to people, they usually reply that if nothing matters, why shouldn't they just stop trying, cross their arms, and do nothing? That response ignores two critical considerations. First, as those who have tried meditation can attest, doing nothing is not that easy. We are not designed for long periods of inactivity. Remember, solitary confinement is considered a punishment, and many people find that even a day at the beach drives them to distraction.

Second, although life doesn't matter, the full statement is that it also doesn't matter that it doesn't matter. Therefore, there are no grounds for changing what you do. You might as well continue to pursue your current goals until or unless you choose different—equally meaningless—goals.

The paradox is that it is the very emptiness of life's canvas that invites us to add our own meanings (Efran, Lukens, & Lukens, 1990). Thus, as human beings operating in language, we exchange stories, set goals, invent games, plan adventures, and celebrate achievements. Problems, too, are linguistic creations. You generate a problem by starting with an unfortunate circumstance and then *making something of it*. For instance, you conclude that it is not okay to disappoint your parents, get a divorce, lose your job, do drugs, spend a night in jail, or give a boring speech. The therapist must comprehend such predicaments but not buy into the importance the client attributes to them. Context-centered therapists keep the big picture in mind—namely, that nothing truly matters and life is never personal. They understand that, in the grand scheme of things, the client's problems are of no great significance. Moreover, there are always more potential solutions than are at first apparent. As George Kelly (1969) noted, "Whatever exists can be reconstrued" (p. 227).

The issue of significance is particularly likely to arise when clients threaten suicide. In our experience, most therapists are as frightened by this prospect as their clients—perhaps more so. At the first mention of the topic, they rush off to find a suicide-prevention contract for the client to sign, sounding alarms and short-circuiting the potentially enlightening conversation about life and death that might otherwise ensue. Such contracts have not been shown to be effective (Goin, 2003; Kroll, 2000). Besides, as more than one client at our clinic has observed, it is a bit idiotic to call something a contract if it cannot be enforced. Furthermore, clients often recognize that the therapists' insistence on negotiating such contracts is as much about their own anxiety as the client's welfare.

In our own work, we operate from the assumption that clients have a perfect right to do themselves in. After all, there is no one right way to live, no sacrosanct objectives to achieve, and no perfect amount of time to spend on earth. The person who commits suicide will have simply used up the one "destructive interaction" to which each of us is entitled (Maturana & Varela, 1987, p. 98). By the way, that person's problems will be over—it is the rest of us who will have regrets.

We wish neither to trivialize suicide nor to dramatize it—we want to provide clients with a forum in which they can think deeply about their lives without having to worry about their therapist's malpractice concerns. Handled correctly, contemplating suicide is at least as likely to herald a clinical breakthrough as precipitate a management crisis. As Nietzsche (1886/2005) pointed out, "The thought of suicide is a great consolation; by means of it one gets successfully through many a bad night" (p. 42).

CONCLUSION

As we have indicated, therapy is a specialized conversation—more rhetorical exercise than healing process. Therapy helps the client break the mind's stranglehold and empowers the self. Sometimes the voice of the self begins as a mere whisper but gains strength as therapy proceeds. The client moves from avoidance and insufficiency to mastery and responsibility—from being "at effect" to being "at cause." Because the context-centered approach is acceptance-based, clients are not asked to eliminate unwanted habits or impulses. The magic is in helping them notice the underlying assumptions that have been limiting their options. Whatever is noticed changes automatically (Efran & Heffner, 1991).

We end with two quotes—the first from family therapist Richard Schwartz (2004) and the second from George Bernard Shaw (1903/2004). Although Schwartz comes from a different theoretical tradition, it is noteworthy that he describes the shift from mind to self in terms that are remarkably similar to our own: "As clients embody more Self . . . they stop berating themselves and, instead, get to know, rather than try to eliminate, the extreme inner voices or emotions that have plagued them. At those times, they tell me, they feel 'lighter' [and] their minds feel somehow more 'open' and 'free'" (p. 39).

Similarly, Shaw's description of the good life parallels the distinctions we have been making. He argues that his life "belongs to the whole community" and that all of us should strive to be "a force of nature instead of a feverish selfish little clod of ailments and grievances complaining that the world will not devote itself to making you happy" (p. 32).

REFERENCES

Bach, R. (1977). *Illusions: The adventures of a reluctant messiah.* New York: Dell.

Beckett, S. (1954). *Waiting for Godot: A tragicomedy in two acts.* New York: Grove Press.

Boszormenyi-Nagy, I. (1987). *Foundations of contextual therapy.* New York: Brunner-Routledge.

Dawes, R. M. (1994). *House of cards: Psychology and psychotherapy built on myth.* New York: The Free Press.

Durkin, J. E. (1981). Foundations of autonomous living structure. In J. E. Durkin (Ed.), *Living groups.* (pp. 24-59). New York: Brunner/Mazel.

Efran, J. S. (1999). The rational self and other myths of daily living. In M. Stoneburner & B. Catchings (Eds.), *The meaning of being human* (pp. 35-56). Indianapolis, IN: The University of Indianapolis Press.

Efran, J. S., & Greene, M. A. (2000). The limits of change: Heredity, temperament, and family influence. In W. C. Nichols, M. A. Pace-Nichols, D. S. Becvar, & A. Y. Napier (Eds.), *Handbook of family development and intervention* (pp. 41-64). New York: Wiley & Sons.

Efran, J. S., & Heffner, K. P. (1991). Change the name and you change the game. *Journal of Strategic and Systemic Therapies, 10*(1), 50-65.

Efran, J. S., Lukens, M. D., & Lukens, R. J. (1990). *Language, structure, and change: Frameworks of meaning in psychotherapy.* New York: W. W. Norton.

Efran, J. S., & Nath, S. R. (2004). The Zen of social phobia: A context-centered group treatment. In J. D. Raskin & S. K. Bridges (Eds.), *Studies in meaning 2: Bridging the personal and social in constructivist psychology* (pp. 185-219). New York: Pace University Press.

Erhard, W. & Gioscia, V. (1977). The est standard training. *Biosciences Communications, 3*, 104-122.

Goin, M. (2003). The "Suicide-Prevention Contract": A dangerous myth. *Psychiatric News, 38*(14), 3.

Gregson, D., & Efran, J. S. (2002). *The Tao of sobriety.* New York: St. Martin's Press.

Harris, J. R. (1998). *The nurture assumption.* New York: Free Press.

Hayes, S. (in press). In the now, but for a purpose. *Psychotherapy Networker.*

Hubble, M. A., Duncan, B. L., & Miller, S. D. (Eds.). (1999). *The heart and soul of change: What works in therapy.* Washington, DC: American Psychological Association.

Kelly, G. A. (1969). Personal construct theory and the psychotherapeutic interview. In B. Maher (Ed.), *Clinical psychology and personality: The selected papers of George Kelly* (pp. 224-264). New York: John Wiley.

Kerr, M. E., & Bowen, M. (1988). *Family evaluation: An approach based on Bowen theory.* New York: W. W. Norton.

Korzybski, A. (1941). *Science and sanity: An introduction to non-Aristotelian systems and general semantics.* Lancaster, PA: Science Press.

Kroll, J. (2000). Use of no-suicide contracts by psychiatrists in Minnesota. *American Journal of Psychiatry, 157*, 1684-1686.

Maturana, H. R., & Varela, F. J. (1987). *The tree of knowledge: The biological roots of human understanding.* Boston: Shambhala Publications.

Mendez, C. L., Coddou, F., & Maturana, H. R. (1988). The bringing forth of pathology: An essay to be read aloud by two. *Irish Journal of Psychology, 9*, 144-172.

Nietzsche, F. (2005). *Beyond good and evil.* Stilwell, KS: Digireads.com Publishing. (Original work published 1886)

Sartre, J. P. (1956). *Being and nothingness.* New York: Philosophical Library.

Schwartz, R. (2004). The larger self. *Psychotherapy Networker, 28*(3): 36-43.

Seligman, M. E. P. (1993). *What you can change and what you can't: The complete guide to successful self-improvement.* New York: Fawcett Columbine.

Shaw, G. B. (2004). *Man and superman.* New York: Penguin Classics. (Original work published 1903)

Smothermon, R. (1979). *Winning through enlightenment.* San Francisco: Context Publications.

Taylor, R. (1984). *Good and evil: A new direction.* Buffalo, NY: Prometheus Books.

Varela, F. J. (1979). *Principles of biological autonomy.* New York: North-Holland.

Watts, A. (1966). *The book: On the taboo against knowing who you are.* New York: Vintage Books.

C3 5 80

Embodiment in Experiential Personal Construct Psychotherapy: Theoretical and Technical Concerns

Larry M. Leitner and April J. Faidley

Personal construct psychology (Kelly 1955/1991a; 1955/1991b) views humans as organisms actively engaged in the process of creating meaning in interaction with the world. However, Kelly's theory often has been misconstrued in that "personal constructs" are seen as intellectual or verbal creations. In reaction to this perceived weakness, many constructivists (e.g. Landridge & Butt, 2005) have been seeking a more explicit understanding of embodiment within personal construct theory. Experiential personal constructivism has elaborated personal construct theory by balancing the cognitive and non-cognitive aspects of the theory. Launched from an exploration of the implications of Kelly's theory for the vital world of highly intimate relationships, experiential personal constructivism has been applied to a wide array of phenomena within the fields of psychopathology and psychotherapy, including diagnosis (Leitner, Faidley & Celentana, 2000), assessment (Leitner, 1995a), resistance to therapy (Leitner & Dill-Standiford, 1993), validation of therapist interventions (Leitner & Guthrie, 1993), levels of awareness (Leitner, 1999), and the therapy relationship (Leitner, 1988, 1995b). This chapter takes a natural further progression, and responds to the theoretical gap that has concerned constructivists, by describing human embodiment and how it can be used in experiential personal construct psychotherapy. First, we will provide a very brief overview of experiential personal constructivism (and psychotherapy). We then will discuss a constructivist understanding of the body and, finally, we will address the therapeutic implications of such an understanding.

This chapter is based upon a Plenary Address delivered to the International Congress on Personal Construct Psychology, Seattle, WA, July, 1997 and a presentation at the American Psychological Association Convention, San Francisco, August, 1998. All clinical material has been falsified to protect confidentiality.

107

EXPERIENTIAL PERSONAL CONSTRUCTIVISM

Based upon Kelly's (1955/1991a) sociality corollary, experiential personal constructivism understands humans as needing to engage in deep, significant, intimate relationships (termed ROLE relationships) in order to have a life filled with richness and meaning. However, such relationships are fraught with potential danger and therefore persons need to retreat in order to protect themselves from serious injury. Thus, the ultimate human dilemma involves developing a ROLE relationship with another (with increased richness yet potential terror of profound injury) versus retreating from the other (with the experience of safety yet emptiness) (see Leitner, 1985; Leitner & Faidley, 1995 for more thorough discussions).

Psychological health and psychopathology then are seen in terms of persons' struggles over intimate connections (Leitner, 1988; Leitner, Faidley, & Celentana, 2000; Leitner & Pfenninger, 1994). Psychological symptoms can be seen as linked to the struggle over ROLE relating. For example, the confusion and disorganization of someone diagnosed as "schizophrenic" can be seen as a way of protecting the self from powerful injury. If the other cannot understand you, he or she cannot get close enough to devastate you. On the other hand, if the other person has enough empathy to grasp aspects of your being despite the confusion and turmoil you present, perhaps that person is worth risking a bit of intimacy with. Psychotherapy, from this perspective, engages the client in this human struggle between intimacy and disconnection (Leitner, 1995b).

For additional clarity, we will take a brief detour to describe what a ROLE relationship is. Intimacy between you and me, from this perspective, is not that I experience the world as you see it. Rather, it is that I have some understanding of the process through which you construe your experiences of the world. For example, I might know that you understand aspects of the world through a construction of "fair versus unfair." However, the extent of intimacy between us is measured more by my ability to grasp what it says about you as a meaning-making being that you created such a dimension to encounter the world. An extensive literature within personal construct psychology suggests that, in order to connect with your process of meaning making, I need to fundamentally grasp your most central (core) constructions (see

Leitner, 1985). These constructions in some ways define life itself for you (Kelly, 1961; Landfield, 1976). Thus, it is little wonder that the affirmation of these core meanings by me can lead to the experience of wonder and awe between us, while their disconfirmation can lead to your feeling profoundly devastated by me (Leitner & Faidley, 1995). Further along, we will discuss how Kelly's notion of core construing has profound implications for the use of the body in psychotherapy. At the moment, we will turn to a theoretical discussion of the central role of the body within personal construct psychology.

THEORETICAL OVERVIEW

Psyche-Soma

It is indeed ironic that Kelly's theory has not been applied more systematically to the body. Kelly (1955/1991a) clearly thought that meaning making (construing) had implications for the soma:

> . . . the notion of construing has a wide range of convenience, if we choose to use it that way. It may even be used within the borderland areas of the realm of physiology. To be sure, it operates somewhat less conveniently there, but the overlapping functions of physiological and psychological systems in this regard help to make it clear that psychology and physiology ought not to try and draw preemptive boundaries between themselves. (p. 36)

As Kelly implied, the traditional construct of "psyche" and "soma" is just that: a construct. This construction, like all created meanings, then can be evaluated as to how useful it is in terms of helping humans meaningfully and richly engage their world. As a matter of fact, much of modern medicine has been re-thinking the utility of such a division. (As an aside, we note that, as modern medicine is becoming more holistic, psychology is abandoning holism in favor of biological reductionism.) We take the position, based upon construct theory, that the notion of "psyche" versus "soma" is a distinction that, at least in the context of psychotherapy, leads to arbitrary, limited, either-or approaches to phenomena. What has traditionally been called "psyche" and "soma" are thoroughly intertwined such that, not only does "psyche" affect "soma" and vice versa, but, even more fundamentally, "psyche" expresses itself through "soma" and "soma" expresses itself through

109

"psyche." In this chapter, we will be focusing specifically on how the psychological process of meaning making is manifested in our physiology.

We believe this position is firmly based upon personal construct principles. For example, Kelly was very clear about his assumption that the entire universe is *integral*, such that any one aspect in the universe ultimately affects all other aspects of the universe. Kelly argued that minor actions in the rural U.S., for example, would affect the price of Yak milk in Tibet. If so, the personal meanings we create (and the implications of these meanings for our life journey) obviously can affect the systems traditionally viewed as "body" in our culture. In such an integral universe, constructs are our ways of separating the flow of interconnected experience. Thus, "psyche" versus "soma" is a way of understanding the complex, interrelated events of our journey through life. This reasoning implies that, as psychotherapists, we need to be fundamentally concerned with body sensations and events.

Core Construing

Kelly was well aware that personal meanings affected bodily integrity. For example, his view of suicide (1961) involved a person choosing death over abandoning core meanings (see Landfield, 1976). His definition of core constructs (those affecting a person's maintenance processes) included vivid illustrations of core construing affecting the body. In other words, core constructs, the most central determiners of a person's "being" (see Leitner, 1985), are experienced through physiological manifestations. (Note: We are not arguing that core constructs are only experienced physiologically. They may very well be known intellectually, verbally, and so on. However, we are arguing that core construing always has a physiological manifestation.) Core constructs are those most frequently shared and risked in the exhilarating, terrifying, yet absolutely essential ROLE relationships central to experiential personal construct psychotherapy. Thus, the body is not a mere "container" of the person. Due to its relationship to core construing, the body is a vital container of meanings. Based upon this reasoning, we believe that clients (and their therapists) should trust the "wisdom of the body." Often meanings central to life, laid down before we had words to describe our experiences, are only accessible to us as they are communicated to us through body messages (Guthrie, 1991).

Since the body is involved in the initial, basic, most core meaning makings, one can see the importance of trusting the body. In essence, bodily responses tell us important things about how we have structured and engaged the world. We believe this is consistent with theorists who have argued that the body has a wisdom that should not be ignored. For example, when faced with an important decision, most persons can muster all sorts of persuasive reasons for acting from either pole of a construct. However, typically, one pole has a felt sense of "rightness" that winds up dictating the decision. This felt sense of rightness is, we believe, a body sensation pointing to the decision that is most consistent with the very core of our meaning making. In other words, psychologically healthy people may be more likely to base decisions not so much on the "rational" reasons for an action but more on the bodily sense of felt rightness.

The Body and Meaning Making

We take the position that the body is the vehicle through which meanings are first constructed. If we are born as meaning-making creatures, early in life, long before we have verbal abilities, we are abstracting meanings through interaction with our world. During this period, many (most? all?) of the confirmations we receive from the world are experienced in the body (e.g. the good satiation of a breast or a bottle, the security of being enveloped in warm, loving arms, etc.). All of the disconfirmations we experience during this critical time also are experienced in the body (e.g. being pulled away from a desired object, not having the satiation of being well fed, etc.). In other words, our original constructs, those that serve as the basis of the entire construct system, have been created in tight relationship to our bodies.

Through the years, these sensed bodily confirmations become more entrenched as we develop a meaning system based upon them. However, as we develop verbally, we can create words that describe some of these bodily meanings. Society also begins to affirm cognitive and, to a lesser extent, affective understandings of self and other. In so doing, we can focus our attention away from the body and elaborate these more intellectualized meanings.

111

This position has direct clinical implications. For example, traditional verbal psychotherapy can change core structures to the extent that words have been linked to body confirmations. However, because many of these structures may lie behind (beyond?) words, they may be less accessible to traditional talk therapies. It may be that Gestalt exercises, sensate focus, and other interventions designed to experience the body more directly will result in more rapid access to such core meanings. Further, people who participate in activities like yoga and certain types of dance may find the bodily movement and felt sensation as integrating and therapeutic; the insertion of the body into the meaning space can allow for core construing to occur. Such experiences may be particularly effective when combined with traditional verbal work.

Body versus verbal reconstructions. This position also can explain a common phenomenon in verbal psychotherapy. It is not uncommon for individuals to be able to apply new verbal labels to experience while not changing at a core level. For example, many psychodynamic approaches have wrestled with the issue of "intellectual" versus "emotional" "insight." Because later, more verbal affirmations, may only be tangentially related to the core, bodily-based, meanings created early in life, it is quite possible (likely?) that verbal meanings will change with little or no change in the core (as mentioned above). These more verbal meanings also might change prior to change on more core structures. If so, one might very well understand verbally (intellectually), for example, that a relationship is safe and worthy of trust while still reacting on a body level as if the relationship was threatening. As a matter of fact, we would expect such a discrepancy as people undergo life changing psychotherapy.

One implication of this position is that true core reconstruction has occurred when the body anticipates differently, not when the person can cognitively reorganize experiences. Until the body anticipations change, there are core meanings that continue to anticipate the world in the older and currently less useful manner. Therapeutic techniques that invite the person to describe the contradictory anticipations may help integrate healthier constructions into the core. However, all too often psychotherapy ceases before such core reconstruction can occur, leaving the person with a contradiction between body anticipations and verbal understandings.

112

Body Invasions

This reasoning points out why, for many people, bodily invasions (e.g. physical and sexual abuse, rape, violent attacks, injuries) are so traumatic. The body's connection to the central definers of identity means that being invaded in such a manner threatens the integrity of the *self* as well as the body. Further, the core distinction between self and other becomes blurred and confused (Leitner, Faidley, & Celentana, 2000). This combination of bodily insult and the threatened annihilation of the self lead many people to freeze psychologically and suspend the construing of such events, resulting in traumatic experiences lying at low levels of awareness (Leitner, 1999). For obvious reasons, events that seem similar to the original trauma (in the sketchy way the original trauma was construed) also can freeze the meaning-making process.

Even body invasions that are less violent threaten core construing due to the body's connection with the central definers of personhood. Organ transplants, reparative surgical procedures, and so on, although for the "good," are invasions of bodily integrity and threaten core meanings. Illnesses (e.g. cancer, cardiovascular accidents, etc.) are also threatening. In all of these traumas, the threat is more than the damage or destruction of our "earthly container"; it is the possible annihilation of the person that is being risked.

Views of the Body

Because it is such a vital container for such central meanings, a person's views of his or her body are important. Persons who describe their bodies as good, healthy, attractive, desirable, and pleasurable may be communicating ways their core meanings are matching the relational challenges being faced in the world. Likewise, persons describing their bodies as bad, unhealthy, unattractive, undesirable, and unpleasurable may be communicating about the ways that core meanings are failing to meet the relational challenges in life. In this context, we often find it useful clinically to ask about the client's experience of the body.

Similarly, it can be important to understand the ways a person's primary relational partner experiences the person's body. First, if the partner finds the client's body unattractive, the client may be dealing with a major trauma due to the connection between the body and core meanings. More fundamentally, because a ROLE relationship involves the affirmation of core meanings and the celebration of the wonder of the other (Leitner & Faidley, 1995), a person cannot have a ROLE relationship with another without experiencing the "awe-fulness" of the other's core meaning-making process. This implies that, as the ROLE relationship develops and the other's psychological beauty is seen, the other may be experienced physically as beautiful due to the connection between core meanings and the body. Thus, if a client's partner fails to find the client's body attractive, the experience may say something important about the depth of the ROLE relationship between them.

The Body and Psychopathology

Because the body is so central in core construing, it is not surprising that emotions are all expressed in sensations in our bodies. However, the current DSM (like its predecessors) is a curious (bizarre?) reversal of this. In the current DSM, the bodily expressions have more *become* the emotion. For example, you may feel sad, blue, down in the dumps, or what have you and not be depressed. Further, even if you do not feel sad, you may be diagnosed as depressed. You can be depressed because you have lost interest in things you used to do, have no appetite, your sleep is disrupted, and so forth. This reversal extracts people from the milieu of persons and interpersonal events and localizes the "disease" within our biology. We would find it ridiculous if we did this with "positive" emotions. For example, we would never say that you are happy because you smile, eat regularly, sleep well, exercise, and have low blood pressure. Rather, we would talk about your interpersonal world as providing the basis for your happiness.

Summary

It is important to note that this elaboration of personal construct psychology implies that the body is absolutely critical in the process of meaning-making. As a matter of fact, construing an event means, by definition, the insertion of the body into that event. Because core constructs govern our physiological processes, any important event in our life has body ramifications. The

experience of threat (the awareness of imminent and comprehensive change in core meanings), for instance, involves profound
physiological manifestations (trembling, heart racing, stomach
falling, bowel excitement, for example). In other words, threat, for
Kelly, was not something confined to the intellect; it was
intimately tied to the body. Similar points could be made about
fear, guilt, hostility, anxiety, and other emotions in personal
construct psychology.

THERAPEUTIC IMPLICATIONS

Body Experiences of Personal Meanings

One of the many therapeutic implications of this position
is the way that personal meanings are experienced within the body.
Many persons, badly injured by massive disconfirmations of core
meanings, may not be aware of their bodies. Such "disembodied"
persons may benefit from exercises (e.g. Gestalt awareness
exercises, sensate focus, psychodrama, mirror work, etc.) that help
them become more aware of their bodies. Further, the theoretical
reasoning presented above implies that being connected to the
body is something that is innate for us. When we are disembodied,
then, we are actually doing things to prevent ourselves from being
aware of the connection. Exploration of how a client prevents the
innate connection also can be useful. With all of these exercises,
the therapist should be very aware that the client "disembodied"
the self for good reasons. Thus, these exercises should be
combined with sensitive work attempting to understand *why*
disembodiment was the elaborative choice for the client. If the
therapist can integrate such exploration with activities designed to
make the client feel safe doing the work, therapeutic growth can
occur.

For example, John presented with high blood pressure that
was unresponsive to medication. He had tried relaxation exercises
previously without success. He knew he worked too hard at an
extremely stressful professional occupation (surgeon), but was
unable to find ways of decreasing his work load. John's therapist
asked him to locate where in his body he experienced stress while
working. When John could not locate any such area, the therapist
asked him to close his eyes and describe a stressful aspect of his
most recent workday. John had a patient who had unexpectedly

died in surgery earlier in the week. The therapist used a "moviola" technique to have John describe the situation like he was scanning the scene with a movie camera (Goncalves, 1995). As the recall of the stressful event became more real, the therapist asked John to pay attention to any changes in his body as the therapist began to describe the patient's death. John described feeling like his stomach had been punched and found it difficult to breathe. The therapist instructed John to breathe deeply and naturally. As John breathed deeply, he began to cry. He recalled how hard it had been to breathe when his father had hit him in the stomach. This recollection led to important therapeutic work for John. Essentially, he began to experientially grasp the ways that he had disconnected from his body in order to minimize the sense of terror around his own abuse. In so doing, he was not hearing the ways his own body was telling him that life was too stressful. As John and the therapist continued to re-live the abuse, John was more able to relax during the day with standard relaxation exercises. More profoundly, he was able to begin to attend to bodily cues and actively do things to minimize stress as it arose. His blood pressure became controllable with medication.

Listening to the body leads to an increased understanding of core meanings. As the client becomes better able to listen to bodily messages about core construing, the client gains a greater felt understanding of the important processes in his or her life. As one gains greater clarity as to whom one is, one also gains a better understanding of the ways that one's meanings facilitate and hinder connections to others. Such awareness of needs and impacts is essential for the formation of ROLE relationships (Leitner & Pfenninger, 1994).

Further, experimenting with bodily movements and sensations can be powerfully therapeutic. Because somatic shifts affect the psyche as much as vice versa, working on shifting bodily experiences can affect core meanings. Thus, relaxation training, hypnosis, biofeedback, and related techniques may reduce the experience of personal threat to core construing by changing bodily sensations. However, these less direct changes are more powerful *if* they are combined with interventions that illustrate the connection between the meaning-making process and the body. A therapist can, for example, hypnotize a client; the bodily relaxation associated with hypnosis, if combined with verbal interventions around how good it is to feel safe and relaxed, can be very powerful. Assurances around the safety of the therapy room and the therapy relationship also are important interventions that can facilitate bodily changes affecting core meanings. John's therapist, for example, connected his lack of awareness of where the stress was felt in his body to his need to minimize the experienced trauma of the abuse. The therapist also kept assuring John that, while the events he was recalling were horrific, the therapy room was safe and nothing bad would happen to him in the therapy room.

The connection between the soma and core construing also means that therapists can gain hypotheses about the client through careful observation of the client's physiological process. Clients presenting physically as restricted and inhibited are communicating the degree of terror they are struggling with in ROLE relationships. As clients feel greater confidence and security in core construing, they often express themselves differently with their bodies. As a matter of fact, observing a client's increasing ease with the body may be an early indication of progress in psychotherapy, particularly for more seriously disturbed clients. In other words, the first validations of the therapist's approach may be non-verbal (Leitner & Guthrie, 1993). Through carefully monitoring such validations, the therapist can develop the confidence that therapy is heading in important and productive directions.

For example, George sought therapy due to troubles making decisions. When he appeared for therapy, he had a way of physically making himself smaller than he was. A colleague termed him "the creeper" for the ways he could creep up the stairs without others seeing him. In therapy, he presented as psychologically petrified, desiring only to determine what his therapist wanted him to say. If he could say that, perhaps the therapist would not focus on him. After three months of therapy, George grew a beard. He allowed the beard to grow so long and disheveled that he essentially drew attention to himself. This beard was the first indication the therapist had of George growing as a result of therapy. He was willing to allow himself to be noticed physically, albeit in ways that took others aback. It was several more months before he could begin to verbally state his experience and insist that it be heard. Shortly thereafter, he trimmed his beard.

Body Meanings

Different bodily sensations may mean different things to different clients. Thus, exploring the meanings of body parts and experiences for the particular client can be very important. For example, Christine presented complaining of heart palpitations. In an attempt to understand what the palpitations meant to her, the therapist asked her to talk to them. Initially, all she could express was her frustration at having the problem. When the therapist asked her to talk "from the heart" as if the heart was telling her something about herself, the heart initially expressed the anxiety Christine was experiencing. When the therapist asked the heart why she was so anxious, Christine became quite tearful and talked about losing her job, how her infant son was suffering from a life threatening illness, and how her husband had dealt with these crises with alcohol. In other words, very specific life meanings were being expressed through her heart palpitations. This symptom, like all, was an expression from herself to herself about herself (Leitner, Faidley, & Celentana, 2000).

Sometimes therapists can facilitate such work by offering tentative hunches as to the meanings of certain body sensations. For example, Tom's therapist speculated that his shallow breathing was his way of expressing how dangerous the world was. Being totally still increased the likelihood of his not being seen and therefore not being injured. Shallow breathing allowed him to be more still. While these interpretations may be useful, it is very important to keep in mind that these are the therapist's guesses about the client's experience. The therapist should be open to the ways the client invalidates such guesses.

Finally, the therapist also will manifest core construing through bodily sensations. Because so much of the therapist's attention is devoted to understanding the client, these bodily experiences often are the first manifestations of the therapist being aware of an aspect of the client's process. In other words, as the therapist focuses on connecting with the client, bodily experiences may tell things about how the therapist's construing process is responding to the client's meaning-making. For example, awareness of physiological signals of anxiety may very well be in response to the client's experience of panic. Thus, paying attention to bodily experiences helps the therapist achieve and maintain optimal therapeutic distance (Leitner, 1995b), that profound blend of closeness and separateness so critical in life changing psychotherapy.

Illnesses

Threats to bodily integrity (e.g. illnesses, injuries, accidents) need to be taken seriously by the therapist. First, given the close connection between the body and core construing, such threats are major stressors in the client's life. The therapist's failure to take such events seriously and caringly could be a major empathic failure. Clients may understandably experience the therapist as not concerned about the important experiences in the client's life if the therapist does not care about these stressors.

Second, illnesses and injuries may be communications about core meanings in jeopardy. In other words, a client may very well be communicating something profoundly important through the illness. In extreme cases, illnesses and accidents may be messages about therapy gone wrong. The client's core processes are being overwhelmingly threatened by the therapy and the illness allows the client the safety of avoiding the therapist. Even if the client attends the therapy session, the client may be too preoccupied with the injury to really be present with the therapist. Thus, the client can protect the self from the terror of further potential core disconfirmation.

Third, the therapist's injuries and illnesses also are important in therapy. Clients know, often better than therapists, the relationship between the body and central meanings. Thus, they know that an injury or illness in the therapist means that the therapist is less available for them. This threatens the dependence they feel on the therapist as reconstructive therapy unfolds. In addition, the client's caring for the therapist in the therapeutic ROLE relationship means he or she has a genuine concern for the well being of the therapist. Honest discussion of these issues combined with the therapist being able to take care of his or her physiological needs can be most therapeutic.

Touch

This reasoning also has implications for touch in psychotherapy. Physical contact in therapy, because it can have implications for the core meaning making process of both parties in the relationship, may be a way in which the being of one person connects with the being of another. My willingness to touch you can be seen as a message about my willingness to have you affect even the most central parts of my being. Such willingness can be a powerful affirmation of the worth, the goodness, of your process of evolution. Not surprisingly, a touch, a pat on the back, a hug, can be experienced as powerfully therapeutic.

However, because many clients have been so injured in their attempts at ROLE relating that they have felt the need to protect themselves from the terrors of intimacy (Leitner, 1985), touch can be profoundly threatening, particularly to seriously disturbed persons. Thus, therapists should be cautious about touching a client prior to understanding the degree of threat involved. As a general rule, we would not touch a client without some direct indication from the client that it will feel safe and caring to the client. Even then, we typically spend time exploring what the touch will mean to the client. Finally, the touch has to feel genuine, authentic, real to the therapist or the therapist is doing things that make him or her phony in the therapy room. Such actions obviously limit ROLE relationship with the client.

For example, George, mentioned earlier, was faced with an important decision about a relationship. He had discovered that his fiancée was having an affair and he was trying to decide what to do. The terror of making a decision was such that he would assume a fetal position and rock back and forth, sobbing. Either decision could (would) be disastrous. As he was leaving the session, his therapist gave him a brief hug and said, "I know how frightening this is for you. I am here if you need me." George almost melted into the therapist's arms and began sobbing uncontrollably. He then pulled back and left the room, a determined expression on his face. He stated the next week that he had gone home and terminated the relationship because "I needed sexual fidelity." Obviously, this open expression of his needs in a conflictual situation is a far cry from the person who had presented determined to be invisible.

Sex

Great intimacy develops in the therapy room as the core processes of therapist and client engage each other. These core meanings often are expressed and experienced through bodily

120

sensations. Further, as these core meanings are confirmed and we see the psychological beauty of the other, the other can become physically attractive as well. Not surprisingly, then, feelings of sexual desire and attraction may be a part of life changing psychotherapy. Because the client is putting more core meanings on the line, the feelings develop in the client for the therapist more often than they develop in the therapist for the client. Sexual feelings can be a tremendous opportunity for personal growth *if* the therapist is not too threatened by sexuality.

For example, Susan reported a dream of having sex with me (LML) that was so intense for her that she woke up having an orgasm. Because the dream was reported at the end of the session, I was able to use the standard therapeutic stall of saying that we could talk about it next time. However, my initial reaction to the dream was horror. I spent time thinking about how I could have allowed a sexual transference to build to the point that she could have such a dream. I had many conversations with spectators judging my inadequacy and blindness as a therapist. I saw her husband discovering the dream and reporting me to the Ohio State Board of Psychology. I saw my wife confronting me about the ways I was encouraging sexual fantasies from my clients rather than keeping my sexuality with her. I knew, though, that, to the extent I stayed stuck in my own anxieties and threats, I would not be available for my client. I therefore sought consultation with a trusted colleague who was able to help me see the ways that the dream was a major step for such an inhibited woman who never allowed herself any spontaneous expressions and joys.

In other words, by sorting out my own issues, I was able to help Susan explore the experience of sexual attraction toward me. These feelings were one of the first indications that she was feeling close, trusting, and intimate in our relationship. They also were an important indication of the emptiness she felt in her marriage. More fundamentally, as my colleague had shown, they pointed to a willingness to be spontaneous and trusting of her bodily sensations, an important step toward psychological health. In other words, to the extent that I was able to be present with her, these bodily experiences could be explored, experimented with, and used creatively to further her growth as a person. Instead of the next session being dominated by her shame at sharing the dream (and/or my anxieties about the content of the dream) we were able to do some very productive work.

THE EMBODIED MEANING-MAKER

We hope this brief overview has clarified the ways that the body is a central component in meaning making. As such, therapists who ignore the body risk turning the therapy into a superficial conversation where no real change can occur. On the other hand, therapists willing to work with the client's visceral, "gut" reactions have the opportunity to transform lives. Our clients, who have entrusted us with their psyches, deserve nothing less than our complete attending to the totality of their being.

REFERENCES

Goncalves, O. F. (1995). Cognitive narrative therapy. In M. J. Mahoney (Ed.), *Cognitive and constructivist psychotherapies* (pp. 139-162). New York: Springer.

Guthrie, A. F. (1991). Intuiting the process of another: Symbolic, rational transformations of experience. *International Journal of Personal Construct Psychology, 4,* 273-279.

Kelly, G. A. (1991a). *The psychology of personal constructs. Vol. 1: A theory of personality.* New York: Norton. (Original work published 1955)

Kelly, G. A. (1991b). *The psychology of personal constructs. Vol. 2: Clinical diagnosis and psychotherapy.* New York: Norton. (Original work published 1955)

Kelly, G. A. (1961). Suicide: The personal construct point of view. In N. L. Farberow and E. S. Schneidman (Eds.), *The cry for help* (pp. 255-280). New York: McGraw-Hill.

Landfield, A. W. (1976). A personal construct approach to suicidal behavior. In P. Slater (Ed.), *Explorations of intrapersonal space* (Vol. 1, pp. 93-108). Chichester, England: John Wiley.

Landridge, D., & Butt, T. W. (2005). The construction of erotic power exchange. *Journal of Constructivist Psychology, 18,* 65-74.

Leitner, L. M. (1985). The terrors of cognition: On the experiential validity of personal construct theory. In D. Bannister (Ed.), *Issues and approaches in personal construct theory* (pp. 83-103). London: Academic Press.

Leitner, L. M. (1988). Terror, risk, and reverence: Experiential personal construct psychotherapy. *International Journal of personal Construct Psychology, 1,* 261-272.

Leitner, L. M. (1995a). Dispositional assessment techniques in experiential personal construct psychotherapy. *Journal of Constructivist Psychology, 8,* 53-74.

Leitner, L. M. (1995b). Optimal therapeutic distance: A therapist's experience of personal construct psychotherapy. In R. A. Neimeyer & M. J. Mahoney (Eds.), *Constructivism in psychotherapy* (pp. 357-370). Washington, DC: American Psychological Association.

Leitner, L. M. (1999). Levels of awareness in experiential personal construct psychotherapy. *Journal of Constructivist Psychology, 12,* 239-252.

Leitner, L. M., & Dill-Standiford, T. J. (1993). Resistance in experiential personal construct psychotherapy: Theoretical and technical struggles. In L. M. Leitner & N. G. M. Dunnett (Eds.), *Critical issues in personal construct psychotherapy* (pp. 135-155). Malabar, FL: Krieger.

Leitner, L. M., & Faidley, A. J. (1995). The awful, aweful nature of ROLE relationships. In G. J. Neimeyer & R. A. Neimeyer (Eds.), *Advances in personal construct psychology* (Vol. 3, pp. 291-314). Greenwich, CT: JAI.

Leitner, L. M., Faidley, A. J., & Celentana, M. A. (2000). Diagnosing human meaning making: An experiential constructivist approach. In R. A. Neimeyer & J. D. Raskin (Eds.), *Construction of Disorders: Meaning-making frameworks for psychotherapy* (pp. 175-203).Washington, DC: American Psychological Association.

Leitner, L. M., & Guthrie, A. F. (1993). Validation of therapist interventions in psychotherapy: Clarity, ambiguity, subjectivity. *International Journal of Personal Construct Psychology, 6,* 281-294.

Leitner, L. M., & Pfenninger, D. T. (1994). Sociality and optimal functioning. *Journal of Constructivist Psychology, 7,* 119-135.

123

PART III

Constructivist Therapy For Specific Issues

∽ 6 ∾

Meaning and Change with Domestic Abusers

James Horley and Amy Johnson

Domestic violence touches the lives of many men, women, and children each year throughout the world. In many cases, lives are ended. Forty-seven percent of the women murdered in the United Kingdom are killed by spouses or lovers (Gilchrist & Blisset, 2002). These figures are very similar to data from the United States, where 25% of all murders occur within the family (Walker, 2000). The past two decades have witnessed a dramatic rise in the number of treatment programs aimed at men who abuse partners, as well as an increase in research into the efficacy of such programs (see Gondolf, 1987a, 1987b). Judging from the results of these evaluations, treating abusers appears to provide a direct and relatively effective route to reducing domestic violence.

The nature and rationale of treatment programs for men involved in domestic violence vary, and there appear to be a number of successful types of programs. Effective programs include cognitive-behavioral (e. g., Woolfus & Bierman, 1996), feminist cognitive-behavioral (e.g. Ganley, 1989; Saunders, 1996), psycho-educational (e. g., Pence & Paymar, 1993), and psychodynamic (e.g. Saunders, 1996). The variety and scope of the successful treatments for male abusers supports Saunders' (1996) conclusion that "one size does not fit all" (p. 411). Such a conclusion would also be anticipated based on various work, especially that of Dutton (1995; Tweed & Dutton, 1998), that domestic abusers do not represent a single, unified group of offenders. Major subgroups of domestic offenders are those who act impulsively and those who act in a more calculated, instrumental fashion—including habitual

An earlier version of this chapter was presented at the 15th International Congress on Personal Construct Psychology in Huddersfield, England, July 2003.

offenders who use violence instrumentally in a wide range of antisocial acts. Devising and implementing new and different approaches to the treatment of domestic abusers appears important.

Most of the existing approaches to domestic violence treatment view abusers through theoretical lenses that do not take into consideration the uniqueness of the individuals who are abusive in domestic situations. Treatment effectiveness depends on consideration of the personal meaning of the insult, the threat, or the blow from the fist. "A punch is a punch is a punch" seems overly simplistic, and the specific meaning of or intention behind any punch should be considered. We outline here a program that considers both the common and unique views of domestic abusers in group therapy. Very preliminary efficacy data are also presented, as is a brief overview of one participant's case.

ADDRESSING MALE ABUSE THROUGH CHANGING WAYS

Our domestic violence intervention program, administered by the Family Violence Action Society (FVAS) of Camrose, Alberta, offers a comprehensive intervention to men, women, and children experiencing domestic violence. One aspect of the program, called "Changing Ways," is aimed at male abusers who admit to a problem involving physical, verbal, and/or emotional abuse of family members. Changing Ways includes two distinct components covering two 12-week periods.

The first program component, "Changing Ways I," is psycho-educational. It is conducted by two facilitators, one female and one male, based on the view that some modeling of appropriate female-male interaction will occur within group presentations (Saunders, 1989). The co-facilitators meet with four to twelve participants once a week for about two hours. During the weekly sessions, discussions focus on a number of topics that include dealing with negative emotions, controlling anger, abuse cycles, control in relationships, becoming less aggressive but more assertive, and self-defeating beliefs. The men in the group are presented with material by facilitators, videotapes, and discussion. Participants are encouraged to examine their own behavior in light of the issues. Although all participants and facilitators can challenge any points raised, the group format is non-confrontational and supportive. All efforts made by group members to improve their lives and relationships, however limited, are encouraged.

Some referrals for the group do come from courts and the local probation office, although no one is forced to attend or to remain in the group. Despite the lack of immediate consequences for dropping out of the group, attrition is relatively low (roughly 20%), especially compared to many North American programs (see Gondolf, 1997). These data, however, do not include "no-shows" (i.e. men accepted for groups but do not attend a single session). The relatively low attrition rates may be due to various factors. FVAS services a large geographical area of east-central Alberta and, while this may appear to be a clear disincentive to men who must drive for an hour or two once a week, it is possible that their resource commitment may make them more likely to continue. Many of the men are self-referred "minor" abusers (i. e. they are emotionally controlling as opposed to physically or sexually abusive), and may have more insight and motivation than batterers. Finally, the men tend to be older (average age mid-thirties), established in careers (most employed), and reporting frustration over years of conflict and dysfunctional relationships. Two of these factors (viz. being self-referred and employed) have been found to be significant predictors of program attendance (Daly, Power, & Gondolf, 2001).

The second component of the program is much more psychotherapeutic than the first. It is this aspect of therapy on which we wish to concentrate. The second stage, "Changing Ways II," typically involves groups of three to eight men. Again, one male and one female therapist facilitate this part of the program. These groups are based on the clinical approach of Kelly (1955) and personal construct theory (PCT), which "can provide a fertile clinical perspective for the analysis of inter-spousal violence" (Hallschmid, Black, & Checkley, 1983, p. 15). We believe that PCT is valuable because of its emphasis on the individual.

Briefly, PCT is concerned with the various binary dimensions, or personal constructs, that individuals use to make sense of their personal experiences. Kelly (1955), unlike most personality theorists, explicitly formulated the epistemological assumptions underlying his approach. Kelly's constructive alternativism asserts that the real world does not reveal itself to us directly, but rather it is subject to as many alternative ways of interpreting it as we ourselves can invent. In this way, we can explain the rich diversity of human experience. Moreover, according to Kelly, all of our current representations of events are anticipatory in function. In order to predict our future experience, each individual develops a unique personal construct system and attempts to accommodate it to the unknown structure of reality. This system, including complex subsystems, affords the underlying ground of coherence and unity in the ongoing experience of each person. Although any particular sequence of events lends itself to a variety of different interpretations, some ways of construing probably will prove more useful for anticipating similar events in the future. As events do not directly reveal their meanings to us, it must be the anticipatory constructions or hypotheses, in essence our units of meaning, that we impose on them which endow them with whatever significance they may have in relation to our own behavior. People have the capacity to represent events, not merely respond to them. Each individual is personally responsible for choosing what specific constructions of events will inform his or her actions. Kelly avoided distinctions between "behavioral scientists" and the "subjects" of their inquiries. He claimed that all persons, as scientists, seek to understand their experience and anticipate future events. In short, Kelly applied a constructivist model of scientific activity to the explanation of all human behavior. Each individual not only constructs his or her own hypotheses for anticipating events, but also evaluates and possibly revises them in the light of the results of behavioral experiments based on these hypotheses. As Horley (2003) pointed out, Kelly "viewed all behaviour as experimental" (p. 4). In addition to a detailed philosophical basis, Kelly (1955) developed a number of psychological assessments and psychotherapeutic techniques that Winter (1992), among others, has presented. For more detailed overviews of PCT, see Adams-Webber (1979), Bannister and Fransella (1971), and Kelly (1970).

PCT has been applied to a variety of forensic situations (e.g. Horley, 2003, in press; Houston, 1998). Hallschmid et al. (1983) presented an intriguing analysis of domestic violence from a PCT perspective. They proposed that domestic conflicts involve a failure to construe the core structure of one's partner (i.e. failure to understand a partner as she/he truly is) and this produces anger. The anger produces a set of hostile constructions of the other (e.g. the partner is viewed as jealous or vengeful) and there is no longer flexibility in the reinterpretation of a partner's core structure.

There appear to be a couple of difficulties with this formulation. While this is a possible if not likely explanation of the psychodynamics of some domestic conflict, it does not seem to hold true of all domestic violence. Like all forms of violence (Winter, 2003), domestic violence can be the result of various dynamics, a point that we discuss later. A more serious and specific issue concerns the question of the necessary role of anger in domestic violence. From our perspective, domestic violence appears to have less to do with anger, especially as seen by Cummins (2003), than it does with manipulation and control of significant others. While most male abusers do indeed report experiencing anger prior to any verbal abuse or assault, careful questioning often reveals no such experience. Abusers often report to us that they "must have experienced anger" rather than stating unequivocally that they actually did. We would suggest that the inclusion of anger in an account of domestic violence is expected to explain the sequence of actions. It is, in effect, part of a "cultural script," or a prescribed set of actions deemed normative in a particular cultural context. A typical initial description of domestic violence in our experience takes the form of "She did x, so I got angry, and I did y." The anger serves as a precursor and direct causal attribution for the reaction. Accounts, too, frequently include important asides (e.g. "You'd be angry if your wife called you an asshole, right?") to make the chain of events more understandable, if not justifiable.

If the abuser does not necessarily experience anger, how can we account for domestic violence? On occasion, the violent response to some slight, whether real or perceived, is simply habitual behavior. Domestic violence can be a reflection of the abuser's violent way of life, where home is one more domain where violent behavior is employed. Dutton (1995) has shown that a subset of batterers use violence in the commission of other criminal acts. We would argue, however, that, rather than an indication that they possess a pathological "impulsivity" trait (Dutton, 1995), these assaultive individuals exhibit a tendency to make quick and extreme judgments (see Winter, 2003). A tendency to make hasty decisions may also be typical of some non-habitual abusers.

Domestic violence can also stem from attempts to quickly and easily control behavior of family members (Tweed & Dutton, 1998). Some abusers use instrumental force on family members, perhaps to validate constructs like "head of the house" or "strong." This instrumentality may be related to a number of constructive dynamics outlined by Winter (2003). Domestic abusers characteristically abbreviate the cycle for considering alternatives prior to choosing a construct and a set of actions. They tend to react violently by suddenly moving to control events. Violence can also be the result of a shared construction, and not just in family situations with mutual violence. In such instances, violent behavior may be expected of the male in a household by all members of the family due to personal histories of abuse.

Self-characterization is a key aspect of this second program component. Kelly (1955) noted the importance and manner by which self-characterization could be employed in therapy. Participants are asked "Who are you?" and "Who would you like to be?" They are encouraged to examine personal beliefs and values, or their personal constructs (Horley, 1991), as well as their relationships with others. Dutton's (1994, 1995; Dutton, Bognarchuk, Kropp, Hart, & Ogloff, 1997) research on childhood experiences of male abusers, particularly paternal rejection, has led to incorporating some exploration of the early life experiences of group members. In our efforts, however, we make a clear effort to avoid having clients label themselves as victims of abuse rather than victimizers.

The major aim of the second 12-week group is to assist male abusers in altering self-construal and interpersonal constructions. The shame experienced by many abusers as children (Dutton, 1995), while not resulting in the development of pathological traits, can result in low self-esteem (Saunders, 1989; Wolfus & Bierman, 1996). Neither FVAS group is intentionally confrontational (see Murphy & Baxter, 1997). Confrontation not only models a similar style of behavior that is viewed as inappropriate in the abusers, but it can threaten the therapeutic relationship. In addition, confrontation can threaten fragile self-esteem that is maintained by denial and repression. Rather than self-condemnation, the aim is to help the participants to accept themselves and their pasts, however troubled, and not victimize vulnerable family members as a means of coping with or distracting themselves from personal threat and torment. It is expected that some changes common to all participants will occur during these weeks (e.g. construing themselves more positively, viewing women more favorably), but personal insights, however minor or fleeting, are major goals. A realistic anticipation is that the men will become more aware of personal deficits and difficulties in their current relationships and will take steps (e.g. individual therapy, marital counseling) to address such issues. If any member of the group wishes to remain in the group for a further 12 weeks, or join again at any time, he is encouraged to do so.

OUTCOME MEASURES AND PRELIMINARY RESULTS

A mixture of traditional and nontraditional outcome measures have been developed to evaluate the two components of the program, both pre- and post-group, as well as between groups. We include client satisfaction surveys and follow-up reports from current spouses/partners. Follow-up data should include input from probation/parole officers and police, although our attempts to collect such data have been unsuccessful due to privacy concerns. To date, with roughly a 75% response rate, 100% of clients have reported themselves either "satisfied" or "completely satisfied" with the assistance that they received in the program. The data from current spouses/partners are very incomplete, in part due to spousal separation during the program, in some cases temporary but in others permanent. This seems to be especially the case for partners of program participants attending counseling/treatment concurrent with the program.

One nontraditional assessment technique that we have developed and used with group participants is based on a psycholinguistics measure from the 1950s, the semantic differential (Osgood, Suci, & Tannenbaum, 1957). This technique, similar to Kelly's (1955) role construct repertory test, is concerned with determining the meaning common terms have for individual respondents, in this instance social role titles. The semantic differential procedure asks respondents to describe various concepts/people/objects by placing a mark between paired adjectives. The technique has been adapted to examine the sexual attitudes of sexual offenders (e.g. Marks & Sartorius, 1967), as well as the sexual and social perceptions of child molesters (Frisbie, Vanasek, & Dingman, 1967; Horley & Quinsey, 1994). Following a review of the literature on batterer feelings and attitudes, we developed a 17-item semantic differential aimed at abusers' perceptions of themselves and others (see Figure 1).

FIGURE 1. PORTION OF THE DOMESTIC VIOLENCE
SEMANTIC DIFFERENTIAL

CONCEPT RATING

Concept to be judged: SELF

Kind	Cruel
Seductive	Repulsive
Bad	Good
Trusting	Suspicious
Beautiful	Ugly
Affectionate	Not Affectionate
Sexy	Sexless
Submissive	Dominant
Even Tempered	Hot Tempered
Big	Small
Deceitful	Truthful
Selfless	Selfish
Pleasant	Unpleasant
Immature	Mature
Happy	Sad
Soft	Hard
Clean	Dirty

The semantic differential can be used with any other psychometric or social measure, and it can replace some familiar ones. It has a number of distinct advantages over many traditional measures. It permits an indirect assessment of self-esteem via discrepancy scores between self-ideal and self-judgments. The semantic differential also provides a measure of attitudes toward women that is less transparent than many existing measures (e.g. Nelson, 1976). Finally, related to the previous point, it permits examination of the personal perspectives of abusers toward women rather than only limited dimensions of those attitudes (e.g. traditional versus gender aschematic attitudes).

We also use a variation of Kelly's (1955) rep test, the role construct repertory grid, or rep grid (see Fransella, Bell, & Bannister, 2004, for details concerning various aspects of the rep grid). The rep grid is essentially a complex sorting task in which a list of elements is categorized dichotomously along a set of bipolar dimensions or personal constructs. We can either elicit a sample of personal constructs from each respondent individually, or simply supply the same set of dimensions to all respondents alike. The data elicited from each respondent are entered into a separate two-dimensional grid or matrix in which there is a column for every element and a row for every construct. Each row-column intersect in this grid contains a symbol (e.g. a binary digit) indicating which pole of a given construct was applied to a particular element.

In our work with abusers, we have used a 20 row by 10 column rep grid with a variety of social elements (see Figure 2). Although the elements in this grid are provided, the personal constructs or the respondents' personal dimensions of meaning are elicited. This grid has been used successfully with forensic clients in the past; it has known and acceptable psychometric properties (Horley, 1996; for a summary, see Horley, 2000). The results of one grid with one domestic abuser are presented below.

The semantic differential, the rep grid, and other measures that we use are still somewhat transparent. As such, they remain vulnerable to respondent misrepresentation because of, for example, social desirability demands. Social desirability effects with such instruments, however, have been found to be insignificant in previous research (e.g. Badesha & Horley, 2000), and we believe that these types of assessment techniques represent a clear step forward over more traditional assessments used with domestic abusers.

Our domestic violence semantic differential requires respondents to complete one set of ratings on seven concepts or social elements (viz. self, ideal-self, man, woman, father, mother, spouse/boyfriend/girlfriend), although any number or choice of elements is acceptable. One of our main concerns was keeping the time/energy demanded of written assessments, especially when repeated three times in our work, to a minimum. Our semantic differential, while limited by a small sample size, has produced some interesting results. Complete data on four small groups ($N = 14$) showed that self-esteem did increase, $t(13) = 3.58$, $p < .01$. This result is even more noteworthy given that most men increased their own standards (i.e. had higher ideal-self ratings after the program).

135

Figure 2. Role Construct Repertory Grid

	Self	Ideal Self	Boy	Girl	Man	Woman	Father	Mother	Authority Figure	Spouse (Boy/Girlfriend)	way alike ⊗	way different ○
1		⊗		⊗		○						
2	○	⊗			⊗							
3			⊗				○	⊗				
4	⊗			⊗			○					
5				⊗		⊗				○		
6	○				⊗					⊗		
7		○		⊗		⊗						
8						○		⊗	⊗			
9		⊗		⊗				○				
10					⊗				○	⊗		
11	⊗		○			⊗						
12				⊗			⊗	○				
13		○				⊗			⊗			
14						⊗	⊗			○		
15			⊗					○		⊗		
16				○	⊗	⊗						
17		⊗			⊗		○					
18	○			⊗					⊗			
19	⊗		⊗							○		
20					○		⊗	⊗				

The results concerning attitudes toward women from the semantic differential are more equivocal. There was only a negligible, statistically non-significant improvement in views of women or a specific woman (viz. spouse/partner). These results may reflect negative emotions experienced by over half of the men to partners who left them during or just prior to their involvement with the program.

THE CASE OF A. C.

One client, A. C., is a typical yet interesting program participant. He is a middle-class, white, married male in his early forties and successful materially. He and his wife have experienced longstanding marital difficulties. They have attended marital and family therapy sessions irregularly for years. A. C. claimed that their relationship had improved recently because they were both addressing the real problem with their relationship, alcohol abuse. A. C. attends Alcoholics Anonymous meetings often and has taken an organizing role in recent months. He reported that the marital problems, including physical assaults, tended to occur when both were intoxicated. A. C. is currently on the waiting list for Changing Ways II.

After attending the first 12-week component of our program, A. C. completed a rep grid and semantic differential. The grid results, superficially at least, seemed to confirm the results of the semantic differential ratings and his self-reports. In terms of his self-descriptions during an open-ended interview, he described himself as more confident, calmer, and more in control of his emotions. Excessive drinking was not a problem now, and the marital problems were being addressed slowly but surely. An analysis of grid results, however, revealed more subtle concerns (see Figure 3).

A. C. used a number of psychological constructs in his grid. In order to reduce the complexity of the information from this matrix, a non-parametric factor analysis was performed (for details, see Adams-Webber, 1979; Kelly, 1955). The first factor, accounting for about 50% of the total variance in the grid, seemed to be concerned with control. The poles of these constructs included "easy-going," "controlling of others" (reflected), "manipulate in actions" (sic), and "thinks of others." The contrasts to some of these poles, however, are revealing. The contrast to

FIGURE 3. REP GRID RESULTS FOR A. C.
(NON-PARAMETRIC FACTOR ANALYSIS)

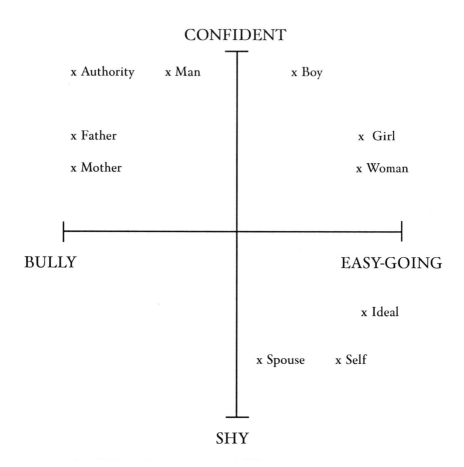

CONFIDENT

x Authority   x Man   x Boy

x Father   x Girl

x Mother   x Woman

BULLY   EASY-GOING

                                   x Ideal

              x Spouse   x Self

SHY

"controlling of others," for example, is "weak." The same was true
for constructs loading on the second factor, accounting for an
additional 20% of the overall variance of the grid. In contrast
to "confident," A. C. provided "shy." He saw himself, his ideal,
and his wife in the easy-going and open-to-change quadrant.
While this may appear positive, it also makes him shy and weak
by his own estimation. Many domestic abusers—indeed, many
criminal offenders—report difficult or traumatic experiences with
authority figures, such as parents, police, and judges. They often

are very ambivalent about authority, seeing it as oppressive and cruel but strong and enviable at the same time. This seems to be the case for A. C., who views authority and both parents as controlling bullies, but also as strong and confident. It is possible that he is able to focus on the positive aspects of his own easy-going flexibility when sober, but the implications of these, a "shy weakness," may become more apparent when drunk. If the couple begin to assert themselves in either a verbal or physical sparring match, A. C. may lash out because of the emotional pain of perceiving weakness in himself.

The social elements in A. C.'s grid were viewed in rather extreme fashion. In terms of the first two factors from Figure 3, all elements were weighted heavily on one pole or another; no elements fell into the center of the graph. This may reflect "black and white" views of people rather than seeing individuals, including himself, more in terms of shades of gray. Certainly in talking to A. C. he was impressive as a man of clear and definite opinions concerning the people around him, yet he admitted that he was quick to judge.

His semantic differential results suggested positive attitudes toward women in general and his wife in particular. In terms of self-ratings, he expressed largely positive views of himself, both present and ideal. A. C.'s only negative ratings concerned his father and mother, whom he rated as similarly cruel, dominant, and unpleasant.

DISCUSSION AND CONCLUSIONS

At present, the role of self-esteem in many areas of criminal offending is complex and unclear. Some investigators (e. g. Marshall & Mazzucco, 1995) have argued that self-esteem is an essential aspect in understanding and assisting a number of offenders, especially child sexual abusers. Other investigators (e. g. Horley, Quinsey, & Jones, 1997), however, have argued that self-esteem is a complex construct, and have presented data suggesting that low self-esteem does not necessarily predict offenses like child sexual abuse. With respect to our program, while we found a significant increase in self-esteem among participants, it may not indicate decreased likelihood of domestic violence in the future. For some abusers, self-esteem may be a buffer variable that, when above a certain level, means that they are less likely to assault intimates because they will be less likely to take offense over off-hand comments or actions. For other abusers, such as individuals who use physical force habitually to gain compliance in everyday affairs, elevation of self-esteem might mean an increased likelihood of abuse because it reinforces a personal identity as a "rotten bastard" or "tough guy." The exact role of self-esteem in domestic violence does indeed demand clarification (Woolfus & Bierman, 1996), but we doubt if the answer will be simple or straightforward.

The case presented above is a good example of the complexity of understanding and intervening in domestic violence. A. C. expressed confidence in his ability not only to avoid alcohol abuse but also the abuse of his wife. There was little perceived distance between his current and ideal selves, suggestive of high self-esteem. There appears to us, however, to be little room for optimism in A. C.'s future. A. C.'s long-term involvement with Alcoholics Anonymous, while it may have provided a sense of meaning and community for him, does not appear to have provided a dramatically new and improved selfhood. Take just the second dimension from his rep grid results as one example. "Confident versus shy," a rather bent construction that is not a logical opposite in a normative sense, seems to present problems for A. C. because of its potentially confounding relationship with constructs like "closed to change versus open to change" and "not easy-going versus easy-going." For A. C., the confident person is also one who is likely narrow-minded and uptight. This is a view that will lead to confusion and conflict for him, if it has not already. Suggesting that he reexamine these construct relations, with a view to realigning them (e.g. a 90 degree shift of "closed-open" with respect to "confident-shy"), would be one focus of our work with him in the second group.

A. C. is not alone in looking to alcohol as a simple explanation for his conflict with his wife. Most of our program participants, and many partners, initially take this position. The zealous nature of many anti-drinking, anti-drug organizations promotes such a view. Clearly, however, alcohol/drug abuse can be as much effect as cause of domestic abuse. Simplistic explanations make our efforts, and the efforts of all who work to eliminate domestic violence, very difficult. This concern about quick and simple answers to complex questions emphasizes our previous point about self-esteem. As mental health professionals, we need to avoid quick and simple psychological explanations of complex psychosocial issues. Domestic violence appears to be much more complex in psychosocial terms for both abusers and victims than many have argued (c.f. Walker, 2000). We would certainly agree with Winter (2003) that there are many "pathways to violence" (p. 16), including domestic violence. Any program for domestic abusers intended to address only one issue will be limited in success to a small subset of offenders. Thus, although there appears to be a sound reason for addressing the self-esteem of some domestic abusers, we would not suggest that it is the only concern for these offenders.

Ganley (1989) appears correct to propose the use of "multiple models" in programs aimed at domestic abusers. This is at the basis of the FVAS program. We have discovered, however, that more complex programs have drawbacks. One problem that must be addressed concerns "selling" the program to both funding sources and potential participants. It is likely that the cost, such as the material cost of facilitators or the increased time commitment of participants, of more complex programs is usually greater than simpler programs. A related problem concerns men who only attend the first group and not the second. To date, we have found that only a small number of participants, roughly 30%, are willing to proceed from the first group to the next. Whether this is due to the change in format (i.e. psycho-educational to psychotherapeutic), the amount of time involved (i.e. roughly six months continuous), or some other issue is difficult to determine. Those who only complete our psycho-educational component seem to be successful in convincing probation/parole officers, and ultimately the courts, that they have fulfilled probation or parole conditions. We wonder and worry whether a participant who just completes Changing Ways I will be successful in convincing family members that they are "cured" or "a different person." We will need to gather more evaluative data in order to argue that the two groups are important together, but our preliminary data and the case of A. C. do not suggest that the first group without the second leads to significant improvements on a number of important indices. Further study will also be required to demonstrate whether our assessment techniques, such as the semantic differential, require further revision.

REFERENCES

Adams-Webber, J. R. (1979). *Personal construct theory: Concepts and applications.* New York: John Wiley & Sons.

Badesha, J., & Horley, J. (2000). Self construal among psychiatric outpatients: A test of the golden section. *British Journal of Medical Psychology, 73,* 547-551.

Bannister, D., & Fransella, F. (1971). *Inquiring man: The theory of personal constructs.* Harmondsworth: Penguin Books.

Cummins, P. (2003). Working with anger. In F. Fransella (Ed.), *International handbook of personal construct psychology* (pp. 83 93). Chichester: John Wiley & Sons.

Daly, J. E., Power, T. G., & Gondolf, E. W. (2001). Predictors of batterer program attendance. *Journal of Interpersonal Violence, 16,* 971-991.

Dutton, D. G. (1994). The origin and structure of the abusive personality. *Journal of Personality Disorders, 8,* 181-191.

Dutton, D. G. (1995). *The abusive personality.* New York: Springer.

Dutton, D. G., Bognarchuk, M., Kropp, R., Hart, S., & Ogloff, J. P. (1997). Client personality disorders affecting wife assault post-treatment recidivism. *Violence and Victims, 12,* 37-50.

Fransella, F., Bell, R., & Bannister, D. (2004). *A manual for repertory grid technique* (2nd edition). Chichester: John Wiley & Sons.

Frisbie, L. V., Vanasek, F. J., & Dingman, H. F. (1967). The self and the ideal self: Methodological study of pedophiles. *Psychological Reports, 20,* 699-706.

Ganley, G. L. (1989). Integrating feminist and social learning analyses of aggression: Creating multiple models for intervention with men who batter. In P. L. Caesar & L. K. Hamberger (Eds.), *Treating men who batter: Theory, practice, and programs* (pp. 196 235). New York: Springer.

Gilchrist, E., & Blissett, J. (2002). Magistrates' attitudes to domestic violence and sentencing options. *The Howard Journal of Criminal Justice, 41,* 348-363.

Gondolf, E. W. (1987a). Evaluating programs for men who batter: Problems and prospects. *Journal of Family Violence, 2,* 95-108.

Gondolf, E. W. (1987b). Changing men who batter: A developmental model for integrated interventions. *Journal of Family Violence, 2,* 335-349.

Gondolf, E. W. (1997). Batterer programs: What we know and need to know. *Journal of Interpersonal Violence, 12,* 83-98.

Hallschmid, C. A., Black, E. L., & Checkley, K. L. (1983). The core boundary: A conceptual analysis of interspousal violence from a construct-systems perspective. *International Journal of Offender Therapy and Comparative Criminology, 29,* 15-34.

Horley, J. (1991). Values and beliefs as personal constructs. *International Journal of Personal Construct Psychology, 4,* 1-14.

142

Horley, J. (1996). Content stability in the repertory grid: An examination using a forensic sample. *International Journal of Offender Therapy and Comparative Criminology, 40*, 26-31.

Horley, J. (2000). Cognitions supportive of child molestation. *Aggression and Violent Behavior: A Review Journal, 5*, 551-564.

Horley, J. (2003). Forensic psychology and personal construct theory. In J. Horley (Ed.), *Personal construct perspectives on forensic psychology* (pp. 1-17). New York: Brunner-Routledge.

Horley, J. (in press). *Sexual offenders: Personal construct theory and deviant sexual behaviour*. Hove: Brunner-Routledge.

Horley, J., & Quinsey, V. L. (1994). Assessing the cognitions of child molesters: Use of the semantic differential with incarcerated offenders. *Journal of Sex Research, 31*, 187-195.

Horley, J., Quinsey, V. L., & Jones, S. (1997). Incarcerated child molesters' perceptions of themselves and others. *Sexual Abuse: A Journal of Research and Treatment, 9*, 43-55.

Houston, J. (1998). *Making sense with offenders: Personal constructs, therapy and change*. Chichester: John Wiley & Sons.

Kelly, G. A. (1955). *The psychology of personal constructs* (2 vols.). New York: Norton.

Kelly, G. A. (1970). A brief introduction to personal construct theory. In D. Bannister (Ed.), *Perspectives in personal construct theory* (pp. 1-29). London: Academic Press.

Marks, I. M., & Sartorius, N. H. (1967). A contribution to the measurement of sexual attitude. *Journal of Nervous and Mental Disease, 145*, 441-451.

Marshall, M. L., & Mazzucco, A. (1995). Self-esteem and parental attachments in child molesters. *Sexual Abuse: A Journal of Research and Treatment, 1*, 279-285.

Murphy, C. M., & Baxter, V. A. (1997). Motivating batterers to change in the treatment context. *Journal of Interpersonal Violence, 12*, 607-619.

Nelson, M. C. (1988). Reliability, validity, and cross-cultural comparisons for the simplified Attitudes Toward Women Scale. *Sex Roles, 18*, 289-296.

Osgood, C. E., Suci, G. J., & Tannenbaum, P. (1957). *The measurement of meaning*. Urbana: University of Illinois Press.

Pence, E., & Paymar, M. (1993). Education groups for men who batter: *The Duluth model*. New York: Springer.

Saunders, D. G. (1989). Cognitive and behavioral interventions with men who batter: Application and outcome. In P. L. Caesar & L. K. Hamberger (Eds.), *Treating men who batter: Theory, practice, and programs* (pp. 77-100). New York: Springer.

Saunders, D. G. (1996). Feminist-cognitive-behavioral and process-psychodynamic treatments for men who batter: Interaction of abuser traits and treatment models. *Violence and Victims, 11*, 393-414.

Tweed, R. G., & Dutton, D. G. (1998). A comparison of impulsive and instrumental subgroups of batterers. *Violence and Victims, 13*, 217-230.

Walker, L. E. A. (2000). *The battered woman syndrome.* New York: Springer.

Winter, D. A. (1992). *Personal construct psychology in clinical practice: Theory, research and applications.* London: Routledge.

Winter, D. A. (2003). A credulous approach to violence and homicide. In J. Horley (Ed.), *Personal construct perspectives on forensic psychology* (pp. 15-54). London: Brunner-Routledge.

Woolfus, B., & Bierman, R. (1996). An evaluation of a group treatment program for incarcerated male batterers. *International Journal of Offender Therapy and Comparative Criminology, 40*, 318-333.

ଓଃ 7 ଅ

A Constructivist Approach to Child-Centered Play Therapy

Richard E. Watts and Yvonne Garza

Suppose you, an adult, went to see a therapist for help with a problem. Suppose your visit to this therapist *feels* mandated and, for reasons beyond your control, you have no choice over which counselor you get to see. This would be difficult enough for most of us. Now suppose that this therapist, during routine intake procedures, discovered that you have a basic knowledge of and facility with a second language. You can speak well enough to "get by" using this second language, but cannot communicate with the level of comfort or emotional depth that you can with your first language. Suppose that this therapist, having discovered your facility with a second language, announces that you may only talk with him or her in your second language. There you are: little sense of control over being there with this stranger who demands that you discuss difficult, personal, emotion-laden content using your second language. How would you feel? Angry, intimidated, and scared are a few feelings that come to mind. One would certainly not feel invited to engage in a fruitful therapeutic process given such a scenario. Yet this is exactly what happens to young children when they are required to sit in a chair and do "talk therapy" with an adult therapist. This is true even when we use toys and play media with young children as a means of "getting them to talk" about their problems. Most young children do not have sufficient cognitive development and expressive language skills to clearly express themselves. They typically are much more comfortable using toys and play media to express themselves. Play therapy allows young children to share their thoughts feelings, reactions, and attitudes in their most natural medium of communication: play (Landreth, 2002).[*]

[*] We believe Landreth (2002) is the best introduction to child-centered play therapy available.

The purpose of this chapter is not to present a model of *constructivist* play therapy. Rather our purpose is to demonstrate the utility of the basic facilitative skills of child-centered play therapy within a constructive (constructivist and social constructionist) therapeutic context with young children. We begin by presenting a rationale for the use of play in child therapy. Next we address points of congruence and resonation between the child-centered perspective and constructive therapies. The remainder of the chapter discusses basic principles and procedures from child-centered play therapy that may be useful for constructive therapists as they work with young children.

WHY USE PLAY IN PSYCHOTHERAPY?

Children of every era have played to cope with and make meaning of the often difficult and meaningless situations in their lives. For example, children in Nazi concentration camps in Auschwitz during the Holocaust of World War II used play to cope as they prepared to die and as they witnessed the horrors of war (Sweeney, 1997). Children living during the "black plague" of the Middle Ages created the game "Ring around the Rosie."

> The "rosie" refers to the red blotches and lesions from contracting the plague; the "pocket full of posies" refers to the flowers for the dead and the practice of putting flowers into the pockets of plague victims to ward off the smell of death; and "ashes, ashes, we all fall down" alludes to the imminent death of the plague-stricken and the practice of burning the bodies of plague victims. (p. 21)

Children use play to comfort themselves and make sense out of their often tragic life situations.

Play is essential to the development of cognitive, language, motor, and social skills in children (Kottman, 2001; Landreth, 2002). Play is the focal activity of childhood and children "do not need to be taught how to play, nor must they be made to play. Play is spontaneous, enjoyable, voluntary, and non-goal-directed" (Landreth, 2002, p. 10). Furthermore, children communicate through play. According to Landreth (2002):

> Children's play can be more fully appreciated when recognized as their natural medium of communication. Children express themselves more fully and more directly through self-initiated, spontaneous play than they do verbally because they are more comfortable with play.

> For children to "play out" their experiences and feelings is the most natural dynamic and self-healing process in which they can engage. (p. 14)

According to Schaefer (1993), play "has the power to not only to facilitate normal child development but also to alleviate abnormal behavior" (p. 3). Most children under age ten do not have the abstract reasoning and verbal abilities to clearly express their thoughts, feelings, reactions, and attitudes. Consequently, many therapists who work with children use toys and other play media to help young children communicate their experiences, reactions to experiences, desires and goals, and perceptions about themselves, others, and the world (Kottman, 2001; Landreth, 2002). According to Caplan and Caplan (1974), there are several unique attributes of play that appeal to children. First, play is a voluntary activity by nature. In a world full of requirements and rules, play is refreshing and provides a respite from everyday tension. Second, play is free from evaluation and judgment by adults. Children are safe to make mistakes without failure and adult reprimand. Third, play encourages fantasy and the use of imagination. In a make-believe world, children can exercise the need for control without competition. Fourth, play increases interest and involvement. Children often have short attention spans and are reluctant to participate in a lower interest, less attractive activity. Finally, play encourages the development of the physical and mental self (Caplan & Caplan, 1974, pp. xii-xvii).

Play therapy is a useful and appropriate method for psychotherapy with young children. According to Kottman (2001), play therapy is useful for establishing and maintaining a therapeutic alliance with children; helping therapists understand children and their interactions and relationships; helping children express feelings that they are unable or unwilling to verbalize; helping children behaviorally and constructively express feelings of anxiety, frustration, or hostility; helping children learn and practice social skills; and creating an environment in which children feel safe to "test limits, gain insight about their own behavior and motivation, explore alternatives, and learn about consequences" (p. 4). Furthermore, Bratton and Ray (2000) presented a comprehensive play therapy literature review of 100 case studies and 82 experimental research studies. The case studies indicated that clients in play therapy consistently show more well-functioning behavior and decreased levels of symptomatic behavior as compared with their behavior prior to entering play therapy. The experimental studies suggest that play therapy can be helpful for children with problems such as social maladjustment, conduct disorder, problematic school behavior, emotional maladjustment, anxiety/fear, negative self-concept, being "mentally challenged," and having a physical or learning disability.

Therapists interested in using play therapy, however, may need to make a paradigm shift. This shift is from a primary therapeutic focus on conversation and verbal skills to a primary focus on using play, toys, play media, and metaphor for communication and to facilitate change. It appears to be a simple change to make, but is actually a complex conceptual shift that many adults find difficult (Kottman, 2001).

> Play therapists look at themselves, children, and the world from a different perspective than talk therapists do. Before they can begin to acquire the skills involved in using play to communicate with children, potential play therapists must learn a completely different way of understanding communication—to a symbolic, action-oriented model in which actions of puppets and animal figures are important pieces of information and in which a shrug, a smile, or a turned back can be an entire "coversation." (p. 20)

This is particularly true for therapists working with children ages three to ten (Landreth, 2002) and children from other cultures (Garza & Bratton, 2005).

CHILD-CENTERED PLAY THERAPY AND CONSTRUCTIVE THERAPIES

We begin this section of the chapter by briefly reviewing our understanding of *constructivism* and *constructive therapies*. There is a wide range of constructive perspectives, from more individually focused views of constructed reality to ones that view reality as socially constructed. According to Mahoney (2002, 2003; Mahoney & Granvold, 2005) major 20th-century constructivists include, but are not limited to, Alfred Adler, Walter Truett Anderson, Albert Bandura, Gregory Bateson, Jerome Bruner, James Bugental, Mary Whiton Calkins, Donald Ford, Viktor Frankl, Kenneth Gergen, Harry Goolishian, Vittorio Guidano, Hermann Haken, Sandra Harding, Yutaka Haruki, Friedrich Hayek, William James, Evelyn Fox Keller, George Kelly, Karin

Knorr-Cetina, Humberto Maturana, Jean Piaget, Joseph Rychlak, Esther Thelen, Francisco Varela, Heinz von Foerster, Ernst von Glaserfeld, Paul Watzlawick, and Walter Weimer.

Constructivist approaches share a common or similar epistemology and may be distinguished by their "operative assumptions about the nature of personal knowledge and its social embeddedness" (Neimeyer, 1995, p. 15). According to Mahoney (1995, 2002, 2003; Mahoney & Granvold, 2005), constructivism is "a family" of theories and therapies that emphasize at least five central features or themes: First, "human experiencing involves continuous *active agency*" (Mahoney, 2003, p. 5) and humans are proactive (and not passively reactive) participants in their own experiences. Second, the majority of human activity is devoted to *ordering processes* or "the organizational patterning of experience; these ordering processes are fundamentally emotional, tacit, and categorical . . . and they are the essence of meaning making" (Mahoney & Granvold, 2005, p. 74). Third, human experience and personal psychological development reflect the ongoing operation of self-organizing or recursive processes that tend to favor the maintenance (over the modification) of experiential patterns. Because the "organization of personal activity is fundamentally self-referent and recursive," the person's body is a "fulcrum of experience and encourages a deep phenomenological sense of *selfhood* or *personal identity*" (Mahoney, 2003, pp. 74-75). Fourth, "self-organizing capacities and creations of meaning are strongly influenced by *social-symbolic processes*; that is, persons exist in living webs of relationships that are typically mediated by language and symbol systems" (Mahoney & Granvold, 2005, p. 75). Thus, one can affirm that knowledge is socially embedded and relationally distributed without emptying the aforementioned sense of selfhood or personal identity (Watts, 2003; Watts & Phillips, 2004). Fifth, human development is a lifelong process of complex cycles and spirals of experiencing that is both "dynamic (always changing) and dialectical (generated by contrasts)" (Mahoney, 2002, p. 749). These complex cycles and spirals can "lead to episodes of disorder (disorganization) and, under some circumstances, reorganization (transformation) of core patterns of activity, including meaning making and both self- and social relationships" (Mahoney, 2003, p. 5).

In regard to constructive therapeutic approaches, there are certainly some distinct differences. However, as Hoyt (1994) suggests, they share some distinct clinical practice characteristics, as well.

These include: (1) A clear emphasis on the development and maintenance of a strong therapeutic alliance; (2) a clear focus on clients' strengths, abilities, and resources rather than their deficits, disabilities, and limitations; and (3) an optimistic and future-oriented perspective.

Person-Centered and Constructive Therapies

Many authors espousing constructive theoretical perspectives have expressed concerns regarding the oppressive and colonialist nature of "traditional" therapies, including various models of play therapy. For example, Smith (1997) delineated four concerns.

1. Therapists using traditional approaches tend to limit the scope of the therapeutic dialogue by attending only to content that is consistent with their theoretical framework and/or is of interest to the therapists.

2. Therapists using traditional approaches may juxtapose their "preferred views of reality upon the clients in the name of empirical science" (p. 20).

3. When operating from the "expert posture" advocated by many traditional therapies, therapists may have difficulty perceiving when genuine change has occurred, as opposed to mere client acquiescence to authority (p. 21).

4. Traditional therapists "may become particularly fixed on certain theoretically predetermined content" (p. 21).

Although these concerns may be accurate for many traditional approaches to therapy in general, and play therapy specifically, they are not appropriate for child-centered play therapy. The theoretical underpinning for child-centered play therapy is Rogers' person-centered therapy. Anyone remotely conversant with the person-centered approach is cognizant that person-centered therapists do not (a) limit the scope of the therapeutic dialogue, (b) juxtapose their preferred view of reality on clients, (c) operate from an expert position, or (d) fixate on theoretically predetermined content. Harlene Anderson (2001), developer of "collaborative therapy," made this abundantly clear in her article comparing

150

person-centered therapy with her approach. Anderson, albeit using different nomenclature, demonstrated that the person-centered theory of Carl Rogers shares with constructive approaches the aforementioned clinical practice characteristics delineated by Hoyt (1994). For example, Anderson (2001) noted that

> The collaborative therapist, similar to Rogers, considers the client as the expert on his or her life and as the therapist's teacher . . . [The therapist] invites, respects and takes seriously *what* a client has to say and *how* they choose to say it. . . . Both approaches share an appreciative and optimistic view of people and their capacity to be experts on their lives, and to resolve their difficulties in ways unique to them and their circumstances. (pp. 349-354)

Although these comments by Anderson are specifically addressing similarities between collaborative therapy and person-centered therapy, we believe these comments are salient for understanding basic similarities between most constructive therapies and the person-centered approach.

Child-Centered Play Therapy and Constructive Therapies

Constructive therapists assert that children are particularly vulnerable to having their voices discounted or ignored because adults wield significantly more power (Freeman, Epston, & Lobovits, 1997; Smith, 1997).

> As children are in a more malleable stage of development compared with adults, it is incumbent upon us that we exercise responsibility regarding the weight of our influence in shaping children's lives and the narratives by which they come to describe their lives. They, too, must be allowed to speak as subjects who have expertise about their own lives, rather than be spoken about as objects who are acted upon by others. (Freeman et al., 1997, p. 8)

Therefore, therapists must be careful to privilege both the voice of child clients and the medium or means by which they are most comfortable sharing their voices (Smith, 1997). Freeman et al. (1997) stated that "conversations can shape new realities" and language "can shape events into narratives of hope" (p. xv). Constructive therapists give a much more expansive definition of "communication" and "dialogue." For example, Anderson noted that she uses "conversation and dialogue, and dialogical conversation, to refer to inner and outer, spoken and unspoken, and silent and out-loud thoughts and communication" (2001, p. 345).

There is significant common ground between the constructive therapy principles briefly addressed above and child-centered play. According to Landreth (2002), children are not miniature adults, and therapists should not respond to them as such. Because children have insufficient cognitive development and expressive language skills to clearly express themselves, play is their natural language and "the medium with which they are most comfortable" (p. 54). Play is their language and toys are their words. By meeting children at their level and allowing them to express themselves in the manner in which they are most comfortable, play therapists help children make sense and give meaning to their experiences and help them give expression to their inner worlds. Child-centered play therapy, congruent with constructive therapeutic approaches, privileges *both the voices of child clients and the medium by which they are most comfortable sharing their voices.*

The relational attitude inherent in the concomitant privileging of the children's voices and their most comfortable means of expression is foundational for building a strong therapeutic relationship. Both child-centered and constructive play therapists seek to accept children unconditionally and establish a warm, caring therapeutic climate where children feel invited to freely express their feelings, thoughts, and experiences. Each child must be understood through the eyes (or voice) of that child. Therefore, play therapists vigorously avoid "judging or evaluation of even the simplest of the child's behaviors" (Landreth, 2002, p. 62). This includes the child's decision not to talk: "Children have the right to remain silent" (p. 54). Furthermore, the play therapist

> . . . works hard to try to understand the child's inner frame of reference. If the therapist is to make contact with the person of the child, the child's phenomenal world must be the point of focus and must be understood. The child is not expected to meet predetermined criteria or fit a set of preconceived categories. (p. 62)

Child-centered play therapy stresses client strengths and allowing clients to direct therapy. This is consistent with the aforementioned emphasis on privileging the child's voice and self-expression. Both child-centered and constructive approaches to play therapy affirm that children are resilient, able to problem-solve, and able to act responsibly (if given opportunities to do so). Children will take the therapeutic experience where they need it to be and the therapist need not tell a child when and how to play. Consequently, a therapist should follow the child client's lead rather than expecting the child to follow the therapist's agenda (Landreth, 2002).

There is significant common ground between constructive therapies and child-centered play therapy. Because of this significant common ground, we believe the knowledge and use of the basic facilitative language of play therapy is a crucial foundation for successful constructive play therapy.

A BRIEF INTRODUCTION TO THE BASIC FACILITATIVE LANGUAGE OF CHILD-CENTERED PLAY THERAPY

Having identified significant points of resonation between constructive therapies and child-centered play therapy, the remainder of this chapter discusses toys and materials necessary for play therapy, and then offers a brief introduction to the basic facilitative language of play therapy that constructive play therapists may use to facilitate "dialogue" with young child clients. In depth discussion of either of these topics (toys or skills) is beyond the scope of this chapter. Readers are directed to Landreth (2002) and Kottman (2001) for more comprehensive presentations.

Toys and Play Media

According to Landreth (2002), toys and materials must be carefully selected—not collected—because they are an essential part of the communication process for children. To help children freely express all aspects of their experiences, play therapists purposefully select toys for their playroom or portable play kit representative of distinct categories. Landreth (2002) lists three categories and Kottman (2003), an Adlerian play therapist, lists five categories. Although both approaches use essentially the same toys, we thought it would be beneficial to present both sets of categories.

Landreth's list of toy categories. Landreth's (2002) three categories of toys include real-life toys, acting-out and aggressive-release toys, and creative expression and emotional release toys. Examples of real-life toys include doll family and puppets, doctor's kit, cash register, pots, pans, dishes, silverware, etc. Examples of acting-out and aggressive-release toys include an inflatable bop bag (Bobo), soldiers, toy guns, toy knives, etc. Creative expression and emotional toy examples include sand, water, clay, newsprint, paints crayons, other art media, and the like. For more complete list, see Landreth (2002).

Kottman's list of toy categories. Kottman (2003) lists five categories of toys: family/nurturing toys, scary toys, aggressive toys, expressive toys, and pretend/fantasy toys. Examples of family/nurturing toys include baby dolls, baby clothes, baby bottle, cradle, doll house, animal families, people puppets, several families of bendable dolls, etc. Scary toy examples include snakes, rats, plastic monsters, dragons, shark, etc. Toys belonging to the aggressive toys category are similar to Landreth's (2002) acting-out and aggressive release toy category (see above). Similarly, toys belonging to the expressive toy category are similar to Landreth's creative expression and emotional release toy category (see above). Finally, examples of pretend/fantasy toys include masks, doctor kit, dress-up clothes, blocks and other building materials, puppets and puppet theater, telephones (have two), zoo and farm animals, etc. For a more complete list, see Kottman (2003).

Regardless of which toy category the play therapist prefers, it is important that play therapists include dolls and doll families from culturally diverse groups so that children can explore similarities and differences between diverse groups of people. Furthermore, when working with culturally diverse clients, the facilitative process of play therapy may be enhanced by including toys and play media specifically indigenous to the child's culture that help capture cultural nuances or familiar elements from their environment (Garza & Bratton, 2005).

It is not necessary to have all of these toys to engage in play therapy. However, it is important to have representative toys from all five categories of play media. Whereas play is the most natural language of children, toys and play media are the words they most naturally use to express themselves. Therefore, the more play media choices children have for expressing themselves, the increased likelihood that they will have sufficient resources to clearly express themselves in play therapy (Kottman, 2003; Landreth, 2002).

Regardless of where play therapy sessions are conducted, the toys should be arranged in an open space and set within easy reach of clients. In addition, toys should be arranged according to their specific categories. In other words, real-life toys should be arranged with other real-life toys, and so forth. This consistent, predictable arrangement helps children experience the play therapy situation as one where they feel safe and comfortable (Landreth, 2002).

The ideal setting for play therapy is a spacious, custom-designed playroom. However, most therapists working with children have limited funds and must share space with other mental health professionals or travel to multiple locations. Fortunately, play therapists can do play therapy in a myriad of locations by bringing with them a box or bag—a portable or play therapy kit—with selected toys from each of the aforementioned categories. Play therapists can work in schools, go to children's homes, or go to hospitals and do play therapy on a hospital bed. What is necessary to engage in play therapy is a relatively quiet, structured play space with sufficient room where the play therapist can set out the toys, and the client and therapist can have sufficient privacy so that the client can be assured of confidentiality in the play therapy sessions (Kottman, 2003; Landreth, 2002).

The most important consideration regarding play therapy space is the comfort level of the therapist. The play therapist must feel comfortable wherever play therapy occurs so that the therapist is able to express his or her creativity and flexibility with clients. Therapists considering the creation of a room solely dedicated to play therapy should consult Landreth (2002) and Kottman (2003) for thorough and practical considerations regarding the "ideal" playroom.

Basic Facilitative Skills

The basic skills of child-centered play therapy help play therapists build a warm, caring and egalitarian relationship with the child and provide an environment whereby the child (a) feels permission to express feelings, thoughts, attitudes, and desires, (b) feels permission to make decisions and test limits, (c) experiences opportunities to assume responsibility and a feeling of control, and (d) feels understood and accepted at the child's level and from his or her perspective (Landreth, 2002). These skills include tracking behavior, reflecting feelings, reflecting content, esteem building, returning responsibility to the child, and setting limits (Carlson, Watts, & Maniacci, 2006; Kottman, 2001; Landreth, 2002).

155

Tracking behavior. When a play therapist tracks behavior, he or she reflects to the child what the child is doing and how the child is using a toy. Tracking behavior is intended to communicate to the child that the child's behavior in the playroom is important and that he or she has the therapist's full attention (Carlson, Watts, & Maniacci, 2006; Kottman, 2001; Landreth, 2002).

- Example: *A child picks up a toy airplane and moves it around in the air.*

     •Response: "You're picking that up" or "You're moving it around in the air."

When tracking a child's behavior, it is important not to label toys, play media, or behaviors. If the play therapist labels something, the child usually feels obligated to go by the therapist's label. By not labeling, the child's imagination is not stifled and the child can decide the identity of toys or behaviors (Carlson, Watts, & Maniacci, 2006; Kottman 2001; Landreth, 2002).

Reflecting feelings. As used in almost all forms of therapy, reflecting feelings is intended to communicate to the client that the affective component of his or her play and words is understood and accepted. The play therapist acknowledges more obvious feelings expressed by the child in play or words and may choose to make tentative guesses about less obvious feelings indicated by the child's nonverbal behavior or based on background information about his or her life situation or experiences (Carlson, Watts, & Maniacci, 2006; Kottman, 2001; Landreth, 2002).

- Example: *A child is playing in the sandbox with a car he calls his "dune buggy." He is having difficulty keeping the sand out of the car, furrows his brow, and makes noises indicative of his annoyance.*

     • Response: "Sounds like you're feeling frustrated."

Reflecting content. Similar to tracking behavior, play therapists use reflection of content to communicate to the child that what he or she says has been heard and is considered important. In reflecting content, the play therapist restates or paraphrases what the child communicated in play or words (Carlson, Watts, & Maniacci, 2006; Kottman, 2001; Landreth, 2002).

- Example: *A child has a little boy doll and a father doll. Using a deep voice, the child has the father doll say, "I know I said I'd take you but I can't right now" and then the child has the father doll turn his back to the child doll.*

  - Response: "That little boy's dad said he would take him but now he has changed his mind."

Esteem building. Esteem building statements communicate that the play therapist believes the child is competent and has strengths and abilities. Esteem building is different than praise in that it focuses on encouraging the child rather than making evaluative statements about the child's behavior. Examples of esteem building statements include:

- "You decided to do something different."

- "You figured that out for yourself."

- "Looks like you've got a plan."

- "You did it all by yourself."

Returning responsibility to the child. It is discouraging and disrespectful to children when adults do or decide things for them that they can do or decide for themselves. The primary way that play therapists avoid doing this is by returning responsibility to the child. When returning responsibility, the play therapist communicates to the child that the child has the capability and responsibility for doing and deciding for him- or herself. Returning responsibility statements help free the child to make decisions and assume responsibility, and facilitate spontaneity and creativity (Carlson, Watts, & Maniacci, 2006; Kottman, 2001; Landreth, 2002).

- Example: *Child asks, "How do you spell truck?"*

    · Response: "In here, you can spell it any way you'd like."

- Example: *Child asks, "Should I paint a picture or play in the sand?"*

    · Response: "That's something you can decide."

- Example: *Child asks, "Will you put my hat on for me?"*

    · Response: "I think that's something you can do for yourself."

- Example: *Child asks, "Can I pretend that this is an airplane?"*

    · Response: "It can be whatever you'd like it to be."

Limit setting. Setting limits in play therapy are therapeutic and have several benefits. These benefits include: Protecting the physical and emotional safety of the child; protecting the play therapist and promoting his or her acceptance of the child; facilitating the child's decision-making, self-control, and self-responsibility; providing consistency in the play therapy environment; anchoring the largely metaphoric and fantasy nature of play therapy to a "here and now" reality; preserving a professional, ethical, and socially acceptable relationship; and protecting the play therapy materials and the room. Non-negotiable limits in play therapy include harming self, the therapist, or others in the playroom; damaging toys or other parts of the playroom; and leaving the playroom before the session is completed. Other limits are negotiated based on the comfort level of the play therapist (e.g. whether or not water is allowed in the sandbox and, if so, how much) but should be reasonable and realistic (Carlson, Watts, & Maniacci, 2006; Kottman, 2001; Landreth, 2002).

Landreth (2002, pp. 260-262) developed a useful and easy to remember "A-C-T" model for setting limits.

A = *Acknowledge the child's feeling, wishes, and wants.*
      Example: "You're so angry you want to hit me."

C = *Communicate the limit.*
      Example: "But I'm not for hitting."

T = *Target acceptable, appropriate alternatives.*
      Example: "The Bobo (bopbag) is for hitting."

- Example: "Jeff, you are so angry you want to hit me, but I'm not for hitting. The Bobo is for hitting."

- Example: "Lori, you think it would be fun to hit the mirror with the hammer, but the mirror is not for hitting. You may hit the woodblock."

If a child persists in breaking a limit, the play therapist may choose to use the *ultimate limit.* This involves, first, placing the item off limits for the remainder of the play therapy session. This is communicated to the child by stating, for example, "Jimmy, if you choose to shoot me with the gun, you choose not to play with it anymore today." If the child continues breaking the limit, then the second, and final step, is removal from the playroom. This is communicated to the child by stating, for example, "Leigh, if you choose to continue to hit the doll house with the hammer, you choose to leave the playroom for today."

THE ROLE OF PARENTS AND TEACHERS: A BRIEF COMMENT

Although thoroughly addressing the role of parents and teachers in the play therapy process is beyond the scope of this book chapter, we thought it important to make a brief statement. Concomitant to the ongoing play therapy process with the child, play therapists consult regularly with parents and, if appropriate, teachers. Parents and teachers can provide invaluable information regarding the child's developmental history, learning styles, and relational patterns. In addition, their support of the child's efforts to change in play therapy can be invaluable. Parental involvement is particularly important in the play therapy process. Children may make some productive changes in play therapy without parental involvement, but substantial and long-lasting progress most often occurs when parents are actively involved (Carlson, Watts, & Maniacci, 2006; Garza & Bratton, 2005; Kottman, 2003). As Landreth (2002) indicated,

> Whether parents need therapy or training in better parenting skills is a question for the play therapist to determine. In most cases, an advisable procedure is to move in the direction of providing parenting skills training or filial therapy if working with the parents is considered necessary. (p. 154)

Teacher involvement is particularly important when the child's presenting problem relates to situations at school or when the problem is hindering the child's academic performance. As with changes in the family system, sometimes changes in the classroom/school interactional patterns are needed to help facilitate or maintain changes in play therapy (Carlson, Watts, & Maniacci, 2006; Kottman, 2003).

With both parents and teachers, consultations can provide at least three valuable experiences. First, parents and teachers experience an empathic ear from the play therapist and also experience a supportive rather than a judgmental or evaluative environment. Second, parents and teachers begin to understand how to experience the child's behaviors, and the narrative from which the behaviors emanate, through the eyes of the child. Third, parents and teachers become aware of subtle changes in the child's behavior that are indicative of progress or the performance of new meanings in the child's narrative.

BEING CHILD-FOCUSED OR PROBLEM-FOCUSED IN PLAY THERAPY: A CLOSING ASIDE

Freeman et al. (1997) stated that their "playful" approach to narrative therapy with children was distinct from most open, unstructured play therapy approaches (e.g. child-centered play therapy). They stated that the distinction is that

> . . . we collaborate closely with children in play that is actively focused on facing a problem. Children's sense of effectiveness

as agents of change clearly increases when they experiment with the possibilities in relationship to an externalized problem. In therapy with families the play is mainly with words, using humor when whenever possible. But an externalizing conversation is easily enhanced with other forms of expression favored by children, such as play and expressive arts therapy. (p. 11)

Freeman et al.'s comments above make a questionable assumption that young child clients will be willing to talk about "the problem" or have the verbal wherewithal and sufficient cognitive development to adequately talk about the situation using the symbolic abstractions we know as "words." Many young children cannot specifically and verbally identify "the problem," and the defining of "the problem" by others may be a surreptitious subjugation of the child's voice. Given the strong emphasis on the therapeutic relationship in constructive therapies, this problem-focused therapeutic engagement appears contrary to basic constructive values and precepts; especially for young children (Kottman, 2001; Landreth, 2002) and culturally-diverse child clients (Garza & Bratton, 2005).

In addition, young children may not have sufficient cognitive development to adequately respond to the types of abstract, *reflexive* questions commonly asked in constructive approaches to child therapy. Thus, the use of these questions may constitute an oppressive environment for young child clients. The skills and procedures commonly used by child-centered play therapists, however, resonate well with constructive theory and allow children to express themselves via a medium that is most comfortable for them: play. That being said, if the child identifies the problem within the context of his or her play (metaphorically or verbally), and the relationship between the child and the play therapist is sufficiently well-developed, then a constructive play therapist may use procedures such as the "magic wand technique" (or "miracle question"), "externalizing questions," and other constructive questions, appropriately worded for the developmental level of the child. Typically, if a child is not ready to address these kinds of questions, he or she will not respond. Furthermore, unless the child has directly and specifically identified him- or herself as one of the characters in the "story," these questions and procedures should be offered indirectly in the context of the child's metaphoric play. For example, suppose five-year-old Sarah is using a family of small dolls to play out a conflict within her family. It is clear to the

161

therapist that one of the doll figures Sarah is presently holding represents Sarah, but she has not identified the doll as herself. In this case, the therapist should ask questions about the little girl doll rather than addressing them directly to Sarah; for example, "I'm wondering how that little girl would . . . ; "Are there times when she and her mommy . . . ? "What would happen if she . . . ?"

CONCLUSION

In this chapter we have attempted to demonstrate that the basic facilitative skills of child-centered play therapy are very useful for constructive therapists who work with young children. We noted that there is clear rationale for use of play in child therapy. Furthermore, we offered support for the notion that there are significant points of resonation between child-centered play therapy—with its theoretical roots in Rogers' person-centered therapy—and constructive therapies. Finally, we discussed toys and play media, and then basic facilitative skills from child-centered play therapy that may be useful for constructive therapy with young children.

Given the notion that play is the language of children and toys are their words (Landreth, 2002), and using the language of constructive therapies, the performance of meaning occurs in play therapy. Typically, young children do not have sufficient cognitive development nor do they have adequate verbal skills to tell their stories. However, when therapists use the basic facilitative skills in play therapy with young children, the children will tell their stories through their play. Play therapy creates space for children to work out problems. With its focus on imagination and fantasy play, play therapy gives children natural opportunities to share their voice, tell their story, and use their strengths and abilities to create and consider—usually on their own—externalizations, exceptions or unique outcomes, solutions, and alternative stories.

REFERENCES

Anderson, H. (2001). Postmodern collaborative and person-centered therapies: What would Carl Rogers say? *Journal of Family Therapy, 23,* 339-360.

Bratton, S., & Ray, D. (2000). What the research shows about play therapy. *International Journal of Play Therapy, 9*(1), 47-88.

Caplan, F., & Caplan, T. (1974). *The power of play.* New York: Anchor Books.

Carlson, J., Watts, R. E., & Maniacci, M. (2006). *Adlerian therapy: Theory and practice.* Washington, DC: American Psychological Association.

Freeman, J., Epston, D., & Lobovits, D. (1997). *Playful approaches to serious problems: Narrative therapy with children and their families.* New York: Norton.

Garza, Y., & Bratton, S. C. (2005). School-based child-centered play therapy with Hispanic children: Outcomes and cultural consideration. *International Journal of Play Therapy, 14*(1), 51-79.

Hoyt, M. F. (1994). Introduction: Competency-based, future-oriented therapy. In M. F. Hoyt (Ed.), *Constructive therapies* (pp. 1-10). New York: Guilford.

Kottman, T. (2001). *Play therapy: Basics and beyond.* Alexandria, VA: American Counseling Association.

Kottman, T. (2003). *Partners in play: An Adlerian approach to play therapy* (2nd ed.). Alexandria, VA: American Counseling Association.

Landreth, G. L. (2002). *Play therapy: The art of the relationship* (2nd ed.). New York: Brunner-Routledge.

Mahoney, M. J. (1995). Theoretical developments in the cognitive and constructivist psychotherapies. In M. J. Mahoney (Ed.), *Cognitive and constructivist psychoterapies: Theory, research, and practice* (pp. 3-19). New York: Springer.

Mahoney, M. J. (2002). Constructivism and positive psychology. In C. R. Snyder & S. J. Lopez (Eds.), *Handbook of positive psychology* (pp. 745-750). New York: Oxford.

Mahoney, M. J. (2003). *Constructive psychotherapy: A practical guide.* New York: Guilford.

Mahoney, M. J., & Granvold, D. K. (2005). Constructivism and psychotherapy. *World Psychiatry, 4*(2), 74-77.

Neimeyer, R. A. (1995). Constructivist psychotherapies: Features, foundations, and future directions. In R. A. Neimeyer & M. J. Mahoney (Eds.), *Constructivism in psychoteherapy* (pp. 11-38). Washington, D. C.: American Psychological Association.

Schaeffer, C. (Ed.) (1993). *The therapeutic powers of play.* Northvale, NJ: Aronson.

Smith, C. (1997). Introduction: Comparing traditional therapies with narrative approaches. In C. Smith & D. Nylund (Eds.), *Narrative therapies with children and adolescents* (pp. 1-52). New York: Guilford.

163

Sweeney, D. S. (1997). *Counseling children through the world of play*. Wheaton, IL: Tyndale.

Watts, R. E. (2003). Adlerian therapy as a relational constructivist approach. *The Family Journal: Counseling and Therapy for Couples and Families, 11*, 139-147.

Watts, R. E., & Phillips, K. A. (2004). Adlerian psychology and psychotherapy: A relational constructivist approach. In J. D. Raskin & S. K. Bridges (Eds.), *Studies in meaning 2: Bridging the personal and social in constructivist psychology* (pp. 267-289). New York: Pace University Press.

⳺ 8 ⳝ

Talking Back to Stuttering: Constructivist Contributions to Stuttering Treatment

Anthony DiLollo and Robert A. Neimeyer

My hands were trembling as I began. . . . I felt very much alone. So great was my fear that I seemed to go into a trance. It was a kind of out-of-body experience: a fluent person seemed to be speaking out of my mouth. I heard his words, but they did not come from me. When I was finished, the teacher complimented me for my fluency and for my courage. I think the class may even have applauded—not in sarcasm but in appreciation for my triumph and also, I imagine, in relief. My feeling of success was fleeting, however, as at my Bar Mitzvah, I had somehow been fluent. But my fluency mystified me. There was no way to remember how I felt being fluent, because my fluency did not seem to come from me. I was beginning to fear fluency. I knew myself when I was stuttering. But I felt estranged from myself when I was fluent. (Jezer, 1997, p. 108).

The problem of stuttering has been addressed by many different professionals, including psychologists, psychiatrists, surgeons, religious healers, and philosophers. Today, speech-language pathologists treat the majority of persons who stutter. Historically, speech-language pathology had its earliest roots in the field of psychology, with many of the pioneers of the field such as Carl Seashore, Lee Edward Travis, Wendell Johnson, and Charles Van Riper holding degrees in clinical psychology (Bloom, 1978). Interestingly, these speech-language pathology pioneers were primarily interested in treating persons who stutter—Charles Van Riper was himself a person who stuttered. As the fields of speech-language pathology and psychology have diverged, however,

165

speech-language pathologists have become increasingly adept at using behavior modification techniques. This has made behavior change their primary focus, perhaps making speech-language pathologists less comfortable with other psychotherapeutic orientations that deal with more global, "counseling" issues (Luterman, 2001; Shames, 2000).

For the problem of stuttering, we believe that simply treating the surface behaviors—the speech disfluencies—cannot address the complexity of the problem or the person experiencing it. For example, Perkins (1979), in reference to lapses by clients who appeared to have mastered behavioral control of their stuttering, stated that, "these lapses seem to have more to do with the person's sense of identity as a stutterer, and his misgivings about relinquishing that identity, than with inability to maintain the skills of normal sounding speech" (p. 109). Perkins' point is that, although behavioral control of stuttering is a useful and generally achievable goal for treatment, it is insufficient for long-term change for most individuals. In this chapter we extend this approach to treatment by offering a constructivist conceptualization of stuttering, summarize the growing evidence base for its major tenets, and outline its novel implications for stuttering therapy. We also provide illustrative material.

STUTTERING TREATMENT AND THE PROBLEM OF RELAPSE

The effectiveness of traditional speech-pathology approaches in the short term appears to be high (Bloodstein, 1995; Harrison & Onslow, 1999; Sheehan, 1975; Van Riper, 1971). However, Silverman (1992) reported long-term relapse rates for stuttering treatment at over 50% for adults and older children, and Craig and Hancock (1995) reported rates in excess of 70%. Unfortunately, these figures appear to be supported throughout the speech pathology literature (Boberg, 1981; Craig, 1998; Craig & Calver, 1991; Culatta & Goldberg, 1995; Perkins, 1983). In fact, relapse has been called the "Achilles heel" of stuttering intervention (Kuhr & Rustin, 1985) and even thought to be "the rule, not the exception for the adult stutterer if long term follow-up investigations are conducted" (Van Riper, 1973, p. 178).

Bloodstein (1995) has suggested that relapse may be most problematic when treatment for stuttering is based predominantly on behavioral approaches to therapy. He stated that the argument against strict behavioral treatment of stuttering is that "it is unreasonable to expect a lifelong problem to be permanently eradicated in the short time it takes to learn to speak fluently in a slow manner by prolonging syllables" (p. 445). Bloodstein raises an issue that appears to be central to the problem of relapse for persons who stutter, namely their ability to maintain changes in a problem behavior that has not only been a "lifelong problem" but, as Perkins (1979) stated, has become a part of their *identity* that they may be unwilling, or unable, to give up.

As an illustration of an individual who stutters' reactions to fluent speech, let's consider the following quote from an interview with Jerry, a 24-year old man who has successfully completed stuttering treatment: *"I often feel like when I'm fluent and people like me, I feel like it's a façade or not, like they're gonna find out I'm not what they thought I was. I'm an imposter."* This quote highlights not only that simply teaching the individual who stutters how to speak fluently may not be sufficient, but also that challenges to an established identity—even an unwanted one such as "the stutterer"—can generate confusion, anxiety, fear, and even guilt. Interestingly, Kuhr and Rustin (1985) reported finding paradoxical evidence of mild *depression* in a number of their clients who had recently completed successful stuttering treatment, while Manning (2001) reported reactions of anxiety, fear, and guilt, citing reports that "some persons who stutter report feeling that they are 'deceiving people' by speaking fluently."

Such observations appear to be related to the difficulty that individuals experience in transition from a "stutterer role" to the new role of a "fluent speaker." Manning (2001) summarized the task for the person who stutters by stating that "in many ways, he must evolve as a person and form a new paradigm, a new view of himself and his possibilities" (p. 423). Similarly, Starkweather (1999) proposed conceptualizing stuttering treatment in terms of "recovery" and suggested that recovery might be viewed as "a search for understanding that will be a foundation for change" and "a journey of discovery that one takes into oneself" (p. 242). According to Starkweather, the result of such an approach to stuttering treatment would lead persons who stutter to "redefine themselves and their disorder" and to "discover new ways of thinking about stuttering and social interaction" (p. 242).

For readers with a constructivist background, the preceding discussion regarding the problems associated with stuttering treatment will likely have generated a few "aha's!" Constructivism is all about change—reconstruction—but more than that, it is about *meaningful* change, and that is clearly what is lacking in traditional speech pathology treatments for stuttering. For behavioral change (i.e. speech fluency) to become "meaningful" it must be accompanied by change at a deeper level that relates to an individual's constructs about self, the world, and the self's role in the world. Current speech pathology treatments, although adept at facilitating behavioral change and even cognitive change in terms of attitudes and avoidances, typically are not designed to address issues related to the reconstruction of the self.

A PERSONAL CONSTRUCT THEORY OF STUTTERING

Fransella (1972) proposed a theory of stuttering based on an application of Kelly's (1955) personal construct psychology to the problem of stuttering relapse following successful treatment. Fransella based her theory on Kelly's *choice corollary* and argued that an individual will continue to stutter "because it is in this way that he can anticipate the greatest number of events: it is by behaving in this way that life is most meaningful to him" (p. 58).

Of course, most persons who stutter do experience significant periods of fluent speech. The question might be asked then, why are these periods of fluent speech not construed as meaningful, thus leading to the development of a meaningful construct system relative to fluent speech? Fransella (1972) suggested that many persons who stutter might fail to abstract meaningful repetitive themes from their fluent periods of speech, thus failing to construe them as meaningful events. In addition, Williams (1995) suggested that, even when fluent, people who stutter may be attempting to gain evidence of support for their stuttering predictions, and thus may perceive their fluent speech as "lucky" or "a fluke." We found evidence of just such perceptions of fluent speech in a study in which we interviewed persons who stutter about stuttering and fluency (DiLollo, Manning, & Neimeyer, 2003).

Many persons who stutter experience negative emotional reactions following successful behavioral treatment for stuttering. Interestingly, a personal construct theory of stuttering predicts just such negative emotional reactions. During successful treatment for stuttering, persons who stutter will experience the awareness of imminent change in their core structures (i.e. "I am a stutterer"). This may produce feelings of *threat* and *fear*, essentially reflecting the subjective incompatibility of the "fluent speaker" role with their core sense of self. Similarly, as such people spend more time in a "fluent speaker" role they may develop an awareness that events that they are experiencing lie outside of the range of convenience of their construct system, generating *anxiety*— being fluent has thrown them into a new and unpredictable interpersonal world in which the old "rules of engagement" no longer seem to apply. These individuals may also feel that they are acting in a way that is contrary to their core role structure, generating feelings of *guilt*. The example cited previously and Manning's (2001) report of persons who stutter stating that they feel as though they are "deceiving" others when speaking fluently may be examples of guilt that can be generated during successful treatment of the surface features of stuttering.

A GROWING EMPIRICAL BASE

In her seminal study, Fransella (1972) conducted personal construct therapy with 16 adults who stuttered, using repertory grids and bi-polar implications grids to assess the relationship between meaningfulness of speaker roles (i.e. fluent versus stuttered) and amount of stuttering. Fransella focused therapy on helping clients develop a more meaningful construction of their experiences of fluent speech and no attempt was made to directly treat speech production. Results supported the hypothesis that speech disfluencies would decrease as the meaningfulness of the fluent speaker role increased across the course of treatment. Follow-up, which varied from three months to one year, was conducted with nine of the 16 participants and revealed one participant who had regressed and eight who had maintained or improved their level of fluent speech.

In order to build an empirical base for her theory, Fransella needed to demonstrate that constructivist counseling could improve long-term outcomes of traditional speech therapy for stuttering. In 1985, Evesham and Fransella combined personal construct counseling with behavioral treatment for stuttering to investigate the effects of the counseling on the relapse rates for two groups of adult persons who stuttered. They again garnered support for Fransella's (1972) theory, with the group who received the personal construct counseling demonstrating significantly lower relapse rates one year following treatment compared to the control group who received only the behavioral intervention. Results from this study must be interpreted with caution, however, as there was a significant difference between the groups with regard to pre-treatment frequency of disfluencies. Despite random allocation of participants to groups, the control group in this study demonstrated a significantly higher mean frequency of disfluencies on initial testing than did the experimental group. According to Craig (1998), such a difference in frequency of disfluencies alone would predict the observed difference in long-term relapse between the groups.

More recently, Stewart and Birdsall (2001), a speech therapist and client working from a personal construct perspective, provided a personal account of constructivist stuttering therapy. In this article, Birdsall recounted his experiences in constructivist therapy for stuttering as "taking the first steps in elaborating a new identity" (p. 224).

In our own research (DiLollo, Manning & Neimeyer, 2003, 2005), we have investigated Fransella's (1972) theory that persons who stutter fail to construe periods of fluent speech as meaningful, thereby failing to develop elaborate construct systems related to a fluent speaker role. To strengthen the design, we employed two convergent methodologies to measure the elaboration of the construct systems of persons who stutter with regard to "stutterer" and "fluent" speaker roles.

Cognitive Anxiety

In a first study (DiLollo et al., 2003), we found support for Fransella's (1972) theory in a systematic content analytic study that examined the cognitive anxiety (Viney & Westbrook, 1976) of 29 persons who stutter and 29 fluent speakers with respect to "fluent" and "stutterer" speaker roles. Cognitive anxiety was defined by Viney and Westbrook as the awareness that one's construct systems are inadequate to allow full and meaningful construing (and, therefore, prediction) of the events with which the person is confronted. That is, cognitive anxiety relates specifically to the inability to *meaningfully integrate* an experience.

In this study, the two groups (i.e. persons who stutter and fluent speakers) were interviewed and asked identical, open ended questions regarding what life was like as (a) a person who stutters and (b) a fluent speaker. Responses to the two questions were transcribed and analyzed using a modified version of Viney and Westbrook's (1976) Cognitive Anxiety Scale.

FIGURE 1. PLOT OF MEAN COGNITIVE ANXIETY (CA) SCORES FOR PERSONS WHO STUTTER (PWS) AND FLUENT SPEAKERS (FS) FOR THE DOMINANT SPEAKER ROLE AND THE NONDOMINANT SPEAKER ROLE (ADAPTED FROM DiLOLLO ET AL., 2003).

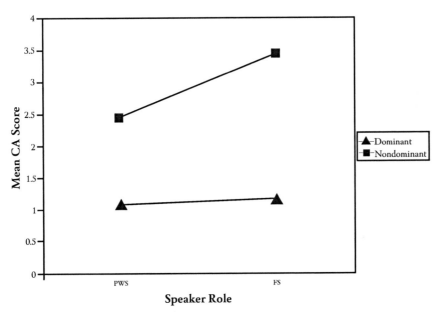

Results (see Figure 1) indicated that both persons who stutter and fluent speakers demonstrated significantly higher levels of cognitive anxiety related to their "nondominant" speaker role compared to their "dominant" role, as they each dismissed experiences of the nondominant role as meaningless. For example, one of the participants from the persons who stutter group referred to his fluent speech as his "lucky fluency" (p. 179), while another referred to fluent episodes only in the context of his prediction of a return to stuttering. In contrast, fluent speakers made little sense of their occasional disfluencies, and reasserted

171

their identities as fluent persons. In other words, both groups tightened their constructs and constricted their perceptual fields, construing speech experiences other than those of their dominant speaker role as outside the range of convenience of their construct systems, thus extracting little meaning from those experiences. The resultant "protection" of the dominant speaker role would appear to be a significant barrier to successful long-term treatment of stuttering if treatment only focused on behavior change. Significantly, qualitative research on the long-term consolidation of fluency across a period of several years suggests that those who substantially overcome stuttering consciously struggle to reorganize a sense of self in the wake of improvement, in keeping with the implications of our model (Plexico, Manning, & DiLollo, 2005).

Cognitive Complexity

A second study utilized the same 29 participants. In this study (DiLollo et al., 2005), we examined the meaningfulness of the fluent speaker role by applying a measure of *cognitive complexity* (Bieri, 1955; Crockett, 1965) to the transcripts. According to Crockett, the number of constructs participants use to describe a domain of interest will be a reflection of the complexity of their construct system with respect to that domain. In this study, the number of constructs used by persons who stutter to describe the domains of their *fluent speaker role* and their *stutterer role* were taken to indicate the cognitive complexity—or meaningfulness—of each role.

According to Fransella's (1972) theory, we would expect that persons who stutter would have less complex construct systems regarding a fluent speaker role compared to a stutterer role. Again, results provided support for Fransella's theory, indicating that the participants in this study demonstrated significantly less complex construct systems related to the fluent speaker role (*Mean CC* = 6.93) compared to the stutterer role (*Mean CC* = 11.66) ($F = 5.201$, $p < .05$).

The themes that emerge from the research on a constructivist theory of stuttering are that persons who stutter appear to have less complex construct systems with regard to a fluent speaker role (DiLollo et al., 2005), resulting in fluency carrying fewer implications than stuttering for their role as a speaker

(Fransella, 1972). Furthermore, the process of invalidating and updating the "stutterer" constructs through experiences of fluent speech appears to be stalled by stout defense of the dominant speaker role—as "stutterer." Typically this occurs through constriction and tightening of identity-defining constructs focusing on their habitual disfluency, and the predictable, if unpleasant, interpersonal experiences to which it leads (DiLollo et al., 2003). In other words, they may cling to their familiar role with all its familiar consequences, rather than consolidate a new role around apparently alien experiences of disfluency.

FUTURE DIRECTIONS

Narrative Therapy

In keeping with a constructivist conceptualization, we have been working to develop a narrative therapy approach to the treatment of stuttering (in conjunction with traditional speech therapy) as one way of facilitating fundamental changes in the ways in which individuals who stutter construe themselves as speakers and communicators (DiLollo, Neimeyer & Manning, 2002). Like other constructivist methods, narrative therapy facilitates elaboration of spontaneous or treatment-induced episodes of desirable change, as represented by temporary excursions into fluency. Once such "sparkling moments" (Winslade & Monk, 1999) are identified, the therapist prompts the client to consolidate a preferred story that challenges the dominant story of the self as symptomatic (Neimeyer & Bridges, 2003). We view this approach as *complementary* to both Fransella's (1972) controlled elaboration approach and traditional speech therapy for stuttering.

The narrative approach described by DiLollo et al. (2002), based on the work of White and Epston (1990), provides a rationale for "externalizing" stuttering, that is, for treating it as if it were a person or agent whose actions have "real effects" on the client. This stands in contrast to the usual assumptions of speech therapy, which foster an identification of the client's self with the symptom, as the term "stutterer" implies. As White and Epston suggested, externalizing language can be useful in encouraging persons to move from feeling like a "problem person" to being a "person with a problem." The process of externalizing stuttering, however, goes far beyond simply using person-first terminology.

173

TABLE 1. EXAMPLES OF QUESTIONS THAT MIGHT BE USED IN
NARRATIVE THERAPY WITH A PERSON WHO STUTTERS
(ADAPTED FROM DILOLLO, ET AL., 2002)

STAGE	SAMPLE QUESTIONS
Mapping the influence of the *problem* in the life of the person:	· What has *Stuttering* persuaded other people to think or say about you? · How does it convince them of these things? · What has it persuaded you to think about yourself? · What decisions does *Stuttering* make for you? · What are its intentions for your future?
Mapping the influence of the *person* in the life of the problem:	
a. Unique Outcome questions	· Have there been times when you have been able to overcome *Stuttering's* hold over your speech? · How did you feel when this happened?
b. Unique Account questions	· How might you stand up to *Stuttering* in the future and refuse its requirements of you?
c. Unique Redescription questions	· By freeing yourself from *Stuttering's* hold over you, do you think in any way that you are becoming less of 'a stutterer'?
d. Unique Possibility questions	· What will the future be like without *Stuttering's* influence dominating your life? · How is this future different from the one that *Stuttering* would have planned for you?
e. Unique Circulation questions	· Of the significant people in your life, who do you anticipate would have difficulty accepting the new life you have chosen, free from *Stuttering's* influence?
f. Questions that historicize Unique Outcomes	· Of the people who knew you growing up, who would have been most likely to predict that you would break free from *Stuttering's* influence? · What qualities would this person have seen in you that would have led him/her to believe that you would have been able to achieve what you have?

Referring to "Stuttering" as an external "entity." using comments like "What did Stuttering say to you to make you avoid that party?" or "Stuttering seemed to be pushing you around yesterday," can help in recruiting the person to be an active participant in the treatment process, rather than feeling like a problem person who requires "fixing" by the clinician.

For the sake of convenience, narrative therapy can be represented as a sequence of logical steps (e.g. DiLollo, et al., 2002; Epston & White, 1995), although, as pointed out by Payne (2000), seldom does real therapy with real clients ever follow such a logical sequence. Initially, the clinician turns to mapping out the influence of "Stuttering" on the life of the person (i.e. How does the problem affect the person's life?), followed by investigating the influence of the *person* on the life of "Stuttering" (i.e. How does the person affect the course of the problem?). Similar to Kelly's (1955) controlled elaboration, investigating the influence of the person on "Stuttering" may involve questioning the client to identify "unique outcomes" (White & Epston, 1990) of fluent speech that contradict the problem story. This might be followed by encouraging clients to make sense of these exceptions to their dominant narrative of disfluency, which might not have previously registered as significant. As the client begins to notice, collect and narrate such exceptions, they ultimately can emerge as part of an increasingly coherent narrative. Further questions can facilitate clients' "redescribing" or reconstruing themselves, and speculating about various personal and relational alternatives that the new narrative makes possible (See Table 1 for examples of questions).

As a new story that is focused on fluency rather than stuttering begins to emerge, the story is told and re-told many times and with many different audiences (Payne, 2000). Each repetition and extension strengthens the meaningfulness of the fluent speaker role for the client and establishes predictions of fluency, not only on the part of the client, but also on the part of significant others in his or her social environment.

The Reconstruction Workbook

DiLollo, Manning, and Neimeyer (2000) developed a workbook to facilitate a constructivist approach to the treatment of stuttering. Based in part on the work of Fransella (1972), White and Epston (1990), Epston and White (1995), and Neimeyer (2000), this workbook is comprised of a series of activities designed to facilitate (1) externalizing the stuttering problem, (2) finding cracks in the armor of the dominant stuttering narrative, and (3) promoting creative problem-solving. For example, one of the activities asks the client to write an autobiography from "Stuttering's" perspective. The following is the response from Nichole, a 22-year old woman seeking therapy for stuttering:

> I have always been with Nichole. Probably so far back that she was too young to know I was there, but I was, lurking. She did not become conscious of me until other people started pointing me out, telling her there was a right way to say things and that she was doing it wrong. She didn't know why I was giving her trouble. One night when she was seven, eight years old, her dad was tucking her into bed. As he walked down the dark hallway he said, "Goodnight, Nichole." What came of her response was, "G-g-g-ggoodnight." Her dad stopped walking and said, "What?" in a tone that sounded like she should know better. It was times like these that Nichole started to feel like I wasn't making things right, and I shouldn't be with her. Likewise on another occasion when her older sister mocked her and she realized what I was making her sound like. I made her feel dumb and ashamed. From this point on, Nichole tried to push me away. She realized I was her weakness and that letting other people discover me came at a social cost.

> Being Stuttering, I want nothing more than to hold Nichole back. I am her reminder of who she is. When she tries to take control, I am her refuge when she comes back in despair. I keep her safe. She does not ever have to grow or explore unknown territory as long as I am with her. With me, she knows who she is, and there is comfort for her in that. She hates me and gets depressed that I exist, but overall I think she appreciates me. When she is challenged in life, she can use me as her excuse to run and hide. I am her measure of herself; I let her know what kinds of people will be accepting of her. I choose her friends. I tell her who she can date. With Jason, I made her settle for less by telling her that was what she deserved. And for a time she believed me. For one year, I made her waste her time with him, deny her potential and engage in destructive behavior. I also decide what kind of job/career she will work, and her potential in that. While other people around her in her company are promoted and being given bigger responsibilities, I keep her down, and I love it! She is embarrassed and ashamed of staying in the same place, but she always goes back to appreciating me, because at least with me she can give an excuse to other people, so she doesn't feel as pathetic.

> *Nichole has plans to get rid of me. More and more each day she knows she deserves better. I feel threatened. I feel her desire to ignore me growing stronger and stronger each day. For one, she lets people know I exist, most of the time anyway. The only thing I have left to hold onto are those times when Nichole loses her confident edge and decides to crawl back to me for safety. These are times that she does not want people to know about me. I can use this to maintain my power. As long as Nichole doesn't like me, I have a chance. I have humiliated her and made her feel worthless many times. As long as I can keep this up, we will be enemies forever. My plan for Nichole: I don't want to lessen my grip on her until she takes her last breath. Then I have won!*

Clearly, this activity highlighted many different aspects of the stuttering problem for Nichole. Most profoundly, it provided a voice for "Stuttering" so that Nichole could, perhaps for the first time, come face-to-face with her tormentor. Nichole's comments following our discussion of this activity focused on the realization that Stuttering was never going to stop while she continued to use it as an excuse and hide from the world. Her renewed resolve to tackle the problem has continued to be evident in her taking more personal responsibility for her life, including her role in stuttering therapy.

Further development, refinement, and testing of the reconstruction workbook are continuing. We hope that it will eventually provide a useful tool to facilitate more widespread constructivist counseling for persons who stutter.

The Lidcombe Program: An Unintended Example of Constructivist Counseling?

In our previous discussion of relapse, we focused on adult stuttering treatment and how relapse rates appear to fall in the 50-70% range. Interestingly, relapse rates from successful stuttering therapy for young children appear to be significantly lower than for adults and older children (Starkweather, Gottwald, & Halfond, 1990; Silverman, 1992). From a constructivist perspective, this observation is not unexpected, as young children are in the process of forming their personal narrative about themselves as communicators, and so their construing of themselves as speakers is more malleable. Conversely, with their more fluid sense of self, young children do not have as great an obstacle in the form of a consolidated identity as "stutterers."

177

One popular and highly successful treatment program designed specifically for young children who stutter is the Lidcombe Program (Onslow, Packman, & Harrison, 2003). The treatment procedure is based on behavior therapy procedures, requiring parents to comment on and praise "stutter-free" speech, while also occasionally acknowledging a moment of stuttering—as the parents are likely to do in any case. Significantly, the recommended ratio of commenting on and praising stutter-free speech compared to stuttered speech is *five-to-one*. In other words, this is a program that focuses both the parents and the child on *fluent* speech production.

Onslow et al. (2003) described the Lidcombe Program as an operant conditioning program. It would appear, however, that the *construction of a meaningful fluent speaker role* for the children, based on the increased attention given to "stutter-free" speech by the child's parents, may also play a significant role in the long-term success of this program. In addition, the Lidcombe Program has also been reported to be less successful with older children who stutter, which could be interpreted as indicating that once constructs (or "stories") about being a "stutterer" have had time to strengthen, it is more difficult for experiences of fluent speech alone to shape one's self-concept.

CONCLUSION

Both George Kelly's (1955) metaphor of the person as scientist and a narrative conception of human beings as the authors of their life stories (Hermans, 2002) emphasize the extent to which people direct their engagement in the social world. Ironically, these very systems of personal meaning can also constrain and constrict their performance on the social stage, sometimes coalescing into seemingly impermeable constructs of identity that equate the person with his or her problem. In this paper we have argued that the problem of stuttering can usefully be viewed in these terms, as involving not merely the behavioral production of disfluent speech, but also the construction, across time, of a sense of self that is problem-saturated and resistant to change. Such a view provides an apt interpretation of the high relapse rates associated with (temporarily) successful behavioral speech modification. It also helps explain the paradoxical sense of distress and deceptiveness that often is voiced following periods of fluency by persons who stutter. Equally important, the constructivist formulation outlined here receives support from a growing body of empirical research, both quantitative and qualitative, that underscores (a) the greater elaboration of a rich, cognitively complex system of meanings for understanding stuttering, but not fluency, for persons who stutter, (b) the anxious struggle to make sense of the self in the unfamiliar role of fluent speaker, (c) the gradual growth in implications of being a fluent speaker for successfully treated clients who tend to preserve their gains over a follow-up period, and (d) the conscious effort to reconstruct a sense of personal identity that characterizes persons who experience impressive and life-long transformations of stuttering.

As clinicians, the parts of this work that most excite us are the rich implications of a constructivist framework for practicing speech pathology. Blurring the lines between speech therapy and counseling, we find ourselves advocating both familiar behavioral methods for fostering fluency and narrative approaches to understanding and surmounting obstacles to long-term success. In our view, one need not be a constructivist or narrative therapist to use these methods—though it helps! Instead, we believe that practical means of externalizing stuttering and countering its influence are within the reach of most practicing speech therapists. As we refine and test these reconstructive methods, we hope they will offer valuable support to a growing number of clinicians and clients who are working together to "talk back" to stuttering.

REFERENCES

Bieri, J. (1955). Cognitive complexity-simplicity and predictive behavior. *Journal of Abnormal and Social Psychology, 51,* 263-268.

Bloodstein, O. (1995). *A handbook on stuttering* (5th ed). San Diego, CA: Singular Publishing Group.

Bloom, L. (1978). Notes for a history of speech pathology. *The Psychoanalytic Review, 65,* 433-463.

Boberg, E. (1981). *The maintenance of fluency.* New York: Elsevier.

Craig, A. (1998). Relapse following treatment for stuttering: A critical review and correlative data. *Journal of Fluency Disorders, 23,* 1-30.

Craig, A., & Calver, P. (1991). Following up on treated stutterers: Studies of perceptions of fluency and job status. *Journal of Speech and Hearing Research, 34,* 279-284.

179

Craig, A., & Hancock, K. (1995). Self-reported factors related to relapse following treatment for stuttering. *Australian Journal of Human Communication Disorders, 23*, 48-60.

Crockett, W. H. (1965). Cognitive complexity and impression formation. In B. A. Maher (Ed.), *Progress in experimental personality research* (Vol. 2, pp. 47-90). New York: Academic Press.

Culatta, R., & Goldberg, S. A. (1995). *Stuttering therapy: An integrated approach to theory and practice*. Needham Heights, MA: Allyn & Bacon.

DiLollo, A., Manning, W., & Neimeyer, R. (2000). *The reconstruction workbook*. Unpublished manuscript.

DiLollo, A., Manning, W., & Neimeyer, R. (2003). Cognitive anxiety as a function of speaker role for fluent speakers and persons who stutter. *Journal of Fluency Disorders, 28*,167-186.

DiLollo, A., Manning, W. H., & Neimeyer, R. A. (2005). Cognitive complexity as a function of speaker role for adult persons who stutter. *Journal of Constructivist Psychology, 18*, 215-236.

DiLollo, A., Neimeyer, R., & Manning, W. (2002). A personal construct psychology view of relapse: Indications for a narrative therapy component to stuttering treatment. *Journal of Fluency Disorders, 27*, 19-42.

Epston, D., & White, M. (1995). Termination as a right of passage. In R. A. Neimeyer, & M. J. Mahoney (Eds.), *Constructivism in psychotherapy* (pp. 339-354). Washington, DC: American Psychological Association.

Evesham, M., & Fransella, F. (1985). Stuttering relapse: The effect of a combined speech and psychological reconstruction programme. *British Journal of Disorders of Communication, 20*, 237-248.

Fransella, F. (1972). *Personal change and reconstruction*. London: Academic Press.

Harrison, E., & Onslow, M. (1999). Early intervention for stuttering: The Lidcombe Program. In R. F. Curlee (Ed), *Stuttering and related disorders of fluency* (2nd ed., pp. 65-79). New York: Thieme.

Hermans, H. J. M. (2002). The person as a motivated storyteller. In R. A. Neimeyer & G. J. Neimeyer (Eds.), *Advances in personal construct psychology: New directions and perspectives* (pp. 3-38). Westport, CT: Praeger.

Jezer, M. (1997). *Stuttering: A life bound up in words*. New York: Basic Books.

Kelly, G. A. (1955). *The psychology of personal constructs*. New York: Norton.

Kuhr, A., & Rustin, L. (1985). The maintenance of fluency after intensive inpatient therapy: Long-term follow-up. *Journal of Fluency Disorders, 10*, 229-236.

Luterman, D.M. (2001). *Counseling persons with communication disorders and their families*. (4th ed.), Austin, TX: PRO-ED.

Manning, W. H. (2001). *Clinical decision making in fluency disorders* (2nd ed.). Vancouver: Singular Publishers.

Neimeyer, R.A. (2000). *Lessons of loss.* Keystone Heights, FL: PsychoEducational Resources.

Neimeyer, R. A., & Bridges, S. K. (2003). Postmodern approaches to psychotherapy. In A. S. Gurman & S. B. Messer (Eds.), *Essential psychotherapies* (2nd ed., pp. 272-316). New York: Guilford.

Onslow, M., Packman, A., & Harrison, E. (2003). *The Lidcombe Program of early stuttering intervention.* Austin, TX: Pro-Ed.

Payne, M. (2000). *Narrative therapy.* Thousand Oaks, CA: Sage.

Perkins, W. H. (1979). From psychoanalysis to discoordination. In H. H. Gregory (Ed.), *Controversies about stuttering therapy.* Baltimore, MD: University Park Press.

Perkins, W. H. (1983). Learning from negative outcomes in stuttering therapy II: An epiphany of failure. *Journal of Fluency Disorders, 8,* 155-160.

Plexico, L., Manning, W., & DiLollo, A. (2005). A phenomenological understanding of successful stuttering management. *Journal of Fluency Disorders, 30,* 1-22.

Shames, G.H. (2000). *Counseling the communicatively disabled and their families.* Needham Heights, MA: Allyn & Bacon.

Sheehan, J. (1975). Conflict theory and avoidance-reduction therapy. In J. Eisenson (Ed.), *Stuttering, a second symposium* (pp. 97-198). New York: Harper & Row.

Silverman, F. H. (1992). *Stuttering and other fluency disorders.* Englewood Cliffs, NJ: Prentice-Hall.

Starkweather, C. W. (1999). The effectiveness of stuttering therapy: An issue for science? In N.B. Ratner & E.C. Healey (Eds.), *Stuttering research and practice: Bridging the gap* (pp. 231-244). Mahwah, NJ: Lawrence Erlbaum.

Starkweather, C. W., Gottwald, S. R., & Halfond, M. M. (1990). *Stuttering prevention: A clinical method.* Englewood Cliffs, NJ: Prentice-Hall.

Stewart, T., & Birdsall, M. (2001). A review of the contribution of personal construct psychology to stammering therapy. *Journal of Constructivist Psychology, 14,* 215-226.

Van Riper, C. (1971). *The nature of stuttering.* Englewood Cliffs, NJ: Prentice-Hall.

Van Riper, C. (1973). *The treatment of stuttering* (2nd ed.). Englewood Cliffs, NJ: Prentice-Hall.

Viney, L. L., & Westbrook, M. T. (1976). Cognitive anxiety: A method of content analysis for verbal samples. *Journal of Personality Assessment, 40,* 140-150.

White, M., & Epston, D. (1990). *Narrative means to therapeutic ends.* New York: Norton.

Williams, R. (1995). Personal construct theory in use with people who stutter. In M. Fawcus (Ed.), *Stuttering: From theory to practice* (pp. 111-113). London: Whurr.

Winslade, J., & Monk, G. (1999). *Narrative counseling in schools: Powerful and brief.* Thousand Oaks, CA: Corwin Press.

❧ 9 ❧

Methods of Reconstruction with Adolescent Substance Abusers: Combining REBT and Constructivism

Robert Adelman

The goal of the reconstruction of young lives given over to severe, chemical substance abuse requires more than personal insight and understanding. It requires a new philosophy for living, and the tools to facilitate adherence to that philosophy. How do we assist young people in arriving at that philosophy, particularly when they may not be motivated to give up drugs, reflect on their behavior, disclose to adults, or work toward personal change? The present chapter will seek to articulate and demonstrate an approach to adolescent treatment using principles of Rational-Emotive-Behavior Therapy (REBT) and Constructivist Psychology.

Albert Ellis' Rational Emotive Behavior Therapy emphasizes how clients actively construct their own disturbed emotional state in relation to frustrating life events, and identifies the core philosophies that maintain their disturbance (Ellis, 1973, 1998, 2002). From a constructivist psychology perspective, REBT may be regarded as a fast track teaching method in construing for novice personal scientists (Adelman, 2006; Cummins, 2004, Personal Communication), and may be most effective with individuals with a particular organization of cognitive structures.

The term "cognitive structure" refers to the concrete ways in which individuals have organized a system for forming meaningful interpretations of the world around them. One important dimension upon which cognitive structures have been categorized is whether they tend to be loosely organized or tightly organized. For example, Bannister (1960) found the construct systems of schizophrenic patients to be loosely organized. Adelman (unpublished doctoral dissertation) validated this finding in a sample of state hospital

183

patients. However, a further unexpected finding was that patients with a diagnosis of schizoaffective disorder had tightly formed construct systems, rather than loosely organized systems. This observation suggested that different diagnostic classes of patients may have differing construction systems that lead to different forms of failed predictions about the environment—a view that was also put forth by Lorenzini, Sassaroli, & Rocchi (1989).

Assuming this to be the case, what kinds of construct systems are likely to be found typical of adolescent substance abusers? This question is important because knowledge of the type of construction system leads us into a more complete consideration of interventions and intervention styles that are likely to be most effective in helping clients move in new directions (Kelly, 1955).

Accounts of REBT in action with clients appear to reflect the tight, all-or-none, forms of construing that Slater (1976) explored empirically and which Button (1985) has identified and described from a clinical perspective. Empirically, these systems are characterized by a high correlation between the majority of system constructs, so that the entire system may sometimes be explained in terms of only one principal factor. Button described this form of system as monolithic in that it is one-dimensional, rigid, and relatively impermeable, due to the lack of alternative views or options that are represented. Thus, when individuals maintain such monolithic construct systems, there is not much differentiation within the system to allow for shadings of meaning, constructive alternatives, or new constructions. This rigidity also reflects an all-or-none perspective on the construing of events. This set of characteristics appears to be highly congruent with the way core irrational beliefs are described within REBT (Dryden & Ellis, 2001).

REBT upholds that the source of these all or none and absolutist constructions is one or more neurotic demands (Ellis, 1973, 1975). A demand may be defined as the belief that the world, self, or others *must* be as one desires them to be (or else it is horrible, awful, etc.). The psychotherapeutic process with REBT helps clients to recognize the centrality of neurotic demands in their psychological functioning, helps them to recognize the destructive aspects of continuing to center themselves in this way, and helps them to open new cognitive pathways for viewing events and constructing their experience. In so doing, their construct systems become altered and they are empowered to anticipate events in fresh ways.

184

Despite these advantages, many constructivist therapists have viewed REBT therapists as imposing their view of what is rational and irrational upon the client (Neimeyer & Raskin, 2001). While REBT is more active-directive and more didactic in its methods than some forms of constructivism (Winter & Waston, 1999), the emphasis on directive or didactic technique may be necessary for reaching adolescent populations. When personal constructions are so limiting or potentially toxic in maintaining a substance abuse lifestyle and associated high-risk adolescent behaviors, it may be ethically necessary to more forcefully talk young people out of their "crooked" thinking. Thus, more persuasive disputational methods than typically used by constructivist therapists may be justified with this population as a means of harm reduction. REBT is frank in calling this "crooked" thinking irrational in the sense that thinking in this manner has a high probability of leading to disturbed emotional states, poor decision-making, and negative outcomes. At the same time, the REBT therapist is making only a probabilistic statement, not an absolute prediction, and encourages the client to test out and compare the contrasting outcomes of acting on irrational thought versus acting on rational thoughts. In addition, the REBT methods are used within the context of a collaborative therapeutic relationship. This means that REBT therapists pace their interventions with the readiness and ability of their clients to identify, dispute, and reconstruct the cognitions that shape their experience.

More persuasive or directive efforts by substance abuse therapists in the early stages of therapy may also be necessary to help alleviate the client's negative, central core construing and get the change process underway. The intense and pervasive negative construing of the client can prevent many interventions from gaining a foothold and delay the formation of a working therapeutic alliance with the therapist. However, once the negative core is alleviated or circumvented, the more gently elaborative interventions common to constructivist therapy may then be potentiated, in which the construct system is more broadly developed and successively differentiated. For example, once the adolescent client no longer views all adult authority figures as negative and controlling, he or she may begin to further develop a construct system that rates adults along a variety of meaningful dimensions.

RATIONAL EMOTIVE BEHAVIOR THERAPY AND
CONSTRUCTIVIST PSYCHOLOGY

Albert Ellis (1998) wrote an article that was published in a collection of commentaries on constructivist approaches to psychotherapy. The article was prompted by an exchange between Ellis and the constructivist psychologist, Michael Mahoney. In the article, Ellis delineates the similarities and differences between REBT and constructivism. He makes the case that while REBT is rationalist in evaluating the likely consequences of cognitions, it has also always been constructivist in the sense of viewing persons as actively involved in constructing their own experiences. Thus, Ellis views REBT as both rationalist and constructivist.

The characterization of individuals as actively engaged in forming (and maintaining) their personal versions of reality opens the door for the consideration of alternatives that have the potential to produce improved therapeutic outcomes. George Kelly, the founder of personal construct psychology, stated this idea in the form of his central notion of constructive alternativism:

> We assume that all of our present interpretations of the universe are subject to revision or replacement. . . . [T]here are always some alternative constructions available to choose among in dealing with the world. . . . [N]o one needs to be completely hemmed in by circumstances; no one needs to be the victim of his own biography. (Kelly, 1955, p. 15).

PCP

It can be argued that Albert Ellis has taken this view a step further in pointing out that victimhood, if accepted uncritically and reinforced by negative self-talk (e.g. "I'm worthless, no good, etc."), leads to a cycle of self-defeat for the individual. Ellis has perhaps most succinctly described his therapeutic method as follows: "I strive to show the client how he does himself in,[1] that he doesn't have to,[2] and how he could do otherwise"[3] (Ellis, 1996, videotape). Thus, the client becomes self-defeating by bringing his or her negative core beliefs to bear on the interpretation of events, without noting or considering the existence of alternative views.

Ellis identified four stereotypical forms of negative core constructions that people adopt that result in emotional upset.

---

[1] negative, core beliefs or constructions
[2] constructive alternativism/ Socratic dialogue and didactic teaching
[3] reconstruction or development of effective, new beliefs

186

These are dogmatic demands, awfulizing and/or negative global-ization, low frustration tolerance, and the negative rating of self or others (Ellis, 1975). Examples of dogmatic demands that clients hold when in residential treatment include "I *shouldn't* have to be here" and "I *must* have special privileges while I'm here." Examples of awfulizing/globalizing include "*Everyone* here is against me" and "This is *awful*. I *hate* it here." Examples of low frustration tolerance are "I'll *never* be able to quit drugs; it's *too* hard" and "I can't stand it here anymore." Examples of negative self-ratings are "Nobody wants me; that's why they brought me here" and "I'm worthless." Additionally, adolescent clients often negatively evaluate direct care staff or authority figures. For example, consider a client who says of a staff member, "She's a real *bitch*; she suspended my pass." In this case, the word "bitch" is a global negative rating of the staff member.

While all these habits of thinking generally have destructive emotional and behavioral consequences for the individual, Ellis (1996, 1998) holds that there are alternatives. In this way, his ideas are compatible with Kelly's (1955) constructive alternativism. These alternatives are initially outside the range of the person's awareness, but can be brought into awareness through processes of didactic teaching, Socratic questioning, and active disputing.

Specific to the therapeutic approach of REBT in amelio-rating these problems with adolescents is the designation of "A" for the activating event and "C" for the emotional and/or behavioral consequences that flow from the interaction of "A" with the core irrational beliefs, "B." Thus, the client's experience of "A" is created depending on how the "A" is evaluated by the client's belief system. At step "D" the evidence for the belief is examined on empirical, logical, and practical grounds. Arguments for overturning the belief are presented. At step "E," the therapist helps the client to constructively elaborate new beliefs that have more promise toward producing favorable life results.

Step E appears to be the part of the REBT model that has undergone the most evolution over the years. In his 1973 book, Ellis calls "E" the cognitive effects of having disputed the irrational belief. Later; "E" is more fully developed as a separate stage of the process and designated as the point at which new, effective beliefs are formulated to replace the irrational beliefs. (The model continues to be referred to as the ABC model for simplicity's sake, even though technically it is the ABCDE model.) Thus, the change process in REBT over time becomes viewed as dependent on the active construction of new meaning, not just insight into the effect of how one's beliefs affect one's emotional experience. It is also here, at point "E", that REBT borrows from other treatment modalities for techniques to facilitate this part of the change process. Some of the techniques are behavioral; hence, the inclusion of "B" into the REBT acronym, which had once stood as RET. Some of these additions are distinctly constructivist; i.e. "what could you tell yourself to help yourself deal more effectively with this event?"

Thus, Kelly's constructive alternatives and Ellis' rational alternatives (or new, effective beliefs) appear to be different ways of facilitating client movement toward increased cognitive flexibility and social adaptation. The constructivist emphasis of REBT is what helps to advance the possibility of change to the client. It guides the treatment technology of the therapist, as all of REBT's methods are geared toward the goal of cognitive reconstruction through the replacement of irrational core beliefs.

A second characteristic common to REBT, constructivism, and CBT as well, is the use of collaborative empiricism (Ellis, 2002, p. 89). This means that rather than the therapist playing the role of an expert, the therapist and client together explore in a scientific manner the evidence for a particular belief or cognition. In constructivist psychology this could involve the technique of fixed-role therapy in which clients define new characterizations of themselves and act them out for a fixed period of time (Kelly, 1955). In REBT, the process may be sped up by exploring the connections between the client's current thoughts, feelings, and behaviors and the linkage of new feelings and behaviors with more rational alternatives for living (Adelman, 2006, Cummins, Personal Communication, 2004). This collaborative empiricism has the practical effect of placing the client and therapist on an equal footing as co-investigators. This new relationship seems to circumvent much of the developmentally built-in resistance and hostility that adolescents often exhibit toward adults and the therapeutic process.

Another feature of REBT, in particular, which appears to be attractive to adolescents, is the philosophy of long-range hedonism (Dryden & Ellis, 2001, pp. 298-299). Adolescent clients learn that it is not the pursuit of pleasure or happiness that gets them into conflict with the adult world, but rather the sacrificing of long-term goals and pleasures for immediate or short-term gratifications. This aspect of REBT helps clients to see that their therapists are not simply controlling or puritanically-minded adults, but instead people genuinely interested in uncovering and advancing their larger aims or goals.

TREATMENT OF ADOLESCENTS: THE NEED FOR AN IMPROVED MODEL

There are particular characteristics of psychological functioning during adolescence that appear to make for a poor fit with much of contemporary psychotherapy. First, as adolescents are striving to demonstrate their personal competence as individuals, it is difficult for them to admit to problems or admit to a lack of confidence. Second, many of them also, rightly or wrongly, do not trust adults. Third, they are a difficult population to assess, as they may intentionally mask feelings of depression. Acting out behaviors may be so distressing to adults that they may overlook the possibility of comorbid depression. Fourth, adolescents may be instinctually reactive toward adults, as they attempt to negotiate the path toward psychological independence. They may bristle at adults' attempts to offer correction or constructive criticism. In turn, as their behavior tests the patience of adults, many adolescents may feel abused or betrayed should adults lose their customary self-control.

Perhaps most importantly, adolescents may not perceive a need for change and thus may require some form of motivational enhancement before they will agree to therapeutic goals with their therapists. Many have great difficulty submitting to any form of unbalanced power arrangement with an adult (expert/novice, authority figure/follower, mentor/apprentice). These issues would seem to require a re-thinking of therapy and the therapist/client relationship. As has been already noted, the model of collaborative empiricism appears to effectively address these problems of treatment engagement with adolescents.

MEASURING PERFORMANCE IMPROVEMENT OF ADOLESCENT SERVICES

A performance quality improvement project in a residential treatment facility revealed client issues with anger to be the most common emotional problem within the client population (Adelman, McGee, Power, & Hanson, 2005). It was hypothesized that unresolved anger might find its expression in the development and maintenance of substance abusing behavior, and that the treatment of anger might be an important component in the treatment of substance abuse. A comparison of five successive quarterly reviews revealed a reduction of almost one standard deviation (1.4 to .45 standard deviations) for the client population on a measure of anger/temper after the introduction of Rational Emotive Behavior Therapy (REBT) into the therapeutic milieu. This improvement was deemed to be highly suggestive of the efficacy of REBT with this clinical population. The remainder of this chapter describes issues that substance-abusing adolescents present in treatment, and gives examples of therapeutic dialogues demonstrating the process of change using constructivist-oriented REBT.

Some of the common frustrating events that typically trigger anger in adolescents in residential care are being brought to treatment against their will, receiving consequences from staff, feeling verbally abused or picked on by peers or staff, and experiencing emotional stress or emotional disturbance. Past issues beyond the immediate triggering event, such as emotional abandonment or physical or sexual abuse, often compound the anger. The adolescent client's response to these events often leads to additional disturbance of emotions and/or behavioral acting out. Some common forms of adolescent acting out in the residential setting include cussing or verbal abuse of others, threatening others with assault, breaking things in anger, and program non-compliance. Common forms of secondary or increasing emotional disturbance include being depressed about being depressed. Thus, when the adolescent is telling him- or herself, "I'll never get over this depression," this generally leads to increased depression and hopelessness.

The ABC problem-solving model of REBT (Ellis, 1973, pp. 55-67) is summarized for the reader below.

a) Activating Event

b) Irrational Core Belief (s)

c) Emotional Consequences & Behavioral Consequences

d) Disputing Irrational Beliefs

e) Effective New Beliefs

The use of the model enables the therapist to zero in on the elements affecting the client's experience of the world and to stay active-directive in moving the client toward the changing of core cognitive structures. The therapist can also visually demonstrate to the client how irrational beliefs play an intermediary role in determining the adolescent's emotional experience of events. The emotional consequences that are experienced often lead to negative behavioral consequences in the lives of adolescents as well, such as substance abuse.

When the adolescent client is first exposed to the ABC model in a psycho-educational format, it can greatly facilitate the client's ability to do therapeutic work in a structured fashion. For this reason, some of the therapeutic dialogues that follow are briefer than one might expect with difficult clients.

CASE EXAMPLES

Case Example 1

This case exemplifies the use of REBT in working with a treatment resistant, adolescent client. The phrases in bold print to the right or below the steps of the dialogue serve to highlight key components of the practice of constructivist-oriented REBT.

Client: I *shouldn't* have to be here (in residential treatment). (*Dogmatic Demand*)

Therapist: Why *shouldn't* you? (*Disputing Statement*)

Client: Because I could be at home where I belong, with my own things, and friends, and doing what I'm used to doing.

Therapist: These are reasons why you would prefer to be home, and I get that, but why *shouldn't* you be here?

Client: Because I *hate* being here, and besides I can quit drugs on my own. (*Negative Globalization*)

Therapist: Again, you would strongly prefer not to be here, but how does that mean you *shouldn't* be here? (*Disputing Statement*)

191

Client: What do you mean? You wouldn't want to be here if you were in my shoes. It's *terrible* being here. (*Negative Globalization*)

Therapist: Where is the evidence that you *shouldn't* be here? (*Disputing Statement*)

Client: This (treatment) is never going to help me! (*Negative Globalization*)

Therapist: Do you really know that? Where is the evidence? (*Disputing Statement*)

Client: (client stays silent looking displeased)

Therapist: Is it possible that you might get something out of treatment without it being your first choice to be here? (*Disputing Statement*)

Client: I guess.

Therapist: Must you always like something for it to have some benefit or value? (*Disputing Statement*)

Client: Maybe not all the time.

Therapist: So I think you might have a more positive experience being here if you told yourself something like, "I can do this and get something out of it for me, whether or not being here suits me at this particular time." (*New Rational Coping Statement*)

Client: Okay, but I still think it is lame that I have to be here.

Therapist: That's okay for you to think that for the time being, but see if you can experiment with it being otherwise.

The therapist has helped the client move from a demand to a preference in regard to the event of coming to treatment. Rather than arguing with the client ("You need treatment!") or attempting to persuade the client ("Treatment won't be as bad as you think"), the therapist asks pointed questions that direct the client toward examining the evidence for his/her beliefs and gives the client suggestions for constructing a more effective, new belief. That is, the client learns that a "should" is a demand that usually results in anger. But by acknowledging one's preference (e.g. "I would prefer not to be here") and giving up the demand, one can begin to diminish anger, accept current circumstances, and behave in more functional ways.

192

As a result of this cognitive shift, the client is much more likely to engage with further treatment goals. Clinical experience at our treatment center has shown that even treatment resistant clients are intrigued by the demonstration of this treatment effect, and want to learn to use the ABC problem-solving method for working on other problems. With enough practice and didactic instruction, clients come to use the process for ongoing self-management of their emotions. This newly developed skill has positive affects on social adjustment in terms of the reduction of anger (Adelman et al., 2005; Adelman, 2006). Increased emotional self-control may translate into a reduced reliance on chemical substances for mood regulation as well.

In contrast, if clients continue to function under the sway of their irrational core beliefs, they will continue to "awfulize" conditions in their lives, continue to be demanding of self and others, and continue to create anguish for themselves and those around them. They may not engage in treatment, and even when they do, their engagement may be short-lived or superficial. Without a change in their maladaptive core beliefs (constructive change), they are likely to show the same disturbed reaction to future activating events.

Case Example 2

This case exemplifies dysfunctional family communication and the use of principles of REBT in modifying the communication impasse. The first phase of the dialogue takes place before parent education in REBT.

Son: I'll *never* be able to keep from relapsing. (*Catastrophizing*)

Mother: Why do you say that?

Son: I've *never* been able to do it before. (*Awfulizing*)

Mother: Well, why can't you think positively about it? Give yourself a chance to succeed.

Son: I've tried *everything*. (*Globalizing*)

Mother: Everything?

Son: (becoming exasperated) I know I can't. Look at all the times I've *failed.* (*Global Negative Self-Rating*)

Mother: (lacking an adequate comeback response, becomes discouraged and gives up)

The dialogue begins again after the therapist provides the mother with parent education in REBT. Now, when the son asserts his inability to avoid relapse, the mother is prepared to respond:

Mother: How do you know that? Has it really been that many times?

Son : I just know it!

Mother: I know you've had some setbacks, but where is it written that because you have failed, you will always fail? (*Disputing statement*)

Son: (grudgingly) Well, I guess I don't know that . . . but it seems too damned hard. (*Low frustration tolerance*)

Mother: Well, all right then. It's hard, but not a foregone conclusion! What can you tell yourself that would help you to work on the problem?

Son: I can tell myself that as hard as it is, I can continue to work toward my recovery.

In this example, before REBT training, the mother's attempts at persuasion and engendering positive thinking have almost the direct opposite effect on the client, producing increased frustration and helplessness. The client's need to resist appears to center around his fear of relapsing again, and experiencing the negative emotional consequences of the global self-rating, "I'm a failure." After REBT education his mother learned to validate his sense of frustration, while simultaneously disputing his conclusion that he will always fail. She also exposed his low frustration tolerance regarding his ability to persevere toward his goal of recovery. In the end she facilitates his developing a new construction of the situation, which enables him to diminish his emotional disturbance, contain his low frustration tolerance, and begin to re-engage with treatment. Again, as with the previous example, it is critical to note that without this process of personal reconstruction the treatment process will likely remain a futile one, resulting in the client being labeled as resistant or unmotivated by staff.

Case Example 3

This case demonstrates the use of REBT to uncover the place of substance abuse within the emotional coping strategy of the adolescent.

Client: I have to have my drugs.

Therapist: Why must you have drugs?

Client: Because it's fun doing drugs. I feel great; on top of everything!

Therapist: How do you feel otherwise?

Client: I'd feel like crap.

Therapist: Why do you think you feel so badly the majority of the time?

Client: Without drugs, I'd be thinking about all my problems, and my hassles with my family.

Therapist: Is that one reason why you do drugs?

Client: Why, yeah. I can forget about all that; escape for a while.

Therapist: What if you could learn to feel better without drugs (by identifying and disputing negative core beliefs) and begin to address some of these problems?

Client: I guess that would be better in the long run.

In this example, rather than arguing with the client over the perceived benefits of his drug use, the therapist exposes the client's emotional avoidance and underlying depression. These issues can now become new targets for intervention. In addition, the therapist has also helped the client to begin to conceptualize the role of chemical substances in his life and to compare the short-range benefits versus the long-term costs of his drug use. Eventually, the decisional balance may be shifted away from the continuation of substance use/dependence, thus setting the foundation for a drug-free lifestyle.

Case Example 4

This case concerns a client with multiple problems (dual diagnosis) who believes that he knows better than the staff and that he can get by with what many others construe to be his current hedonistic, self-centered lifestyle without regard to its effects on others. Whenever challenged about his behavior, attitude, or lifestyle he reacts indignantly and makes derisive and defensive comments declining responsibility for his actions. The client is referred for crisis counseling due to his extreme anger over the perception that he was "threatened" with behavioral consequences by staff.

Client: This isn't going to help me (*the REBT Self-Help Form*).

Therapist: You may be right, but let's take a look.

Client: (No response.)

Therapist: You're angry at staff, correct?

Client: Yes, he shouldn't have treated me that way! He's an "expletive deleted."

Therapist: Okay then, let's just take the worst-case scenario. Suppose he did treat you poorly? (Instead of entering into an argument about who did what to whom, the therapist begins a line of questioning that prepares the client to handle his frustrations in life from a more empowering point of view.)

Client: He threatened me. He's got no business doing that.

Therapist: Maybe he did, maybe he didn't, but do you think you can count on all people to treat you the way you want all the time? (By the therapist admitting the possibility that staff was out of line, the client doesn't feel compelled to keep making his point. At the same time, the therapist has been careful not to side with the client, while he continues to collaborate with the client on examining his beliefs about the event.)

Client: But he's staff!!

Therapist: Well, sometimes even staff falls short in achieving standards, but it doesn't make him a horrible person because he disappointed you by the way he treated you.

Client: Are you telling me I shouldn't be angry about this?

196

Therapist: I'm suggesting that people don't always treat us the way we would like, but that it doesn't mean the end of the world; and that he is probably not a horrible person, but a fallible human being who makes mistakes.

Client: But I've always been too impulsive a person to keep from acting on my feelings.

Therapist: Your impulsivity is just one part of who you are. If we can work to bring it into balance with the rest of you, it could have a dramatic impact on how things go for you.

Client: It's too much trouble to learn this stuff (REBT and other coping skills).

Therapist: You're right in one way. It does take increased effort right now, but it will probably save you from more hassles in the long run.

Client: But I'll never need these skills on the outside.

Therapist: Is it reasonable to think that you can always depend on your family to get you by in the world, even if you do start out working for your dad? It might be simpler to deal with this issue now, and have something to show for your time in treatment.

Client: I guess I see your point. (Client completes self-help form with the assistance of the therapist).

This client had several key beliefs that were interfering with the process of change and which REBT nicely addresses. These included the dogmatic demand that one must never be treated unfairly, narcissistic entitlement and low frustration tolerance beliefs in a number of areas (e.g. believing that one shouldn't have to work to earn achievements, adapt to other people in a work setting, or be bothered with the task of self-improvement). When the client was able to consider the perspective that ultimately these beliefs were likely to be self-defeating, his anger and resistance turned to a diminishing of his emotional upset, acceptance of a difficult situation, and the beginnings of a problem-solving orientation.

CONCLUDING STATEMENTS

The personal core constructions of substance abusing adolescents are by definition rigid and difficult to change (Button, 1985; Kelly, 1955). As a result, they interfere with the consideration of

197

new data that can lead to the higher levels of cognitive differentiation and psychological functioning that adolescents typically need to acquire. This deficit in the ability to effectively cope with the inevitable frustrating events that life presents leads to the creation of disturbed emotional states (Ellis, 1975). Drug use, anger, and conduct disordered and avoidant behaviors appear to be the typical substitutes for the insufficiency of available coping mechanisms possessed by the adolescent client. Unfortunately, the life pattern of habitual drug use only leads to a greater lack of frustration tolerance, and a continued loss of opportunities for learning or developing more effective coping mechanisms and adaptive, reconstructed views of the social world.

In conclusion, REBT emphasizes the ways that clients actively construct their own disturbance in relation to frustrating life events, and identifies the core philosophies that maintain their disturbance. From a constructivist perspective, REBT techniques may perhaps be most effective with individuals with a particular form of cognitive structure. Accounts of REBT in action with clients appear to reflect the tight, all-or-none forms of construing that Button (1985) identified. In turn, these structures may be more typical of particular clinical populations such as adolescent substance abusers. When individuals maintain such tightly organized constructions of the social world as seem to be tied to the structure of core irrational beliefs, there is not much differentiation within the system to allow for shadings of meaning, constructive alternatives, or new constructions. It becomes imperative for the therapist to help facilitate a cognitive shift in the adolescent's core constructions of irrational beliefs for the change process to begin.

These types of one-dimensional, rigid, cognitive structures, and the dire consequences for living that they perpetuate in adolescents, justify the use of more persuasive disputational methods within the context of a collaborative therapeutic relationship. It is considered essential that adolescent clients learn to understand their complicity in their emotional disturbance. Sustained change appears to be contingent upon their coming to identify and replace maladaptive, core beliefs through a process of personal reconstruction. This key change in these basic and foundational structures of experiencing may then make possible, and encourage, further elaboration of the client's wider system of personal constructions. From the REBT perspective, both healthy and unhealthy emotions stem from underlying constructions.

Thus, it is essential to assist adolescents in developing new constructs that are supportive of healthier emotions, better choices in living, and more differentiated, mature views of the world, self, and others. When these larger changes begin to take place, the saliency of substance abuse as a source of adolescent identity and as a strategy for emotional coping may progressively lose its luster.

REFERENCES

Adelman, R. (1998). *Changes in construct systems of recovering psychiatric patients.* Unpublished doctoral dissertation, Texas A&M-Commerce, Commerce, Texas.

Adelman, R., McGee, P., Power, R., & Hanson, C. (2005). Reducing adolescent clients'anger in a residential substance abuse treatment facility. *The Joint Commission Journal on Quality and Patient Safety, 31,* 325-327.

Adelman, R. (2006). The angry adolescent and constructivist REBT. In P. Cummins (Ed.), *Working with anger: A constructivist approach* (pp. 99-114). London: John Wiley.

Bannister, D. (1960). Conceptual structure in thought disordered schizophrenics. *Journal of Mental Science, 108,* 825-842.

Button, E. (1985). *Personal construct theory and mental health.* London: Croon Helm.

Dryden, W., & Ellis, A. (2001). Rational Emotive Behavior Therapy. In K. S. Dobson (Ed.), *Handbook of cognitive-behavioral therapies* (2nd ed., pp. 295-348). New York: Guilford Press.

Ellis, A. (1973). *Humanistic psychotherapy: The rational-emotive approach.* New York: Julian Press.

Ellis, A. (1975). *A guide for rational living* (3rd ed.). New York: Wilshire.

Ellis, A. (1996). *Dealing with addictions* (Master therapists video series). New York: Albert Ellis Institute.

Ellis, A. (1998). How rational emotive behavior therapy belongs in the constructivist camp. In M. F. Hoyt (Ed.), *The handbook of constructive therapies: Innovative approaches from leading practitioners* (pp. 83-99). San Francisco: Jossey-Boss.

Ellis, A. (2002). *Overcoming resistance.* New York: Springer Publishing.

Kelly, G. A. (1955). *The psychology of personal constructs* (2 vols). New York: Norton.

Lorenzini, R., Sassaroli, S., & Rocchi, M. (1989). Schizophrenia and paranoia as solutions to predictive failure. *International Journal of Personal Construct Psychology, 2,* 417-432.

199

Neimeyer, R. A., & Raskin, J. D. (2001). Varieties of constructivism in psychotherapy. In K. S. Dobson (Ed.), *Handbook of cognitive-behavioral therapies* (2nd ed., pp. 393-423). New York: Guilford Press.

Slater, P. (1976). *Explorations of intrapersonal space.* New York: John Wiley.

Winter, D. A., & Watson, S. (1999). Personal construct theory and the cognitive therapies. *Journal of Constructivist Psychology, 12,* 1-22.

☞ 10 ☜

Constructivist Treatment of Divorce

Donald K. Granvold

The whole process is shrouded in mystery, with the beginning and ending difficult to ascertain because of the absence of clearly demarcated rites of passage and rituals. Most often, modern people must celebrate, mark and facilitate their own transition. (Catron & Chiriboga, 1991, p. 124)

Divorce. It is occurring at record setting rates in America and in countries across the world. This life transition is an incredibly unique crisis in the lives of the couple experiencing it. The direct and ripple effects in the lives of those in the couple's intimate personal domain are deep, persistent, permeating, and sustaining. There are no blueprints to follow in this journey of coming apart and, as noted above, painfully little societal sanctions exist as guideposts to help with transitioning.

This chapter discusses the process of divorce and the application of constructivist philosophy and practice to those engaged in this life transition. After some introductory remarks, I will address constructivist caveats that inform my clinical conceptualizations and intervention selections when working with divorcing clients. The remainder of the chapter will focus on constructive applications potentially viable in clients' evolution through the pervasive changes inherent in divorce.

I have often stated that divorce is to couple treatment as pathology is to the practice of medicine. Divorce is conceptualized as the "death" of a committed union. In many cases, working with divorcing individuals or couples is the consequence of "failed" couple therapy. Despite the efforts of couple therapists to promote the preservation of marital relationships, divorce is the likely

outcome. Gottman (1999), reporting on the findings of longitudinal research, states that "we have consistently found significant
correlations between going for marriage counseling and getting
a divorce" (p. 5). His research findings indicate that only 11% to
18% of couples receiving treatment in controlled study programs
show lasting clinically significant change.

Historically in the couple treatment field, treatment was
terminated when the decision was made to dissolve the union
(Brown, 1976). Fortunately, therapists of today recognize that if
ever people could benefit from counseling, it is during the time
they are struggling with the decision to divorce and beyond.

PRINCIPLES OF CONSTRUCTIVE PRACTICE

Constructivist approaches to psychotherapy are comprised
of a "fuzzy" set of principles and practices that are dissonant in
many ways with modern psychology both philosophically and
methodologically (Neimeyer & Raskin, 2000). Although distin-
guishably postmodern, there are many varieties of constructivism
reflecting differences in semantics and terminology, conceptual
variability, and methodological biases (Neimeyer & Raskin, 2001;
Raskin, 2002). Although the intent of this chapter is not to discuss
the philosophic bases of the interventions presented, it may be
helpful to the reader to have a sense of the principles that inform
my approach to constructivist practice. Several principles are
explicated below. The spirit of both client and therapist creativity
and respect for the idiosyncratic nature of human experiencing
and human change are inherent in the approaches to intervention
presented.

Meaning Making

The principle of multiple meaning making is the
cornerstone of constructivist theory and practice (Granvold,
2001). Individual mental health is, in large part, a product of the
individual's capacity to generate multiple meanings for the same
event. The dichotomous approach to meaning making, driven by
logical positivism, would have the individual replacing irrational
thoughts (constructions) with rational ones (Granvold, 1996b).
The constructive approach is based on no such dichotomy, but
rather encourages the development of multiple meanings with

202

attention devoted to various consequences, both active and potential, of each meaning.

It is assumed that people are active participants in meaning making. "Reality" is subjective, the co-creation of the individual and the stimulus condition. Meanings are socially embedded and are constructed out of life experience. "Reality" is dynamic, rather than a static condition. Consequently, while some meanings are rather inexorable over time, other meanings are highly subject to reconstruction. The passage of time, altered circumstances, and selfhood changes have tremendous potential impact on meaning reconstruction. Socialization promotes the tendency in people to form rather restrictive, often singular views of complex life events, circumstances, and processes. Furthermore, negative constructions often prevail over more positive meanings. These simplistic, absolutistic, and negative biases in human meaning making are readily challengeable psychotherapeutically.

Emotions as Change Agents

A second caveat is that emotion often plays a powerful role in human change. Emotions are operatives in effecting change and, as such, it is preferable to therapeutically support and encourage emotional experience. Mental health professionals label as "negative" many human emotions—such as depression, anxiety, anger, and resentment. I, along with countless others, have received excellent training in the application of intervention methods to control, limit, decrease, and stop emotions. In postmodern psychotherapy practice, emotions should neither be labeled as negative, nor should they be therapeutically targeted for extreme limitation or eradication. Although deep depression, feelings of loss, aloneness, anxiety, fear, and the like may be uncomfortable, untoward, or subjectively undesirable, there is potential utility in these feelings. For example, in the postdivorce recovery period, intense anger is oftentimes helpful in the process of "letting go" of the ex-mate. The realization, experiencing, and expression of emotions such as anger, hurt, resentment, and loathing advance the process of de-attachment. Emotions are emotions, the effects of which may be immediately unappealing to the client while holding the promise of long-term gain. The disclaimer appropriate to this discussion is that extreme emotions associated with suicidal ideation/planning or homicidal ideation/planning obligate the

203

therapist to take steps to protect the client from acting on these urges. Hospitalization for protection and medication for control may be desirable options under these circumstances.

3rd) Selfhood Processes

A third constructivist caveat relates to the definition of self. The self is not singular or fixed, but rather is a multifaceted and ever-changing "system" of identity meanings. Selfhood is a process reflecting a history of development and accumulated meanings forged through tacit and explicit cognitive operations (Guidano, 1988). The evolutionary elaboration of self results in a multifaceted self comprised of self-schemata which are variably activated in a social context. Since schemata are seldom "purged" from our memory system, we have ever-increasing sets of self-conceptions. Due to cognitive limitations, only a partial set of self-schemata can be activated at a given time. The activated "self" is the one that "reflects meaningful links between the demands of the situation and self-conceptions related to those cues" (Nurius & Berlin, 1994, p. 255). Thus, the socially embedded nature of self-schemata plays a powerful role in the activation of one set of self-conceptions over another. From the above conceptualization, it can be concluded that multiple "possible" selves exist among stored schemata (Markus & Nurius, 1986). One's "active" sense of self is *never a complete representation of one's being.* Furthermore, one's sets of self-conceptions are continuously expanding as the experience of life is translated into selfhood development.

4th) Activity

Humans are active participants in their own evolution, not merely "passive pawns in life" (Mahoney & Granvold, 2005, p. 75). Individuals are seen as ripe with potential to assume a proactive role in their experiencing of life. Past may be revisited and given new meaning through the application of current perspectives and preferential ways of construing past "realities." Life in the moment reflects the intersection of external demands and human choice. While not within total human control, individual agency is a powerful influence on the meaning and experience of life in the moment. As with the past and the present, constructive focus on the future is biased with hope, possibilities, and rejuvenation.

204

Constructive conceptualizations of human change emphasize client awareness and expression of creative potential, self-efficacy, and activity. Life and psychotherapy are about possibilities—those "realized" but perhaps lacking form, recognition, or acknowledgement; and possible futures with the potential for achievement, revitalization, and revisioning of self and life experience.

Strengths and Possibilities

The pathology conceptualization of mental health so central to the dominant models of psychotherapy practice reflects views of the human condition that constructivists eschew. The pathology model objectifies human functioning, reducing to a diagnostic label human adaptation, coping, and evolution (Leitner & Faidley, 2002). The necessary unrest that is life at its personal best when humans are confronted with loss, exposed to trauma, or challenged with personal or interpersonal crisis is construed as dysfunction, disability, and disorder. In contrast to such conceptualizations, constructivists maintain that the world cannot be known "as it is" in an objective sense, independent of personal and social constructions (Anderson, 1995; Gergen, 1991; Raskin & Lewandowski, 2000). The focus on individual limitation, liability, flaw, incapacity, and shortcoming produces a remarkable negative bias, one of deviance, debilitation, and disorder. Furthermore, labeling people as "disordered" promotes an artificial division between normal and abnormal experiencing of life.

Rather than emphasizing what is "wrong" with the individual, constructive practice wisdom would have us look for client strengths. The identification of and placement of emphasis on client strengths, resiliency, coping capacities, and interpersonal and social resources holds rich promise for meeting the challenges of human adaptation and change. Saleebey (2006) states that to practice from a strengths perspective means that everything you do as a practitioner "will be predicated, in some way, on helping to discover and embellish, explore and exploit clients' strengths and resources in the service of assisting them to achieve their goals, realize their dreams, and shed the irons of their own inhibitions and misgivings, and society's domination" (p. 1). Clients are to be viewed as ripe with the capacity to draw on personal, interpersonal,

205

and socio-environmental resources in accommodating past and present losses, disappointments, and regrets. The future is an expression of human resiliency, regenerative potential, realized human resources and activity.

Constructive psychotherapy is about possibilities, a stance that emphasizes the present and future. McNamee (2002) poses the question, "What would happen if therapists were to shift the psychotherapeutic conversation from the realm of charting the history of a problem to the realm of future images?" (p. 164). It is my belief that such a shift coupled with an emphasis on personal, interpersonal, and socio-environmental assets will erode the power of negativity, doubt, hopelessness, despair, and inactivity.

DIVORCE AS PROCESS

Divorce is not an event. It is a process characterized both by discrete stressful events and by a cumulative set of losses and adaptation demands. The self systems and family system are thrust into an extreme state of disequilibrium as pervasive change demands are realized (Granvold, 1989). The process is typically extreme in its emotional consequences, necessarily self-identity changing, and produces change across most domains of the individual's life. Few transitions in life are more emotionally evocative and these emotions are often lived to extremes. That is to say that people are driven by their emotions to behave in ways that are extreme, with logical abandon, and in personally uncharacteristic fashion. For example, an attorney going through the early separation phase of his divorce stated that, "I found myself in the bushes outside the bedroom of my own home, peering in the window at my wife—as if I was a peeping Tom!" This man saw himself as a law abiding, rule compliant, "well-adjusted" person behaving "crazily." Emotion driven behavior may take clients into uncharted territory. These forays may prompt subsequent emotive reactions, views of self as highly unstable, and new self-conceptualizations.

The distress and emotional pain associated with the dissolution of a committed love relationship is rivaled only by the death of a loved one. (Paradoxically, many going through divorce have said that it would have been easier had the spouse died.) For most, coming apart carries with it extreme emotional consequences. Divorce is simultaneously an ending punctuated by loss, estrangement, and detachment, and a new beginning characterized by fear of the unknown; challenging novel roles, responsibilities, and behaviors; and promising future possibilities. Client treatment goals can be expected to fluctuate. The desire for a sense of closure regarding the past may prompt a focus on the estranged or ex-mate and the associated family and social networks. Alternatively, the focus may be on the development of novel or expanded "selves" to meet current and evolving demands and possibilities.

STAGES OF THE DIVORCE PROCESS

For clarity of expression purposes, the divorce process will be conceptualized in stages. This categorization is not intended to say that the divorce experience is the same for all. To the contrary, the experience of divorce is unique to the individual. That stated, there are commonly experienced challenges at various points in the divorce process. A number of stage theories have been suggested in which divorce is collapsed into various categories. I prefer to conceptualize the divorce process as broadly composed of three overlapping stages: 1) *decision making*, 2) *transition*, and 3) *postdivorce recovery* (Granvold, 1994, 2000a, 2000b). Each of these stages poses unique challenges to the individual.

 *Decision Making*

Reaching the decision to divorce is a most difficult deliberation for an individual or couple. As difficult as it is for those directly affected by the decision, it is also incredibly challenging for therapists whose counsel is sought to assist in the decision making process. For many therapists it can be said that when the client(s) has the greatest need for input, the therapist has the least to give. It has been my view for some time that there is a paucity of techniques for decision-making intervention (Granvold, 1994). By far, the therapeutic bias in treating couples is working to keep them together. A powerful value is placed in our society on the maintenance of committed relationships. Most people continue to consider divorce to be an ethical violation. Like it or not, "get married and stay married" is the mainstream message resonating within most individuals who are "coupled"—even those who are unhappily coupled.

207

In addition to a therapeutic bias (reflective of a social bias) to help couples stay together, few specific decision making methodologies have been developed. Typically, one or both partners continue their marriage in a state of high dissatisfaction and protracted indecision before ultimately arriving at a decision to divorce. The state of indecision is stressful in itself, characterized by high levels of frustration, anxiety, uncertainty, fear, worry, insecurity, distrust (particularly for the mate who is more greatly committed), hurt, resentment, depression, hopelessness and impending doom, and feelings of disempowerment. Consistent with constructivist philosophy, the experiencing of these emotions is highly significant and desirable in some measure as the individual struggles with the decision to remain in the relationship or leave it. Most endure frustration and discomfort with protracted ambivalence. To avoid premature decision making out of sheer frustration with indecision, therapists should attend to low frustration tolerance.

Often, there is erosion in feelings of love, intimacy, sexual desire, and sexual satisfaction during decision-making. Individuals who are emotionally fragile, highly dependent upon the mate, and/or evidence low self-esteem experience discussions of divorce to be highly threatening to their current and future well being. Such individuals, typically more committed and less likely to leave their relationships, are far more vulnerable to divorce related crisis responses.

The decision to divorce is almost always an emotionally driven decision. It is interesting that most decision making intervention procedures reported in the literature are cognitive and behavioral by design. This is not to say that they do not access emotions. The frequently utilized balance sheet procedure (Janis & Mann, 1977) is a cognitive exercise in which the perceived costs and benefits of either remaining married or divorcing are delineated. Although list generation is cognitive, the *content* of the lists is often emotion based (e.g. fear of the unknown, feelings of loss, relief, elation). Ingredients of the list may be weighted in importance and concessions and compromise factors determined. This procedure is useful in gaining better definition of the issues, values, and emotional elements associated or anticipated with either decision.

Structured marital separation is a viable approach for select couples who are having difficulty cohabitating (Granvold, 1983;

Granvold & Tarrant, 1983). This procedure affords a variety of benefits of time apart without forcing a premature decision to divorce.

The gravity of the decision on the lives of the couple, their children, extended family and friends effect great pressure on the decision maker(s). The ultimate decision to divorce may be a collateral decision of the couple or the unilateral decision of one partner. There is typically intense and protracted pain in both the decision maker and the "rejected" partner. It is noteworthy that today divorce appears to be far more likely the consequence of a loss of intimate connectedness than the result of intense conflict (Stanley, 2001). Infidelity, incompatibility, and alcohol and drug use are other common reasons for divorce (Amato & Previti, 2003). In situations where erosion in emotional connectedness is the primary decision making factor, the absence of overt signs of disagreement and dissatisfaction may be confusing to both the partners and to those close to the couple, particularly offspring.

Although couples may struggle with their decision in therapy, the decision to divorce is usually the product of an extratherapeutic event or realization, not the product of a therapeutic discussion or procedure. Often, the deciding factor is of crisis proportions. The trauma resulting from a divorce decision-making crisis (e.g. infidelity, violence) may serve to compound the difficulty of coming apart. Curiously, however, in some instances the effects of a crisis facilitate closure.

The following are examples of therapeutic goals during the decision making stage (adapted from Granvold, 2002):

- Specify factors eroding the relationship

- Optimize relationship functioning (specify and implement strategic change)

- Promote frustration tolerance for indecision (i.e. combat low frustration tolerance)

- Limit impulsive decision making

- Carefully determine and weigh the factors of satisfaction and dissatisfaction

209

- Clarify values and life goals related to coupling

- Clearly identify perceived advantages and disadvantages of divorce relative to remaining married (balance-sheet procedure; Janis & Mann, 1977)

- Consider structured marital separation to interrupt maladaptive patterns of interaction, re-evaluate the relationship from an altered perspective, and move more gradually to singlehood (a treatment of choice only for select couples) (Granvold, 1983; Granvold & Tarrant, 1983)

Transition

Once a decision to divorce is made, the couple enters the transition phase of the divorce process. The decision sets in motion remarkable change demands, demands that are typically highly emotionally charged. Divorce is emotionally painful to the couple and their children, and to extended family and friends as well. A major therapeutic objective at this time is damage control in the lives of the couple and, as important, in their children's lives. Effort is made to avoid or to greatly limit adversarial conduct and to promote more "healthy" family reconstitution. Unless a mate moved out during the decision-making period, physical separation occurs. Aside from one partner's physical relocation, the major practical considerations during this time are legal divorce proceedings, division of property, child support, and child visitation. Each of these issues is an indicator that divorce is taking place. Children's needs for parental involvement, support, and emotional engagement tend to be high at this time. Their accommodation of this typically unwanted change may result in clinginess, withdrawal, or acting out behavior. Parents' resources during this transition period are often spent on their own needs leaving them less capable of effective parenting. It has been said that when children of divorce have their greatest need for parental involvement and nurturing, parents have the least to give (Wallerstein & J. B. Kelly, 1980).

As noted earlier, divorce is often a consequence of an erosion of love, a shift from feeling "in love" to simply "loving" or "caring."

Despite this shift, interpersonal attachment tends to persist (Donovan & Jackson, 1990; Kitson, 1982; Weiss, 1975). Repetitive separations and reconciliations are evidence of the strength of attachment and the difficulty of the decision to come apart. There is a sense of comfort in the relationship and in the shared physical environment. Dissolving the partnership and physically separating may well have a concomitant profound sense of loss even for those who are no longer "in love" and who *want* the divorce.

Divorce may be conceptualized as a "death" of an intimate partnership. As with the death of a loved one, the losses associated with divorce engage individuals in the grieving process. While grieving is a necessary, adaptive process, and unique from person to person, it may become debilitating to those who lack personal or social resources to effectively address loss. A meaning-making model of grief and loss represents a potential personal resource the client may not realize. Neimeyer (2001) postulates that, "meaning reconstruction in response to a loss is the central process in grieving" (p. 4). This reconstruction process may focus on past, present, or future. Consideration of outstanding interactions and events throughout the course of the early relationship and marriage, as well as review of the decision making process, allow opportunities for meaning reconstruction. Bereavement has been identified as a "choiceless event" in which one is "victimized" by loss (Neimeyer, 1998). The noninitiating partner, in particular, may be feeling victimized by the divorce. Meaning reconstruction may result in the displacement of the sense that one has been "victimized." If the individual retains the view that the ex-mate has victimized him or her, the therapist may shift the focus of the elaboration of meaning to include "survivor" and ultimately "thriver" self views.

I have experienced a common theme among many who attempt to reconcile their sense of loss regarding the ex-mate. It is confounding to have initiated the divorce, to have "fallen out of love" with the ex-mate, and to have no desire to reconcile, and yet to feel such intense sadness, dysphoria, and loss. In exploring this state, rather than the partner being the object of the feelings of loss, the meaning of the loss is best stated as, "*the illusion of what might have been.*" The dream of marrying and remaining together "*'til death do us part*" is a powerful ethic, a standard that persists in the face of relational emptiness. The reconstruction of this meaning has been valuable in clients' efforts to gain better "closure" on the marriage.

211

There is an associated reduction in the intensity of the feelings of loss, particularly as the client produces other meaningful beliefs that mitigate the "intrinsic permanence" view of marriage (Scanzoni, 1972).

The current and future life of the individual is even more subject to meaning reconstruction than is the past. During the transition period, however, the focus on meaning making may be biased toward making meaning out of the past, getting through today and tomorrow, and short-term future planning. In the divorce recovery period, after the initial adjustment has been accomplished, clients may be more ready to proactively reconstruct their current lives and revision their future.

Divorce related crises may occur at any point in the process and far after the divorce has been legally finalized (Granvold, 2000a, 2000b). Although risk assessment is an important consideration at any point in a treatment process with divorcing/divorced clients, it is particularly critical during transition. Vulnerabilities during this period include depreciated sense of self, depression, hopelessness, anxiety and fear of the unknown, substance abuse, loneliness, isolation, alienation, exploitation, violence, and sexually transmitted disease. This combination of vulnerabilities coupled with a depletion in coping abilities make the population particularly at risk of suicide, extreme depression, substance abuse, and, in rare instances, homicide. For example, the suicide rate of separated and divorced is far higher than their married or single counterparts (Stack, 1989; Trovato, 1987; Zeiss, Zeiss, & Johnston, 1980). Although subject to many vulnerabilities as noted above, depression, suicidal ideation and planning, and substance abuse are most commonly evident among separated and divorced individuals. Clients should be carefully evaluated for their ways of dealing with stress in the event they are putting themselves or others at risk, or alternatively, are experiencing significant maladjustment.

The following are examples of therapeutic goals during the transition phase (adapted from Granvold, 2002):

Goals of Transition phase

- Assess and treat suicidal and homicidal ideation and planning

- Assess death wishes (passive suicide)

- Assess alcohol use and prescription and illicit drug use

- Complete strengths and resiliency assessment

- Strategize about informing children, family and friends regarding the divorce

- Promote the expression of loss (emotionally, cognitively, behaviorally)

- Develop adaptive strategies for stress management during transition (for example, limit alcohol/drug use; check excessive investment in work; engage in deep muscle relaxation and healthy exercise)

- Facilitate effective relationships with children, family and friends

- Address effecting legal action to dissolve the marriage contract

As noted above, the transition phase requires attention to the specifics of the division of property, physical relocation, child custody, and child support—all of which stimulate emotional reactions. These considerations pose remarkable opportunities for conflict, divorce decision doubt, uncertainty regarding the future, and intense feelings of loss.

Postdivorce Recovery

Postdivorce recovery, as identified earlier, involves pervasive change. In addition to dealing with losses of a physical and emotional nature, one is challenged with redefining oneself and revisioning one's life. Now it is necessary to establish a monadic identity, independent of the "self" that evolved and was forged through years of intimate connectedness with the ex-mate. The path of life that had been relatively established and "known" no longer fits the novel territory in which one now travels. It is time for change. Among the changes being experienced are new role relationships with children (for example, single parenting), work mates, extended family, and friends. Dating, perhaps something one hasn't experienced in years, is being strongly considered or

213

actually being experienced. Dating provides opportunities for sexual expression, experimentation, and renewed views of self as a sexual being.

Commonly, self-esteem and feelings of self-worth markedly diminish during the entire divorce process, particularly for the noninitiator. In response to low self-appraisals and feelings such as depression, hurt, loss, and hopelessness, those in postdivorce recovery often withdraw and become isolated. Loneliness and preoccupation with loss prevail. Even though the individual may have remarkable personal qualities, a ready and varied support system, and a plethora of social and recreational opportunities, his or her experience in the moment may result in immobilization. Tom Glover, a resident of Pine Ridge Reservation, perhaps said it best. Reflecting on the enormity of problems on the reservation and the available opportunities, he observed: "We're surrounded by insurmountable opportunity" (Glover, 2004, p. 12). Although their challenges are very, very different, this quote captures the sentiment of so many dealing with divorce.

In postdivorce recovery, the remnants of the attempt to gain "closure" on the past may continue to receive attention. The preferential focus, however, is on generating and realizing new beginnings, revisioning oneself in a state of singlehood, and promoting the many new possibilities today and into the future. Constructivist theory and treatment strategies are extremely well suited for postdivorce issues. Lifespan orientation, multiple possible selves, strengths and possibilities perspectives, and activity—the proactive role one may assume in the experience of life—inform the therapist with efficacious approaches for application with postdivorce recovery clients. While grieving is a necessary, adaptive process, and unique from person to person, it may become debilitating to those who allow it to become "all-consuming." The following are examples of therapeutic goals during postdivorce recovery (adapted from Granvold, 2002):

- Delineate and dedicate efforts to the evolution of "possible selves" consistent with the revisioning of one's life

- Establish a quality relationship with children as a single parent (attend to their emotional needs and their need for structure in the reconstituted family)

214

- Develop an effective parallel parenting relationship with the ex-spouse

- Gain "closure" on the marriage (grieve and seek to "emotionally" accept the marriage as over)

- Promote efficacy expectations regarding present and future life satisfaction

- Generate rejuvenation goals across various categories of life (career, education, hobbies, interests, relationships, lifestyle, geographic and environmental circumstances)

- Seek intimate connectedness with others through clear delineation of partner/relationship qualities, active pursuit, deliberate relationship evaluation, and proactive decision making to terminate or maintain the relationship(s)

- Activate a lifestyle in which physical health and exercise are priorities

- Develop and rejuvenate sexuality

INTERVENTION

The divorce experience is viewed in the context of the life span. States of extreme disequilibrium, although discomforting, may produce remarkable adaptive change in the individual's on-going evolution. Divorce is conceptualized as a self-system perturbation with tremendous opportunity for constructive change and rejuvenation. Its positive potential is emphasized. The crisis potential of the experience may optimally result in increased knowledge of self and, if capitalized on, may stimulate the proactive establishment and movement toward creative change in the individual's course of life.

Therapy is focused on the personal meanings of clients' explicit statements with the objective to gain insight into broader systems of personal constructs (R. A. Neimeyer, 1993). The develop-

215

mental dimensions of the client's experience and its context are examined with attention given to primary attachment relationships, significant intimate relationships, and remarkable life events that may have strongly influenced self-schemata. Emotions, rather than being considered "negative," are treated as highly informative. Intervention tends to be "reflective, elaborative, and intensely personal, rather than persuasive, analytical, and technically instructive" (R.A. Neimeyer, 1993, p. 224). This is not to say that there isn't a persuasive motive in some forms of intervention. The goal of cognitive elaboration, for example, is to limit the strength of isolated meanings through the generation of "competing" constructs. I purposefully act energized and supportive of the constructs my clients specify that produce greater immediate positive consequences and future promise.

Although there is no narrowly defined model, the following enumeration is reflective of constructivist treatment of divorce:

1. Conceptualize divorce as a self-system perturbation.

2. Seek to access self-schemata activated by the divorce process with the objective of modifying core ordering processes through construct elaboration.

3. Explore primary attachment relationships as they relate to views of self and the world including the attachment relationship with the ex-spouse.

4. Promote a view of self as a multifaceted and ever-changing "system" of identity meanings, rather than a singular, fixed self.

5. Promote emotional expressiveness through guided discovery, imagery, imaginary dialogues (empty chair technique), and therapeutic rituals.

6. Utilize personal narratives and journaling as change mediums.

7. Accentuate client strengths, personal and social resources, creativity, coping capacities, and resiliency.

8 Collaborate with the client in constructing change mediums, models, and techniques with which the therapist has an expertise and that "fit" the client.

Although the therapist has expertise regarding both the process of divorce and human change processes, a non-authoritarian role is assumed in relation to the client (Granvold, 1996a; Mahoney, 1991; Neimeyer, 1996). The intervention is strategically the co-construction of the client and therapist.

CLINICAL EXAMPLES

In this section, several treatment approaches will be demonstrated, each reflective of constructivist theory and practice. The exemplars represent intervention with clients at various stages of the divorce process.

Journaling

Lorna and Ralph initiated counseling uncertain whether or not they wanted to remain married. Ralph expressed strong leanings toward divorce while Lorna strongly wanted to remain married. The initial treatment goal was to optimize the relationship. To this end, a variety of changes were sought (cognitive and behavioral) to improve their communication, intimacy (sensual and sexual), social life, and general quality of time together. After a time period, Ralph initiated a separation indicating feeling intensely smothered living together. He also expressed a need for space "to allow an opportunity for his feelings to grow." As part of the intervention, the couple used journaling to record the experiences with one another and while alone during the separation. The following are poignant excerpts of their struggle. The couple used journaling to bring their own thoughts and feelings into better focus, and a portion of our therapy sessions were devoted to journal content.

> *Lorna:* I wish I understood what you wanted. What you're doing. This situation has gotten me going so many different directions emotionally . . . the more I think about your choice to separate, the more disgusted I feel. . . . You may think

217

that because I show my anger, that I don't feel crushed. Well you have crushed my spirit many times, but never like this.

Lorna: While I do feel anger, it's love that I most want to show you. They can both be very intense, love and anger. Actually one sort of stems from the other. In this case, anger comes from pain/hurt, pain comes from caring/loving.

Ralph: This morning she cried me into staying. But why am I staying? For more abuse? More stress? We both say we'll change, but do we? "If I change any more, I'll lose myself. If she changes any more, she'll lose her mind." Daily. I feel it growing with each passing day. The anger. The cool glow of a deep burning. That which pushes me towards my decision. With every session, it grows. It is enough to make me want to make the decision *now*. Right now, there is only one decision, rather, one choice. I guess that doesn't make it much of a choice. Words are becoming harder and harder to come by as everyday my emotions run deeper. They are less expressible in ordered thoughts and more expressible as chaotic action.

Ralph: Did you realize you didn't love her?
Did you realize you couldn't live with her?
Did you realize how she was changing you?
Or was life just a little more empty with her in it?
Why live a life of regret when you can nip it in the bud?
Nobody wins.

Perhaps you, too, can sense the agony in this couple's words. The journaling excerpts communicated Lorna's love for Ralph, her uncertainty of what he wants, her disgust toward him for seeking the separation, her feelings of anger and an explanation of her passion. In other excerpts, Lorna expressed increasing frustration, hurt, resentment and a sense of impending doom. Ralph's entries trace his journey toward the decision to divorce. He sees futility in change and questions himself regarding the relationship. Ultimately, Ralph tearfully asked Lorna for a divorce. He had arrived at the decision and asked Lorna to "let me go."

Journaling appeared to be a very useful tool for this couple as they navigated their separation and the ultimate decision to divorce. Journal entries were used routinely in conjoint sessions and served as the basis for much of the deliberation as the couple sought a decision. Once the decision was made, the emotional responses of each partner to the decision were the primary focus of treatment. The couple was seen individually as well as conjointly during this time. The course of treatment shifted from efforts to optimize the marriage and decision making to the emotional and practical requirements of coming apart.

Cognitive Elaboration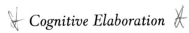

In the following example, a client who has been separated from her husband for seven months is approaching the legal finalization of the divorce. Although she did not initiate the divorce, she has felt "empty" in the relationship for several years. She was reared to believe the "intrinsic permanence" view of marriage: marriage has inherent value and one is morally obligated to sustain it despite one's satisfaction level (Scanzoni, 1972). The predominant construct she has in relation to the divorce becoming legally final is, "I'm a loser," a thought that is highly compatible with the philosophy about marital commitment that she has integrated. In the following excerpt, the objectives are: (1) to demonstrate the unappealing consequences of the predominant belief, (2) to introduce the idea that there may be other ways of viewing the situation (that her "reality" of the divorce may take on several meanings), and (3) to determine the consequences of one of the alternative meanings. Connecting her initial construct with other beliefs such as the intrinsic permanence of marriage ethic and other self-schemata followed this early cognitive elaboration effort.

> *Therapist*: What crosses your mind when you think of the divorce being final?
>
> *Client*: What a loser I am.
>
> *Therapist*: I see. What are the consequences of thinking of yourself as a loser?
>
> *Client*: Well I don't feel very good about it. . . . I feel down . . . depressed. And I don't want to see anyone.
>
> *Therapist*: So the thought, "I am a loser because I'm divorced" results in feeling down, depressed and you want to withdraw from people.
>
> *Client*: That's right.
>
> *Therapist*: Do you like these results—depression and withdrawal?
>
> *Client*: Not really, but I don't see myself changing any time soon.

219

Therapist: Since you really don't like these consequences, suppose we explore your situation and see if there are any other ways of looking at it. Think back once again to the divorce being final, what other thoughts do you have about it, besides "I'm a loser."

Client: I guess that I am somewhat relieved because we really hadn't been getting along for years.

Therapist: Okay, so one other thought is, "I'm relieved." What other thoughts do you have? Perhaps you can come up with several more.

Client: Let me see (pauses to think). Well, I got married when I was 19 years old so I have never been on my own as an adult. This will give me an opportunity to sort of find out who I am. I've been Joe's wife for ten years. Also, I will be free of Joe's criticism. I could never seem to do things right in his eyes.

Therapist: Let's go over these thoughts now. In addition to "I'm a loser," you have added, "I'm relieved," "I'll have an opportunity to find out who I am as a single adult", and "I'll be free of Joe's criticism." Have I missed anything, or stated anything incorrectly?

Client: No, I think those are the other thoughts that I mentioned.

Therapist: Something important has happened here, Sue. You've established that there is more than one way of looking at the divorce. And perhaps you've only begun to scratch the surface of the many, many thoughts you may actually have about the divorce. Earlier I asked you for the consequences of the thought, "I'm a loser." Now, take one of the other thoughts and let's see what the consequences are of that thought. For a moment, contemplate the thought, "I'll be free of Joe's criticism." (Pause). What kinds of feelings do you have now?

Client: I feel somewhat relieved. I can't say that I feel good, but I don't feel worthless like I sometimes did when Joe would start in on me.

Therapist: So, rather than feeling down, you feel relieved, and not *bad* about yourself.

Client: That's right.

Therapist: Again keeping the thought, "I'll be free of Joe's criticism," do you feel as inclined to stay away from people, to withdraw?

220

Client: No, not really. I'm not ready to party or anything, but I have a few girl friends that I wouldn't mind seeing.

This example demonstrates the following:

- Exposure of a negative construct, "I'm a loser."

- Determination and analysis of the consequences of the thought (both feelings and behavior).

- Personal appraisal of the *consequences* ("Do you like these consequences?").

- Generation of alternative constructs as a means of elaborating on the active meaning.

- Selection of one of the alternative constructs to demonstrate the benefits of cognitive elaboration.

- Determination and analysis of the *consequences* of the new construct (feelings and behavior).

Therapeutic Rituals

Mahoney (2003) provides an extensive description of rituals and their many functions in constructive therapy. Among their potential qualities, rituals are trial and error endeavors; may reflect symbolic meanings of past, present and future; may be aimed at skill development; reflect basic contrasts in life (e.g. ending and beginning); and may involve support group or significant others. I believe that rituals aptly reflect the constructive perspective that, "*the power to change lies in processes* rather than in specific procedures" (Mahoney, 2003, p. 58). Change takes place in "curious" ways. The processes of change know no one path. Many different actions may be taken to achieve a desired outcome; there is no "right" way. Also, when invoking the use of rituals and many other techniques as well, timing is a critical consideration. For example, implosion therapy techniques used in postdivorce recovery to overcome the loss of the loved one may promote regression if they are employed too soon, and are rather impotent in effect if employed too late (Granvold, 1994).

Rituals are active elements in life experience. People are already engaged in ritualized behavior and activities when they become our clients. Family rituals around such events as birthdays, holidays, graduations, quinceañeras, and bar mizvahs are part of relationship history and are often redesigned following divorce. Therapeutic rituals may be used to mark important transitions and events (Ahrons, 1994). The development of therapeutic rituals with divorcing clients involves creative therapist-client interchange in the generation of possible enactments followed by client experimentation to determine if desired change results from the ritual(s).

Wedding ring ritual. Arlene was having difficulty overcoming her sense of loss following her divorce from Tim. She viewed her strong family values and dedication to Tim and their marriage as current barriers to letting go. She was particularly distressed about what to do with her wedding ring—the symbol of the never-ending bond and commitment she *thought* she and Tim had in common. The thought of disposing of the ring represented views of the marriage as valueless and illegitimate. She treasured many aspects of the years that she and Tim had shared, the most meaningful being their two children. The fate of the ring—the symbol of many loving, meaningful years—was discussed in session. Many alternative courses of action were considered, including saving the ring in its current state to pass on to her daughter. Finally, Arlene decided to have the ring melted down, re-designed as a necklace in a contemporary style, and the diamonds re-set. The transformation of her ring became a metaphor for the transformation of her relationship with Tim. The sentimental value of the "ring" was retained but its shape, use, and personal meaning were altered as a reflection of Arlene today.

Unsent letter technique. Sally's husband began dating another woman during their separation. Now divorced, she has continued to see her ex-husband and his girlfriend at her son's sporting events. Although she has no interest in reconciliation, their open displays of affection in Sally's presence have triggered extreme emotional reactions in Sally immediately and later. Among the actions taken to process her feelings of betrayal, sadness, hurt, and anger, Sally has found the unsent letter ritual to be effective. Sally concluded that direct confrontation of her ex-husband would, in effect, let him know of her struggle. After several iterations of the unsent letter ritual, Sally found herself less aroused by her ex-husband's "public display of affection" behavior.

CONCLUSION

The demands and potential for change that result from divorce provide incredible opportunities to implement a wide range of constructive therapy interventions. These clients are already experiencing remarkable change. Our tasks are to introduce, promote, and support change processes that take form and meaning through creative and collaborative interchange between client and therapist. Practice decisions should be informed by our knowledge of the divorce process, constructive conceptualization of the divorce experience, and constructive practice procedures. Beyond knowledge, constructivists view client and therapist human creativity as necessary ingredients in realizing paths to change that, although potentially discomforting, honor flexibility in meaning making and stimulate clients' proactive participation in their lives.

REFERENCES

Ahrons, C. R. (1994). *The good divorce: Keeping your family together when your marriage comes apart.* New York: HarperCollins.

Amato, P. R., & Previti, D. (2003). People's reasons for divorcing: Gender, social class, the life course, and adjustment. *Journal of Family Issues, 24,* 602-626.

Anderson, W. T. (Ed.). (1995). *The truth about the truth.* New York: Tarcher/Putnam.

Brown, E. M. (1976). Divorce counseling. In D. H. L. Olson, (Ed.), *Treating relationships* (pp. 399-429). Lake Mills, IA: Graphic Publishing.

Catron, L. S., & Chiriboga, D. A. (1991). Passage through divorce: A transitions perspective. In D. A. Chiriboga, L. S. Catron, & Associates, *Divorce: Crisis, challenge, or relief?* (pp. 97-124). New York: New York University Press.

Donovan, R. L., & Jackson, B. L. (1990). Deciding to divorce: A process guided by social exchange, attachment, and cognitive dissonance theories. *Journal of Divorce, 13,* 23-35.

Gergen, K. J. (1991). *The saturated self: Dilemmas of identity in contemporary life.* New York: Basic Books.

Glover, V. (2004). *Keeping heart on Pine Ridge: Family ties, warrior culture, commodity foods, rez dogs, and the Sacred.* Summertown, TN: Keeping Voices.

Gottman, J. M. (1999). *The marriage clinic: A scientifically based marital therapy.* New York: Norton.

Granvold, D. K. (1983). Structured separation for marital treatment and decision-making. *Journal of Marital and Family Therapy, 9*, 403-412.

Granvold, D. K. (1989). Postdivorce treatment. In M. R. Textor (Ed.), *The divorce and divorce therapy handbook* (pp. 197-223). Northvale, NJ: Aronson.

Granvold, D. K. (1994). Cognitive-behavioral divorce therapy. In D.K. Granvold (Ed.), *Cognitive and behavioral treatment: Methods and applications* (pp. 222-246). Pacific Grove, CA: Brooks/Cole.

Granvold, D. K. (1996a). Challenging roles of the constructive therapist: Expert and agent of social responsibility. *Constructivism in the Human Sciences, 1*, 16-21.

Granvold, D. K. (1996b). Constructivist psychotherapy. Families in Society: *The Journal of Contemporary Human Services, 77*, 345-359.

Granvold, D. K. (2000a). Divorce. In F. M. Dattilio & A. Freeman (Eds.), *Cognitive-behavioral strategies in crisis intervention* (2nd ed., pp. 362-384). New York: Guilford.

Granvold, D. K. (2000b). The crisis of divorce: Cognitive-behavioral and constructivist assessment and treatment. In A. R. Roberts (Ed.), *Crisis intervention handbook: Assessment, treatment, and research* (2nd ed., pp. 307-336). New York: Oxford University Press.

Granvold, D. K. (2001). Constructivist theory. In P. Lehmann & N. Coady (Eds.), *Theoretical perspectives for direct social work practice* (pp. 303-325). New York: Springer.

Granvold, D. K. (2002). Divorce therapy: The application of cognitive-behavioral and constructivist treatment methods. In A. R. Roberts & G. J. Greene (Eds.), *Social Workers' desk reference* (pp. 587-590). New York: Oxford.

Granvold, D. K., & Tarrant, R. (1983). Structured marital separation as a marital treatment method. *Journal of Marital and Family Therapy, 9*, 189-198.

Guidano, V. F. (1988). A systems, process-oriented approach to cognitive therapy. In K. S. Dobson (Ed.), *Handbook of cognitive-behavioral therapies* (pp. 307-354). New York: Guilford.

Janis, I. L., & Mann, L. (1977). *Decision making: A psychological analysis of conflict, choice, and commitment.* New York: Free Press.

Kitson, G. C. (1982). Attachment to the spouse in divorce: A scale and its application. *Journal of Marriage and the Family, 44*, 379-391.

Leitner, L. M., & Faidley, A.J. (2002). Disorder, diagnoses, and the struggles of humanness. In J. D. Raskin & S. K. Bridges (Eds.), *Studies in meaning: Exploring constructivist psychology* (pp. 99-121). New York: Pace University Press.

Mahoney, M. J. (1991). *Human change processes: The scientific foundations of psychotherapy.* New York: Basic Books.

Mahoney, M. J. (2003). *Constructive psychotherapy: A practical guide.* New York: Guilford.

Mahoney, M. J., & Granvold, D. K. (2005). Constructivism and psychotherapy. *World Psychiatry.* 4(2), 74-77.

Markus, H., & Nurius, P. S. (1986). Possible selves. *American Psychologist, 41,* 954-969.

McNamee, S. (2002). The social construction of disorder: From pathology to potential. In J. D. Raskin & S. K. Bridges (Eds.), *Studies in meaning: Exploring constructivist psychology* (pp. 143-168). New York: Pace University Press.

Neimeyer, R. A. (1993). An appraisal of constructivist psychotherapies. *Journal of Consulting and Clinical Psychology, 61,* 221-234.

Neimeyer, R. A. (1996). Process interventions for the constructive therapist. In H. Rosen & K. T. Kuehlwein, (Eds.), *Constructing realities: Meaning-making perspectives for psychotherapists* (pp. 371-411). San Francisco, CA: Jossey-Bass.

Neimeyer, R. A. (1998). *Lessons of loss: A guide to coping.* New York: Primis Custom Publishing.

Neimeyer, R. A. (2001). Meaning reconstruction and loss. In R.A. Neimeyer (Ed.), *Meaning reconstruction and the experience of loss.* Washington, DC: American Psychological Association.

Neimeyer, R. A., & Raskin, J. D. (2000). On practicing postmodern therapy in modern times. In R. A. Neimeyer & J. D. Raskin (Eds.), *Constructions of disorder: Meaning-making frameworks for psychotherapy* (pp. 3-14). Washington, DC: American Psychological Association.

Neimeyer, R. A., & Raskin, J. D. (2001). Varieties of constructivism in psychotherapy. In K. S. Dobson (Ed.), *Handbook of cognitive-behavioral therapies* (2nd ed., pp. 393-430). New York: Guilford.

Nurius, P. S., & Berlin, S. B. (1994). Treatment of negative self-concept and depression. In D.K. Granvold (Ed.), *Cognitive and behavioral treatment: Methods and applications* (pp. 249-271). Pacific Grove, CA: Brooks/Cole.

Raskin, J. D. (2002). Constructivism in psychology: Personal construct psychology, radical constructivism, and social constructionism. In J. D. Raskin & S. K. Bridges (Eds.), *Studies in meaning: Exploring constructivist psychology* (pp. 1-25). New York: Pace University.

Raskin, J. D., & Lewandowski, A. M. (2000). The construction of disorder as human enterprise. In R. A. Neimeyer & J. D. Raskin (Eds.), *Constructions of disorder: Meaning-making frameworks for psychotherapy* (pp. 15-40). Washington, DC: American Psychological Association.

Saleebey, D. (2006). Introduction: Power in the people. In D. Saleebey (Ed.), *The strengths perspective in social work practice* (4th ed., pp. 1-22). Boston: Allyn and Bacon.

Scanzoni, J. (1972). *Sexual bargaining*. Englewood Cliffs, NJ: Prentice-Hall.

Stack, S. (1989). The impact of divorce on suicide in Norway, 1951-1980. *Journal of Marriage and the Family, 51*, 229-238.

Stanley, S. (2001, January). *Helping couples fight for their marriages: Research on the prediction and prevention of marital failure*. Paper presented at the Annual Conference of the Texas Association for Marriage and Family Therapy, Dallas, TX.

Trovato, F. (1987). A longitudinal analysis of divorce and suicide in Canada. *Journal of marriage and the family, 49*, 193-203.

Wallerstein, J. S., & Kelly, J. B. (1980). *Surviving the breakup: How children and parents cope with divorce*. New York: Basic Books.

Weiss, R. S. (1975). *Marital separation*. New York: Basic Books.

Zeiss, A. M., Zeiss, R. A., & Johnston, S. M. (1980). Sex differences in initiation and adjustment to divorce. *Journal of Divorce, 4*, 21-33.

PART IV

PROFESSIONAL ISSUES IN CONSTRUCTIVIST THERAPY

Personal Construct Psychotherapy in a National Health Service Setting: Does Survival Mean Selling Out?

David A. Winter

need for
emp. proof
of Frtmnt.

The world in which constructivist therapists practice may at times appear all too "real." Particularly in public health systems, the demands of this world include the sheer volume of individuals referred for treatment of psychological problems, and the severity and complexity of the latter. Other demands derive from the requirements of purchasers of health services for the provision of "evidence-based" or "empirically validated" therapies, with associated pressures for manualization of treatments, and for these to be targeted at particular diagnostic groups. In the view of some constructivist and humanistic therapists, the likely result is the "empirical violation" of their treatments (Bohart, O'Hara, & Leitner, 1998).

In this chapter, I shall focus on the provision of one form of constructivist therapy (personal construct psychotherapy) in a setting (the British National Health Service) characterized by several of these demands. Particular consideration will be given to whether the issues concerned can be addressed without selling out constructivist principles and sacrificing the integrity of the therapeutic approach.

VOLUME OF REFERRALS

Faced with a very high demand for psychological therapies, and consequent lengthy waiting lists, the response of some services has been to place stringent time limits on treatments or to increase the use of group therapies. This has implications for personal construct psychotherapy, which are discussed next.

Time-Limited Therapy

Various features of personal construct psychotherapy render it conducive to a time-limited approach. Among these are the inclusion in the personal construct psychotherapist's repertoire of assessment techniques that may allow focusing of the therapy on particular aspects of the client's construing; the encouragement of experimentation in the outside world, both during and following the therapy contract; and the sharing with clients of concepts and tools that facilitate their becoming effective "personal scientists" and integrating the therapist's construct system with their own systems (Semerari, 1989).

Repertory grid technique is one method that may reveal aspects of a client's construing at a low level of awareness on which therapy might usefully focus. For example, Bell, Winter, and Watson (2004) have developed a method that allows the identification of elements (usually people) in a grid that present a conflict in that constructs are applied to them in a way that differs from their application to other elements in the grid. Alternatively, consideration of similarities and differences in the way in which elements are construed may be fruitful. For example, Ali's puzzlement at recurrent nightmares in which he was being attacked by a cobra was lessened when a grid revealed that the cobra was viewed as very similar to his ex-wife. Discussion of this finding allowed the focus of therapy to shift to a productive consideration of issues concerning guilt.

However, it is the identification of conflictual relationships between constructs in a repertory grid that provides one of the clearest examples of a focused personal construct approach amenable to brief therapy. This may be illustrated by a method developed by Feixas and colleagues (Feixas & Saúl, 2005; Feixas, Saúl, & Sánchez, 2000) to allow the resolution of dilemmas, particularly those involving positive implications of the client's symptoms. In this method, the client's dilemmas are defined by relationships in a grid between two types of constructs: *discrepant constructs*, in which the self and ideal self are situated at opposite poles; and *congruent constructs*, in which the self and ideal self are at the same pole. A dilemma occurs when the correlation between a discrepant and a congruent construct is such that movement of the self towards the ideal self on the former would imply movement away from the ideal self on the latter. Consider the case of Tom, who construed himself as "passive" and his ideal self as "assertive." "Assertive" was the contrast pole for this discrepant construct, which was positively correlated with a congruent construct of "unselfish-demanding," on which Tom placed both himself and his ideal self at the "unselfish" pole. He was faced by the dilemma that to construe himself as assertive would necessitate seeing himself as more demanding. Therefore, his lack of response to an assertiveness training program was hardly surprising (Winter, 1987).

Feixas and Saúl (2005) initially reformulate the client's problem in terms of the dilemma, namely as "a conflict between the desire to change and the difficulty to do that" (p. 139). They then employ various techniques to elaborate the dilemma, elucidating its meaning. For example, the implications of the dilemma may be traced by laddering (Hinkle, 1965), in which superordinate constructs are identified by successively asking the client at which pole of a construct he or she would prefer to be located and why; or Tschudi's (1977) ABC technique, in which the client is asked to indicate the advantages and disadvantages of each pole of a construct. Controlled elaboration of the dilemma may then be attempted by viewing it from the perspective of Kelly's (1955) Experience Cycle, in which the person's anticipation concerning an event is either confirmed or disconfirmed by an encounter with the event, with the possibility of subsequent reconstruing. Thus, the therapist might explore with the client occasions when constructs relating to the dilemma have been validated or invalidated. In addition, the therapist might explore whether particular individuals in the client's life served as prototypes for the two poles of the dilemma. In some cases, these individuals might be the client's parents. In Tom's case one parent, his mother, was the prototype for both poles of the dilemma. When he was a child she oscillated between occasions when Tom saw her as extremely passive and unselfish and rarer occasions when she was assertive to the point of being physically violent. Identification of prototypes for a dilemma may allow the use of time binding or person binding (Kelly, 1955), in which the therapist indicates that the client's construing was entirely appropriate in anticipating the people concerned at that particular point in time, but is now anachronistic. It may also allow the use of narrative elaboration methods, such as the consideration of dialogues between the prototypical people. A related method of elaboration of the dilemma is to dramatize it by using two-chair technique (Greenberg, 1979) to carry out a dialogue between the two poles of the dilemma.

Following elaboration of the dilemma, various methods may be used in an attempt to resolve it. The client may be asked to identify individuals who are exceptions to the dilemma (for example, in Tom's case, people who are able to be assertive but unselfish). Discussion of these individuals may allow alternatives to the dilemma to be elaborated. Such alternatives may also be elaborated in imagination or by asking the client to write a characterization of the self as if the dilemma were resolved or to role play situations in which he or she is characterized by the previously incompatible preferred poles of the two constructs involved in the dilemma. A more elaborate role play procedure would be the application of Kelly's (1955) fixed-role therapy, in which the client takes on for two weeks a role outlined in a character sketch, in this case one exemplifying the resolved dilemma.

 Fixed-role therapy is but one of several methods involving homework assignments that can be used by the personal construct psychotherapist to encourage experimentation in the outside world, consistent with Kelly's (1955, p. 1067) view that "the therapy room can be a laboratory and the client's community a field project." As R. A. Neimeyer and Winter (2005) have described, such methods may include journaling, in which clients are asked, with the aid of facilitative questions, to reflect upon the results of a laddering exercise (R. A. Neimeyer, Anderson, & Stockton, 2001) or upon their experiences of some other assignment, such as spending a period of time in front of a mirror. They may also include exercises designed to elaborate an alternative to the symptom in clients for whom this has become their "way of life" (Fransella, 1970). Thus, the client might be asked to write a characterization of the self without the symptom or to engage in activities that may facilitate the elaboration of a symptom-free self. For example, Rodney, who was unable to ejaculate, was given various assignments with the aim of increasing his awareness, and elaborating his construing, of pleasurable bodily sensations—including his sexual responses. These exercises included keeping a daily record of the frequency, and degree of pleasure associated with, his sexual urges; going to the gym; and luxuriating in the bath (Winter, 1988).

good analogy

Case Example: "Barry Potter"

Some of the methods described above may be illustrated by the six-session treatment of Chris, who had sought out personal construct psychotherapy after unsatisfactory experiences with various other forms of therapy. Chris experienced anxiety following difficulties in his work situation, which led to his early retirement. Chris's repertory grid indicated that susceptibility to anxiety carried various positive implications for him, being associated with the following preferred poles of some of his other constructs: "emotional" (as opposed to "stoical"), "visceral" (as opposed to "cognitive"), "selfless" (as opposed to "calculating"), "transparent" (as opposed to having a "hidden agenda"), "trustworthy" (as opposed to "untrustworthy"), and "questioning" (as opposed to "conformist"). To explore these dilemmas further, two of his constructs were laddered. On the first of these, "susceptible to anxiety" versus "doesn't feel anxious," the superordinate implication of the latter pole, which he preferred, was "responding better to situations," which implied, in turn, "finding a way of pursuing interests and through or round difficulties," "feeling better about self," "being employable," "having a sense of satisfaction and fulfillment, and being part of the social fabric," and "providing welfare and wellbeing." On the second construct, "selfless" versus "calculating," the former pole implied "feeling better about self from a moral perspective," which implied "always thinking about the consequences of my behavior on other people." However, his dilemma was clearly indicated by the fact that the contrast pole that he provided for the latter construct, laughing as he realized what he was saying, was "successful and held in high regard," which in turn implied being employable. For Chris, then, while feeling better about himself in terms of his ability to respond to situations and difficulties carried the implication of being employable, feeling better about himself morally carried the implication of being unemployable. The laddering was followed by exploration of the historical roots of his construing of anxiety by the identification of people who had served as the prototypes of his constructions. He was also encouraged to think of people who might be able to combine lack of anxiety or success with selflessness.

Much of Chris's life was structured around ruminating and "ranting" in self-talk, often in the early hours of the morning, about the injustices that he considered that he had suffered at the hands of his employers and, subsequently, the mental health system. He wrote a stream of letters to government departments about the former and papers for psychotherapy journals about the latter. Virtually his only oasis was provided by his ventures into ceramics. Partly in order to help him to experiment with an alternative way of life, we decided to embark upon fixed-role therapy. In view of his concerns about the power differential in psychotherapy, a collaborative approach was adopted in which both he and I prepared a fixed-role sketch, with the intention that we would agree on a final sketch combining features of the two. Coincidentally, but also perhaps revealing a degree of commonality in our construing that might have been conducive to a facilitative therapeutic process (Landfield, 1971), the names that we chose for the fixed-role character both reflected his interest in ceramics: in Chris's sketch, this was Cassius Clay and in mine, Barry Potter. There were various other similarities between the two sketches, but it was eventually decided that he would take on for a short period the Barry Potter role, the sketch of which read as follows:

> Barry Potter has not had the easiest of lives, but every setback that he has suffered seems to have strengthened his resolve, as well as providing a well of experience and emotion from which he is able to draw in his creative art. This does not mean that he is always, or even most of the time, able to identify explicitly the roots and meaning of his art work, only that he is aware that one aspect of this work is that it enables him to give expression to some of his feelings concerning his life experiences, as well as to explore ways of resolving conflicts. His art has also allowed him to develop contacts with a number of like-minded people, who have generally not been very accepting of social conventions but for whom the world of art has provided a social niche. In some cases, this has involved opportunities to achieve a degree of success; in others, merely an oasis in the midst of a more conventional working life.

> Barry is always eager to explore new ideas, which he does energetically and with commitment, although usually also with a healthy skepticism. Indeed, he sometimes wakes early, thinking about the latest area that has excited his considerable intellectual curiosity. One such area has been Eastern philosophy, and in particular the Buddhist notion that suffering may be reduced by letting go of attachments, whether these be to material things or fixed ideas and feelings about oneself or one's past. He is interested in the way in which such an approach may provide more of a sense of acceptance, freedom, and control while not requiring one to discount one's past experiences.

234

He has not always suffered fools gladly, but he attempts, with varying degrees of success, to see the world through the eyes of the people with whom he comes into contact. He therefore generally values, and tries to understand the opinions of, other people, even those with whom he disagrees. He finds that this provides the best basis for communication with others, including the occasional possibility of some satisfying and productive relationships. In such relationships, his sense of humor and confidence often emerge, and he is able not to feel particularly anxious, while remaining caring, trustworthy, and transparent.

Rather than fully embarking on fixed-role therapy, Chris's use of the role was, when he next engaged in an early morning rant, to have a conversation between Barry and his ranting self, which he called Billy. This enabled him to take a humorous perspective on his situation, which, as Viney (1985) has indicated, may facilitate the consideration of alternative constructions. His post-treatment repertory grid indicated a considerable reduction in the number and intensity of his dilemmas.

Although it has proved possible to practice personal construct psychotherapy effectively with some clients on the basis of a six- or twelve-session renewable treatment contract, this is not to say that such brief therapy is appropriate with every client. For example, in clients with whom a dependency transference on the therapist has been encouraged, or whose construing has loosened considerably during therapy, a more lengthy period of therapy may be necessary. This is also likely to be the case in approaches, such as experiential personal construct psychotherapy (Leitner, 1988), that focus on role relationships, including that between therapist and client.

Group Therapy

Personal construct psychotherapy was originally adapted for use in a group format by Kelly (1955), and there has been a burgeoning of such applications by post-Kellyan personal construct psychotherapists. While the use of therapy groups makes economic sense when the demand for treatment is high, it also has a theoretical rationale from a personal construct perspective. Thus, the therapy group may provide an interpersonal laboratory for relatively controlled social experiments, and as Kelly (1955) indicated, it may enable the client to develop a more comprehensive social role; to revise the limiting constructions that Kelly

235

termed preemptive and constellatory; and to disperse dependencies rather than, for example, focusing these on one individual. In addition, there is considerable research evidence from repertory grid studies that group therapy can facilitate reconstruing, including viewing the self more favorably and as more similar to other people (Winter, 1997). The latter finding is relatively specific to group therapy, and is consistent with Yalom's (1970) view that the experience of "universality" is a principal curative factor in this form of treatment.

Kelly's original stage model of group psychotherapy is now rarely used, and those therapists who have attempted to do so have expressed frustration that their groups did not follow a neat pattern of development from one stage to the next (Dunnett & Llewellyn, 1988; Morris, 1977). More useful than approaching therapy groups in terms of a fixed sequence of stages is a more superordinate view of Kelly's group stages as involving a progression from experimentation within, to experimentation outside, the group. In order to facilitate, as well as to provide some control over, such experimentation, personal construct psychotherapy groups have generally employed structured exercises, one of the most commonly used of which has been Landfield and Rivers' (1975) Interpersonal Transaction (IT) Group. Sessions of such a group commence with "rotating dyads" in which each group member has a brief interaction with every other on a theme provided by the therapist. Members then discuss their experience of the interactions in a plenary phase of the group. A wide range of other structured approaches have been used in personal construct psychotherapy groups with children and adolescents (Agnew, 1985; Jackson, 1990; Truneckova & Viney, 2005; Viney & Henry, 2002), adults of working age (Cummins, 2005; Dunnett & Llewellyn, 1988), and older adults (Botella, 1991); and in clients with physical health issues (Foster & Viney, 2005; Lane & Viney, 2005a, 2005b) as well as those presenting with psychological problems. These have included modifications of fixed-role therapy for use in the group setting (Beail & Parker, 1991; Epting & Nazario, 1987; Kelly, 1955). In addition, Forster's (1991) dependable strengths articulation procedure, which has been used to develop more positive self-construing in non-clinical populations, may be of value in the clinical setting.

Both theoretically and in terms of research evidence, there are arguments for the transition of a therapy group from a structured to a relatively unstructured format. As G. J. Neimeyer and Merluzzi

(1982) have described, initial structuring of the group can facilitate self-disclosure and the use and testing out of psychological constructions of others, which in turn is likely to lead to enhanced ability of members to construe each others' construction processes and increased group cohesion. An approach of this type was attempted by Gordon and Giles (1999) in their National Health Service group for women survivors of childhood sexual abuse, which initially employed an interpersonal transaction group format but then dispensed with this because "it was interfering with the developing group process and the flow of discussion and exploration" (p. 498). Their experience contrasts with more positive reports of the use of such groups with this client population (Alexander, R. A. Neimeyer, Follette, Moore, & Harter, 1989; R. A. Neimeyer, Harter, & Alexander, 1991). The poor attendance at Gordon and Giles' group following cessation of the interpersonal transaction group sessions may perhaps be related to the fact that the therapists switched to the use of a group analytic model. An investigation of the interventions of personal construct and group analytic therapists has indicated significant differences between these two approaches (Winter, 1997), and the transition from one to the other may have been confusing and anxiety-provoking for clients. For example, although the therapists indicate that they "avoided in-depth interpretations and comments that could be construed as critical" (p. 498) in the second phase of the group, that they may not have exactly adopted Kelly's (1955) credulous attitude in this phase is indicated by such statements about dropouts as that she "left the group prematurely, purporting to be better" (p. 500). A therapy group in which there is a transition from structured to less structured sessions, but in which a personal construct model is consistently applied in both these phases, may be likely to be more effective. Two examples will now be given of National Health Service groups that did adopt such an approach.

Example 1

A series of repertory grid studies of agoraphobia have consistently indicated that clients presenting with this problem constrict their worlds to avoid situations of interpersonal conflict, their construing of which is poorly elaborated and which are therefore likely to be anxiety-provoking (Winter & Gournay, 1987;

Winter, 1989; Winter, Gournay, & Metcalfe, 1999). This constriction tends to limit their worlds to partners whose construing is very similar to their own, and who are therefore likely to be constant sources of validation. These studies also provided evidence that agoraphobics and their partners tended to share an idealistic fantasy of what the future would hold if only the client lost his or her agoraphobic symptoms, except that this might carry a risk of marital infidelity. On the assumption that the aspects of construing identified in these studies served to maintain clients' agoraphobic symptoms, a manualized group treatment approach targeting these areas was developed (Winter & Metcalfe, 2005), to be employed in conjunction with behavioral exposure therapy as a means of encouraging experimentation (Kelly, 1970). The first three personal construct group sessions were structured in an interpersonal transaction group format, focusing on elaboration of construing of interpersonal conflict; exploration and reconstruction of negative implications of independence and the ability to go out; and elaboration of a favorable yet realistic construction of the non-phobic self. Three further personal construct group sessions were conducted in a less structured manner, with clients' partners being invited to the first two of these. Research investigation of this intervention indicated that it resulted in greater improvement in symptoms, coupled with changes in construing, than when clients were on the waiting list, and was associated with a more facilitative treatment process than supportive therapy, and at least a comparable outcome (Winter, Gournay, Metcalfe, & Rossotti, 2006).

Example 2

"Borderline personality disorder" is the latest in a long list of psychiatric nosological categories developed to accommodate people who do not comfortably fit in the existing diagnostic system. The *DSM-IV* criteria for this diagnosis may be reframed in terms of such characteristics as preemptive construing; slot rattling, the reconstruing of a person or event at the opposite pole of a construct to that which was previously applied to it; and impulsivity reflected in foreshortening of the "Circumspection-Preemption-Control Cycle," which Kelly considered to characterize decision-making (Gillman-Smith & Watson, 2005; Winter, Watson, Gillman-Smith, Gilbert, & Acton, 2003).

This latter cycle, in which there is consideration of all the constructs involved in a decision, followed by focusing on the most superordinate of these constructs, and the application of one pole of this construct to the issue in question, has been used to delineate the phases of a personal construct group psychotherapy approach for clients with this diagnosis. The initial experiment with this approach, in which it has been compared with dialectical behavior therapy, alternates 30 group sessions with 30 individual personal construct psychotherapy sessions. The first phase of the group, located in the circumspection phase of the cycle, employs an interpersonal transaction group format, with such topics as "pros and cons of sharing emotional difficulties" and "when and when not to trust others." The second phase, also characterized by circumspection, involves elaboration of the complaint and of construing of the self and ideal self, as well as the facilitation of propositional construing. The third phase, with its encouragement of experimentation both within and outside the group, represents the preemption phase of the cycle. It includes the use of time-binding and of fixed-role sketches. In the final phase of the group, the focus is on control, and there is tightening of construing as well as consideration of potential difficulties in maintaining alternative constructions, and possible ways of overcoming these difficulties. At the last session of one of the groups, the members brainstormed the following list of what they would take away from the group experience (Gillman-Smith & Watson, 2005, p. 196):

- The knowledge that I am not alone in how I feel;

- New friends;

- The realization that life is worth living;

- Stuff I've learned about myself;

- The ability to challenge myself;

- Coping techniques;

- Our lunacy, or "accepting how mad I am";

- Accepting that some things cannot change

Although the examples of personal construct group psychotherapy presented above have been conducted with homogeneous client groups, as has been the case with several other applications of this treatment approach (Winter, 1992), the therapist needs to be attentive to the danger that groups of like-minded individuals may only serve to validate members' construing and to elaborate the "way of life" presented by their symptoms. Heterogeneous groups may offer greater possibilities for experimentation.

SEVERITY AND COMPLEXITY OF CLIENT PROBLEMS

Problem Severity

The treatment by Gillman-Smith and Watson (2005) of clients diagnosed with "borderline personality disorder" is consistent with Kelly's (1955, p. 1156) view that "group psychotherapy may be the treatment of choice for seriously disturbed clients." It also indicates that personal construct psychotherapy is by no means contraindicated for clients with severe problems. Indeed, one of the first reports of the use of personal construct psychotherapy in the British National Health Service setting concerned clients diagnosed as thought disordered schizophrenics (Bannister, Adams-Webber, Penn, & Radley, 1975), and several other examples from this setting have been provided of its application with clients in the "psychotic" spectrum (Allen, 2005; Bannister, 1985; Procter, 1987). Other groups of clients whose problems may be regarded as of considerable severity are those who pose a risk to others or themselves. Personal construct approaches have been applied with the former group in National Health Service forensic settings (e.g. Houston, 1998), but it is on the latter group, those who deliberately harm themselves, that we shall focus. Such behavior is on the increase in the United Kingdom, as in several other countries, particularly in young men, and it places considerable demands on the National Health Service. A personal

240

construct psychotherapy approach developed for deliberate self-harmers will now be described.

Personal Construct Therapy and Deliberate Self-Harm

The extension of Kelly's (1961) classification of different forms of suicide to encompass types of deliberate self-harm has provided the basis for a personal construct psychotherapeutic intervention for people presenting at a National Health Service Accident and Emergency Department following self-harm (R. A. Neimeyer & Winter, 2006; Winter, 2005a; Winter, Bhandari, Metcalfe, Riley, Sireling, Watson, & Lutwyche, 2000). This commences with two sessions, the second of which may include one of the client's significant others, in which a personal construct formulation of the client's self-harm is developed. The therapeutic approach that is adopted in the next four sessions of the renewable six-session treatment contract is tailored to this formulation. For example, with clients whose self-harm occurred in the context of persistently tight construing and a deterministic view of the world, techniques such as brainstorming, aimed at loosening construing, may be employed. In marked contrast, with clients whose self-harm occurred in the context of persistently loose construing and a chaotic view of the world, the techniques used, such as self-monitoring assignments, are likely to be directed at tightening construing. With those for whom self-harm provides a "way of life," the therapeutic focus is on the development of an equally well elaborated alternative way of life. A research study of this intervention indicated that it resulted in greater reductions in suicidal ideation, hopelessness, depression, and frequency of repetition of self-harm than did normal clinical practice, coupled with changes in construing indicative of a more favorable view of the self and a less constricted view of the world and of the future (Winter et al., 2007).

The Intrusion of the "Real World" in Therapy

Many of the clients referred to state health systems such as the British National Health Service are from backgrounds characterized by high levels of deprivation or abuse. Therefore it may be difficult for therapists, let alone clients, to always heed Kelly's (1955) dual maxims that (1) clients need not be victims of their biographies and that (2) everything in the world is potentially subject to some kind of reconstruction. This is the case, for example, with asylum seekers, who, having survived horrific events in their countries of origin, may find themselves faced with a whole new series of traumas as they negotiate the asylum process.

> For Farouk, the asylum process had taken six years and ten court hearings. He described it as a situation of "not knowing what's going to happen, just waiting, waiting, not being free to work or study—how can you think or study properly if you think that the police might always come and send you back and your life is in danger if you go back—that's the limbo." In view of this unpredictability, and the consequent constant anxiety that he faced, coupled with a cultural background in which any sign of vulnerability by a male was anathema, therapy initially was dominated by what Kelly called the "palliative" techniques of reassurance and support. For example, I provided explanations for the somatic symptoms that he was experiencing, so that he would have at least some means of construing these; and wrote letters to government departments and to housing agencies. Only then, and in a very gradual manner, was it possible to begin to explore alternative constructions of events. Similarly, Ravi, who had suffered torture and witnessed the murder of members of his family in his country of origin, had little opportunity of passing his time apart from brooding upon these events because the asylum system prohibited him from working, even voluntarily. Therapy sessions, conducted through an interpreter, therefore initially focused on us giving each other language lessons, this providing some validation for a view of himself as a productive individual, as well as the additional structure for his life that was provided by practicing his English. As he gradually developed trust that therapy would not be yet another abusive experience, we were able to explore core issues concerning interpersonal relationships and loss.

If an individual considers that his or her psychological problems are a result of the circumstances to which he or she has been subjected, the therapist may need to take care that a focus on the former is not construed as attributing psychopathology to the client and thereby colluding with an abusive environment. This was the case with Chris, aspects of whose therapy were described above, and whose self-characterization indicated that he viewed his anxiety and anger as "related to instances of perceived selfishness in others and an obligation to undertake unnecessary tasks" and "being forced by deteriorating working conditions from the occupation to which he devoted the first half of his adult life." Thus, in one of his sessions, there was the following interaction:

> *Chris*: The grievance I have is about the role of psychiatry and psychotherapy to manage and marginalize me in the sick role as a way of accounting for my behavior. I can account for my behavior in other ways but it doesn't amount to anything. As I have done, I can talk about bullying managers, harassed and aggrieved colleagues, gratuitous bureaucracy, meaningless tasks, ageist attitudes in the workplace but nobody will look at that because while ever I am held by my involvement in psychotherapy it's always a deficiency in me, it's never a deficiency in them.
>
> *David*: But you don't have to, do you? To a large extent it was your choice to go down the psychotherapy road.
>
> *Chris*: Well, I don't accept that. . . . I think that that kind of argument is a part of the insidious nature of this exercise that all the time it's a matter of making this a matter of individual responsibility.

Chris's predicament, and mine as his therapist, can perhaps be viewed in terms of Kelly's notion of hostility, the extorting of evidence for his predictions. Thus, by accepting him for psychotherapy, I was validating his sense of alienation, although equally had I not taken him on as a client I would have validated his view of others as not caring about him. He and I have therefore agreed to collaborate on a paper exploring issues such as this which arose over the course of his therapy.

EVIDENCE BASE FOR PERSONAL CONSTRUCT PSYCHOTHERAPY

The British National Health Service is no different from many other contemporary healthcare settings in demanding that its clinicians provide evidence-based (empirically validated or supported) treatments. As stated in its review of strategic policy on psychological therapies,

> it is unacceptable . . . to continue to provide therapies which decline to subject themselves to research evaluation. Practitioners and researchers alike must accept the challenge of evidence-based practice, one result of which is that treatments which are shown to be ineffective are discontinued. (Parry & Richardson, 1996, p. 43)

243

Big Problem— providing evidence
that therapy effective.

The personal construct psychotherapist need no longer feel threatened by such statements because there is growing evidence of the effectiveness of this approach. For example, we have not only demonstrated significant improvement in our agoraphobic clients over the course of our combined personal construct and exposure therapy (Winter et al., 2006), and that self-harmers treated by personal construct psychotherapy have a better outcome than those receiving normal clinical practice (Winter et al., 2007), but also that a less selected group of clients, typical of those referred to National Health Service Clinical Psychology Departments, fare at least as well in personal construct psychotherapy as they do in cognitive-behavioral or psychodynamic therapy (Watson & Winter, 2005). The results of these studies are consistent with those of a larger body of research that has indicated that clients treated by personal construct psychotherapy improve significantly more than do those receiving no, or a non-active, intervention, and that their degree of improvement is comparable to that in other forms of therapy, including those that are commonly regarded as evidence-based (Holland & R. A. Neimeyer, 2005; Metcalfe, Winter, & Viney, 2007; Viney, 1998; Viney, Metcalfe, & Winter, 2005; Winter, 2005b).

The National Health Service review of strategic policy on psychological therapies was published in conjunction with a book entitled *What Works for Whom?* (Roth & Fonagy, 1996), designed to assist health commissioners to decide on the appropriate mix of psychological therapies for their populations. There was no mention at all of personal construct psychotherapy in this book, readers of which would therefore be likely to conclude that this form of therapy works for no one. Hearing that a second edition of the book was being prepared, I provided the authors with details of the "evidence base" for personal construct psychotherapy, and this has led to a footnote to a statement in the text that the authors "do not imply that one design should automatically be privileged over another without consideration of the context from which such evidence is drawn" (Roth & Fonagy, 2005, p. 492). The footnote reads as follows:

> A further example is offered by personal construct therapy (PCT). Practitioners of this approach tend to eschew psychiatric diagnosis, which means that an already small literature is usually based on mixed patient samples. In addition, most reports are of single-case studies or uncontrolled trials, using measures that are designed to detect

shifts in process and meaning, rather than shifts in symptomatic functioning (Winter, 2003a). This compounds the fact of a small evidence base with the problem that what is available is philosophically at variance with a conventional review such as this one. This latter point could be used to argue that the absence of reports of evidence for PCT in this book reflects our selection bias rather than a real absence of evidence, and this would be a reasonable point for debate (e.g. Viney, 1998).

DOES SURVIVAL REQUIRE THE SACRIFICE OF INTEGRITY?

Some of the earliest clinical research studies from a personal construct perspective were carried out by Bannister (1960, 1962) in a National Health Service setting. These caught the attention of the psychiatric establishment because they led to the development of a diagnostic repertory grid test for schizophrenic thought disorder (Bannister & Fransella, 1966). As such, they demonstrated the worst fears of those personal construct psychologists who have expressed concerns that compliance with the demands of the real world may lead to the theory being compromised, in this case by the seeming acceptance of a psychiatric diagnostic system that Kelly (1955) viewed as "all too frequently an attempt to cram a whole live struggling client into a nosological category" (p. 775). However, the principal message to emerge from Bannister's research was that the processes that operate in people who are labeled as thought disordered schizophrenics, for example loosening of construing as a response to persistent invalidation, are no different from those that may be used by anyone else under similar circumstances. Indeed, the research also pointed to ways in which these processes might be reversed by personal construct psychotherapy (Bannister, Adams-Webber, Penn, & Radley, 1975). Arguably, then, by displaying sociality and speaking the language of his psychiatric colleagues, Bannister was able to promulgate a theory that indicated that diagnostic systems are no more than human constructions (Raskin & Lewandowski, 2000) and that they need not be used in a preemptive manner.

A similar point may be made in regard to the evidence that is being collected for the effectiveness of personal construct psychotherapy. In evaluating whether this has led, as feared, to the "empirical violation" of this form of therapy, it is instructive to consider that those outcome studies discussed above that have also

245

incorporated   investigation of the treatment process have indicated the distinctiveness of the personal construct approach, differentiating it from supportive therapy for agoraphobic clients (Winter et al., 2005), from dialectical behavior therapy for those with a diagnosis of "borderline personality disorder" (Winter et al., 2003), and from cognitive-behavioral therapy with the more mixed client group (Winter & Watson, 1999). Thus, even though therapy in these studies has been offered on time-limited contracts, and in one case was manualized, this does not appear to have significantly compromised the integrity of the personal construct approach. Unlike much psychotherapy research, designed according to "gold standards" that produce tightly controlled studies of highly selected clients at the expense of very limited external validity, our investigations have been carried out with minimal interference to normal clinical practice and often on client groups "depicting the researcher's worst nightmare in terms of comorbidity, complexity and levels of motivation" (Watson & Winter, 2005, p. 346). Although conventional symptom measures have been used in most of these studies, providing the type of information on treatment outcome that is likely to be most meaningful to commissioners of health services (and indeed to clients), they have been complemented by measures, such as repertory grid technique (Winter, 2003b), that allow exploration of change at the level of personal meaning. The use of a range of measures, both of treatment process and outcome, has also allowed statistical examination of changes in group means to be complemented by intensive single case studies of reconstruing during personal construct psychotherapy.

George Kelly (1955) emphasized the versatility that is required of the personal construct psychotherapist, largely because "the individuality and variety of ways different persons have of construing their worlds" imply that "the ways of assisting people may vary quite widely" (p. 631). The personal construct psychotherapist working in a health service setting now needs to adapt his or her approach not only to the variety of ways in which clients construe their worlds but also to the ways in which the world of the health service is construed by its various other stakeholders, including those in control of its purse strings. It is hoped that the examples provided in this chapter will indicate that such a stance may lead to the gradual incorporation of personal construct psychotherapy into guides for health service commissioners and clinicians (such as *What Works for Whom?*), but that it need not imply selling out on the basic principles of the personal construct approach. The alternative, for example a refusal to speak the language of empirical validation with those who construe the world in this way, is only likely to lead to the extinction of personal construct psychotherapy and therefore to a health service that is even more dominated than at present by more mechanistic forms of therapy that pay minimal attention to personal meaning.

References

Agnew, J. (1985). Childhood disorders or the venture of childhood. In E. Button (Ed.), *Personal construct theory and mental health* (pp. 224-245). London: Croom Helm.

Alexander, P. C., Neimeyer, R. A., Follette, V., Moore, M. K., & Harter, S. (1989). A comparison of group treatments of women sexually abused as children. *Journal of Consulting and Clinical Psychology, 57,* 479-483.

Allen, D. (2005). Working with people who hear voices. In D. A. Winter & L.L. Viney (Eds.), *Personal construct psychotherapy: Advances in theory, practice and research* (pp. 212-225). London: Whurr.

Bannister, D. (1960). Conceptual structure in thought-disordered schizophrenics. *Journal of Mental Science, 106,* 1230-1249.

Bannister, D. (1962). The nature and measurement of schizophrenic thought disorder. *Journal of Mental Science, 108,* 825-842.

Bannister, D. (1985). The psychotic disguise. In W. Dryden (Ed.), *Therapists' dilemmas* (pp. 167-179). London: Harper and Row.

Bannister, D., & Fransella, F. (1966). A grid test of schizophrenic thought disorder. *British Journal of Social and Clinical Psychology, 5,* 95-102.

Bannister, D., Adams-Webber, J. R., Penn, W. I., & Radley, P. L. (1975). Reversing the process of thought disorder: a serial validation experiment. *British Journal of Social and Clinical Psychology, 14,* 169-180.

Beail, N., & Parker, S. (1991). Group fixed role therapy: a clinical application. *International Journal of Personal Construct Psychology, 4,* 85-96.

Bell, R., Winter, D., & Watson, S. (2004). *Figures in conflict.* Paper presented at the 35th Annual Meeting of the Society for Psychotherapy Research, Rome.

Bohart, A. C., O'Hara, M., & Leitner, L. M. (1998). Empirically violated treatments: disenfranchisement of humanistic and other therapies. *Psychotherapy Research, 8,* 141-157.

Botella, L. (1991). Psychoeducational groups with older adults: an integrative personal construct rationale and some guidelines. *International Journal of Personal Construct Psychology, 4,* 397-408.

Cummins, P. (2005). The experience of anger. In D. A. Winter & L. L. Viney (Eds.), *Personal construct psychothrapy:Advances in theory, practice and research* (pp. 239-255). London: Whurr.

Dunnett, G., & Llewellyn, S. (1988). Elaborating personal construct theory in a group setting. In G. Dunnett (Ed.), *Working with people: Clinical uses of personal construct psychology* (pp. 186-201). London: Routledge.

Epting, F. R., & Nazario, A., Jr. (1987). Designing a fixed role therapy: issues, technique, and modifications. In R. A. Neimeyer & G. J. Neimeyer (Eds.), *Personal construct therapy casebook* (pp. 277-289). New York: Springer.

Feixas, G., Saúl, L. A., & Sánchez, V. (2000). Detection and analysis of implicative dilemmas: implications for the therapeutic process. In J. W. Scheer (Ed.), *The person in society: Challenges to a constructivist theory* (pp. 391-399). Giessen, Germany: Psychosozial-Verlag.

Feixas, G., & Saúl, L. A. (2005). Resolution of dilemmas by personal construct psychotherapy. In D. A. Winter & L. L. Viney (Eds.), *Personal construct psychothrapy: Advances in theory, practice and research* (pp. 136-147). London: Whurr.

Forster, J. R. (1991). Facilitating positive changes in self-constructions. *International Journal of Personal Construct Psychology, 4,* 281-292.

Foster, H., & Viney, L. L. (2005). Personal construct workshops for women experiencing menopause. In D. A. Winter & L. L. Viney (Eds.), *Personal construct psychothrapy: Advances in theory, practice and research* (pp. 320-332). London: Whurr.

Fransella, F. (1970). Stuttering: not a symptom but a way of life. *British Journal of Communication Disorders, 5,* 22-29.

Gillman-Smith, I., & Watson, S. (2005). Personal construct group psychotherapy for borderline personality disorder. In D. A. Winter & L. L. Viney (Eds.), *Personal construct psychothrapy: Advances in theory, practice and research* (pp. 189-197). London: Whurr.

Gordon, D., & Giles, S. (1999). From May to November: A six-month group for women survivors of childhood sexual abuse. *Group Analysis, 32,* 495-506.

Greenberg, L. S. (1979). Resolving splits: The two-chair technique. *Psychotherapy: Theory, Research and Practice, 16,* 310-318.

Hinkle, D. N. (1965). *The change of personal constructs from the view-point of a theory of construct implications.* Unpublished dissertation, Ohio State University.

Holland, J. M., & Neimeyer, R. A. (2005). *The efficacy of personal construct therapy: a quantitative review.* Paper presented at 16th International Congress on Personal Construct Psychology, Columbus, Ohio.

Houston, J. (Ed.) (1998). *Making sense with offenders: Personal constructs, therapy and change.* Chichester, UK: John Wiley.

Jackson, S. (1990). A PCT therapy group for adolescents. In P. Maitland & D. Brennan (Eds.), *Personal construct theory, deviancy and social work* (pp. 163-174). London: Inner London Probation Service and Centre for Personal Construct Psychology.

Kelly, G. A. (1955). *The psychology of personal constructs* (2 vols.). New York: Norton

Kelly, G. A. (1961). Theory and therapy in suicide: The personal construct point of view. In M. Farberow & E. Shneidman (Eds.), *The cry for help* (pp. 255-289). New York: McGraw-Hill.

Kelly, G. A. (1970). Behaviour is an experiment. In D. Bannister (Ed.), *Perspectives in personal construct theory* (pp. 255-269). London: Academic Press.

Landfield, A. W., & Rivers, P. C. (1975). An introduction to interpersonal transaction and rotating dyads. *Psychotherapy: Theory, Research and Practice, 12,* 365-373.

Lane, L. G., & Viney, L. L. (2005). Group work with women living with breast cancer. In D. A. Winter & L. L. Viney (Eds.), *Personal construct psychothrapy: Advances in theory, practice and research* (pp. 310-319). London: Whurr.

Leitner, L. M. (1988). Terror, risk and reverence: Experiential personal construct psychotherapy. *International Journal of Personal Construct Psychology, 1,* 299-310.

Metcalfe, C., Winter, D. A., & Viney, L. L. (2007). The effectiveness of personal construct psychotherapy in clinical practice: A systematic review and meta-analysis. *Psychotherapy Research, 17,* 431-442.

Morris, J. B. (1977). Appendix I: The prediction and measurement of change in a psychotherapy group using the repertory grid. In F. Fransella & D. Bannister (Eds.), *A manual for repertory grid technique* (pp. 120-148). London: Academic Press.

Neimeyer, G. J., & Merluzzi, T.V. (1982). Group structure and group process: personal construct therapy and group development. *Small Group Behavior, 13,* 150-164.

Neimeyer, R. A., Anderson, A., & Stockton, L. (2001). Snakes versus ladders: A validation of laddering technique as a measure of hierarchical structure. *Journal of Constructivist Psychology, 14,* 83-103.

Neimeyer, R. A., Harter, S. L., & Alexander, P. C. (1991). Group perceptions as predictors of outcome in the treatment of incest survivors. *Psychotherapy Research, 1,* 148-158.

Neimeyer, R. A., & Winter, D. A. (2006). To be or not to be: Personal constructions of the suicidal choice. In T. E. Ellis (Ed.), *Cognition and suicide: Theory, research and practice* (pp. 149-169). New York: American Psychological Association.

Neimeyer, R. A., & Winter, D. A. (2007). Personal construct therapy. In N. Kazantzis & L. L. A'bate (Eds.), *Handbook of homework assignments in psychotherapy* (pp. 151-171). New York: Springer.

Parry, G., & Richardson, A. (1996). *NHS Psychotherapy Services in England: Review of Strategic Policy.* London: NHS Executive.

Procter, H. G. (1987). Change in the family construct system: Therapy of a mute and withdrawn schizophrenic patient. In R. A. Neimeyer & G. J. Neimeyer (Eds.), *Personal construct therapy casebook* (pp. 153-171). New York: Springer.

Raskin, J. D., & Lewandoski, A. M. (2000). The construction of disorder as human enterprise. In R. A. Neimeyer & J. D. Raskin (Eds.), *Constructions of disorder: Meaning-making frameworks for psychotherapy* (pp. 15-40). Washington, DC: American Psychological Association.

Roth, A., & Fonagy, P. (1996) *What works for whom? A critical review of psychotherapy research* (2nd ed.). New York: Guilford.

Semerari, A. (1989). *The construction of therapeutic relationship: A theoretical model.* Paper presented at 8th International Congress on Personal Construct Psychology, Assisi, Italy.

Truneckova, D., & Viney, L. L. (2005). Personal construct group work with troubled adolescents. In D. A. Winter & L. L. Viney (Eds.), *Personal construct psychotherapy: Advances in theory, practice and research* (pp. 271-286). London: Whurr.

Tschudi, F. (1977). Loaded and honest questions: a construct theory view of symptoms and therapy. In D. Bannister (Ed.), *New perspectives in personal construct theory* (pp. 321-350). London: Academic Press.

Viney, L. L. (1985). Humor as a therapeutic tool. In F. R. Epting & A. W. Landfield (Eds.), *Anticipating personal construct psychology.* Lincoln: University of Nebraska Press.

Viney, L. L. (1998). Should we use personal construct therapy? A paradigm for outcomes evaluation. *Psychotherapy, 35,* 366-380.

Viney, L. L., & Henry, R. M. (2002). Evaluating personal construct and psychodynamic group work with adolescent offenders and non-offenders. In R. A. Neimeyer & G. J. Neimeyer (Eds.), *Advances in personal construct psychology: New directions and perspectives* (pp. 259-294). Westport, CT: Praeger.

250

Viney, L. L., Metcalfe, C., & Winter, D. A. (2005). The effectiveness of personal construct psychotherapy: A meta-analysis. In D. A. Winter & L. L. Viney (Eds.), *Personal construct psychotherapy: Advances in theory, practice and research* (pp. 347-364). London: Whurr.

Watson, S., & Winter, D. A. (2005). A process and outcome study of personal Construct Psychotherapy. In D. A. Winter & L. L. Viney (Eds.), *Personal construct psychotherapy: Advances in theory, practice and research* (pp. 335-346). London: Whurr.

Winter, D. (1997). Personal construct theory perspectives on group psychotherapy. In P. Denicolo & M. Pope (Eds.), *Sharing understanding and practice* (pp. 210-221). Farnborough: EPCA Publications.

Winter, D., & Gournay, K. (1987). Constriction and construction in agoraphobia. *British Journal of Medical Psychology, 60*, 233-244.

Winter, D., Gournay, K., Metcalfe, C., & Rossotti, N. (2006). Expanding agoraphobics' horizons: An investigation of the effectiveness of a personal construct psychotherapy intervention. *Journal of Constructivist Psychology, 19*, 1-30.

Winter, D., Bhandari, S., Metcalfe, C., Riley, T., Sireling, L., Watson, S., & Lutwyche, G. (2000). Deliberate and undeliberated self-harm: Theoretical basis and evaluation of a personal construct psychotherapy intervention. In J. W. Scheer (Ed.), *The person in society: Challenges to a constructivist theory* (pp. 351-360). Giessen, Germany: Psychosozial-Verlag.

Winter, D. A. (1987). Personal construct psychotherapy as a radical alternative to social skills training. In R. A. Neimeyer & G. J. Neimeyer (Eds.), *Personal construct therapy casebook* (pp. 107-123). New York: Springer.

Winter, D. A. (1988). Reconstructing an erection and elaborating ejaculation: Personal construct theory perspectives on sex therapy. *International Journal of Personal Construct Psychology, 1*, 81-99.

Winter, D. A. (1992). *Personal construct psychology in clinical practice: Theory, research and applications.* London: Routledge.

Winter, D. A. (2003a). The evidence base for personal construct psychotherapy. In F. Fransella (Ed.), *International handbook of personal construct psychology* (pp. 265-272). Chichester: John Wiley.

Winter, D. A. (2003b). Repertory grid technique as a psychotherapy research measure. *Psychotherapy Research, 13*, 25-42.

Winter, D. A. (2005a). Deliberate self-harm and reconstruction. In D. A. Winter & L. L. Viney (Eds.), *Personal construct psychotherapy: Advances in theory, practice and research* (pp. 127-135). London: Whur.

Winter, D. A. (2005b). The evidence base for personal construct psychotherapy. In F. Fransella (Ed.), *The essential practitioner's handbook of personal construct psychology* (pp. 123-132). Chichester: John Wiley.

Winter, D. A., Gournay, K., & Metcalfe, C. (1999). An investigation of the effectiveness of a personal construct psychotherapy intervention. In J. M. Fisher and D.J. Savage (Eds.), *Beyond experimentation into meaning* (pp. 146-60). Lostock Hall: EPCA Publications.

Winter, D. A., & Metcalfe, C. (2005). From constriction to experimentation: Personal construct psychotherapy for agoraphobia. In D. A. Winter & L.L. Viney (Eds.), *Personal construct psychotherapy: Advances in theory, practice and research* (pp. 148-164). London: Whurr.

Winter, D., Sireling, L., Riley, T., Metcalfe, C., Quaite, A., and Bhandari, S. (2007). A controlled trial of personal construct psychotherapy for deliberate self harm. *Psychology and Psychotherapy: Theory, Research and Practice, 80,* 23-37.

Winter, D. A., Watson, S., Gillman-Smith, I., Gilbert, N., & Acton, T. (2003). Border crossing: A personal construct therapy approach for clients with a diagnosis of borderline personality disorder. In G. Chiari & M. L. Nuzzo (Eds.), *Psychological constructivism and the social world* (pp. 342-352). Milan: FrancoAngeli.

Yalom, I. D. (1970). *The theory and practice of group psychotherapy.* New York: Basic Books.

↶ 12 ↷

Counseling Multiracial Clients in Context: A Constructivist Approach

Ronnie Priest and Nancy Nishimura

Helping professionals are being challenged to work with an increasingly diverse clientele (Hall, 1996; Jackson, 1995; Sue & Sue, 2003). Professional codes of ethics (APA, 2002; ACA, 2005; NASW, 1999) clearly state that psychologists, counselors and social workers must be culturally competent in order to provide quality psychological services to their clients. In response, the current professional literature highlights the importance of acknowledging and addressing multicultural issues that impact the therapeutic relationship and treatment planning (Axelson, 1999; Parham, 1997; Pedersen, Draguns, Lonner, & Trimble, 2002; Sue, Ivey, & Pedersen, 1996). While counselors are strongly encouraged to be culturally competent, what that actually means and how practitioners are to achieve this goal is not always clearly outlined (Sue & Sue, 2003). One explanation as to why cultural competence is a difficult concept to grasp is due, in part, to the fact that it consists of multiple components: awareness, knowledge, and skills (Sue, Ivey, & Pedersen, 1996; Sue & Sue, 2003). For the purposes of clarity, cultural competence is operationally defined as awareness of cultural distinctions across groups and the utilization of clinical skills to acknowledge the distinctions and incorporate them into interventions that empower the client (Paniagua, 2001, p. 57).

The focus of this chapter is an examination of race as an aspect of culture; specifically, the counseling issues that confront multiracial individuals (persons whose parents are from two or more racial groups). Our premise is that therapists who utilize a constructivist counseling approach within a multicultural context will likely be more culturally competent than therapists who do not when working with multiracial clients. The following areas are addressed: (1) The role race holds in society; (2) Basic concepts of constructivist therapy; (3) Basic concepts of the theory of multicultural counseling therapy; (4) The impact of therapists' attitudes toward multiracial individuals; (5) Complex issues that challenge many multiracial persons; (6) A case study describing a constructivist-multicultural counseling approach with a multiracial individual, and; (7) The strengths and weaknesses of utilizing a constructivist approach in working with a multiracial clientele.

THE ROLE OF RACE IN SOCIETY

In the United States, race is a component of culture. Historically, racial classifications have been determined by relying on biological/phenotypical considerations (i.e. skin color, hair texture, etc.) (Sue & Sue, 2003). Operationalizing race in this manner became a means of visually identifying members of certain groups in order to distinguish which groups had access to benefits and opportunities and which groups did not (Gillem & Thompson, 2004; Korgen, 1998). As group interaction/intermarriage became a reality, however, the racial characteristics of subsequent generations became less and less distinct. Even so, race currently remains an extremely sensitive societal, economic, and political issue (Korgen, 1998; Sue & Sue, 2003).

With physical characteristics becoming less and less distinct as a means of group identification, race has become a construct; a concept that represents an individual's perception as opposed to an "iron clad" category (Fernandez, 1996). Interestingly, while distinct racial characteristics are blurred, the racial group with which one identifies remains a salient issue of utmost significance (Korgen, 1998).

The burgeoning number of multiracial persons constitutes evidence of the growing diversity in the United States. An increased number of Americans have biological parents from different racial groups (i.e. Caucasian/African American, Asian American/Hispanic American, etc.) (Korgen, 1998; Root, 1996; Sue & Sue, 2003; Wehrly, 1996). The racial identity development of multiracial persons is not as readily discernible as it seems to be for monoracial individuals (Nishimura, 1998; 2004; Roberts-Clarke, Roberts, & Morokoff, 2004; Root, 1996; Sue & Sue, 2003; Wehrly, 1996). The identity development process becomes an individualistic endeavor, often to such an extent that members of the same family may self-identify in ways dramatically different from each other (Root,

1992; 1996). A complex question that often confronts multiracial individuals is summed up in the self-reflective query: "Who should I identify with—my mother or my father or both?" (Tizard & Phoenix, 1993, p. 49).

One reason why the process of racial identity development has the potential to be complicated is because two dimensions impact it: racial definition and racial identity (Nishimura, 1998). Racial definition is group identification that is *externally* imposed and focuses on tangible differences (physical features), that is, how other people perceive one's group affiliation (Nishimura, 1998). In contrast, racial identity is identification that is *internally* framed and based on perceptions of shared characteristics with the chosen group (Nishimura, 1998). We focus on the latter dimension in keeping with constructivist paradigms encompassing the perspective that individuals have the capacity to construct meaningful solutions for their own lives (Mascolo, Craig-Bray, & Neimeyer, 1997). Given this context, we contend that multiracial persons' racial group choice has the potential to be a complex and challenging issue that can best be addressed by working closely with the individual.

Despite there being important multiracial contributions throughout American history, multiracial identities have only recently been formally acknowledged—as evidenced by the inclusion of the multiracial choice option in the 2000 U.S. census (Sue & Sue, 2003; Wehrly, 1996). Specific socio-political factors impacted the reticence to formally acknowledge this rapidly growing racial group (Fernandez, 1996; Sue & Sue, 2003). One such factor was the "One-Drop" Rule which stated that if a person had "one-drop of blood" (genetic heritage) from a racial minority group, that person was automatically relegated to being a member of that racial group (Wehrly, 1996). This "rule" was established during slavery in the United States and, to some extent, continues on to present day (Daniel, 2003; Korgen, 1998; Sue & Sue, 2003; Tizard & Phoenix, 1992). An equally compelling factor is the realization that the amount of government funding of social services provided to various racial minority groups is often dependent on the census number of persons reported to be members of that racial group (Fernandez, 1996; Gillem & Thompson, 2004; Sue & Sue, 2003). Consequently, when individuals acknowledge their multiracial group status on government documents instead of choosing a traditional monoracial "box," there is the potential that specific minority groups will be in danger of losing federal funds when it appears that that their population (as noted by the U.S. Census) has decreased.

A third factor that has influenced recognition of multiracial identities is the conscious and unconscious messages that are conveyed by family, community, media, and society in general regarding the negative perception of multiracial persons (Cruz-Janzen, King & Wardle, 2005; Korgen, 1998; Sue & Sue, 2003; Tizard & Phoenix, 1993; Tomishima, 2003). Multiracial individuals are often viewed as persons who are forever consigned to live marginalized lives (Korgen, 1998; Nakazawa, 2003; Tizard & Phoenix, 1993). While a limited number of case studies in the professional literature suggest that multiracial persons experience lives filled with adversity, the alternative perspective that multiracial children have the opportunity to experience a "doubly rich heritage" is not as widely noted (Korgen, 1998; Nakazawa, 2003; Suyemoto, 2004). According to one biracial teenager, "Being biracial isn't hard because we're confused about our racial identity—it's hard because everyone else is confused" (Gaskins, 2003, p. 44).

THE DYNAMICS OF CONSTRUCTIVIST THERAPY

The core of constructivist therapy includes an emphasis on "hearing" clients' stories and inviting clients to articulate the meanings events hold for them (Mascolo, Craig-Bray, & Neimeyer, 1997). A core belief of constructivist therapists is that clients construe individually; if the therapist does not grasp the client's constructions, empathy and effective intervention will be impossible (Kelly, 1969). Therefore, the ability of the therapist to accurately reflect back the client's feelings and meanings is of critical importance (Bridges, 2004).

THE ROLE OF THE CONSTRUCTIVIST THERAPIST

According to Kelly (1969):

> . . . only as the therapist approaches his client's problem as a scientist, and invites his client to do the same . . . can he avoid the tyranny of dogmatism and the professional exploitation of his clients . . . [the] psychologist is his [the client's] fellow experimenter, not an unctuous priest. (p. 53)

The counseling relationship, then, is the central means by which the therapist is encouraged to work in a collaborative therapeutic alliance with the client, as opposed to fostering an expert-client interaction. Additionally, the goal of constructivist therapists is to "pay attention to the existing core constructs that both help clients to make life meanings and also stop them from finding the life satisfaction they seek" (Bridges, 2004, p. 444). Logically extended, therapists must be wholly involved, therapeutically, in the client's world. They must strive to see through their clients' perspective (Stevens & Walker, 2002).

THE THEORY OF MULTICULTURAL COUNSELING AND THERAPY

The Theory of Multicultural Counseling and Therapy (Sue, Ivey, & Pedersen, 1996) outlines six propositions. Specifically, Proposition 3 states:

> Cultural identity development is a major determinant of counselor and client attitudes toward the self, others of the same group, others of a different, group, and the dominant group. . . . The level or stage of racial/cultural identity will both influence how clients and counselors define the problem and dictate what they believe to be appropriate therapeutic goals and processes. (p. 17)

Sue, Ivey, and Pedersen (1996) believe that the counselor's cultural self-perception directly impacts how clients and presenting problems are perceived. In turn, a client's cultural self-perception similarly impacts how the counselor, as well as the therapeutic approach, will be viewed. To disregard the relevancy of these dynamics represents a denial of key components of both the counselor and the client.

There are notable commonalities between Personal Construct Psychology and Multicultural Counseling Theory. Both counseling approaches highlight the importance of the involvement of the client and therapist in the counseling relationship. Additionally, both emphasize the influence of the therapist's "sense of self" and "self in relation to the client" related to the extent the counselor can be "present" to accurately reflect back the client's reality (Stojnov & Butt, 2002; Sue, Ivey, & Pedersen, 1996). A counselor's self examination of his or her attitudes and assumptions is a key component of being a skilled therapist. "Counselor, know thyself" is a fitting professional expectation, especially for therapists who view their professional role as helping clients to "get in touch" with themselves and their personal realities (Sue, Ivey, & Pedersen, 1996).

THERAPISTS' ATTITUDES RELATED TO MULTIRACIAL PERSONS

Both Personal Construct Psychology and Multicultural Counseling Theory place heavy emphasis on therapists' self-awareness and involvement with clients (Stojnov & Butt, 2002; Sue, Ivey, & Pedersen, 1996). We contend that in order to effectively accomplish these dual mandates when working with multiracial clients, there are crucial questions that therapists must address in terms of their own attitudes and beliefs. Specifically:

- "How do you view your racial heritage?"

- "How do you believe other people view you in terms of your racial heritage?"

- "Do you embrace a "color blind" attitude in regards to persons with different racial backgrounds?

- "What is your attitude about interracial romantic relationships?"

- "What is your attitude related to multiracial persons?"

- "How do you identify multiracial persons (by appearance, by minority group membership, etc)?"

These questions, coupled with therapists' subsequent responses to them, are pertinent because they afford therapists opportunities to become more aware of their attitudes and perceptions regarding multiracial individuals and their families. This heightened sense of awareness will enable therapists to better intuit how their impressions of multiracial clients are being influenced by their own biases (Sue, Ivey, & Pedersen, 1996).

COMPLEX ISSUES RELATED TO BEING MULTIRACIAL

Others often greet multiracial persons with the demand to know "what they are" (Root, 1996; 2004; Sue & Sue, 2003). There appears to be the need to satisfy one's curiosity that motivates people (often perfect strangers) to approach multiracial individuals to inquire about their racial heritage. The impact of such encounters often leaves multiracial individuals feeling detached, marginalized, or reduced to little more than a racial category representation.

> What are you?' Boy, that's a question I try to dodge every day of my life. I don't like to answer it. I try to feel out the person, you know, their motives and stuff. I really think that what I represent turns other people's worlds upside down. Some |people| get really angry at me for not giving them the answer they want to hear, insisting that I belong to this group or that group. (Williams, 1996, p. 204)

Another issue that impacts multiracial persons is their physical features. The stereotype that multiracial people are attractive and/or beautiful is both a blessing and a curse (Nakashima, 1992; Nishimura, 2004). Possible blessings associated with being multiracial include being viewed as special and desirable by potential dating partners or employers.

> 'I get a lot of attention from guys and potential partners based on my looks . . .' She |a biracial woman| seemed to recognize the preference for women of lighter skin (and straighter hair) among some men of color, and she seemed to be conflicted that her biracial appearance had provided social benefits. (Roberts-Clarke, Roberts, & Morokoff, 2004, p. 112)

The "curse" associated with the perception that multiracial persons are beautiful presents challenges to multiracial clients. "The men who would be attracted to me because of the way I look are men that I find disgusting. It's almost like I'm always in a trick bag" (Funderburg, 1994, p. 197). Depicting multiracial individuals as "beautiful objects" risks dehumanizing them and reducing them to exotic status (Edwards & Pedrotti, 2004; Nakashima, 1992; Nishimura, 2004). And what happens to multiracial persons whose physical features do not match stereotypical images? When multiracial persons are characterized by their physical appearance, essential aspects of who they are as individuals are overlooked.

While establishing a sense of identity is a developmental stage confronted by most adolescents, identity development has the potential to be significantly more complex for multiracial children. Monoracial parents of multiracial children do not have comparable life experiences upon which to draw in order to empathize or guide their children (Cauce, Hiraga, Mason, Aguilar, Ordonez, & Gonzales, 1992). "I don't think they [parents] understood what it was like to be me. When I said "I'm different" they just kind of dismissed it. It was almost denial, or maybe they didn't know how to deal with it" (Nishimura, 1998, p. 49). Speaking from a parent's perspective, one mother explained that her strategy was to "encourage her children to make little of such incidents [racist encounters]. The positive strategies she implemented centered around telling her children that they must work 'that little bit harder' to succeed, and to encourage them to feel good about themselves" (Tizard & Phoenix, 1993, p. 142). Not being able to discuss what it means to be multiracial with their monoracial parents, however, often results in multiracial children having a sense of being stranded and devoid of any guidance in finding their own way (Tizard & Phoenix, 1993). "If someone had been there to guide me through, encouraging me to accept being biracial, it would have been so much easier" (Nishimura, 1998, p. 49). Consequently, some multiracial persons believe that their loving parents did them a disservice by not helping them address their racial heritage (Buckley & Carter, 2004). "Sometimes parents want to communicate to their children that you are just a wonderful person and they do the color doesn't matter thing and this is so damaging" (Nishimura, 1998, p. 49). By not addressing the difficult parent/child dialogues related to race and being multiracial, these adolescents and or young adults often believe that they are ill prepared to function in a race conscious society.

It should be noted, in the interest of balance, that there are significant numbers of parents who do openly talk with their multiracial children about their racial or cultural heritage, providing a foundation upon which to develop a sense of self (Lee, 2004). Early parent-initiated discussions related to race have a positive impact on the racial identity development of their multiracial children. One mother's strategic plan was to provide her daughter with a clear understanding of racism, to encourage educational achievement, and "to help develop self-esteem, she had told her daughter to 'reject any attempt on the part of the external world to impose a view of inferiority on her'" (Tizard & Phoenix, 1993, p. 141).

A unique issue that frequently challenges multiracial persons from the time they are children through adulthood is pressure from others (extended family, teachers, peers, community, etc.) to declare themselves as being a member of a single racial group. In describing one of the forms in which this pressure is manifested, a young woman shared: "The woman told me if I did not check the box to say I was black I was going to be suspended" (Funderburg, 1994, p. 85). These pressures are often fostered by good as well as not-so-good intentions with the primary intent of protecting multiracial persons from the reactions of society. While identifying with one racial group may in fact avoid "rocking the boat" in terms of societal norms, when the choice is made for the comfort of others instead of the individual's internal fit, the result is often disequilibrium for the individual.

Being able to "belong" to a group, an aspect of adolescence that seems to rate extremely high on the priority list of young people in general, has its challenges for multiracial youths. "There were times I did not feel like I totally belonged to that group [African American students] . . . the White kids saw me as Black, and the Black guys saw me as White, either way I was screwed" (Nishimura, 1998, p. 49). This dilemma exemplifies the impact of distinct racial categorization within an increasingly diverse society. Role models who encourage young people to explore and appreciate their multiple identities (athletics, music, hobbies, etc) might greatly impact adolescent racial "divides."

For many individuals, the potential benefits derived from being multiracial outweigh the challenges. The experience of being a multiracial person often provides the opportunity to grasp that the world is full of complexities (Tizard & Phoenix, 1993). "[Being multiracial] allows you to have perspective that they [monoracial people] can't have. It's not always easy growing up. Now, I know a lot about identity, but maybe because I have had to deal with it a lot more" (Nishimura, 1998, p. 50).

Being able to meet and interact with other multiracial persons has the potential to be a very affirming experience that is often described as being with "family" (Nishimura, 1998). This may be partially understood, when it is considered that many people do not comprehend what is involved in being multiracial in the United States. During interviews, multiracial college age individuals consistently articulated a sense of sharing a common bond based on experiences that they thought were unique, only to find that other multiracial persons had gone through similar situations (Nishimura, 1998).

In summary, there are a number of potential challenges that multiracial persons face that are unique to their multiple racial heritages:

1. There was always the question, "What are you?" or "Are you something—you look kind of exotic?"

2. Multiracial persons are impacted because their physical features are both a blessing and a curse.

3. Monoracial parents of multiracial children do not automatically have equivalent life experiences upon which to draw in order to empathize or guide their children. Interestingly, for some of these children, their loving parents inadvertently did them a disservice by not helping them address their racial heritage. There are many parents, however, who do openly talk with their multiracial children about their racial or cultural heritage providing a foundation from which to develop a sense of self.

4. Multiracial individuals face pressure from others (extended family, teachers, peers, community, etc.) to declare themselves as being a member of a single racial group and this is a difficult challenge to address.

COUNSELING IMPLICATIONS

Researchers have noted that there is a paucity of professional literature addressing the area of counseling multiracial persons and a need for counselor competency in working with this growing client population (Suyemoto, 2004; Wehrly, 1996). In order to provide an empathic therapeutic environment when working with multiracial persons, therapists must be able to grasp their clients' worldviews and demonstrate in-depth understanding of how their clients make meaning of their experiences.

Buckley and Carter (2004) noted that multiracial clients often do not specify multiracial concerns as part of the presenting problem. It is much more likely that the presenting problem will be based on dissatisfaction in other areas of their lives, such as relationships, professional choices, physical appearance, and so forth. We wish to caution therapists not to automatically assume that all multiracial clients are grappling with their racial/cultural heritage regardless of their presenting concerns. Instead, therapists are strongly encouraged to listen to their clients with an open mind, allowing the client's "story" to unfold as it will.

A Case Study of Constructivist Therapy with a Multiracial Client

Reiko Thompson (not the client's actual name) is a 19-year-old college freshman enrolled in a southern university who presents to the university's counseling center with problems associated with adjusting to being away from home and attending college. On her intake form, she requests a female counselor and is subsequently assigned to see Dr. Charlene Smith (not her actual name). Reiko's mother is a 41-year-old Japanese American and her father is a 43-year-old African American.

Reiko grew up in the Pacific Northwest, where she was very involved in the Japanese community. Physically, she looks Asian with the exception of her very wavy black hair. She applied to a university far from home because she felt her parents were too old fashioned and over protective. She expressed a desire to "be on her own" and saw going to college as an opportune time to be independent. When she arrived at college however, she was not prepared for the reaction of students in her classes and dorm, including her roommate. Reiko noted that people seemed to stare at her when she entered a room and maintained a curious distance from her. Several students had asked her "What are you?" When Reiko asked them "what do you mean?" The response was usually, "you know, are you Black or Mexican, or what?"

When Reiko returns to the counseling center for her first counseling appointment, Dr. Smith asks her about her request for a female counselor. Reiko states that she is more comfortable talking with women, and because coming to the counseling center was a big step for her, she wanted to talk with someone with whom she would hopefully feel comfortable. Dr. Smith says that it is a high priority for her as well that Reiko feels she is in a safe emotional environment. Dr. Smith asks if there was anything that Reiko wants to ask her before they address what brought Reiko to counseling. (*Multicultural Counseling Emphasis on Acknowledging that the Counselor is an Integral Part of the Relationship*). Reiko is relieved by Dr. Smith's genuine demeanor.

Dr. Smith focuses on Reiko's presenting problem. Reiko discloses that she finds herself becoming apprehensive and angry when she encounters new people, although she never outwardly demonstrates her anger—not even in those instances when she is asked the "What are you?" question. Reiko also notes that it is particularly unsettling in those instances when she replies she is biracial in response to the "What are you?" question. If the interrogator persists and attempts to have Reiko align herself with either her father's or her mother's ethnic identity, she becomes both frustrated and angry. She also notes that the number of severe headaches she experiences has increased in the past two months.

Dr. Smith suggests Reiko complete a counseling homework assignment that involves writing a personal statement related to what racial identity means to her and how it impacts how she views herself. (*Narrative Therapy*) The following session, Reiko reads her statement aloud in Dr. Smith's office. Reiko describes how the concept of racial identity was not a part of her world until she arrived at school and began interacting with people outside of her extended family. It seems to her that her racial heritage is something that others are more concerned about than are she or her parents. She attended public schools that had large Asian American student populations and while her friends were chosen according to shared interests (e.g. chess club, pep band, girl scouts), most of them were Asian American. Additionally, Reiko attended Japanese language school because her mother wanted her to learn how to speak Japanese in order to communicate with her maternal grandparents. Reiko's involvement in the Asian American community and her Asian physical features led people in her hometown to assume that her racial identity was Asian American. For the most part, Reiko did not contradict them; it just seemed easier to "go with the flow." But when she left home to attend college, Reiko decided to acknowledge both of her parents' heritage starting with the acceptance of a scholarship for African American students.

The rest of the session is spent on processing what it was like for Reiko to write and read her essay. She notices that her sense of racial identity has been externally focused throughout her life. It seems that how she views herself has been more a function of how others view her. As her self-awareness increases, Reiko notes her level of frustration decreasing. She acknowledges that her overall situation hasn't changed, yet she is starting to see it differently. (*Goal of Constructivist Therapy*)

Dr. Smith shares with Reiko that while her (Reiko's) life experiences are truly her own, there are aspects to which she could relate. Mainly, Dr. Smith has experienced people seeing her only as an African American based on her physical features, without acknowledging numerous other unique aspects of her personhood, such as her love of classical music, Greek food, and scuba diving. (*Tie in with MC Therapy*)

During subsequent sessions, Dr. Smith asks Reiko to relate specific troubling incidents that have recently occurred. Reiko describes an incident that occurred the previous week. Reiko notes she had attended a Black Student Union meeting where new students were invited to come and get acquainted. When she arrived, someone asked her if she had mistakenly come to the wrong room and that the Asian Student group was meeting down the hall.

Dr. Smith asks Reiko what that incident meant and felt like to her. Reiko states that the message was clear: "You don't belong here." She felt rejected. At a time when she wanted to explore her African American heritage, she felt "short circuited." As she processes her feelings further, Reiko describes this experience as "an important door being shut in her face." Dr. Smith (1) addresses with Reiko what it was like to be talking to an African American therapist about her recent unpleasant experience with African American students (*MC Therapy, Addressing Impact of Therapist's Race*); and (2) invites Reiko to visualize her "closed door" analogy and to envision an adjoining open door asking her to describe where that door might lead (*Constructivist Therapy*).

Through these explorations, Reiko comes to view her situation and her options differently. Working with Dr. Smith allows Reiko to experience an affirming relationship with an African American woman, as well as to identify other ways she might become involved with African American groups. She subsequently finds an African American women's book club sponsored by a local book store. Reiko makes several friends through this experience. The experience of being involved in the African American community gives Reiko an opportunity to appreciate her African American heritage.

By the time Reiko terminates her therapeutic relationship with Dr. Smith, her interactions with students have changed. While their questions and reactions to her are essentially the same, Reiko responds to them differently. Her increased self-awareness leads to heightened self confidence. In the past, she interpreted the "What are you?" question as an affront. She now responds to the "What are you?" question with an assumption that she has a valued heritage to share with others. Her responses reflect a self-confidence that attracts people. By the end of her second semester, Reiko develops a small circle of friends from diverse backgrounds based on common interests.

THE STRENGTHS OF A CONSTRUCTIVIST THERAPEUTIC APPROACH

Because racial identity is an internally directed cultural construct, many multiracial persons perceive their racial identity as a developmental process that evolves and changes well into adulthood (Edwards & Pedrotti, 2004, Nishimura, 1998). The client's peer group and environment change during various life circumstances and different aspects of one's cultural identity are prioritized. Take for example, a situation where at one point the client may self identify as African American and, at another point, as multiracial (Korgen, 1998; Nishimura, 1998).

Kelly (1969) noted that "constructivists perceive clients' personal growth as being brought about through changing constructs; that is, events are not unique occurrences, but recurrences" (p. 230). Constructivist therapists are acquainted with the concept of evolving client perceptions and place a high value on clients' interpretations of how they experience themselves, others, and their situations. Because it is advisable that therapists not assume that a multiracial client's physical features signify personal affiliation or that the racial groups a client embraces will indeed be a "safe harbor" for that person, a constructivist therapeutic approach has its merits (Buchanan & Acevedo, 2004).

266

Butt (2005) articulates the reality that "constructivism challenges both the individual/social and mind/body dualisms and insists on constructing events in psychological terms" (p. 1).

A number of authors (Edwards & Pedrotti, 2004; Henriksen & Trusty, 2004; Rockquemore & Brunsma, 2004) discussed the merits of utilizing a narrative approach when working with biracial clients. They noted that each person creates a personal reality that is in a state of constant flux as the person gains new information and perceptions related to what each life experience means. In order to allow the client's perspective to unfold, clinicians can encourage their clients to share their stories verbally and or in writing. As such, a narrative approach represents a logical counseling intervention.

THE LIMITATIONS OF A CONSTRUCTIVIST THERAPEUTIC APPROACH

The strength of a constructivist approach has the potential to be its greatest challenge. The focus of a constructivist therapist is on facilitating the client's task of articulating his or her perception of the problem situation and viable solutions (Mascolo, Craig-Bray, & Neimeyer, 1997). In those instances where the therapist lacks the ability to perceive or empathize with the multiracial client's situation, however, it will be difficult to make progress (Sue, Ivey, & Pedersen, 1996). Monoracial therapists, much like the monoracial parents of multiracial children discussed earlier, have the potential of lacking a frame of reference from which to grasp the complexities that multiracial persons face on a day to day basis (Nishimura, 1998). Clinicians' self-awareness is a personal resource from which to draw when providing advanced empathy to multiracial clients.

An additional concern regarding a constructivist approach is related to the tenet that solutions to clients' problems reside within themselves. This viewpoint, clearly, has the potential to be very empowering for clients; however, sometimes the problems that confront multiracial clients may have solutions that reside outside of the clients' direct control. Examples of such situations include but are not limited to media representations of multiracial persons and the expressed attitudes of persons in authority (e.g. teachers, church leaders, etc.).

SUMMARY

Multiracial clients potentially present a unique challenge to traditional mental health delivery systems. Constructivist therapy expands traditional helping paradigms by affording multiracial clients an array of opportunities to address individual/personal and social experiences while interpreting and understanding those experiences in ways that are meaningful to clients. We caution that the challenge for clinicians is to foster an environment wherein clients are able to meaningfully examine the complexities of their lives.

REFERENCES

American Counseling Association (2005). *Code of ethics and standards of practice.* Alexandria, VA: Author.

American Psychological Association (1997). *Ethical principles of psychologists and code of ethics.* Washington, DC: Author.

American Psychological Association (2002). *Guidelines on multicultural education, training, research, practice, and organizational change for psychologists.* Washington, DC: Author.

Axelson, J. A. (1999). *Counseling and development in a multicultural society* (3rd Ed.). Pacific Grove, CA: Brooks/Cole.

Bridges, S. K. (2004). Personal and social responses to tragedy: A case for "both/and" constructivism. In D. Raskin & S. K. Bridges (Eds.). *Studies in meaning 2: Bridging the personal and social in constructivist psychology.* New York: Pace University.

Buchanan, N. T., & Acevedo, C. A. (2004). When face and soul collide: Therapeutic concerns with racially ambiguous and nonvisible minority women. In A. R. Gillem & C. A. Thompson (Eds), *Biracial women in therapy: Between the rock of gender and the hard place of race* (pp. 119-131). New York: The Hawthorne Press.

Buckley, T. R., & Carter, R.T. (2004). Biracial (Black/White/ women: A qualitative study of racial attitudes and beliefs and their implications for therapy. In A. R. Gillem & C. A. Thompson (Eds.), *Biracial women in therapy: Between the rock of gender and the hard place of race* (pp. 45-64). New York: The Hawthorne Press.

Butt, T. (2005). Editorial foreword: The construction of sexualities. *Journal of Constructivist Psychology, 18,* 1-2.

Cauce, A. M., Hiraga, Y., Mason, C., Aguilar, T., Ordonez, N., & Gonzales, N. (1992). Between a rock and a hard place: Social adjustment of biracial youth. In M.P.P. Root (Ed.), *Racially mixed people in America* (pp. 207-222). Thousand Oaks, CA: Sage.

Cruz-Janzen, M. I., King, E. W., & Wardle, F. (2005). The challenge of declaring an interethnic and/or interracial identity in postmodern societies. In F. Schultz (Ed.), *Annual editions: Multicultural education 05/06* (12th ed.) (pp. 110-117). Dubuque, IA: McGraw-Hill.

Daniel, R. G. (2003). *More than black? Multiracial identity and the new racial order*. Philadelphia: Temple University Press.

Edwards, L. M., & Pedrotti, J. T. (2004). Utilizing the strengths of our cultures: Therapy with biracial women and girls. In A.R. Gillem & C.A. Thompson (Eds), *Biracial women in therapy: Between the rock of gender and the hard place of race* (pp. 33-43). New York: The Hawthorne Press.

Fernandez, C. A. (1996). Government classification of multiracial/multiethnic people. In M. P. P. Root (Ed.), *The multiracial experience: Racial borders as the new frontier* (pp. 15-36). Thousand Oaks, CA: Sage.

Funderburg, L. (1994). *Black, white, other: Biracial Americans talk about race and identity*. New York: William Morrow & Co.

Gaskins, P. F. (2003). My quest for what my identity is. In M. P. P. Root & M. Kelley (Eds), *Multiracial child resource book: Living complex identities* (pp. 43-46). Seattle: Mavin Foundation.

Gillem, A. R., & Thompson, C. A. (2004). (Eds), *Biracial women in therapy: Between the rock of gender and the hard place of race*. New York: The Hawthorne Press.

Hall, C. C. I. (1996). 2001: A race odyssey. In M. P. P. Root (Ed) (1996). *The multiracial experience: Racial borders as the new frontier* (pp.395-410). Thousand Oaks, CA: Sage.

Henriksen, R. C., Jr., & Trusty, J. (2004). Understanding and assisting Black/White biracial women in their identity development. In A. R.Gillem & C. A. Thompson (Eds), *Biracial women in therapy: Between the rock of gender and the hard place of race* (pp.65-83). New York: The Hawthorne Press.

Jackson, M. L. (1995). Multicultural counseling: Historical perspectives. In J. G. Ponterotto, J. M. Casas, L. A. Suzuki, & C. M. Alexander (Eds.), *Handbook of multicultural counseling* (pp. 3-16). Thousand Oaks, CA: Sage.

Kelly, G. A. (1969). The psychotherapeutic relationship. In B. Maher (Ed.), *Clinical psychology and personality: The selected papers of George Kelly* (pp. 216-223). New York: Wiley.

Korgen, K. O. (1998). *From Black to Biracial: Transforming racial identity among Americans*. Westport, CT: Praeger.

Lee, W. M. L. (2004). Therapeutic considerations in work with biracial girls. In A. R. Gillem & C. A. Thompson (Eds), *Biracial women in therapy: Between the rock of gender and the hard place of race* (pp. 203-216). New York: The Hawthorne Press.

Mascolo, M. F., Craig-Bray, L., & Neimeyer, R. A. (1997). The construction of meaning and action in development and psychotherapy: An Epigenetic Systems perspective. In G. J. Neimeyer & R. A. Neimeyer (Eds), *Advances in personal construct psychology*, (Vol. 4, pp. 3-38). Greenwich, CT: Jai Press.

Nakashima, C. L. (1992). An invisible monster: The creation and denial of mixed-race people in America. In M. P. P. Root (Ed.). *Racially mixed people in America* (pp. 162-178). Thousand Oaks, CA: Sage.

Nakazawa, D. J. (2003). *Does anybody else look like me? A parent's guide to raising multiracial children.* Cambridge, MA: Perseus.

National Association of Social Workers (1999). *Code of ethics.* Washington, DC: Author.

Nishimura, N. (1998). Assessing the issues of multiracial students on college campuses. *Journal of College Counseling, 1,* 45-53.

Nishimura, N. (2004). Counseling biracial women: An intersection of multiculturalism and feminism. In A. R. Gillem & C. A. Thompson (Eds), *Biracial women in therapy: Between the rock of gender and the hard place of race* (pp. 133-145). New York: The Hawthorne Press.

Paniagua, F. A. (2001). *Diagnosis in a multicultural context.* Thousand Oaks, CA: Sage.

Parham, T. A. (1997). An African-centered view of dual relationships. In B. Herlihy & G. Corey (Eds.), *Boundary issues in counseling* (pp. 109-112) Alexandria, VA: American Counseling Association

Pedersen, P. B., Draguns, J. G., Lonner, W. J., & Trimble, J. E. (Eds.) (2002). *Counseling across cultures* (5th ed.). Thousand Oaks, CA: Sage.

Roberts-Clarke, I., Roberts, A.C., & Morokoff, P. (2004). Dating practices, racial identify, and psychotherapeutic needs of biracial women. In A. R.Gillem & C. A. Thompson (Eds), *Biracial women in therapy: Between the rock of gender and the hard place of race* (pp. 103-117). New York: The Hawthorne Press.

Rockquemore, K. A., & Brunsma, D. L. (2004). Negotiating racial identity: Biracial women and interactional validation. In A. R. Gillem & C. A. Thompson (Eds), *Biracial women in therapy: Between the rock of gender and the hard place of race* (pp. 85-102). New York: The Hawthorne Press.

Root, M. P. P. (1992). *Racially mixed people in America.* Thousand Oaks, CA: Sage.

Root, M. P. P. (Ed). (1996). *The multiracial experience: Racial borders as the new frontier.* Thousand Oaks, CA: Sage.

Root, M. P. P. (2004). From exotic to a dime a dozen. In A. R. Gillem & C. A. Thompson (Eds.) *Biracial women in therapy: Between the rock of gender and the hard place of race* (pp. 19-31). New York: The Hawthorne Press.

Stevens, C. D., & Walker, B. M. (2002). Insight: Transcending the obvious. In R. A. Neimeyer, & G. J. Neimeyer (Eds.) *Advances in personal construct psychology: New directions and perspectives* (pp. 39-79). Westport, CT: Praeger.

Stojnov, D., & Butt, T. (2002). The relational basis of personal construct psychology. In R. A. Neimeyer & G. J. Neimeyer (Eds) *Advances in personal construct psychology: New directions and perspectives* (pp. 81-110). Westport, CT: Praeger.

Sue, D. W., Ivey, A. E., & Pedersen, P. B. (1996). *A theory of multicultural counseling and therapy.* Pacific Grove, CA: Brooks/Cole.

Sue, D. W., & Sue, D. (2003). *Counseling the culturally diverse: Theory and practice* (4th ed.). New York: John Wiley & Sons.

Suyemoto, K.L. (2004). Racial/ethnic identities and related attributed experiences of multiracial Japanese European Americans. *Journal of Multicultural Counseling and Development, 32,* 206-221.

Tizard B., & Phoenix, A. (1993). *Black, White or mixed race? Race and racism in the lives of young people of mixed parentage.* New York: Rutledge.

Tomishima, S. (2003). When and how families can disrupt mixed race identity. In M. P. P. Root & M. Kelley (Eds), *Multiracial child resource book: Living complex identities.* (pp. 95-101). Seattle: Mavin Foundation.

Wehrly, B. (1996). *Counseling interracial individuals and families.* Alexandria, VA: American Counseling Association.

Williams, T. K. (1996). Race as process: Reassessing the "What are you?" encounters of biracial individuals. In M. P. P. Root (Ed.) *The multiracial experience: Racial borders as the new frontier* (pp. 191-210). Thousand Oaks, CA: Sage.

෬ 13 ෭

When Constructs Collide: Constructivist Research on When and How to Challenge Clients

Daniel C. Williams & Heidi M. Levitt

Once thought to be an objective process, many now consider psychotherapy to be a value laden endeavor. The literature on multiculturalism has highlighted the danger of value imposition when therapists are unaware of their cultural biases (Sue & Sue, 1990). However, other research has demonstrated that therapy, unavoidably, does change clients' values (T. Kelly, 1990). Consequently, therapists face the dilemma of deciding when they should work within clients' belief systems and when they should challenge clients' ideas. In this chapter, findings from constructivist research studies exploring therapists' and clients' perspectives will be compared to elucidate practice-based principles to guide therapists' conceptualizations and moment-to-moment decisions around dealing with therapist-client differences.

It seems likely that all psychotherapists, at some point, will encounter moments in therapy when they are uncomfortable or ardently disagree with a client's stance or course of action. Although psychotherapy often is seen as a co-constructed process in which clients' and therapists' perspectives come together (Monk, 1997; Neimeyer, 1995, 1996), there is bound to be the occasional disagreement and divergence in constructs as well. A question rarely answered, however, is *what should therapists do in moments of therapist-client difference?* Should therapists respect clients' expertise in their own lives and try to place their differences to the side? Or should they more actively challenge clients' stances and directly encourage specific courses of action? It might be that therapists' potentially healthier perspectives would benefit clients, but therapists' advocating certain paths also might damage the alliance

The authors would like to thank the Social Sciences and Humanities Council of Canada for their support

273

when clients are committed to different paths. This chapter highlights how constructivist research can inform therapy practice and guide therapists through pressing clinical dilemmas. To better understand the issues involved in the decision of when to challenge clients and when to work within their perspectives, we review the literature on this topic. Findings drawn from two research studies—one from the perspective of the client, and the other from that of the therapist—are compared.

Creative Versus Corrective

Neimeyer (1995) provided a useful heuristic to differentiate how constructivist therapists challenge their clients as opposed to therapists who work within more of a foundationalist framework, when he wrote that constructivists are "creative, not corrective" (p. 17). By this he meant that constructivist therapies seek novel solutions that may be idiosyncratic to each client rather than attempting to guide clients to adopt a preconceived solution or correct action. Using this heuristic, we will identify and describe beliefs about client-therapist differences from both a creative and a corrective approach and consider how each can inform therapists' responses to client-therapist differences.

Creative approaches. Carl Rogers (1957) provides an example of a creative approach to challenging clients. His three necessary therapeutic conditions are: *genuineness,* or therapists' ability to accurately express their internal experience; *unconditional positive regard,* or therapists' unreserved acceptance and respect for clients; and *empathy,* or the ability of therapists to sense and communicate clients' subjective experiences. Rogers challenged his clients, not by providing solutions to their problems, but by guiding them to internally reflect, more accurately and genuinely understand themselves and their experiences, and find their own direction. For instance, in the following segment from a well-known videotaped session (Shostrom, 1964) with a client, Gloria, she put forward a concern about whether she should be honest with her daughter, Pam, about her sexual relations and Rogers challenged the focus of this concern:

> *Gloria:* Do you feel that that [telling her I am having sexual relations with men] could hurt her [my daughter, Pam]?

> *Rogers:* I guess, I am sure this will sound evasive to you, but it seems to me that perhaps the person you are not being fully

honest with is you? Because I was very much struck by the fact that you were saying, "If I feel all right about what I have done, whether it's going to bed with a man or what, if I really feel all right about it, then I do not have any concern about what I would tell Pam or [about] my relationship with her."

Gloria: Right. All right. Now I hear what you are saying (pause). Then all right, then I want to work on accepting me, then. I want to work on feeling all right about it. That makes sense. That that will come natural and then I won't have to worry about Pammy.

His questioning tone, demeanor and pace encouraged Gloria to introspect and to come to a new understanding of her problem, one centered upon her own beliefs about relationships rather than her daughter's beliefs. In doing so, he referenced her prior thoughts and challenged her to synthesize them in a new way.

Corrective approaches. One clear example of a corrective approach is Albert Ellis' Rational Emotive Therapy (RET), in which he helps clients modify thoughts guided by a list of 12 core irrational beliefs. According to Ellis (1979), "The most elegant and probably the most common cognitive method of RET consists of the therapist's actively-directively disputing the client's irrational beliefs. If there is any fundamental rational-emotive method, this is probably it" (p. 67). Ellis viewed his role as an authoritative educator on adaptive thinking and beliefs.

In a similar session with the same client (Shostrom, 1964), Ellis challenged Gloria to develop a new understanding of her problem attracting desirable men:

Gloria: What I was hoping, is whatever this is in me —why I don't seem to be attracting these kind of men, why I seem more on the defensive [with them], why I seem more afraid— you could help me with what it is I'm afraid of so I won't do it so much.

Ellis: Well, my hypothesis is, so far, that what you're afraid of is not just failing with this individual man, which is really the only thing at issue when you go out with a new—and we are talking about eligible male (now we are ruling out the ineligible ones)— you are not just afraid that you will miss this one. You're afraid that you will miss this one and therefore you'll miss every other; and therefore you've proved that you are really not up to getting what you want and wouldn't that be awful? You are bringing in these catastrophes.

Gloria: Well, you sound more strong at it, but that's similar [to how I feel]. I feel like this is silly if I keep this up.

275

While Rogers was tentative and built a new understanding from the story emerging in the moment, Ellis speaks with an authority and conviction that may enhance his ability to teach the client the extant strategies he had developed. In contrast to the creative approach to challenging, which seeks to avoid leading clients to a preconceived solution by the therapist, the corrective approach is based on the assumption that the therapist has a prior understanding of what solution is healthy and should educate the client about that solution.

Values Literature

Psychology's understanding of the nature of psychotherapy has continued to evolve over the past half century. Once thought of as a scientifically objective procedure for changing human behavior and experience, many now understand psychotherapy as a value laden enterprise (e.g. Bergin, 1980). This importance of values is supported by empirical research demonstrating that clients' values become more like their therapists' through the course of therapy (Beutler, 1979; T. Kelly, 1990; Tjeltviet, 1986), and that therapists do not rate their clients as improved until clients' values have shifted closer towards their own (Rosenthal, 1955). In fact, values typically thought to be out of the purview of psychotherapy, such as religion, have been found not to be exempt from this phenomenon (Beutler, 1979; T. A. Kelly & Strupp, 1992). Despite the shifting of clients' values, however, therapists' values do not seem to be so easily influenced as research shows that they do not shift throughout therapy, leading Tjeltveit (1986, 1999) to term this phenomenon *value conversion*. Thus it seems that no matter how hard therapists try, the previously perceived ideal of value neutrality may not be possible. This literature tends to suggest that client-therapist value differences should be dealt with by encouraging therapists to be generally cautious about their influence on clients (e.g. Tjeltveit, 1999), although a postmodern approach is developing in which therapists are advised to be upfront about their personal values with clients and to openly discuss differences (Doherty, 1995; Slife, Smith, & Burchfield, 2003; Slife, 2004).

Multiculturalism Literature

Similar to the values literature, the multicultural movement is infused with an understanding that psychotherapy is a value laden enterprise that has been shaped largely without input from minority voices. As a result, many multiculturalists share concerns about the potential for value conversion and potential abuse that could result from it. Addressing this concern, one of the multicultural competencies (Sue et al., 1998) is that counselors become "aware of how their own cultural background and experiences, attitudes, values, and biases influence psychological processes" (p. 38). The danger is that therapists' lack of awareness of their values could result in a culturally oppressive act of value imposition (Sue & Sue, 1990). In response to these potential dangers, multiculturalists have sought to end oppression not only at an individual level, but also at a societal one by promoting the value of social justice (Sue et al., 1998; Vera & Speight, 2003; See Fowers & Richardson, 1996 for discussion of multiculturalism as value imposition). The multicultural movement offers a necessary reminder that the stakes are potentially high when therapists challenge clients, as there is the possibility that therapists can further the social oppression of minorities by misunderstanding clients' needs and perspectives. This movement tends to advocate, on one hand, that therapists act cautiously about challenging clients' values that might be embedded in their cultural context (Pederson, 1997; Roysircar, Arredondo, Fuertes, Ponterotto, & Toporek, 2003), but, on the other hand, they encourage therapists to challenge clients to explore racist or other xenophobic beliefs (Tinsley-Jones, 2003). Their concern, therefore, is not to eliminate the process by which therapists might shift client values, but to eliminate oppressive elements within that process.

STUDY ONE: THERAPISTS' PERSPECTIVES ON CHALLENGING CLIENTS' IDEAS

Fourteen eminent psychotherapists, from four major psychotherapy orientations, were interviewed to explore their understanding of the process of change (see Table 1 for list of participants). The interviews were transcribed and analyzed using a qualitative method called grounded theory (Glaser & Strauss, 1967). This inductive method was designed to develop an empirically-based model of a phenomenon based on participants' experiences. In this process, the interviews were broken down into "meaning units"—segments of text that each contain a single main idea (Giorgi, 1970). Next, the meaning units were compared to

277

each other and formed into categories according to perceived similarities. The categories were then compared to one another, based on their similarities, to form higher-order categories. This process, called constant comparison, continued until a hierarchical model of therapists' experience of the process of change was developed. The hierarchy became saturated, meaning that the final interviews did not add new information to the hierarchy and the data collection process was considered complete. This saturation suggested that the hierarchical model was comprehensive. Throughout the analysis, a process of "memoing" was used to record shifts in hypotheses and conceptualizations in an attempt to record and bracket theories that developed, and to restrict the influence of a priori ideas upon the analytic process.

TABLE 1. THERAPISTS' APPROACHES AND CATEGORIZED
ORIENTATIONS

THERAPIST NAME	APPROACH
Arthur Bohart	Humanist
Laura Brown	Constructivist
Gerald Davison	Cognitive-behavioral
Morris Eagle	Psychodynamic
Bruce Ecker	Constructivist
Arthur Freeman	Cognitive-behavioral
Marvin Goldfried	Cognitive-behavioral
Leslie Greenberg	Humanist
Steven Hollon	Cognitive-behavioral
Adelbert Jenkins	Psychodynamic
Robert Neimeyer	Constructivist
Donald Polkinghorne	Constructivist
David Rennie	Humanist
Donald Spence	Psychodynamic

Several checks were conducted to ensure the credibility of the findings. First, at the end of each interview, the interviewee was asked about the process of the interview to determine if any information was withheld due to the interviewer. Participating therapists denied withholding any pertinent information and reported feeling comfortable during the interview. Second, the analysis was conducted by both authors and consensus was reached on the analysis. Third, following the analysis, the participants were asked to provide feedback on the results. Half of the participating therapists responded and provided positive feedback about the analysis. These checks increased the credibility of the analysis. In order to indicate how widely different themes were discussed across orientations, the number of participants who contributed to a theme according to participants' general orientations are provided in text for each major theme and in Table 1, while their specific, self-identified orientations are listed following their names in the text. For further details on the method for this study please see Williams and Levitt (2007).

Findings from Research on Therapists

Despite the fact that there was some consensus that their values did influence therapy, therapists disagreed on how values in therapy should be managed. Their disagreement was captured within the following question: Should therapists attempt to situate themselves within clients' perspectives, or should they challenge clients to adopt their own, potentially healthier, views?

Value judgments as inevitable. For all the therapists who addressed the question of the role of values ($N = 9$; 3 = Humanist, 3 = CBT, 2 = Constructivist, 1 = Psychodynamic), psychotherapy was understood as value laden, and values were assumed to influence the course of therapy. When asked whether his values influenced his therapy, Arthur Bohart (Humanist) stated:

> I am sure they do, though I would like to say they don't, but I'm sure they do. . . . Even with Carl Rogers you could see his values. . . . And I don't think that there's any way that the client being an intelligent human being isn't going to say "Here's this other human being who is an authority figure and they think this and think that and I'm sure going to consider that." So yeah, I don't think there's any question that our values—I don't think you can hide them. . . . But having said that that doesn't mean that you can't create an environment as much as possible [with] some degree of freedom of choice.

279

> There's still a difference between the degree of freedom they
> have to consider and [to] accept.

Although values were acknowledged as influential and perceptible by clients, therapists still sought to ensure that clients would choose their own values.

Therapist defers to client's values. The majority of therapists (N = 9; 3 = Constructivist, 3 = CBT, 1 = Psychodynamic, 2 = Humanist) described taking, at least at certain times, a morally relativistic stance in which they tried to situate themselves within clients' perspectives while guiding the therapy. One way of accomplishing this goal was to place clients in the driver's seat. Laura Brown (Constructivist) described her practice of this approach:

> So the important thing as a feminist therapist is *not* to make
> my values be the values of what happens in the therapy, but to
> support clients in the development of their own voice again—
> own voice, own values. What's important to them?

Asking clients to make important therapeutic decisions was thought to lead to the development of clients' values.

Sometimes, however, it was not easy for therapists to avoid interjecting their own values when they believed that clients might be off course. Marvin Goldfried (CBT) described such a struggle and how he was able to maintain his focus on working toward the client's goal.

> I try to make every effort not to let that [my perspective]
> interfere, but sometimes it's very, very hard to do that. And
> sometimes in the process of doing that it becomes distressful.
> For example, I saw a guy who . . . was having an affair and was
> getting ready to divorce his wife, and she didn't know about it.
> And what he was really upset about was that his grown kids
> would not want to have anything to do with him. . . . But I
> worked with him to help him to maintain a decent relationship
> with his kids by encouraging him . . . to explain to his kids that
> he and his wife no longer had enough shared interests, so he was
> not leaving her for another woman, which I thought would be
> the best way of him achieving his goals of having his kids
> maintain a relationship with him, so it would be less of a blow.
> And then only later on report that he was involved with
> somebody else. So that was very stressful to me, but I had the
> allegiance to him and what his goal was. And he was in great
> distress too about his family. So values certainly do play a role in
> either saying "I can't work with you" more or less—but I chose to
> work with him on this.

280

Acting in what he perceived to be the client's best interest was prioritized over his own personal discomfort about the client's choices.

When therapists felt like their biases might be coming through, therapists sometimes reported disclosing this struggle to their clients (N = 4; 1 = Psychodynamic, 1 = Humanist, 1 = CBT, 1 = Constructivist). Morris Eagle (Psychodynamic) shared an example of his disclosure:

> I'm just working with a man. I've seen he and his wife together, they've been separated. . . . And he also has a girlfriend and they've been separated, a mistress. And I realized that my own bias was to hope that they would get back together, his wife and him. And I don't know that that's necessarily the best thing for him. But it was definitely my bias. And at a certain point I think I needed to make that clear to him, but also try to make clear to him that I really wanted to focus on what was best for him. But that's a very clear, concrete example of my own values, biases being present and having to be dealt with. . . . In this case I openly acknowledged it, yes. I thought it was more helpful to do that rather for it to come across in subtle ways, some of which I myself was not aware of. Like a kind of subtle reinforcement.

Instead of challenging clients to adopt their own beliefs, by disclosing their biases, some therapists seek to empower their clients, minimizing the influence of therapist values and avoiding implicit persuasion.

Therapist challenges client's position. Although generally therapists seemed to want to work within clients' frameworks and accomplish their goals, therapists reported times when they clearly disagreed with clients and would strongly challenge their clients' perspectives (N = 11; 4 = CBT, 3 = Humanist, 2 = Psychodynamic, 2 = Constructivist). These situations seemed to occur when therapists thought clients' perspectives would impede change or when they strongly clashed with therapists' own values about therapeutic change. Gerald Davison (CBT) recounted one experience that exemplified the importance of challenging clients.

> I would just discuss with the patient the value components of decisions like this—tell them where I stand and they should know that. Then I have to make clear what changes I'm prepared as a professional and as a person to help them work towards. Not all changes are going to be acceptable to me. . . .
> [I had a client] who wanted to be desensitized to her husband's running around with other women. She knew about desensitization and she wanted to not feel so bad when she would be

> sitting at home knowing that he was out screwing another
> woman. I found this unacceptable and I told her so. I said 'No, I
> can't do that with you.' Then it turned out once I said that, it
> turned out that's not really what she wanted anyway, and she
> wanted to talk about why she was putting up with this crap, and
> maybe she should get out of the marriage. . . . But most
> importantly I told her from the get go, 'No, I don't think that
> that's something I'd feel comfortable working on, in fact I know
> it wouldn't, so is there something else you would like to talk
> about?'

In deciding whether to accept or challenge a client's goal, these
therapists attuned themselves to their own comfort level, based
on their values, to determine its acceptability. When the goal
was not acceptable, they openly challenged clients to find a
more acceptable one.

Another cognitive-behavioral therapist, Arthur Freeman,
recounted an experience highlighting the importance of challenging
clients' maladaptive behavior:

> As an example I had a referral of a woman in her eighties,
> her daughter says "I can't stand her anymore," you know.
> "Unless you get some help, I'm just going to put you in a home."
> She was living with the daughter and the daughter's family.
> And this [elderly] woman comes into my office and. . . [there]
> are pictures of my family, my children, my grandchildren.
> And she walks in and kind of stops and looks at the pictures
> and says "are those your children?" Obviously, I said "yes."
> She says, "They're very unattractive. . . . " I say, "Why would you
> say that?" She says, "Well, because it's true." I said, "Well, yeah,
> I understand, even were it true, why would you say that?" But
> for her to walk into my office and say, "You have ugly children,"
> is really, in a microcosm, why her daughter doesn't want her to
> live at home, because this woman is insulting and nasty. . . .
> [She replied] "Well, I've always believed in telling the truth."
> [I said] "Well I understand that. Are you willing to tell the truth
> no matter what the consequences? If the consequence is for
> example, that your daughter says, 'Mom, because you're such a
> great truth teller, I don't want you to live here anymore, you're
> going to have to go live in a home?'" If she says, "Yes, I'd rather
> live in a home and be honest," you know the old Shakespearean
> injunction, "To thine own self be true." Fine, that's a decision.
> As a therapist, I would not try to work on that. I mean, that's a
> choice people make.

Because the client's insulting behavior was strongly interfering
with the therapeutic process as well as her external interactions,
the therapist believed it was important to challenge the client's

282

behavior and encouraged evaluation, but without insisting on compliance with his beliefs.

As a final example of challenging clients, two therapists reported challenging clients to act more socially responsible. Donald Polkinghorne (Constructivist) articulated this position,

> I think people have responsibility for their children, responsibility not to hurt other people and in working out things to be done that would enter into my looking and working through the options with the person. . . . If their [the client's] point is basically, "I don't care, that's not my job, my job is to take care of me," I terribly wouldn't be supportive of that. . . . I would say I really have different values. I think it's very important what happens when you have responsibility. I'd try to remind them of that, with the hope that that's just something they had forgotten or had heard somewhere, that they should just look out for number one (Levitt, Neimeyer, & Williams, 2005; Williams & Levitt, 2007).

In these cases when the client may be hurting someone who might not be able to protect him/herself, not only did the therapists seek to challenge clients' actions, but also to lead them toward a specific, self-identified solution.

Thus, there were two main approaches to challenging clients, although they were not mutually exclusive. In the first approach, therapists sought to work within clients' perspectives by challenging them to direct the course of therapy. Within the second approach, therapists openly challenged clients' behavior or values and provided more direction on how to change.

STUDY TWO: CLIENTS' PERSPECTIVES ON BEING CHALLENGED BY THEIR THERAPISTS

In this study, twenty-six participants were interviewed who varied in terms of their gender (6 men and 20 women), age (mean age = 29.23, SD = 13.90, range 18 - 79), careers (including blue collar, white collar, and student occupations), and presenting problems (including varied concerns such as familial issues, assertiveness, depression, rape, anxiety, anger, attention deficit disorders, and eating disorders). These differences within participants are considered a strength by grounded theorists, who seek to diversify sources of information and develop results that are as rich and encompassing as possible (Glaser & Strauss, 1967). Participants were involved in individual psychotherapies that were, at minimum,

283

eight sessions in duration (mean = 15.80 months, *SD* = 23.54 months, range = 1 month–10 years). All clients completed their course of psychotherapy two months prior to the interview, allowing time to reflect upon and assess their experience, but not greater than one year prior, so that details of their experience remained accessible.

To facilitate a sense of comfort about disclosure, participants were not asked to disclose the identity of their therapist or the context in which they practiced, and most could not describe their therapists' orientation or professional degree. The researchers surmised, however, from the descriptions of gestalt chairing exercises, assertiveness training, early childhood exploration, cognitive thought records, pillow-beating, hypnosis, and paraphrasing that therapies ranged across major therapeutic orientations.

Clients in this study were asked to describe whatever was significant or important to them about their general psychotherapy, specific psychotherapy moments, and therapeutic relationship—although the results presented here focus specifically on their reactions to being challenged by therapists. The grounded theory method (Glaser & Strauss, 1967) described already in Study 1 was used in this analysis as well. Similar credibility checks were used in this study as well, although the authors had difficulty obtaining feedback at the end of the analysis from the participants due to the lengthy transcription of the data (one year) and analytic process (eight months) required by this intensive method and the mobility associated with a university city that made participants difficult to reach. For more information on the method of this study, please see the original study (Levitt, Butler, & Hill, in press).

Findings from Research on Clients

Therapists' challenging as problematic. Generally, therapists' challenging was not well received by clients. Nineteen of the 26 participants described being challenged in negative terms. Sometimes the challenging was unwelcome because it posed a set of external demands. One client described,

> I had a really hard time opening up to my therapist and talking with her. Felt a little like she was pushing me at times, giving me books to read, and "Have you read this book?" and "Read this book", and "Alright, let's try this, now I want you to write a letter to your father". It was like — (laughing) "Hold on a minute!". . . . I felt all in all it was demanding. (Participant 08)

This challenging could keep clients from expressing and exploring what they needed. Another client conveyed this succinctly:

> You know a lot of people when they give you counseling they want to teach you, they try to teach you. To a certain degree that's good, I mean, if you need it. If somebody's trying to teach you all the time [though], you feel like you're not being heard, they're not recognizing what you're. . . . What you're thinking, what you're feeling, [they are more] involved in what they think you need. Rather than being more attentive and listening to what's going on [for you]. (Participant 05)

It was interesting that clients resisted challenging even when the therapists were attempting to support them. For instance, one rape victim described resenting her therapist's strong advocacy:

> I didn't expect her to say good things about him [the rapist], but I kind of just wanted her to be like, I don't know . . . supportive but not too, too — not overbearing in her supportiveness. . . . She would just be talking about it too much and be driving me crazy. And I didn't want to go in there and have this lady being like, "All rapists are assholes, blah blah, blah." . . . I needed her to be calmer. . . . You know what I mean? It's like I don't need a big parade, put it that way, and a big entourage with what she has to say. (Participant 25)

One client described when she would let her therapist know that her "annoying" persistence was disruptive: "After a while, if she kept like pushing me, like too much. [Then] I'm going to be like umm, 'This is really an option I'm not considering so can you, can we like please move on. Can you like suggest something else?'" (Participant 26). More typically, however, clients admitted being reluctant to convey their discomfort to their therapists at all.

Therapists' challenging as needed. In contrast, challenging was interpreted differently when it was used to confront clients who were being manipulative within the therapeutic context or were avoiding important aspects of their experience. Often clients liked being challenged when they felt that they actively were avoiding some important issue in their lives.

> [My therapist and I], we were always not fighting, but not agreeing. Like she told me something and I was like "you you're wrong, you're totally wrong. I like my father, I don't like my mother," for example. And she told me "No, you don't like your father you have a little problem with your mother." And that was good. . . .because when I was finished the hour I was at

home you know thinking and thinking "Why, why did she say that?" . . . It's like when you don't want to see something like she's right. Why, why did I tell her "No, you're wrong"? Because I don't want to face it. (Participant 08).

This challenging could be about engagement in the therapy itself:

I'm always very private when I'm first going to therapy, and um, I think my last therapist was the only one who really uh, took the time to, to say to me "Ok, see, it's time to stop doing what you're doing, because you're not doing anything". Um, and I think that's, that's the real reason why — I started going forward but it took almost a year to get to the point where we were going forward. . . . I think I resisted doing it a little longer, and she kept badgering me, and she continued to throughout therapy anytime that she saw that I was starting to, to do that again. . . . You know, "You're, you're disconnecting", or "You're . . . not being . . . honest with your emotions" (Participant 18).

An eating disordered client compared two therapists she had:

[The first] was just a nice man, you know. I cared about him as a person and he did help me in the beginning because when I first came to him. . . . I needed that, that understanding that he had. . . . But in order for me to get better, I need to know that the person I'm talking to is stronger than this thing [eating disorder] inside me, so that I can trust them with my life and I couldn't trust him [to be strict with me]. [The second therapist] he just knew that he couldn't get too close because, like. . . [then] I couldn't manipulate him. This man was like, even when I was not lying, he said I was lying. . . . He put me on it [bedrest] for four or five days. I was miserable, and he showed me. . . . He was so condescending, too. . . . And finally I would just start to do it [eat], and that's what, I guess in a way he put ideas in my head and then it would get to where I chose it. . . . I just, I felt like he gave me direction, I felt like, in a way, he just really gave me direction, I just really respected him. (Participant 23).

When clients were manipulating therapists, lying, or avoiding working, they reported wanting therapists to challenge them on these points and feeling distressed when this did not occur.

DISCUSSION

In both studies, principles to describe the main patterns of interaction were developed from the hermeneutic analysis of the hierarchy that was formed. While rules are specific, mechanistic

286

prescriptions for guiding conduct across contexts, principles are contextually situated directives in which conduct changes depending on changing circumstances (see Levitt, Neimeyer & Williams, 2005 for a discussion of the term *principles*). In both studies, the authors examined the patterns and assumptions in the responses that could lead to the identification of principles within the interview text. Principles were reviewed and consensus was developed by the authors conducting that analysis.

From the study on the therapists, the following principle was formed: *Eminent therapists desired to respect clients' values by allowing their use during explorations unless these values were thought to actively impede change, as based upon therapists' personal or professional values about the therapeutic change process. In that case, therapists would directly engage clients in evaluating that value.* This principle was created to distill the thoughts that expert therapists used in deciding what course of action to take when deciding if a therapist-client difference should lead to challenging or not. When therapists thought that the clients were impairing their own development, hurting vulnerable significant others, or blocking the therapy process, the therapists considered challenging clients on their actions or ideas.

The study on clients' experience in therapy led to the developing of this principle: *Confrontation was thought to disrupt trust and compromise the therapy in most cases, with the exception of when the client was being manipulative or avoidant of difficult material—then it was desirable.* Typically, clients disliked being challenged. However, they prized this behavior when they were not doing the work they knew they should be doing in session. This principle differentiated the contexts in which clients are resistant to challenges from the therapist and when they desire to be pushed and confronted.

The qualitative constructivist methods used in these studies are attuned to contextual and covert factors in psychotherapy, helping researchers to construct principles for practice at the moment-by-moment level. These principles suggest directions that can guide therapists' intentionality in session by increasing their awareness of the rationale underlying both expert clinicians' decision making and clients' experiences. As such, they can be used to justify a variety of possible interventions and are not intended as behavioral prescriptions for treatment. The guidelines suggested in the principles are complementary to one another and can help therapists assess when it might be good to aggressively challenge clients, to find a gentler way of encouraging self-examination, or to work within clients' own values and beliefs.

CORRECTIVE VERSUS CREATIVE CHALLENGING REVISITED: FINDING THE BEST IN BOTH WORLDS

Going back to the construal of corrective and creative therapeutic approaches, it would appear that both therapists and clients agree that the creative approaches are better more of the time. Within both data sets, and from therapists using a variety of modalities and from clients with a variety of issues, challenges were thought to be better avoided in general.

In his personal construct theory, George Kelly highlighted the co-constructive nature of the therapeutic relationship and advocated a process of guiding clients to determine their own values:

> Instead of assuming, on the one hand, that the therapist is obliged to bring the client's thinking into line, or, on the other, that the client will mysteriously bring his own thinking into line given the proper setting, we can take the stand that the client and therapist are conjoining in an exploratory venture. The therapist assumes neither the position of judge nor that of sympathetic bystander. He is sincere about this; he is willing to learn along with his client. He is the client's fellow researcher who seeks first to understand, then to examine, and finally to assist the client in subjecting alternatives to experimental test and revision (Kelly, 1969, p. 82).

Kelly eschewed the role of the therapist as the teacher with all the correct answers. Still, he did not present himself as never challenging clients either. Instead of challenging clients to adopt a specific solution, he challenged them to experiment with and revise their own constructs, in whichever direction that may lead them.

And indeed, within both the therapists' and clients' interviews, experiences often brought to light a differentiated answer to the dilemma of therapist-client differences. As the principles in the study suggested, therapists viewed the challenging approach as destructive at times and the creative approach as insufficient at other times. An advantage of

288

qualitative constructivist work is that it can help examine the therapy at the moment-to-moment level, creating guidelines more sensitive to the ever-shifting therapy context. Further, it can develop a more nuanced understanding of what really unfolds within the therapists' intentionality as their interventions are being generated and provides a window into clients' experience—even accessing covert experiences that may not be shared with the therapist in the session (e.g. Levitt & Rennie, 2005; Rennie, 1994).

REFERENCES

Bergin, A.E. (1980). Psychotherapy and religious values. *Journal of Consulting and Clinical Psychology, 48,* 95-105.

Beutler, L. E. (1979). Values, beliefs, religion and the persuasive influence of psychotherapy. *Psychotherapy: Theory, Research, and Practice, 16*(4), 432-440.

Doherty, W.J. (1995). *Soul Searching: Why psychotherapy must promote moral responsibility.* New York: Basic Books/HarperCollins.

Ellis, A. 1979). The practice of rational-emotive therapy. In A. Ellis and J. M. Whiteley (Eds.), *Theoretical and empirical foundations of rational-emotive therapy* (pp. 61-100). Monterey, CA: Brooks/Cole.

Fowers, B. J., & Richardson, F. C. (1996). Why is multiculturalism good? *American Psychologist, 51,* 609-621.

Giorigi, A. (1970). *Psychology as a human science: A phenomenological approach.* New York: Harper & Row.

Glaser, B.G., & Strauss, A.L. (1967). *The discovery of grounded theory: Strategies for qualitative research.* Hawthorne, New York: Aldine.

Kelly, G. A. (1969). Man's construction of his alternatives. In B. Maher (Ed.), *Clinical psychology and personality: The selected papers of George Kelly* (pp. 66-93). New York: Wiley.

Kelly, T. (1990). The role of values in psychotherapy: A critical review of process and outcome effects, *Clinical Psychology Review, 10,* 171-186.

Kelly, T. A., & Strupp, H. H. (1992). Patient and therapist values in psychotherapy: Perceived changes, assimilation, similarity, and outcome. *Journal of Consulting and Clinical Psychology, 60*(1), 34-40.

Levitt, H. M., Butler, M. & Hill, T. (in press). Clients' retrospective recall of significant principles in psychotherapy. *Journal of Counseling Psychology.*

Levitt, H. M., Neimeyer, R. A., & Williams, D. (2005). Rules vs. principles in psychotherapy: Implications of the quest for universal guidelines in the movement for empirically supported treatments. *Journal of Contemporary Psychotherapy, 35,* 117-129.

Levitt, H. M, & Rennie, D. L. (2004). The act of narrating: Narrating activities and the intentions that guide them. In L. Angus & J. McLeod (Eds.), *The Handbook of Narrative and Psychotherapy: Practice, Theory, and Research.* Thousand Oaks, CA: Sage.

Monk, G. (1997). How narrative therapy works. In G. Monk, J. Winslade, K. Crocket & D. Epston (Eds.), *Narrative therapy in practice: The archaeology of hope* (pp. 3-31). San Francisco: Jossey-Bass.

Neimeyer, R. A. (1995). Constructivist psychotherapies: Features, foundations, and future directions. In R. A. Neimeyer & M. J. Mahoney (Eds.), *Constructivism in psychotherapy* (pp. 11-38). Washington, DC: American Psychological Association.

Neimeyer, R. A. (1996). Process interventions for the constructivist psychotherapist. In H. Rosen & K. T. Kuehlwein (Eds.), *Constructing Realities: Meaning-making perspectives for psychotherapists* (pp. 371-411). San Francisco: Jossey-Bass.

Pederson, P. B. (1997). Culture-centered counseling interventions: Striving for accuracy. Thousand Oaks, CA: Sage.

Rennie, D. L. (1994). Clients' deference in psychotherapy. *Journal of Counseling Psychology, 41*(4), 427-437.

Rogers, C. R. (1957). The necessary and sufficient conditions of therapeutic personality change. *Journal of Consulting Psychology, 21,* 95-103.

Rosenthal, D. (1955). Changes in some moral values following psychotherapy. *Journal of Consulting Psychology, 19,* 431-436.

Roysircar, G., Arredondo, P., Fuertes, J. N., Ponterotto, J. G., & Toporek, R. L. (2003). *Multicultural counseling competencies 2003: Association for multicultural counseling and development.* Alexandria, VA: American Counseling Association.

Shostrom, E. (1964). *Three approaches to therapy.* Santa Ana, CA: Psychological Films.

Slife, B. D., Smith, A. F., & Burchfield, C. (2003). Psychotherapists as crypto-missionaries: An examplar on the crossroads of history, theory and philosophy. In D.B. Hill & M.J. Kral (Eds.), *About Psychology: Essays at the crossroads of history, theory, and philosophy* (pp. 55-69). Albany, NE: SUNY Press.

Slife, B. D. (2004). Theoretical challenges to research and practice: The constraint of naturalism. In M. Lambert (Ed.) *Handbook of psychotherapy and behavior change* (pp. 44-83). New York: Wiley.

Sue, D. W., & Sue, D. (1990). *Counseling the culturally different*. New York: Wiley.

Sue, D. W., Carter, R. T., Casas, J. M., Fouad, N. A., Ivey, A. E., Jensen, M., LaFromboise, T., Manese, J. E., Ponterotto, J. G., & Vasquez-Nutall, E. (1998). *Multicultural counseling competencies: Individual and organizational development*. Thousand Oaks, CA: Sage.

Tinsley-Jones, H. (2003). Racism: Calling a spade a spade. *Psychotherapy: Theory, Research, Practice, Training, 40*(3), 179-186.

Tjeltveit, A. C. (1986). The ethics of value conversion in psychotherapy: Appropriate and inappropriate therapist influence on client values. *Clinical Psychology Review, 6*, 515-537.

Tjeltveit, A. C. (1999). *Ethics and values in psychotherapy*. London: Routledge.

Vera, E. M., & Speight, S. L. (2003). Multicultural competence, social justice, and counseling psychology: Expanding our roles. *Counseling Psychologist, 31*(3), 253-272.

Williams, D. C., & Levitt, H. M. (2007). A qualitative investigation of eminent therapists' values within psychotherapy: Developing integrative principles for moment-to-moment psychotherapy practice. *Journal of Psychotherapy Integration, 17*, 159-184.

PART V

CONSTRUING CONSTRUCTIVIST THERAPY IN EVERYDAY LIFE

⋈ 14 ⋈

Everyday Constructivism

Michael F. Hoyt

We are what we think,
Having become what we thought.

The Buddha,
opening lines of *The Dhammapada*
(c. 500 B.C.E./1967, p. 39)

Because our perception of the world influences how we live
in it, our consciousness sculpts reality. Conversely, our
experience shapes our thinking, so our reality molds con-
sciousness. Our minds create what is real, and our lived
experiences generate our thoughts. There is a reciprocity
between beliefs and observations—what we look for affects
what we see. . . .

Harriet Beinfield and Efrem Korngold,
Between Heaven and Earth: A Guide to
Chinese Medicine (1991, p. 17)

As far as constructivism is concerned, only the name is modern.
Paul Watzlawick
(in Watzlawick & Hoyt, 2001, p. 151)

The doors of therapeutic perception and possibility have
been opened wide by the recognition that everyday we are actively
constructing our mental realities rather than simply uncovering or
coping with an objective "truth." According to Michael Mahoney
(2003):

> Constructivism is a view of humans as active, meaning-making
> individuals who are afloat on webs of relationships while they are

This chapter is based upon a Keynote Address delivered at the 12th Biennial
Conference of the Constructivist Psychology Network in San Marcos, CA, July
2006. Figure 1 © *The New Yorker Collection* 2004 Harry Bliss from cartoonbank.com.
All rights reserved.

moving along streams of life that relentlessly require new directions and connections. Whether they realize it or not, most clients are constructivists. They construct meanings, and they live their lives from an invisible web of meanings they have woven thus far. A large part of what therapists and clients do together in constructive psychotherapy is to weave new possibilities for experiencing. (p. xii)

This largely happens through language. While I could cite any number of excellent authorities (including Efran, Lukens, & Lukens, 1990; Gergen, 1994a; Mahoney, 2003; Neimeyer & Mahoney, 1995a; Neimeyer & Raskin, 2000a; Raskin & Bridges, 2002, 2004; and Rosen & Kuehlwein, 1996), my favorite explanation of narrative constructivism is still the famous joke about the three baseball umpires disputing their acumen:

The first, the honest ethicist, says "I call 'em the way I see 'em." The second, the accurate objectivist, says "Well, that's good—but I call 'em the way they are." Finally, the third ump, the narrative constructivist, says: "They ain't nothin' until I call 'em!"

There are options to the ways we "call 'em," to how we put our stories together. Some stories are better than others, some ways of looking and thinking and acting are more invigorating and rewarding than others. Indeed, some stories define us and sustain us, serving as vessels that allow us to "carry water in the desert and fire through a blizzard" (Olson, 1995, p. 6).

Stories are the vehicle that moves metaphor and image into experience. Like metaphors and images, stories communicate what is generally invisible and ultimately inexpressible. In seeking to understand these realities through time, stories provide a perspective that touches on the divine, allowing us to see reality in full context, as part of its larger whole. Stories invite a kind of vision that gives shape and form even to the invisible, making the images move, clothing the metaphors, throwing color into the shadows. Of all the devices available to us, stories are the surest way of touching the human spirit. (Kurtz & Ketcham, 1992, p. 17)

How we look influences what we see, and what we see influences what we do (Hoyt, 2000). Everyday we construct our view of the world. People often come to therapy when their ways of looking aren't getting them what they want—they're telling themselves a story or constructing a worldview or a narrative that isn't satisfying to them. They come looking, in essence, for a new

296

story, a new perception, a new way of understanding—which can lead to new experiences, new behaviors, and new outcomes.

This chapter reviews some of the personal and professional experiences that have influenced my viewpoint. My hope is that by listening to some of these in an "invitational mood" (Kelly, 1969; McWilliams, 2004; Raskin, 2004), other people may get some ideas to help them expand their own awareness of possibilities and challenges when using constructivist therapeutic approaches with clients. As the novelist Stephen King (2000, p. 174) says, "Description begins in the writer's imagination, but should finish in the reader's."

How I Got Here

How'd I get to be a constructive therapist? How did you? I think that in some ways, I was born to it. I grew up in a largely secular Jewish home, my parents had a diversity of friends, there was a lot of storytelling, and my father had an interest in anthropology and archeology and would take me to museums—so I quickly learned that there was not just one "right way" to see the world. I'm now 57 years old. I was born in 1948, and came of age in the zeitgeist of the 1960s and 70s. In addition to a growing political and social awareness, I heard the call to "Blow your mind and come to your senses" and experimented with some ways, Western and Eastern, to alter my consciousness. The details aren't important, but the lesson was clear— this phenomenon we experience as "reality" is subject to change depending on our set and setting.

In the 1970s I did the *est* training. I know that many people nowadays barely know about *est* or think it was just some 1970s cult in which you were locked in a room, insulted, and not allowed to go to the bathroom. I also know that *est* has fallen out of favor and that the personal life of the founder, Werner Erhard, seems to have turned out to be a mess, but for many of us who were there, the actual training was a wonderful, life-affirming experience. Over two long weekends and a mid-week evening, we were led through a series of processes, drawing from Gestalt, psychodrama, psychoanalysis, psychosynthesis, hypnosis, Eastern religions, group therapy, and so on, in which we came to recognize undeniably how much of how we experience life is of our own making. We talked a lot about *It*, the realization that we make our reality in the sense that we are responsible for our perceptions and thoughts. This understanding is fundamental and pivotal. We were confronted and empowered with our abilities to choose and the consequences of keeping our agreements and having integrity. By the end, when the trainer went around the room and asked, "Did you get *It*?" I had become a confirmed constructivist and responded: "Did I get *It*? I brought *It* with me!"

When I attended the first Evolution of Psychotherapy conference in Phoenix back in 1985, I had another mind-blowing experience. The first speaker was brilliant and right on. The second speaker was equally brilliant and convincing—and contradicted the first! The third was also brilliant and convincing—and contradicted both of the others! By the time I was on the bus going back to the hotel, my mind was racing and kind of spilling out on the floor. "But . . . but . . . but!" I experientially realized that all of my cherished theories were just that—theories, ways of thinking, interesting constructs but only as real as my perception made them. I really got it![1]

In an interview I did with Michael White and Gene Combs a few years ago (Hoyt & Combs, 2001), Michael said something that impressed me profoundly. Paraphrasing the Spanish poet Antonio Machado, he remarked, "We do not just walk a path but, rather, we create our path as we walk it."[2] This echoed for me an experience I had had some years earlier when I initially met one of my mentors, Bob Goulding, at that first Evolution of Psychotherapy Conference. I was talking with Bob about his training program and asked what I would experience if I attended. He smiled, and then replied, "Well, that will depend a lot on what you do." There may be many possibilities, but we make our path as we go.

Here are a few short stories from the Hoyt family archives about everyday constructivism:

(1) I was standing at the car wash on Santa Monica and Vine in Hollywood one day in the 1960s. I was with my father waiting for his car and turned to the man standing next to me,

---

[1] As Lynn Hoffman (1993, pp. 90-91) has cogently written: "Social construction theory is really a lens about lenses. . . an awareness that what you thought looked one way, immutably and forever, can be seen in another way. You don't realize that a 'fact' is merely an 'opinion' until you are shocked by the discovery of another 'fact,' equally persuasive and exactly contradictory to the first one. The pair of facts then presents you with a larger frame that allows you to alternate or choose. At the cost of giving up moral and scientific absolutes, your social constructionist does get an enlarged sense of choice."

[2] Machado's (1983) words: "*Caminante No Hay Camino, Se Hace Camino al Andar.*"

298

who was black, and nonchalantly said "Hi, how you doing?" It was a sunny late Saturday morning and everything should have been pleasant and easy, but he looked at my pale face in a way that said there was a large distance between us. It was like walking into a wall. From my naïve, white-privileged perspective, that may have been the day I first discovered the baleful effects of the cultural construct we call race.

(2) When I received my Ph.D. degree in 1976, my proto-constructivist grandmother asked, "A *Ph.D.*? So what kind of disease is philosophy that it needs a doctor?" (Hoyt, 1995, p. 217)

(3) At age 6, my son Alexander said: "Dad, there's a nation in my head. It's called imagination!" Like the old baseball player and manager Leo Durocher used to say, you can look it up— it's the epigraph that opens the first volume of the *Constructive Therapies* books (Hoyt, 1994, p. v).

(4) A couple of years later, I had one of the worst days of my life. Twelve hours earlier, my older brother had died in the hospital after an emergency liver transplant surgery had failed. His wife was holding one of his hands and I was holding the other when he passed. He had been ill for many years, but my mother did not know anything about this last episode, and I had to drive to where she lived and tell her. Awash in my own grief, I was filled with dread as I rang her doorbell. As soon as she saw me and the look on my face, she knew something awful had happened and wailed, "Billy's dead, isn't he?" I nodded, then followed her into her place. She cried as she asked questions. I tried to comfort her. After a while, she announced that she had to call her friends. I watched as she shared the bad news, each time crying and accepting sympathy as she told the story over and over. I had not yet read Bob Neimeyer's (2002a) excellent edited volume, *Meaning Reconstruction and the Experience of Loss*—nor had my mother—but as I sat and heard phrases such as "no longer suffering," "a courageous fighter," "a good man," "in a better place," and so on I could see social construction in action as she and her friends sifted and shifted memories and incorporated one another's perspectives and reflections to construct a meaningful narrative with which they could live.

(5) My dog, Ranger, and I have a thing going: if he looks at the door a certain way, I'll put on my shoes and walk around the block! I read a fascinating *New Yorker* article (Gladwell, 2006) about the ways dogs size up a situation, cuing their behavior by

making meaning of the subtle actions of both other dogs and the creatures on the other end of the leash, and it is clear that every day Ranger and I co-construct our signals and our relationship.

I also like the way David Abrams (1996, pp. 53-54) explains things in *Spell of the Sensuous: Perception and Language in a More-than-Human World*:

> Where does perception originate? I cannot say truthfully that my perception of a particular wildflower with its color and its fragrance, is determined or "caused" entirely by the flower—since other persons may experience a somewhat different fragrance, as even I, in a different moment or mood, may see the color differently, and indeed since any bumblebee that alights on that blossom will surely have a very different perception of it than I do. But neither can I say truthfully that my perception is "caused" solely by myself—by my physiological or neural organization—or that it exists entirely "in my head." For without the actual existence of this other entity, of this flower rooted not in my brain but in the soil of the earth, there would be no fragrant and colorful perception at all, neither for myself nor for any others, whether human or insect. . . . Neither the perceiver nor the perceived, then, is wholly passive in the event of perception. . . . Perception, in this sense, is an attunement or synchronization between my own rhythms and the rhythms of the things themselves, their own tones and textures.

(6) I love supercharged language. As James Hillman (1992, p. 157) has written:

> All words have roots, histories, genders, off-spring. They reach back through the centuries to the dead tongues of ancient peoples, and they go on accumulating wealth and shedding outworn baggage as they travel from region to region. . . . Because words are so laden with hidden messages, they cannot help but be metaphors, by nature "poetic," opening beyond their commonsense definitions into mystery and myth. In fact, the Italian philosopher Giambattista Vico wrote, "a metaphor is a myth in brief."

In *The Principles of Psychology*, William James (1890, p. 293) wrote: "Each world whilst it is attended to is real after its own fashion." Recently my wife and I, along with our son and his girlfriend, went to the Berkeley Repertory Theater to see Tennessee Williams' "memory play," *The Glass Menagerie*. The acting and staging were excellent, and the playwright began to work his dramaturgic legerdemain from the narrator's opening incantation:

> Yes, I have tricks in my pocket, I have things up my sleeve. But I am the opposite of a stage magician. He gives you illusion that has the appearance of truth. I give you truth in the pleasant disguise of illusion. (Williams, 1945/1999, p. 4)

We became quickly entranced, engrossed in the scene before us. Afterwards, when the lights came back up, we came back to our regular, familiar selves. As we discussed our various perceptions and experiences, I had yet another glimpse of how the gloss of my everyday reality is a construction.

DOING THERAPY

While many members of the Constructivist Psychology Network have a "homepage" in George Kelly's (1955) personal construct theory, my own professional development has been based in several other major systems of psychotherapy. With special nods toward Milton Erickson, Steve de Shazer, Bob and Mary Goulding, Carl Whitaker, Michael White, and others (see Hoyt, 2004, especially pp. 230-244), my approach to psychological intervention can be subsumed under the general rubrics of *brief therapy* and *constructive therapies*. For me the hallmarks of brief therapy are the development of a collaborative alliance and the emphasis on clients' strengths and competencies in the service of the efficient attainment of co-created goals. *Brief therapy* has come to mean, generically, any therapeutic approach that is problem-driven; that is focused on resolving the presenting complaint, with the therapist responsible for creating and maintaining the focus (O'Hanlon, in Hoyt, 2001, p. 35). In this sense, *brief therapy* can include psychodynamic, solution-oriented, problem-focused, and lots of family therapy and systemic and interactional approaches—all having a goal-directed emphasis on resolving the presenting problem:

> The goal of brief psychotherapy, regardless of the specific theoretical approach or technical method, is to help the client resolve a problem, to get 'unstuck' and to move on. Techniques are specific, integrated, and as eclectic as needed. Treatment is focused, the therapist appropriately active, and the patient

> responsible for making changes. Each session is valuable, and
> therapy ends as soon as possible. Good outcomes, not good
> process, are most valued. More is not better; *better* is better. The
> patient carries on, and can return to treatment as needed. (Hoyt,
> 1995, pp. 326-327)

In addition to meaning "efficient" and "to the point,"
I would add that *brief therapy* is also used sometimes to refer
particularly to time-sensitive intervention based on certain
(generally social constructionist) theoretical principles, not on the
length of treatment.[3] Directly or indirectly, these approaches
involve a wide variety of creative methods that operate at the
level of cybernetics and hermeneutics, strategies and "language
games," all more-or-less intended to influence how clients
recursively interact and construe (or "story") their experience (Hoyt,
2001, p. xiv).

I never really set out to be a *brief therapist*. I'm just
attracted to things that are efficient in reducing suffering and
that are lively and creative and respectful of people's existing
talents and abilities. I'm interested in being an *expander*, not a
shrink (Hoyt, 1985/1995, pp. 209-211). I'm interested in what works.
I try to attend to intrapsychic as well as interpersonal aspects.
Most of the time I'm my solution-focused/narrative/client-centered
self (with an existential-experiential strategic twist). I try to
assist people to use better what they've got. Sometimes I teach
skills, like communication and relaxation; sometimes I'll try to
bring to awareness what appears to be a limiting unconscious
belief or conflict; sometimes I'll do something akin to a form of
problem-solving cognitive therapy; occasionally I'm downright
directive and even confrontational. If simple rationality was all

---

[3] Neimeyer and Raskin (2000b, pp. 7-8) comment that the "tension between the
demands of a belt-tightening system of managed care and its apparent resistance
by many constructivist, social constructionist, and narrative therapists may lead
some readers to question the practicality of a postmodern therapy in light of the
economic realities imposed by living in a modern world," but then go on to note
that "[these] therapies have frequently been on the cutting edge in the development
of brief therapies that refuse to sacrifice subtlety of discourse for speed of delivery."
Because I do my clinical practice within a health-maintenance organization, I also
have come to have a quotidian awareness of certain inherent contradictions or
dilemmas between the theoretical underpinnings of constructivist/postmodern
therapy and managed care (which wants quick results). My colleague, Steven
Friedman, and I have discussed four of these dilemmas in a chapter that appears in
Some Stories Are Better than Others (Hoyt, 2000, pp. 109-117): (1) Possibility vs.
Certainty, (2) Egalitarian vs. Expert, (3) Competency vs. Pathology, and (4) Systemic vs.
Unilateral.

that was needed, all my OCD patients would get better in a single visit. They don't.

When I edited the first volume of *Constructive Therapies* (Hoyt, 1994; also see Hoyt, 1996, 1998), I was initially going to call it *Building Solutions*, but the publisher wanted a different title, something broader (not sounding like it only covered solution-focused therapy). *Building* = *Constructive* and *Solutions* = *Therapies*, plus *constructive* refers to the theoretical basis of constructivism and social constructionism and also has the connotations of positive, productive, creative, and so on (Hoyt, 2000, p. 139). If asked about my theoretical orientation, I usually reply that I don't quite know, although when pushed, I'll finally say something like "Narrative constructivism—helping people see how they're putting their story together and how they might do it in a way that gets them more of what they want." For me, the term *narrative constructivism* refers to the idea that we are each actively building our worldviews, our stories about ourselves and others, our psychological realities. Technically, I suppose that I'm what some folks call a *social constructionist* or a *critical constructivist* (see Neimeyer & Mahoney, 1995b, p. 403; Raskin, 2002). It's important to keep in mind that it is not all languaging and perception. Knowing involves construal, construction, interpretation, meaning-making, and so on; but there is a *there* there—even if we can only know it through a glass (darkly or otherwise). It gets filtered, mediated through our lenses, and we can influence that process. As George Kelly wrote (1955, pp. 6-8):

> We assume that the universe is really existing and that man [sic] is gradually coming to understand it. By taking this position we attempt to make clear from the onset that it is a real world that we shall be talking about, not a world composed solely of the flitting shadows of people's thoughts. But we should like, furthermore, to make clear our conviction that people's thoughts also really exist, though the correspondence between what people really think exists and what really does exist is a continually changing one. . . . Any living creature, together with his perceptions, is a part of the real world; he is not merely a near-sighted bystander to the goings-on of the real world.

Theories are stories. They are useful; indeed, essential. Both George Kelly (1969) and Gregory Bateson (1972, 1980) reminded us that you cannot *not* have an epistemology, even if you are unaware of what it may be; and it was Kurt Lewin (Marrow, 1977) who often

remarked that "That there is nothing as practical as a good theory."[4]
Some theories—like some stories—are more helpful than others.
The skillful practice of therapy is craft-like in its application, and we
all need some framework to orient our intention and response.
As Ecker and Hulley (1996, p. 6) have written:

> A constructive therapist assumes that there are any number
> of viable ways the client's view of reality could change that
> would dispel the presenting problem, and in a spirit of
> collaboration, the therapist and client consider and try out
> such possibilities. The differences among constructivist
> therapies are differences in how they select an alternative,
> symptom-free view of reality for the client to experimentally
> inhabit, and in how they invite and assist the client to do so.

One effective way to guide clients toward new perceptions
is to ask good questions. We can arouse people's imagination
and curiosity and invite them to refocus their attention and
resourcefulness toward where they want to go using a variety of
methods, such as:

- When a solution-focused therapist asks the Miracle
  Question (de Shazer, 1985): "Suppose tonight, while
  you're sleeping, a miracle happens and the problem you
  came to see me about is gone—how will you notice?"

- When a redecision therapist (Goulding & Goulding,
  1979) asks the basic contract question: "What are
  you willing to change today?"

- When a narrative therapist (White & Epston, 1990)
  asks the relative influence question: "When are you
  able to influence the problem, and when does it
  influence you?"

[4] As Carlos Sluzki (1988, pp. 80-81, emphases in original) has noted, "Constructivism
is a way of *talking about* therapy, rather than of *doing it.* Being a theory of knowledge
rather than a set of techniques, constructivism offers us not a particular way of
helping clients, but a way of understanding how we use our clinical tools and
the interplay between practitioners' beliefs and their practice." Speaking of theory,
Mary Catherine Bateson (in Simpkins & Simpkins, 2005, p. 26) remarked: "My
sense is that [Milton] Erickson was highly improvisational. One of the things
that sometimes concerns me about therapists is that they would like to have
formulas to deal with the great ambiguity of the relationship. . . . [I]t is important
to have a theory, and there are lots of theories about what is happening in
psychotherapy. It turns out that having a theory is very helpful, but you have to
hold that theory lightly and flexibly."

We can also use directives, as when Milton Erickson (1954) had a client gaze into an imaginary crystal ball to see the answer to their problem; or when Jay Haley (1984) prescribed an ordeal that forced the clients to develop new ways of solving their problems; or we can arrange a situation, à la narrative therapist Michael White (1995; also see Friedman, 1995) that allows clients to listen to (and possibly incorporate and modify) the multiple perspectives of a reflecting team.

Constructive therapists often focus on how language builds our worldview and the practical consequences (utility) of these constructions.[5] Every day we attempt to fashion "silk purses from sows' ears" as we suggest different meanings for a particular set of events and circumstances, whether it be relabeling a teenager's rude intransigence as efforts toward "adolescent independence"; positively connotating a husband's somewhat domineering manner as his (albeit) clumsy efforts at "'caring'"; recasting a heavy drinker's relative alcohol tolerance as a sign not that they can safely "hold their liquor'" but, rather, than they are at serious risk (Miller & Rollnick, 1991, pp. 107-108); or reframing a substance abuser's relapse as the client's internal reminder that he or she is still a "recovering person" who needs to be more vigilant about the recovery process (Berg, 1994, p. 213).

Consider which description of *reframing* is richer, more inviting, and more redolent with possibilities. This one—from my fine colleagues at the Mental Research Institute (Watzlawick, Weakland, & Fisch, 1974, p. 95):

> To reframe, then, means to change the conceptual and/or emotional setting or viewpoint in relation to which a situation is experienced and to place it in another frame which fits the "facts" of the same concrete situation equally well or even better, and thereby changes its entire meaning.

Or this, from Walt Whitman's *Leaves of Grass* (1891-92/1940, Stanza 21):

> I am the poet of the Body and I am the poet of the Soul.
>
> The pleasures of heaven are with me and the pains of hell are with me.
>
> The first I graft and increase upon myself,
>
> The latter I translate into a new tongue.

[5] It is important to keep in mind that *language* and *languaging* need to be conceived

305

Other ways of thinking about this are possible, of course. In *The Heart of the Dragon*, Alasdair Clayre (1984, p. 108) writes:

> The Chinese have a favorite term, *banfa*, meaning any stratagem for getting around an obstacle; and the chief skill of a mediator often lies in his capacity to think of a solution that will get people out of a conflict while saving everyone's "face": avoiding a quarrel and achieving a reconciliation by making people see things differently, preferably in such a way that no one's dignity is lost.[6]

I also like what Cloé Madanes (1990, pp. 213-214) says about reframing:

> The therapist explains to the family that the origin of the problem, the motivations of the characters, and the nature of the conflict are not as they appear. That is, family members come to the therapy with one view of the obstacles that they find overwhelming. The therapist transforms these obstacles into new difficulties that can be resolved. . . . With reframing, magic is introduced. . . . [R]eframing introduces to the family meaning, drama, and the possibility of being someone else, of relating and living in ways that have gone unsuspected. The truth of the reframing depends on its own persuasive powers, on the skill of the magic. Every good therapy tells the truth and every bad therapy lies. Truth in therapy is to make the client experience an illusion; manipulation and lies mean to be unable to accomplish that trickery. Therapy has its own ethic, one in which truth and falsehood are secondary concepts.

---

more broadly than mere talk or talking; stories are usually told in words—prose, poetry, and song—but they can also be expressed in other forms of language, such as art and dance. Thus, Ecker and Hulley (1996, p. 3) call for "active engagement with *full* phenomenology—emotional, cognitive, somatic (kinesthetic and somesthetic), and behavioral, conscious and unconscious."

[6] Rick Foster and Greg Hicks (1999, pp. 110-111) describe the related concept of *recasting*, in which a person moves through a painful experience to a new understanding. They write: "Recasting has two phases. First, happy people dive into negative feelings head on and experience them deeply. . . . Once they are fully engaged with their emotions they move into the second phase. They begin to transform their feelings with new reactions and insights. What lessons can they learn? What new meaning can they create for their lives? What opportunities for the future can they create from this experience? . . . When we recast we put the event and our reactions into a psychological furnace and melt them down. Over time, we allow ourselves to feel the heat of the negative emotions *and* forge a richer, deeper meaning from the trauma." This would appear to be quite different from what Horowitz (1975) refers to as a "sliding of meanings" in which narcissistic patients exaggerate information which might enhance the self and minimize information that might reflect poorly on the self. From his psychodynamic framework, these "face saving" maneuvers are seen as "distortions" that serve to protect the client's fragile self-esteem at the expense of communicating realistically.

Reframing is, by nature, social and intersubjective rather than strictly individual and solipsistic (Coyne, 1985). Constructive therapy is a bipersonal endeavor that involves careful listening and active engagement, sometimes with a willing suspension of disbelief and a desire to bend one's ear toward the parable.[7] Thus, Lois Parker (2006) refers to the "oral-aural" nature of narrative, and Henry David Thoreau (1849/1980, p. 267) wrote: "It takes two to speak the truth—one to speak, and another to hear."

Reframing may offer clients a "preferred view" (Eron & Lund, 1996), but Efran, Lukens and Lukens (1988, p. 34) delineate the asymptote:

> "Reframes" sometimes work, and make sense, because they evoke alternative, viable, and socially acceptable frameworks of interpretation. However, some "reframes" are little more than cheap carnival tricks. For example, telling a teenager that cutting school was really his or her way of keeping the family together, or of distracting attention from an extramarital affair, strikes us as disingenuous and foolhardy—unless, of course, one really and truly believes such a thing. As we have attempted to make clear, constructivism is not a license to fabricate indiscriminately for immediate effect.

Circumstances and motivations are often ambiguous and subject to different interpretations (see Empson, 1930/1966; Perlman, 2003), but facts are stubborn, and "spin doctors"—whether they are therapists reframing behavior or a president claiming weapons of mass destruction—need to have their revision be both internally cohesive and correspond to external realities.[8] For reframes to endure, they must be proposed in such a manner that they validate people's interactions with their everyday environments— see Figure 1.

---

[7] Paralleling the process of my introductory remarks about hoping that readers would receive my comments in an open-minded "appreciative mood," constructive therapists, being keenly respectful of the idea that another person has at least a somewhat different construction of their personal 'truth,' often endeavor to use "experience close" language (Freedman & Combs, 1996) and to adopt a "not knowing" perspective (H. Anderson & Goolishian, 1992). For a good discussion of some narrative therapy methods for creating "care-full" listening and conversations, see Shalif (2005).

[8] For a good laugh, go to YouTube.com and search for the video of political commentator Stephen Colbert roasting George W. Bush! Sometimes "An Inconvenient Truth" requires attention before it's too late—see climatecrisis.net.

FIGURE 1.

"I know what you're thinking, but let me offer a competing narrative."

How you look influences what you see, and what you see influences what you do. As Brad Keeney (1983, p. 98) put it: "Any act of epistemology affects how you act as well as perceive—the two are linked as a recursive process." There are "virtuous cycles" as well as "vicious cycles" (Wender, 1968). One can help construct a therapeutic reality by interviewing a couple in a variety of ways that elicit positive images of each partner; for example, one could ask directly about what they like in the other person, or guide them into a happy reminiscence, or assign an activity—such as an observation task or a role-play enactment—that requires them to focus on positives rather than negatives (de Shazer, 1985, 1991; also see Selvini Palazzoli, Boscolo, Cecchin, & Prata, 1978; Roth & Chasin, 1994). Getting each partner to see the other person in a more positive light helps inspire them to act more positively toward one another, and what goes around comes around (Hoyt & Berg, 1998; Hoyt, 2002; Ziegler & Hiller, 2002).

How you recall and relate to past events is malleable, but unless you're younger than 18 years old, your childhood isn't really going to change (Hoyt, 2006, p. 123). However, there are different "histories of the present," to use Michael White's (1993) excellent term, different tales of the past that could be evoked to support different constructions of the present. One could practice the "archeology of hope" (Monk, Winslade, Crocket & Epston, 1997), looking for a history of the present recovery rather than stopping with a history of the present complaint. Instead of (or in addition to) constructing the usual genogram of suicides, alcoholics, and cut-offs, one could develop a solution-focused genogram (e.g. "Who in your past would be glad to hear that you are beginning to treat your wife and kids better?") to help support healthy and happy relationships.[9]

If an emergency arises, I like to take care of my own patients, of course, rather than having them seen by the on-call crisis worker. One time, however, Maria arrived when I just couldn't see her. It turned out that a colleague, "Dr. Noel," was on-call. He's not really a bad guy, but he tends to be a pathologizing logical positivist. Telling him that Maria has a chronic paranoid psychotic disorder, speaks broken English, and works at the post office wasn't going to help the collaborative alliance that she needed. I only had a couple of moments to brief Dr. Noel before I had to attend to another pressing commitment, so I quickly filled him in: "She's sensitive, and when she gets upset, she tends to get suspicious of people she doesn't know well. She's very creative and imaginative, and often uses symbols and poetic language, especially with strangers, and sometimes takes long pauses to think of just how to express things. She's bilingual, and her English is much better than your Spanish, so she'll have to work with you in her second language—but she'll be patient if you try." When I saw Dr. Noel a couple of hours later, he told me his meeting with Maria had gone well. He never mentioned "thought blocking" or "long latency of response" or even "cognitive distortions" or "psychosis"— he said she had an interesting way of articulating things, that they

---

[9] Remembering involves living (re)production (Bartlett, 1932; Neimeyer, 1995), a process more akin to a play or a painting than a videotape or a photograph. It was St. Augustine, in his 4th Century *Confessions* (quoted in Boscolo & Bertrando, 1993, p. 34), who wrote: "What is by now evident and clear is that neither future nor past exists, and it is inexact language to speak of three times—past, present, and future. Perhaps it would be exact to say: there are three times, a present of things past, a present of things present, a present of things to come. In the soul there are these three aspects of time, and I do not see them anywhere else. The present considering the past is the memory, the present considering the future is expectation."

had figured out what she needed to do to handle a situation at work that was bothering her, and that they had scheduled a regular appointment with me for the next week.

How you look influences what you see, and what you see influences what you do. However, while constructivist approaches strongly emphasize the role of language and the idea that our sense of reality is mediated through awareness, there is also an external world with which to reckon. Existence determines consciousness and consciousness determines existence. The situation can be very significant, and it is very important not to confuse perceptions and beliefs with the hard realities in which some people are living. Back in 1982 the journal *Family Process* carried a banner which read "The Invasion of the New Epistemologists" and in 1988 the *Family Therapy Networker* heralded "The Constructivists Are Coming!" Some family therapists (such as Minuchin, 1991, 1992; and Pittman, 1999) became alarmed that constructivists would obscure power dynamics and simply try to rename things rather than working to change actual dysfunctional behavioral patterns and right wrongs.

They didn't really need to worry. "Story" is not the whole story. The map is not the territory. As the title of Michael White and David Epston's well-known 1990 book, *Narrative Means to Therapeutic Ends*, indicates, "story reauthoring" is the vehicle, not the destination. This was spelled out in their subsequent 1992 book:

> Thus, the stories that we enter into with our experience have real effects on our lives. . . . This is not to propose that life is synonymous with text. It is not enough for a person to tell a new story about oneself, or to assert claims about oneself. Instead, the position carried by these assertions about the world of experience and narrative is that life is the performance of texts. And it is the performance of these texts that is transformative of persons' lives. (Epston & White, 1992, p. 81)

Moreover, as Chris Beels (2001, pp. 254-255; also see Flaskas, 2002) wrote:

> . . . a strangely intense debate . . . took place inside the circle of narrative "schools." Some postmodern thinkers were so taken with the idea of the narrator as the ultimate authority that they began to believe that no other perspective was valid, or even knowable, and they found scientific support for this in the biology of Humberto Maturana. . . . [However,] every clinician has the dual and inescapable responsibility to comprehend both

the knowledge of the outside world and the knowledge that is in the patient's head. If they conflict, whatever is useful of each has to be somehow brought together, and that is no more a matter of simply joining the patient's experience than it is of simply appealing to medical authority. The combination of the art and the science is more difficult than that, and the path of doing no harm lies through the middle of the conflict, a path one must follow with one's eyes open." [10, 11]

SOME OTHER CONSTRUCTIVIST CONUNDRUMS

(1) Healing vs. Treatment

It was Shakespeare, in *All's Well That Ends Well* (Act 1, Scene 1, line 216) who said, "Our remedies oft in ourselves do lie." Constructive therapists operate from a belief that clients often have the capacities, perhaps with skillful facilitation, to solve their problems. Thus, Milton Erickson advised, "Let patients know that they *are* going to be cured and that it will take place *within* them (as quoted in Short, Erickson & Klein, 2005, p. 19). He also counseled:

> The fullest possible utilization of the functional capacities and abilities and the experiential and acquisitional learnings of the patient . . . should take precedence over the teaching of new ways in living which are developed from the therapist's possibly incomplete understanding of what may be right and serviceable to the individual concerned. (Erickson, 1980, p. 540)

[10] As Freedman and Combs (1996, p. 26) note, Lynn Hoffman (1993) initially assumed constructivism and social constructionism were synonymous but then, following Gergen (1985), shifted her alliance to the latter when she realized "that social constructionists place far more emphasis on social interpretation and the intersubjective influence of language, family, and culture, and much less on the operations of the nervous system."
[11] Beels (2001, p. 255) goes on to caution: "I have watched narrative therapists— myself included—do damage by sticking exclusively to the client's own story when a darker possibility needed to be investigated. Childhood autism, affective disorders, and addictions are easy to miss if the therapist is paying attention only to the hopeful side of the family's narrative." As noted above, reframing also carries the possibility that one may simplistically rename rather than redress serious issues. Hence, one thoughtful reviewer (G. Neimeyer, 1996) questioned whether some of the solution-oriented reframes I listed in a table in *Constructive Therapies* (Hoyt, 1994, p. 4), which were offered as part of an introductory discussion about a shift towards competency-based future-oriented therapy, might be hollow, patronizing, or plain silly.

Short et al. (2005, italics in original) elaborate:

> Healing is the activation of inner resources during the process of recovery . . . a great deal of healing comes from emphasizing positive attributes located in the individual and then building on it incrementally. This is why Erickson argued throughout his career that cures are not the product of suggestion but instead result from the reassociation of experience. (pp. 16-17)

> . . . Thus healing is something separate from treatment. Treatments are interventions coming from the outside. Healing is something that occurs from within and involves all of the body's systems . . . The essential point to be understood is that, whether biological or psychological, it is the capacities and resources of the patient that produce sustainable health. (p. 19)

Recently there has been a lot of discussion about empirically validated treatments and evidence-based practice (see APA Presidential Task Force, 2006; Bohart, O'Hara, & Leitner, 1998; Marquis & Douthit, 2006; www.talkingcure.com), and one commentator (Barlow, 2004) has proposed that we reserve the term *psychological treatment* for interventions that are severe enough to be included in health care systems worldwide, and that these interventions be differentiated from more generic psychotherapy. The need to make sense of what we see and do requires disciplined observation and disciplined creation, art *and* science (O'Donohue, Cummings & Cummings, 2006), but let me quote Erickson again:

> And I do wish that all Rogerian therapists, Gestalt therapists, transactional therapists, group analysts, and all the other offspring of various theories would recognize that not one of them really recognizes that psychotherapy for person #1 is not psychotherapy for person #2. I've treated many conditions, and I always invent a new treatment in accord with the individual personality (quoted in Zeig, 1980, p. 104)

I agree with Jay Efran and Mitchell Greene (2005, pp. 35-36) who argued that the move to carefully scripted, manualized treatment misses the point. They wrote:

> Undoubtedly, one can specify general principles and guidelines, and therapy can be anchored in a contract that defines roles and sets boundaries. However, therapy also requires a certain creative ambiguity that can't be reduced to stock exercises or "bottled" like an antidepressant. . . . We can trace the current conundrum we're in—over the difficulty of making real therapy fit into a scientific paradigm—to the "slow-acting poison pill"

that former American Psychological Association president George Albee says the mental health profession ingested several decades ago. With this pill, we swallowed the deeply flawed medical/psychiatric assumptions about diagnoses and dosages, culminating in the unrealistic expectation that forms of psychotherapy can be administered with the reliability of, let's say, a surgical protocol. The belief that this level of consistency can be obtained derives from a serious confusion of models—what philosopher Gilbert Ryle called "a category mistake."
In other words, psychotherapy has been misclassified; it should never have been a treatment in the first place. Rather, it's a specialized form of inquiry—more philosophical journey than medical procedure. . . . In fact, if Jungian James Hillman had his way, the therapy enterprise would be categorized "as an art form rather than a science or a medicine." At root, therapy is just two people conversing.[12]

(2) Direction vs. Discovery

Constructivist therapists need to stay keenly aware of the ambiguous and inchoate nature of the therapeutic enterprise (Mahoney, 1995), knowing how to direct and structure a session in a manner that allows clients to make genuine discoveries rather than simply confirming the already known (White, Hoyt, & Zimmerman, 1996). We try to utilize whatever the client brings, but therapists should know a variety of things that would benefit our clients. We can sometimes teach particular skills (such as relaxation, communication, and problem-solving); and it is important to know when medication might be helpful to control psychiatric symptoms and thus restore the capacity for restorying (Hoyt, 2000, p. xv).

To my mind, invitation, not imposition, is the key—insistence produces resistance, and imposition produces opposition. In the brief and constructive therapy literature that I am familiar with—especially the worlds of solution-focused therapy, narrative

[12] Neimeyer and Raskin (2000b, pp. 8-9) write: "Although constructivist, narrative, and social constructionist therapists are as concerned as any with the quality of services they provide, they generally rest uneasily with the EVT [empirically validated treatments] trend. These misgiving are anchored in numerous concerns, among which are (a) the common preference of constructivists for more individualized criteria of change that focus on personal meanings as much as observable actions, (b) an interest in qualitative research on processes of change more than 'horse race' comparisons of preferred and nonpreferred theories, (c) a distrust of reified clinical diagnostic categories as a basis for demonstrating treatment specificity, and (d) suspicions about the political agenda of powerful groups attempting to marginalize other approaches in a bid to consolidate their hegemony over funding for both research and clinical practice."

therapy, strategic-interactional therapy, Ericksonian therapy, and the like—the term *countertransference* isn't much used. Rather, recognizing that "some stories are better than others," brief therapists tend to think more in terms of how to frame and constructively utilize whatever emerges in their work with clients. *Client-inspired therapist contributions* (Hoyt, 2004, p. 9) can be very useful, although there needs to be keen recognition of the power gradient and the importance of honoring clients' goals and not imposing our values while maintaining a collaborative client-therapist relationship. I like the way Michael White (in Hoyt & Combs, 2001, p. 77) expressed it: "And, because the impossibility of neutrality means that I cannot avoid being 'for' something, I take the responsibility to distrust what I am for—that is, my ways of life and my ways of thought—and I can do this in many ways." Constructive therapists are very cognizant of the politics of experience and appreciate the entire therapeutic venture as an exercise in ethics.

(3) Joining vs. Believing

We can join with clients and treat them respectfully without necessarily believing everything they say. As a clinical strategy, we may choose to overlook or not confront or even to utilize or "work with" a blatant symptom. We can use "psychojudo" and "humor the resistance" (Cummings & Sayama, 1995) without gainsaying the pathology. When Milton Erickson (see Haley, 1973), in his famous case of the mental patient who thought he was Jesus, put the patient to work in the hospital carpentry shop, he may have "accepted" the patient's delusional thinking but didn't come to believe it himself.

While not always, I generally find that the harder I listen, the smarter the client gets—there is an internal logic to what they're thinking and doing. We all need our polestars and lodestones, but we also need to have faith in our clients and in the process. I tend to take things as I find them, at face value. Sometimes I get enmeshed, or duped, but those open-hearted risks are better than starting out seeing the "Other" as a diagnostic specimen or a nut-case or a medical-legal risk.

> It is the ability to see health amid sickness that gets the treatment under way. Surgeons, for example, do not operate unless there are sufficient signs of life. . . . We in psychiatry are

not so fortunate: there are few if any tests of healthy mind or spirit. Freud spoke of the ability to love and work. Existentialists wrote of affective attunement, imaginative freedom, the ability to tolerate death and the random. Erik Erikson wrote of intimacy, autonomy, and generative abilities. The problem is that we have no clear, quantitative tests of these conditions, like the rate of respiration or the range of motion in a limb. The result is a morbid outlook on even healthy people, a tendency to look for hidden problems rather than hidden strengths. The whole field is in the untenable position of attempting to define sickness before it has defined health. If I had a magic wand to wave over psychiatry and clinical psychology, I would call forth usable measures of health and strength, measures of capability in all the psychic parts and functions. Then we would know how much neurosis or schizophrenia someone had and where, not laying those sad words across the whole person like a thunder cloud, especially when we can't agree on what they are. Patients would be less afraid of us; we would be more enthusiastic about the patients. The work could start up quickly and strongly. (Havens, 1989, pp. 40-41)

(4) Intra- vs. Inter-

When I was in the London Underground a few years ago and saw all the signs saying "MIND THE GAP" I thought I had wandered into some kind of social constructionist's subway! As numerous authors—Homans and Mead, Vygotsky, Wittgenstein, Bateson, and others—have suggested, the mind is social. In his foreword to *The Handbook of Constructive Therapies*, Ken Gergen (1998, pp. xiv-xv) elaborated:

> Central to the modernist tradition is the assumption of the individual as the fundamental atom of society. It is the individual's capacity for independent thought upon which our democratic institutions are based; it is on the basis of the individual's capacity to love that we trust our institutions of intimacy; and it is the individual's capacity for free agency that forms the foundation for our conceptions of moral responsibility. Yet as the dialogues on constructive therapy unfold, we find the presumption of independent self-contained individuals increasingly problematic. To construct an intelligible world essentially requires relationship; indeed, out of relationship emerges the very intelligibility of the individual self. In effect, the fundamental material out of which society emerges, from which institutions of democracy, intimacy, and moral responsibility derive, is that of relational process.

315

Knowledge is interpersonal. As Aristotle said, "Man is a social animal." Everyday 24/7/365 we co-create our relationships; like the famous Escher print, "one hand draws the other" (Matthews, 1985). Thus, William Butler Yeats (1928/1989, p. 217) wrote:

> O chestnut-tree, great-rooted blossomer
> Are you the leaf, the blossom or the bole?
> O body swayed to music, O brightening glance,
> How can we know the dancer from the dance?

(5) Idiomorphic vs. Nomothetic

For constructivist therapists, there is an "essential tension" between focusing on the "local knowledge" and particularities of individuals rather than simplifying into broad categories or metanarratives (Held, 1995; Neimeyer & Bridges, 2003). Indeed, practicing psychotherapy in a pluralistic world keeps us keenly aware of the enduring tensions between *affirmation* and *critique*, between embracing a point of view and recognizing that it is *only* a point of view (Bernstein, 1992; Downing, 2004).

Neimeyer (1998) warns about mixing theoretical assumptions lest we produce an "indiscriminate gallimaufry [ragout or hodgepodge] of deconstructive rules," although Neimeyer and Bridges (2003, p. 272) refer to a "loose confederation of contemporary approaches" that fall under the postmodern rubric. They write:

> [W]e use the term "postmodern" when we explicitly wish to emphasize the broad range of this orientation, and the terms "constructivist," "narrative," and "social constructionist" when we are speaking principally about one of its variants, which themselves subsume many specific therapies. However, we are less interested in getting bogged down in terminological nuances than in conveying the sorts of ideas and practices associated with this perspective. . . . Although this immense variety of postmodern approaches frustrates any attempt to offer a single definition of their features, in general they tend to be more collaborative than authoritarian, more developmental than symptom oriented, more process oriented than content focused, and more reflective than psychoeducational.

I agree. We could talk more about the names of psychotherapy schools, but what is really important—and I think much more interesting—is what using a particular lens does to our practice and how we relate to and intervene with clients. I'd like to suggest that

316

what is most important is finding ways for therapists and clients to work together effectively, ethically, and aesthetically. Preferring the related theories of constructivism and social constructionism means viewing constructive psychotherapy as a relational and conversational process involving collaboration oriented around the clients' theories and meanings, as well as the power of language and imagination (Hoyt & Ziegler, 2004). Again, as Neimeyer (2000b, p. 259) has wisely written, "Psychotherapy training should critically deconstruct such discourse and focus attention on human change processes irrespective of their 'brand name' pedigree."

(6) The Ineffable Lightness of Being

In *Shakespeare: The Invention of the Human*, Harold Bloom (1998) discusses the tradition of *humanism*, which appreciates individual personalities, selves with rich and variegated interior lives. He writes:

> Like Kierkegaard, Shakespeare enlarges our vision of the enigmas of human nature. Freud, wrongly desiring to be a scientist, gave his genius away to reductiveness. Shakespeare does not reduce his personages to their supposed pathologies or family romances. In Freud, we are overdetermined, but always in much the same way. In Shakespeare . . . we are overdetermined in so many rival ways that the sheer wealth of overdeterminations becomes a freedom. . . . Perhaps Hamlet, like Kierkegaard, came into the world to help save it from reductiveness. If Shakespeare brings us a secular salvation, it is partly because he helps ward off the philosophers who wish to explain us away, as if we were only so many muddles to be cleared up. (p. 730)

I find myself thinking about a wonderful keynote speech I heard Ken Gergen (1994b) give some years ago at a Therapeutic Conversations conference held in Reston, Virginia. He spoke of a "relational sublime," a sense of connection beyond word and stories to relatedness itself. Eckhart Tolle (2006, pp. 25-27) says something similar:

> Words, no matter whether they are vocalized and made into sounds or remain unspoken as thoughts, can cast an almost hypnotic spell upon you. You easily lose yourself in them, becoming hypnotized into implicitly believing that when you have attached a word to something, you know what it is. The fact is: You don't know what it is. You have only covered up the mystery with a label. Everything, a bird, a tree, even a simple stone, and certainly a human being, is ultimately unknowable.

> This is because it has unfathomable depth. All we can perceive, experience, think about, is the surface layer of reality, less than the tip of an iceberg. . . . The quicker you are in attaching verbal or mental labels to things, people, or situations, the more shallow and lifeless your reality becomes, and the more deadened you become to reality, the miracle of life that continuously unfolds within and around you. In this way, cleverness may be gained, but wisdom is lost, and so are joy, love, creativity, and aliveness. They are concealed in the still gap between the perception and the interpretation. Of course we have to use words and thoughts. They have their own beauty—but do we need to become imprisoned by them?

Perhaps the meditators and others who see Mind for what it is—and isn't—will understand. I do think that there is a wordless truth but, paradoxically, I can refer to it only through language. Thus, Ralph Waldo Emerson (1844/1950, p. 374), describing both the power and the limits of words, eloquently wrote: "We are painting the lightning with charcoal." In a similar vein, Czeslaw Milosz (2001, p. 2), who in 1980 won the Nobel Prize in Literature, said about books:

> Their learned terms are of little use when I attempt to seize naked experience, which eludes all accepted ideas. To borrow their language can be helpful in many ways, but it also leads imperceptibly into a self-contained labyrinth, leaving us in alien corridors which allow no exit.

BEFORE CLOSING

Knowing that every day I am constructing my version of this world has helped me to open my vision. If we look, there is more to see. However, although I live in Northern California, in Marin County, there is a lot that seems too mystical and flaky for me; but at the same time, I also recall the Hasidic story Martin Buber (1947, p. 53) told about the fiddler who

> played so sweetly that all who heard him began to dance and whoever came near enough to hear, joined in the dance. Then a deaf man, who knew nothing of music, happened along, and to him all he saw seemed the action of madmen—senseless and in bad taste.

318

In this world, we need more rationality, to be sure, but I have also been suggesting that we need more curiosity and flexibility and humanity. Creativity is a "necessary angel" (Stevens, 1951). Some people seem to think that precision can replace imagination. As Robert Frost said (reported in Roethke, 2001, p. 120), "Let's be accurate, but not too accurate." I'm pretty smart and I can think critically and analytically, but I almost drove off the road laughing one morning on the way to work when I heard Garrison Keillor on the radio say, "Being intelligent doesn't make you happy. It just means you can get stuck in more remote places!"

Narrative constructivism, which highlights the everyday language-based meaning-making aspects of awareness, has made me more appreciative of both what is really real and what is often assumed and taken-for-granted but can be examined and questioned and sometimes changed. A constructivist position may hold that we are always part of the equation, that there is no knowing without the knower; but there are extra-linguistic forces to be reckoned with. The constructive therapist gives up "temptations of power and certainty," maintains "curiosity" and a "healthy irreverence," is "inspired by incompleteness" and is "suspicious of great subjects and all-encompassing theories." The constructive therapist recognizes that psychotherapy is a "process of semiosis," an exercise in "aesthetics" and "clinical epistemology"; that it is hermeneutics rather than engineering, and poetics rather than physics, that are the fields of study that examine the warp and weft of human life. The constructive therapist forgoes the dryness of the positivist shore, joining the collaborative flow of "the third wave" as an intersubjective "co-participant" or "co-author" (see Hoyt, 2004).

In his famous poem, "To a Skylark," Percy Bysshe Shelley (quoted in Oliver, 1998, p. 176) wrote:

> Like a Poet hidden
> In the light of thought,
> Singing hymns unbidden,
> Until the world is wrought

We are all more verbs than nouns and, as we construct our daily realities, we all get to decide: *Will our life be prose, or poetry?*

My hope is that considering what I have been describing will help you (and reality) to allow for the growth of more stories that bring what is wanted. Please let me conclude with four final suggestions:

1. Keep in mind that ultimately, the power is in the patient. We don't really change people—we create contexts in which they can change themselves.

2. Be open to others, but find your own way. Poet Mary Oliver (1998, pp. 82-83) advises that we learn the basic moves *and* become distinct individuals: Your own style will take time. It will reveal itself. You cannot force it. . . . You can, however, suppress it when it begins to appear, and this you should guard against. In an effort to be rule-abiding, you may smooth out your work too fiercely. Just those distinctions that often accrue finally to a style are, at first, often rough and hard to handle. But cherish them. Do you seek small perfections, which are not so hard to come by once you know the rules? Rather be patient, and make room always for those oddities that are your own manner, your own voice.

3. Pay attention to what you pay attention to. How we look influences what we see, and what we see influences what we do, 'round and around. What you focus on tends to grow, so notice your noticing and be mindful of your language and what you choose to emphasize. To use a metaphor from the world of computers, one of the keys to happiness is knowing where to double-click!

4. It may be later than we think—every day we should seize the moment and get on with it. If reality is just an illusion and time is just a theoretical construct, let me ask you: Why didn't we make more of it?

REFERENCES

Abrams, D. (1996). *The spell of the sensuous: Perception and language in a more-than-human world.* New York: Vintage.

Anderson, H., & Goolishian, H. (1992). The client is the expert: A not-knowing approach to therapy. In S. McNamee & K. J. Gergen (Eds.), *Therapy as social construction* (pp. 25-39). Newbury Park, CA: Sage.

APA Presidential Task Force on Evidence-Based Practice (2006). Evidence-based practice in psychology. *American Psychologist, 61,* 271-285.

Barlow, D.H. (2004). Psychological treatments. *American Psychologist, 59,* 869-878.

Bartlett, F.C. (1932). *Remembering. Cambridge,* England: Cambridge University Press.

Bateson, G. (1972). *Steps to an ecology of mind.* New York: Ballantine.

Bateson, G. (1980). *Mind and nature: A necessary unity.* New York: Dutton.

Beels, C.C. (2001). *A different story: The rise of narrative in psychotherapy.* Phoenix: Zeig, Tucker & Theisen.

Beinfield, H., & Korngold, E. (1991). *Between heaven and earth: A guide to Chinese medicine.* New York: Ballantine/Random House.

Berg, I.K. (1994). *Family-based services: A solution-focused approach.* New York: Norton.

Bernstein, R.J. (1992). *The new constellation: The ethical-political horizons of modernity/postmodernity.* Cambridge, MA: MIT Press.

Bloom, H. (1998). *Shakespeare: The invention of the human.* New York: Riverhead Books.

Bohart, A.C., & O'Hara, M., & Leitner, L.M. (1998). Empirically violated treatments: Disenfranchisement of humanistic and other psychotherapies. *Psychotherapy Research, 8,* 141-157.

Boscolo, L., & Bertrando, P. (1993). *The times of time.* New York: Norton.

Buber, M. (1947). *Tales of the Hasidim: Early Masters.* New York: Schocken.

Buddha (1967). *The Dhammapada* (P. Lal, Trans.). New York: Farrar, Straus & Giroux. (Original work c. 500 B.C.E.)

Clayre, A. (1984). *The heart of the dragon.* Boston: Houghton Mifflin.

Coyne, J. C. (1985). Toward a theory of frames and reframing: The social nature of frames. *Journal of Marital and Family Therapy, 11,* 337-344.

Cummings, N.A., & Sayama, M. (1995). *Focused psychotherapy: A casebook of brief, intermittent psychotherapy throughout the life cycle.* Philadelphia: Brunner/Mazel.

de Shazer, S. (1985). *Keys to solution in brief therapy.* New York: Norton.

de Shazer, S. (1991). *Putting difference to work.* New York: Norton.

Downing, J. N. (2004). Psychotherapy practice in a pluralistic world: Philosophical and moral dilemmas. *Journal of Psychotherapy Integration, 14,* 123-148.

Ecker, B., & Hulley, L. (1996). *Depth-oriented brief therapy.* San Francisco: Jossey-Bass.

Efran, J. S., & Greene, M. (2005, November/December). The art of therapeutic conversation. *Psychotherapy Networker, 29*(6), 35-36.

Efran, J. S., Lukens, M. D., & Lukens, R. J. (1990). *Language, structure, and change: Frameworks of meaning in psychotherapy.* New York: Norton.

Efran, J. S., Lukens, R. J., & Lukens, M. D. (1988). Constructivism: What's in it for you? *Family Therapy Networker, 22*(5), 27-35.

Emerson, R. W. (1950). Self-reliance. In *The selected writing of Ralph Waldo Emerson* (pp. 145-169). New York: Modern Library/Random House.

Emerson, R. W. (1950). *The selected writings of Ralph Waldo Emerson* (B. Atkinson, Ed.). New York: Modern Library/Random House. (Original work published 1844)

Empson, W. (1966). *Seven types of ambiguity* (revised ed.) New York: New Directions. (Original work published 1930)

Epston, D., & White, M. (1992). *Experience, contradiction, narrative and imagination: Selected papers of David Epston and Michael White, 1989-1991.* Adelaide, Australia: Dulwich Centre Publications.

Erickson, M. E. (1954). Pseudo-orientation in time as a hypnotic procedure. *Journal of Clinical and Experimental Hypnosis, 6*, 183-207.

Erickson, M. (1980). *Collected papers* (Vol. 1). New York: Irvington.

Eron, J. B., & Lund, T. W. (1996). *Narrative solutions in brief therapy.* New York: Guilford Press.

Flaskas, C. (2002). *Family therapy beyond postmodernism: Practice challenges theory.* New York: Brunner-Routledge.

Foster, R., & Hicks, G. (1999). *How we choose to be happy: The nine choices of extremely happy people—their secrets, their stories.* New York: Perigee/Berkley.

Freedman, J., & Combs, G. (1996). *Narrative therapy: The social construction of preferred realities.* New York: Norton.

Friedman, S. (1995). (Ed.). *The reflecting team in action: Collaborative practice in family therapy.* New York: Guilford Press.

Gergen, K. J. (1985). The social constructionist movement in modern psychology. *American Psychologist, 40*, 266-275.

Gergen, K. J. (1991). *The saturated self: Dilemmas of identity in contemporary life.* New York: Basic Books.

Gergen, K .J. (1994a). *Realities and relationships: Soundings in social construction.* Cambridge, MA: Harvard University Press.

Gergen, K. J. (1994b). *Between alienation and deconstruction: Re-envisioning therapeutic conversation.* Keynote address at Therapeutic Conversations 2 Conference, Reston, VA.

Gergen, K. J. (1998). Foreword. In M.F. Hoyt (Ed.), *The handbook of constructive therapies* (pp. xi-xv). San Francisco: Jossey-Bass.

Gladwell, M. (2006, May 22). What the dog saw: Cesar Millan and the movements of mastery. *The New Yorker*, 48-57.

Goulding, M. M., & Goulding, R. L. (1979). *Changing lives through redecision therapy.* New York: Brunner/Mazel.

Haley, J. (1973). *Uncommon therapy: The psychiatric techniques of Milton H. Erickson, M.D.* New York: Norton.

Haley, J. (1984). *Ordeal therapy: Unusual ways to change behavior.* San Francisco: Jossey-Bass.

Havens, L. (1989). *A safe place: Laying the groundwork of psychotherapy.* Cambridge, MA: Harvard University Press.

Held, B. S. (1995). *Back to reality: A critique of postmodern theory in psychotherapy.* New York: Norton.

Hillman, J. (1992). Language: Speaking well and speaking out. In R. Bly, J. Hillman, & M. Meade (Eds.), *The rag and bone shop of the heart: Poems for men* (pp. 153-159). New York: HarperCollins.

Hoffman, L. (1993). *Exchanging Voices: A Collaborative Approach to Family Therapy* (pp. 86-102). London: Karnac Books.

Horowitz, M. J. (1975). Sliding meanings: A defense against threat in narcissistic personalities. *International Journal of Psychoanalytic Psychotherapy, 4,* 167-180.

Hoyt, M. F. (1994). (Ed.) *Constructive therapies.* New York: Guilford Press.

Hoyt, M. F. (1995). *Brief therapy and managed care: Readings for contemporary practice.* San Francisco: Jossey-Bass.

Hoyt, M. F. (1996). (Ed.). *Constructive therapies* (Vol. 2). New York: Guilford Press.

Hoyt, M. F. (1998). (Ed.). *The Handbook of Constructive Therapies.* San Francisco: Jossey-Bass.

Hoyt, M. F. (2000). *Some stories are better than others: Doing what works in brief therapy and managed care.* Philadelphia: Brunner/Mazel.

Hoyt, M. F. (2001). *Interviews with brief therapy experts.* Philadelphia: Brunner-Routledge.

Hoyt, M. F. (2002). Solution-focused couple therapy. In A.S. Gurman & N.S. Jacobson (Eds.), *Clinical handbook of couple therapy* (3rd ed., pp. 335-369). New York: Guilford Press.

Hoyt, M. F. (2004). *The present is a gift: Mo' better stories from the world of brief therapy.* New York: iUniverse.com.

Hoyt, M. F. (2006). The temporal structure of therapy: Key questions often associated with different phases of sessions and treatments (plus twenty-one helpful hints). In W. O'Donohue, N. A. Cummings, & J. L. Cummings (Eds.), *Clinical strategies for becoming a master psychotherapist* (pp. 113-127). San Diego, CA: Elsevier/Academic Press.

Hoyt, M. F., & Berg, I. K. (1998). Solution-focused couple therapy: Helping clients construct self-fulfilling realities. In M.F. Hoyt (Ed.), *The handbook of constructive therapies* (pp. 314-340). San Francisco: Jossey-Bass. Reprinted in M. F. Hoyt, *Some stories are better than others* (pp. 143-166). Philadelphia: Brunner/Mazel, 2000.

Hoyt, M. F., & Combs, G. (2001). On ethics and the spiritualities of the surface: A conversation with Michael White. In M. F. Hoyt (Ed.), *Interviews with brief therapy experts* (pp. 71-96). Philadelphia: Brunner-Routledge.

Hoyt, M.F., & Ziegler, P. (2004) The pros and cons of postmodernism: Stepping back from the abyss. In M.F. Hoyt, *The present is a gift: Mo' better stories from the world of brief therapy* (pp. 132-181). New York: iUniverse.com

James, W. (1890). *The principles of psychology* (Vol. 2). Troy, MO: Holt, Rinehart & Winston.

Kelly, G. A. (1955). *The psychology of personal constructs.* New York: Norton.

Kelly, G. A. (1969). *Clinical psychology and personality: The selected papers of George Kelly* (B. Maher, Ed.). New York: Wiley.

Keeney, B. P. (1983). *The aesthetics of change.* New York: Guilford.

King, S. (2000). *On writing: A memoir of the craft.* New York: Simon & Schuster.

Kurtz, E., & Ketcham, K. (1992). *The spirituality of imperfection: Storytelling and the search for meaning.* New York: Bantam.

Machado, A. (1983). "Caminante No Hay Camino, Se Hace Camino al Andar"/ "There is No Way, the Way is Made by Walking." In *Times alone: Selected poems of Antonio Machado* (R. Bly, Trans.). Middletown, CT: Wesleyan University Press.

Madanes, C. (1990). *Sex, love, and violence: Strategies for transformation.* New York: Norton.

Mahoney, M. J. (1995). The psychological demands of being a constructivist psychotherapist. In R. A. Neimeyer & M. J. Mahoney (Eds.), *Constructivism in psychotherapy* (pp. 385-399). Washington, DC: American Psychological Association.

Mahoney, M. J. (2003). *Constructive psychotherapy: Theory and practice.* New York: Guilford Press.

Marquis, A., & Douthit, K. (2006) The hegemony of "empirically supported treatment": Validating or violating? *Constructivism in the Human Sciences,* 11(1), 108-141.

Marrow, A.J. (1977). *The practical theorist: The life and work of Kurt Lewin*. New
    York: Teacher's College Press.

Matthews, W.J. (1985). A cybernetic model of Ericksonian hypnotherapy: One hand
    draws the other. *Ericksonian Monographs, 1*, 42-60.

Matthews, W. J. (2002). Reality exists: A critique of antirealism in brief therapy.
    In J.K. Zeig (Ed.), *Brief therapy: Lasting impressions* (pp. 147-168).
    Phoenix: The Milton H. Erickson Foundation Press.

McWilliams, S. A. (2004). Constructive alternativism and the self. In J. D.
    Raskin & S. K. Bridges (Eds.), *Studies in meaning 2: Bridging the personal
    and social in constructivist Psychology* (pp. 291-309). New York: Pace
    University Press.

Miller, W. R., & Rollnick, S. (1991). *Motivational interviewing: Preparing people to
    change addictive behavior*. New York: Guilford Press.

Milosz, C. (2001). *To begin where I am: Selected essays*. New York: Farrar,
    Straus and Giroux.

Minuchin, S. (1991). The seductions of constructivism. *Family Therapy
    Networker, 9*(5), 47-50.

Minuchin, S. (1992). The restoried history of family therapy. In J.K. Zeig (Ed.), *The
    evolution of psychotherapy: The second conference* (pp. 3-12). New York:
    Brunner/Mazel.

Monk, G., Winslade, J., Crocket, K., & Epston, D. (1997). *Narrative therapy in
    practice: The archeology of hope*. San Francisco: Jossey-Bass.

Neimeyer, G. J. (1996). Changes in attitudes, not in the platitudes. [Review of the
    book Constructive Therapies]. *Contemporary Psychology, 41*, 697-698.

Neimeyer, R. A. (1995). Constructivist psychotherapies: Features, foundations,
    and future directions. In R. A. Neimeyer & M. J. Mahoney (Eds.),
    Constructivism in psychotherapy (pp. 11-38). Washington, DC: American
    Psychological Association.

Neimeyer, R. A. (1998). Cognitive therapy and the narrative trend: A bridge too far?
    Journal of Cognitive Psychotherapy, 12, 57-65.

Neimeyer, R. A. (2002a). (Ed.). *Meaning reconstruction and the experience of loss*.
    Washington, DC: American Psychological Association.

Neimeyer, R. A. (2000b). How firm a foundation? A constructivist response to
    Mahrer's archeology of beliefs about psychotherapy. In J. D. Raskin & S. K.
    Bridges (Eds.), *Studies in meaning: Exploring constructivist psychology*
    (pp. 247-264). New York: Pace University Press.

Neimeyer, R. A., & Bridges, S. K. (2003). Postmodern approaches to psychotherapy.
    In A.S. Gurman & S.B. Messer (Eds.), *Essential psychotherapies: Theory
    and practice* (2nd ed., pp. 272-316). New York: Guilford Press.

Neimeyer, R. A., & Mahoney, M. J. (1995a). (Eds.). *Constructivism in psychotherapy*.
    Washington, DC: American Psychological Association.

Neimeyer, R. A., & Mahoney, M. J. (1995b). Glossary. In R. A. Neimeyer & M. J. Mahoney (Eds.), *Constructivism in psychotherapy* (pp. 401-409). Washington, DC: American Psychological Association.

Neimeyer, R. A.., & Raskin, J. D. (2000a). (Eds.). *Constructions of disorder: Meaning-making frameworks for psychotherapy.* Washington, DC: American Psychological Association.

Neimeyer, R. A., & Raskin, J. D. (2000b). On practicing postmodern therapy in modern times. In R. A. Neimeyer & J. D. Raskin (Eds.), *Constructions of disorder: Meaning-making frameworks for psychotherapy* (pp. 3-14). Washington, DC: American Psychological Association.

O'Donohue, W., Cummings, N., & Cummings, J. (2006). The art and science of psychotherapy. In W. O'Donohue, N. A Cummings, and J. L. Cummings (Eds.), *Clinical strategies for becoming a master psychotherapist* (pp. 1-10). San Diego, CA: Elsevier/Academic Press.

Oliver, M. (1998). *Rules for the dance: A handbook for writing and reading metrical verse.* New York: Mariner/Houghton Mifflin.

Olson, D. L. (1995). *Shared spirits: Wildlife and Native Americans.* Minnetonka, MN: NorthWord Press.

Parker, L. (2006). Narrative psychotherapy as effective story-making: An introduction. In W. O'Donohue, N. A Cummings, and J. L. Cummings (Eds.), *Clinical strategies for becoming a master psychotherapist* (pp. 55-70). San Diego, CA: Elsevier/Academic Press.

Perlman, E. (2003). *Seven types of ambiguity.* New York: Riverhead/Penguin.

Pittman, F. (1992). It's not my fault. *Family Therapy Networker, 16*(1), 56-63.

Raskin, J. D. (2002). Constructivism in psychology: Personal construct psychology, radical constructivism, and social constructionism. In J. D. Raskin & S. K. Bridges (Eds.), *Studies in meaning: Exploring constructivist psychology* (pp. 1-25). New York: Pace University Press.

Raskin, J. D. (2004). The permeability of personal construct psychology. In J. D. Raskin & S. K. Bridges (Eds.), *Studies in meaning 2: Bridging the personal and social in constructivist psychology.* (pp. 327-346). New York: Pace University Press.

Raskin, J. D., & Bridges, S. K. (2002). (Eds.) *Studies in meaning: Exploring constructivist psychology.* New York: Pace University Press.

Raskin, J. D., & Bridges, S. K. (2004). (Eds.) *Studies in meaning 2: Bridging the personal and social in constructivist psychology.* New York: Pace University Press.

Roethke, T. (2001). *On Poetry and Craft: Selected Prose.* Port Townsend, WA: Copper Canyon Press.

Rosen, H., & Kuehlwein, K. T. (1996). (Eds.). *Constructing realities: Meaning-making perspectives for psychologists.* San Francisco: Jossey-Bass.

326

Roth, S., & Chasin, R. (1994). Entering one another's worlds of meaning and imagination: Dramatic enactment and narrative couple therapy. In M. F. Hoyt (Ed.), *Constructive therapies* (pp. 189-216). New York: Guilford Press.

Selvini Palazzoli, M., Boscolo, L., Cecchin, G., & Prata, G. (1978, July). A ritualized prescription in family therapy: Odd days and even days. *Journal of Marriage and Family Counseling*, 3-9.

Shalif, Y. (2005). Creating care-full listening and conversations between members of conflicting groups in Israel: Narrative means to transformative listening. *Journal of Systemic Therapies, 24*(1), 35-52.

Short, D., Erickson, B. A., & Klein, R. E. (2005). *Hope and resiliency: Understanding the psychotherapeutic strategies of Milton H. Erickson, M.D..* Norwalk, CT: Crown House Publishing.

Simpkins, A. M., & Simpkins, C. A. (2005). Interview: Mary Catherine Bateson. *The Milton H. Erickson Foundation Newsletter, 25*(3), 1, 26-28.

Sluzki, C. (1988). Case commentary II. *Family Therapy Networker, 12*(5), 77-79/

Stevens, W. (1951). *The necessary angel: Essays on reality and the imagination.* New York: Vintage/Random House.

Thoreau, H. D. (1980). *A week on the Concord and Merrimack Rivers* (C. F. Hovde, W. L. Howarth & E. H. Witherell, Eds.). Princeton, NJ: Princeton University Press. (Original work published 1849)

Tolle, E. (2006). *A New Earth: Awakening to your life's purpose.* New York: Plume/Penguin.

Watzlawick, P., & Hoyt, M. F. (2001). Constructing therapeutic realities. In M. F. Hoyt (Ed.), *Interviews with brief therapy experts* (pp. 144-157). Philadelphia: Brunner-Routledge.

Watzlawick, P., Weakland, J. H., & Fisch, R. (1974). *Change: Principles of problem formation and problem resolution.* New York: Norton.

Wender, P. (1968). Vicious and virtuous circles: The role of deviation amplifying feedback in the origin and perpetuation of behavior. *Psychiatry, 31*, 309-324.

White, M. (1993). Commentary: Histories of the present. In S.G. Gilligan & R. Price (Eds.), *Therapeutic conversations* (pp. 121-135). New York: Norton.

White, M. (1995). *Re-Authoring lives: Interviews and essays.* Adelaide, Australia: Dulwich Centre Publications.

White, M., Hoyt, M. F., & Zimmerman, J. L. (2000). Direction and discovery: A conversation about power and politics in narrative therapy. In M. White, (Ed.), *Reflections on narrative practice: Essays and interviews* (pp. 97-116). Adelaide, Australia: Dulwich Centre Publications. (Reprinted in M.F. Hoyt, *Interviews with brief therapy experts* (pp. 265-293). Philadelphia: Brunner-Routledge, 2001.)

Whitman, W. (1940). "Song of Myself." In *Leaves of grass* (rev. ed., pp. 29-74). New York: Modern Library: Random House. (Original work published 1891-92)

Williams, T. (1999). *The glass menagerie* (Intro. by R. Bray). New York: New Directions. (Original work published 1945)

Yeats, W. B. (1989). "Among School Children." In *The collected poems of W.B. Yeats* (R. J. Finneran, Ed.; pp. 215-217). New York: Collier. (Original work published 1928)

Zeig, J. K. (1980). *A teaching seminar with Milton H. Erickson.* New York: Brunner/Mazel.

Ziegler, P., & Hiller, T. (2001). *Recreating partnership: A solution-oriented, collaborative approach to couples therapy.* New York: Norton.

Looking for the Context:
Therapy as Social Critique

Mark Eliot Paris

INTRODUCTION

thesis

Social constructionism and personal construct theory address two different levels of what is the same overall process—the construction of meaning (Paris & Epting, 2004). They not only complement each other, but are necessary to each other as a way of filling in what would otherwise be lost pieces in our understanding of how meaning-making works—those pieces being, on the one hand, the role of relationships and the larger social context and, on the other hand, the role of the person and personal process. I seek to establish a strong and compelling connection between social context and social meaning and the kinds of personal problems and concerns that both theorists and practitioners see as the domain of their own professional expertise.

This chapter clarifies how social context, social meaning, and psychological process go together, and how they give us a different picture of what is happening with at least some of our clients and what we might do in response. We always encounter our clients in a place—the therapy room—in which they are physically removed from the complex social, cultural, political, and relational contexts in which they live. Even in family therapy, we encounter clients whose everyday worlds all too often remain invisible to us, out of sight and out of mind. What we see are *problems* and certain kinds of psychological and/or relational processes, which we place in the context of our own theoretical frames of reference and professional expertise. More often than not, the manifold connections between our clients' problems and process, on the one hand, and the larger world in which they live, on the other, go unattended. However, as constructivists (or constructionists), we are in a particularly good position to trace out connections between social meaning and personal meaning processes because meaning is the very substance of the connections that exist. I offer a workable *constructionist* framework— a synthesis of personal construct psychology and social constructionism—that can help practitioners *see* the social, cultural, and political contexts that serve as the ground against which clients' problems and processes emerge as figure. If we are able to use the therapeutic process to illuminate some of these contexts with our clients, then we will be in a better position to help them unravel those meanings, both personal and social, that tie them inextricably to the demands of the problems that have brought them to us.

In Kelly's approach to therapy (Epting, 1984), we begin by elaborating the problem; that is, we try to get a more fully developed notion of what the problem is like, how the problem is affecting the client, and what she or he is trying to do about it. Then we move on to elaborating the person. We stop talking about the problem as such and starting trying to get a sense of who the client is, what he or she is up to, and what his or her relationships to other people are like. This gives us a better sense of how the problem fits into the person's life and what it is like to be this kind of person having this kind of problem. It is a natural extension of this approach, although one not usually undertaken, to move on to an elaboration of the client's social world, to see how the person who has the problem fits into the larger social context and how that context can help us to understand more fully both the person and the problem. Just as personal construct psychology helps us to understand how clients' personal constructions have everything to do with both the problems they bring to therapy and who they are as persons, so social constructionism can help us to see larger *social* meanings as having everything to do with the kind of social world in which therapists and clients find themselves living. Thus, social constructionism is a theoretical framework that we can use to elaborate the social context, just as we use personal construct psychology to help us elaborate both the problem and the person.

However, when we elaborate the social context, and the person *in context*, we may find that what look and feel like personal problems are, in fact, social problems that have exacted a high personal toll. We arrive at our own sense of personal meaning, at our own personal constructs, by engaging with the meanings that define the world around us and that define what a *person* is or ought to be. Sometimes these meanings are deeply problematic in a way that is analogous to what Rogers (1961) calls "conditions of worth," only these are conditions of worth writ large. As a result, we can become captured by the confusions, contradictions and *violence* that belonging to and participating in the larger social world entails. We must, however, participate in some kind of social world if we are to remain sane (or even alive), and so the question becomes what can we do if the terms that seem to define us in that world commit a kind of violence against us or require that we establish our own worth by committing a similar kind of violence against others? We are caught in a dilemma in which to escape this violence means exile from the very social world that sustains us, while participating in that world requires that we, in some measure, "internalize" the violence that characterizes it. This violence, then, is a social problem that can be deeply problematic for the person, depending, in part, on the extent to which she or he is exposed to it. In this way, problems that feel personal or that seem to characterize particular relationships may have at their center a *social* problem—in particular, a problematic and violent *social meaning*—that none of the parties involved knows how to challenge or overcome.

When our sense of self, our personal constructions of who we are, are constrained by the violence inherent in our world, then *change* begins with challenging those social constructions that constitute our sociality in destructive terms. Change, in this sense, is both personal and social. The goal is to forge an alternative social space, between clients and therapists, between clients and other important people in their lives, in which the rules are different and violence, of whatever kind, is rejected. This is why we, as therapists, need to learn to think *critically* about social realities and social meanings that both we and our clients might otherwise take for granted. We need to ask genuinely critical questions about the consequences of dominant discourses that seem to make doing some kind of violence to oneself or to others a sort of pre-condition for entering into the larger social world and becoming a genuinely social being. These critical questions can become the basis for a different kind of shared inquiry with our clients, one that allows them to entertain and experiment with genuinely *constructive* alternatives that make it

331

possible for them to transform a negative personal process and move out of or alter a social or relational context that has proved to be destructive to them. This different kind of inquiry begins with simply being more curious about the *world* our clients bring with them into the therapy room, realizing that this world is much bigger and more powerful than they are, and asking ourselves what the requirements of this big, powerful world have to do with the difficulties and distress our clients are experiencing. The point, ultimately, is not simply to be more "critical," but to be more *sensitive* (Hardy & Laszloffy, 1995) to our clients' actual experience, which is one of living in a "real world" that has stretched them beyond whatever constructive (and relational) resources they currently have available to them to move their lives in a direction they prefer.

In what follows, I offer my own take on how politics as a form of social process intersects with the kind of concerns addressed in therapy. I want to bridge the disconnect that many of us experience between thinking about politics and thinking about personal (or interpersonal) process, and I argue that one way to do this is to look at how certain kinds of *violence* are inherent in the social construction of everyday life. To begin, I provide a more explicitly theoretical framework in which to look at these issues, a synthesis of social constructionism and personal construct psychology that gives us a way of talking about how social process and personal process fit together. Following that, I try to give a fuller account of the personal side of this equation by offering an elaboration of Kelly's (1963) concept of sociality that includes the larger social world—the world of social meanings that we, necessarily, participate in—and our sense of our own "role" in that world. I argue that the exercise of a healthy and necessary sociality can easily trap us in the violence that characterizes how certain kinds of human differences are construed socially, so that our own "role-governing" constructions become deeply problematic. Therefore, as therapists, we need some way of critiquing *social* constructions that are violent and de-humanizing, in order to be able to help clients formulate alternative constructions—social and personal—that allow them to reconnect to their own sociality in positive and hopeful ways. Next, I use Judith Butler's (2004) notion of a socially constructed differential between the human and the less-than-human to talk about where I believe critical practice and therapeutic practice come together. Finally, I offer what I think are some of the therapeutic implications of thinking this way about context, meaning-making and process.

POLITICS AND VIOLENCE

One of my main goals in talking about "context" is to help more mental health professionals to see the kinds of social and political concerns addressed by feminist and multicultural counseling theories (among others) as central to their own thinking and practice. According to Goodman, Liang, Helms, Latta, Sparks, and Weintraub (2004),

> both feminist and multicultural counseling psychology (a) emphasize the ways in which social oppression (e.g. racism, classicism, ethnocentrism, and/or sexism) contributes to the mental health problems that clients present . . . (b) argue that survival responses under oppressive conditions are often mistaken for pathology . . . and (c) provide ways to help clients directly address various oppressive conditions in their lives (p. 796)

Goodman et al. (2004) argue that counseling professionals have an obligation to engage in social justice work both inside and outside the therapy room because life difficulties rooted in social, political, and cultural oppression "cannot truly be resolved without changing the systems and structures from which they arise" (p. 798).

These authors are right to point out that "oppressive conditions" (Goodman et al., 2004) have everything to do with the emotional, relational, health, and general life problems that many people experience. Contemporary American society is built upon increasingly brutal disparities that, to those of us not immediately impacted by them, can be dangerously easy to ignore, or to rationalize away as matters of individual or social breakdown caused by the pathologies and/or misguided values of those who find themselves at the bottom of the heap. That is, we may not *see*, or *want* to see, what some people are up against.

For instance, Patricia J. Williams (2006) discusses the ongoing legacy of "the Jim Crow principle of 'separate but equal'" in terms of the profound *inequalities* that continue to define the

333

conditions of life for far too many African-Americans (and other minorities), including

> the disgraceful and immoral rates of segregation that still exist in housing and schools, now rationalized as a mere matter of "choice"; or the horrendous disparity in health and longevity statistics, attributed to inherent mysteries; or the high school dropout rate of young minorities, dismissed as laziness; or the dismal disparities in employment rates, shrugged away as a collective failure of "individual responsibility"; or, of course, the appalling rates of minority incarceration. (p. 9)

As mental health professionals, we *must* recognize that life is simply far more difficult and/or dangerous for those who live at the margins or beyond the bounds of a social contract that the rest of us usually take for granted. By "social contract," I mean those underlying social arrangements by which people who play by society's rules supposedly receive, in their turn, the protection of society (Joxe, 2002) and the opportunity to succeed in accord with their own efforts.

However, while it makes sense to some mental health professionals to address social oppression as an intrinsic part of their work, for most of us, therapy is still about helping individuals, couples, and families overcome what are primarily personal and/or relational problems. It is difficult for many therapists and clients alike to connect large, abstract concepts like oppression, privilege and power to the kinds of personal and relational difficulties that seem to define everyday life, or to think about racism, sexism, homophobia, etc. in terms of anything more than the attitudes and behaviors of particular people. Furthermore, the general tendency of the therapeutic process is to focus on clients as individuals, couples, or families, and on the difficulties and struggles that they, themselves, have identified as the reason why they have come to therapy. So while a strong and committed minority of mental health professionals believe that addressing oppression, privilege, and power is a crucial part of their work as therapists, others may view this as an inappropriate and unwanted intrusion of a particular brand of politics into a process that should be only about the client's, and not about the therapist's, political beliefs. Seen in this way, providing "ways to help clients directly address various oppressive conditions in their lives" (Goodman et al., 2004) can seem like little more than telling clients what their politics should be. What happens when neither therapists nor clients share the political point of view that feminist and multicultural counseling theories, for instance, seem to prescribe?

Given that we live in a very diverse society comprised of people who have very different political, ethical, and religious points of view, it may be difficult, if not impossible, to elaborate any kind of overtly political conception of the therapeutic process, and the therapist's role in that process, which will not alienate a significant part of the intended audience. Even those who are sympathetic politically to the concerns raised by feminist and multicultural theorists may still feel that a therapeutic focus on *social* oppression and injustice only serves to diminish the *personal* uniqueness and agency of the client. As therapists, we are dealing with individuals (or couples and families) who have their own histories, their own beliefs, and must make their own decisions. The only reasonable conclusion would seem to be to make therapy politically neutral and to let both therapists and clients determine their politics for themselves.

The problem is that politics intrudes itself into the lives of both clients and therapists, whether they want it to or not. Politics is not only about left and right. Politics is a *process* that people are unavoidably caught up in as a part of living together in a large and complex society. Politics is about the *social contract* and about how the terms of that contract are defined and will be defined in the future. It is about who *counts* within the terms of that contract, about who has more *say* in how those terms will be defined; and, conversely, it is about who does *not* seem to count for much and who has little or no say. For instance, African-Americans, as a *class* of persons, count for less and have less say in how our underlying social arrangements are constructed, as evidenced by the fact that the *rules* that govern society (both written and unwritten) do not sufficiently protect them; and they have, proportionally speaking, less opportunity to succeed. That is, they are more exposed to physical violence, incarceration, health problems, social dysfunction and even chaos. They have less opportunity to make use of the benefits that society offers to many other kinds of persons. Again, lesbians and gay men count for less and have less say in how those social arrangements pertaining to intimate relationships are constructed. Their relationships are less protected by society and they do not have access to many

335

(or sometimes any) of the benefits that, for instance, the institution of marriage confers on heterosexual couples.

Political *arguments* are usually about whether the underlying social contract is proper and necessary (the "conservative" point of view), or whether it ought to be changed (the "liberal" point of view). As therapists, however, we need only ask ourselves what the *consequences* of these arrangements are for the people who use our services and how we might go about trying to address these consequences within the therapeutic process. (This is not to say that an awareness of the consequences will not lead us to want to take greater action in the larger community.) Talking about politics, in the context of therapy, is not a way of imposing politics where it does not belong, but of opening up more space to talk about what is actually there and about what is going on in the world that makes a difference in clients' lives and in how they see themselves (and others).

In very basic terms, we might think of a skewed social contract as creating two distinct worlds, a world of opportunity and a world of trouble (in any particular person's life, of course, there may be considerable overlap between these two worlds.) In the world of trouble, trouble is always inviting (or even pushing) people to go along with the ways of trouble, which is to say, the ways of the world they live in, so that even when they "know better," they may find trouble the only partner that is readily available to them. In the world of opportunity, on the other hand, opportunity is always there inviting people to discover different avenues for success. To escape from the world of trouble, people need *more* creativity, *more* social support, *more* inner strength and determination, and *more* plain good luck than are needed for people to succeed in the world of opportunity, where there are multiple roads to success, and where the only possible constraints are the given abilities and aptitudes of the individual person. What is more, different social groups—racial and ethnic minorities, women, poor and other less affluent or less educated people, lesbians and gay men, transgendered people, etc.—may find themselves invited (or pushed) into different kinds of trouble, so that the trouble that insinuates itself into their lives has contours, dimensions, and *meanings* that are not the same. Seen in this way, it seems both insensitive and irresponsible to rely on some standardized, "universal" conception of human psychology, of psychological health and pathology, and of appropriate

336

therapeutic interventions, that does *not* take into account these wildly divergent worlds in which different people must try to make a life for themselves.

There is a social *violence* at work in a social contract that operates by offering some people a world of opportunity while constantly pushing other people into a world of trouble dictated by their class, race, ethnicity, sex, sexual orientation, gender identity, age, health, level of education, etc. I want to emphasize the concept of "violence" instead of more overtly political concepts like "oppression," "privilege," and "power," because "violence" clearly names a kind of relation in which, very simply, someone gets hurt. Violence is a process word; it describes something that is happening between people or, in this case, between the person and the larger social order. Where there is violence, our personal processes will necessarily organize themselves, in one way or another, around that violence. How people respond to violence is by no means uniform, and for some, it may be the kind of challenge that, for better or for worse, arouses their own fighting spirit. For others, however, this kind of larger *systemic* violence just means getting hurt, sometimes on a daily basis.

We often try to talk about this larger systemic violence by using terms like "racism," "sexism," and "homophobia" (among others). The problem with these terms, as far as the kind of intimately personal work that therapists do with individuals, couples, and families is concerned, is that the complexities and nuances of personal and interpersonal process are subordinated to concepts that are much better suited to describe large-scale social, cultural, historical, and political processes that people participate in to different degrees and in different ways. Even at a social level, they describe processes of *meaning-making* only in the broadest terms and are useful primarily as a way of issuing an explicitly political and moral challenge to an unacceptable status quo. I believe that using the concept of "violence" gives us a more direct, immediate, and less overtly ideological way of talking about what the problem actually is because it describes both a kind of interaction and a kind of effect on the person that is quite demonstrable. Furthermore, as therapists, we are often keenly aware of how overt or covert interpersonal violence, particularly within families—be it physical and sexual abuse or a violence of words and threats that devalue, demean and intimidate— translates into many of the kinds of problems that our clients present. It only requires a broadening of awareness and a little more imagination to see the kinds of social, cultural, political, and economic violence that make the world a troublesome one for clients. What therapists are in the best position to address, then, is the intersection between certain kinds of violence that, for some people, seem written into the very social contract under which they live, and the difficulties they experience in terms of their own personal and interpersonal processes.

Goodman et al. (2004) are right to say that mental health (and other kinds of) problems resulting from oppression "cannot truly be resolved without changing the systems and structures from which they arise" (p. 798). The practice of therapy, as they point out, only operates at the "micro-level" (Goodman et al., 2004). It does not change the surrounding social conditions that clients will continue to have to cope with, regardless of the work that we do with them. However, we should not lose sight of the role therapy can play in helping clients to identify the social violence that often permeates their lives, to talk about how this violence affects them and their own understanding of themselves and those around them, and to explore how they might respond differently, which is to say, how they might make a different kind of sense of themselves and their world that does *less* violence to them and that helps them to find the strength and hope they need to get on with their lives.

In this regard, a model of therapy that focuses on *meaning-making* is especially useful because it allows clients to look more closely at problematic meanings they have taken for granted, and to experiment with other constructions that may allow them to move beyond or to transcend *social* meanings that can only constrain them and do violence to their own personal process. The focus on social meaning, or "discourse," and on the language through which various discourses are conveyed, is central to the practice of narrative therapy (Freedman & Combs, 1996; White & Epston, 1990), which has a strong social constructionist bias. In what follows, this kind of social constructionism plays an important part. I see social constructionism as a theoretical tool that can help us to think about how social meaning serves to construct both social and personal realities. This is especially important if we are to get a handle on how social meaning becomes an instrument of violence that damages lives above and beyond

338

whatever material and institutional constraints with which people must contend.

However, we also need some way of talking about how this kind of social violence actually impacts personal process. It is all too easy to look at social problems as simply one possible cause of personal pathology, and it is difficult to distinguish between symptoms that are "survival responses" (Goodman et al., 2004) and symptoms that are the result of supposedly genuine "mental disorders." Furthermore, while social constructionist approaches such as narrative therapy eschew the language of disorder, they say surprisingly little about personal process. They also do not offer much about how "narratives" function in any kind of psychological sense. I think that Kelly's personal construct psychology can be of tremendous help in this regard. This is why I argue for the need to create a synthesis between social constructionism and personal construct psychology.

SOCIAL AND PERSONAL CONSTRUCTION AS SOCIAL AND PERSONAL PROCESS

Social constructionism and personal construct psychology each offer theoretical perspectives that are indispensable to the larger project of trying to understand the *person in context.* George Kelly (1955/1991) helps us to see meaning-making as a process that, at the level of the person, goes all the way down, into our thoughts, feelings, actions, and even into the functioning of the body itself. To construe is to engage the total workings of our physical, mental, and emotional being. Construing is also how we engage with other people. For Kelly (1963), we involve ourselves with others to the extent that we try to construe the ways in which *they* construe the world. This includes construing how they construe *us*, which has everything to do with what kinds of relationships we are able or unable to establish with them. Personal construct psychology allows us to see both personal and interpersonal processes as organized in terms of the meaning-making activities of the people involved. Social constructionists help us to see the construction of meaning as a process that goes all the way out to the farthest reaches of our social world. To construe is to construe with and among other people in a social context that already has its own structure, culture, politics, and history. From a social constructionist

339

perspective, all meaning-making is necessarily an elaboration, disruption, or alteration of those already existing social constructions that make the world an intelligible place, and ourselves an intelligible part of that world (Burr, 2003; Gergen, 1994). Seen in this way, meaning-making is *always* social, no matter how deeply it may engage and affect our personal processes. Social constructionism gives us a framework for talking about the ways in which large-scale social, cultural, historical, and political processes of meaning-making subsume (in the sense of serving to organize) the constructive activities of individual persons as they strive to make sense of themselves and engage with others.

A social constructionist perspective is both useful and necessary because an individual's personal processes of meaning-making only make sense in terms of her or his participation in *larger* contexts of social meaning, so that we cannot fully enter into the former without having some understanding of the latter. Furthermore, we cannot understand the ways in which social meanings enable people in certain ways, and constrain them in others, without adopting a perspective in which we, ourselves, do not take certain dominant *constructions* for granted, or as representing natural givens. For instance, terms like homosexual and heterosexual, black and white, and man and woman, are often seen as describing something *essential* about people, something that is found in the way nature has molded them, rather than as culturally loaded categorical distinctions that establish and perpetuate a certain kind of social valuing process and that open up certain life possibilities while closing down others. Social constructionists say, in effect, that meaning serves social purposes, so that we should always ask ourselves what kind of purposes are being served by asserting that various widely accepted categorical distinctions (and by extension, everything those distinctions connote) represent *natural givens*. The point is to challenge the power of dominant constructions in order to introduce the possibility of other ways of construing and other ways of life.

Social constructionism, then, is a way of unpacking the ways of looking at things that most of us take for granted in order to try to effect change in the larger *social* processes in which we all participate. A social constructionist perspective is essential to the kind of *critical* practice discussed later. However, social constructionism, in and of itself, does not give us a way of talking about meaning-making at the level of the person or a way of thinking about connections between meaning and *psychological* process. It is, in fact, relatively easy to come away with the impression that social constructionists have done away with the person altogether because their argument seems to imply that we have no way of standing outside of the available social constructions in order to get directly at something called the "person." The "person," it would seem, is just another social construction.

This version of the social constructionist argument, however, depends on the idea that constructions function like *representations* that have no referent but themselves or other representations, so that all meaning circles back upon itself without ever touching *terra firma*. Kelly's (1963) notion of *construction* is somewhat different and more useful, in that he sees human beings as trying to *do* something with reality rather than make a picture of it. Our constructions are a form of *action* upon the world, in that by making sense of it in some way, we actually make of the world something it could not have been otherwise. Constructions always embody some purpose; different constructions embody different purposes and have different *consequences* in the *real world*. Kelly's conception of truth and reality is purely pragmatic; as he says, "the open question for man is not whether reality exists or not, but what he can make of it. If he does make something of it he can stop worrying about whether it exists or not" (Kelly, 1969, p. 25). This pragmatic understanding of reality holds whether the constructions we are talking about are personal or social.

For instance, Kenneth Gergen (1994) argues that "truths" are something that we work out *with each other* for what are essentially pragmatic purposes—i.e. to improve our collective lot in life. For Gergen, this means that we ought to attend, first and foremost, to the *relationships* in which this working out takes place—*how* we, in fact, work with each other. The end result will always be the best we can do right now, but the better we work with each other, from the point of view of "going on together" (McNamee, 2004), the more likely the current end result can work well for *all* involved. Conversely, the kind of social violence I have been discussing is the very opposite of the ideal that Gergen has in mind. What matters, then, is not whether or not our constructions actually represent reality, but what we are trying to *do* with them *in* reality and what they have *us* doing, be it at the

341

level of society and our collective relationships with each other, or at the level of the individual person.

Personal construct psychology, operating within this pragmatic epistemological framework, gives us a way of talking about psychological process that is analogous to, although not identical with, the way that social constructionism addresses social processes. What sets Kelly apart from any other psychological theorist is that he sees people as being, first and foremost, meaning-making beings, so that everything about us develops out of how we construe the events, circumstances, and relationships that comprise our lives. While it makes sense to talk about the construction of meaning as a social process, Kelly helps us to see that it also makes sense to talk about *construing* as a foundational psychological act, one that is oriented around the concerns of the person in her or his efforts to find a way to live.

For Kelly, focusing on personal meaning-making is the only way of engaging with the *whole* person and of gaining an understanding of what he or she is really up to. Psychological *process* is characterized by intentionality; that is, our thoughts and feelings are always directed toward the task of making some kind of sense of what is going on around us and inside us, so that we can take some type of action. This means that we must find a way of "reading" the world and our place in it that works for us. This is an ongoing, life-long project that involves both dealing with constant change and getting hold of something that makes for a stable foundation. It is this sort of finding our way in the world project that Kelly (1963) describes in terms of personal meaning-making, or "personal constructs." Personal construct psychology does not try to answer questions about *why* we are we the way we are or why do we do what we do. For Kelly (1963) we must always be and do *something*; we are always already in motion, so that there is no need to try to figure out what *made* us move one way or another. We move ourselves. What does interest Kelly is *where* we are trying to go, *how* we are trying to get there, and *what* else we might be able to do if we construed our circumstances a little differently. Kelly's theory is a psychology of *possibility*, in which *psychological* process is opened up or changed through the invention of *alternative* constructions that provide a fresh approach to otherwise knotty problems.

For Kelly, construing is also an *embodied* process, so that the consequences of our constructions are written on the body.

Thus, meaning-making involves (or interferes with) the "elaboration of all our psychological processes, including the so-called 'bodily' processes" (Kelly, 1991, p. 246). Another way of putting this is to say that *meaning orients process*. The idea of process, of course, includes not only conscious thought but emotion and the myriad of other things inside of us that operate at a low level of awareness or beyond the range of what we are able to say to others or even to ourselves. For Kelly, process cannot be abstracted from our efforts to meaningfully construe our immediate experience. If we want to understand another person's psychological process, then we must understand what the world looks like to her or him. Therefore, the entry point for any kind of therapeutic engagement is the effort to understand the personal constructions of the client. However, because constructs are not only linguistic, but also non-verbal and "pre-verbal" (Kelly, 1963), we must pay close attention to the client's overall process (i.e. feelings, non-verbal communication, etc.). After all, *process discloses meaning*.

The further argument that I am making is that personal process also discloses our participation in contexts of *social* meaning and the nature of our role in larger social and *political* processes. As McNamee (2004) points out, while the thrust of Kelly's theory is more individual than social, he does move out into the social realm through his conception of "sociality" (Kelly, 1963). In fact, sociality is a key concept because it allows us to see how larger social and political processes show up in personal process through the construction of meaning.

SOCIALITY AND "ROLE"

Many of the personal meanings that are most important to us are what might be called "self-in-relation" constructions. For Kelly (1963), our sociality, which is our psychological connection to other people, depends on "the extent" to which we are able to "construe the construction processes of another" (p. 95). This is how we go about defining our "role" (Kelly, 1963), which is to say, *who we are*, in relation to others. Much of what is *core* for us has to do with how we construe what our *role* is in relation to family, peers, and others who are important to us. These constructions are core because they are the living tissue of our connection to others.

We can extend this understanding of sociality and say that we must also construe the constructions of the social world around us. The rules we perceive as governing that world have a lot to do with how we go about construing the construction processes of others, including those who are closest or most important to us and, thus, with how we construe who *we* are in relation to them. That is, we can only achieve a sense of psychological connection to a *community* of others by construing the constructions that define the terms of membership in that community, in a way that is analogous to what Kelly (1963) calls "role relationships." Put simply, having a role in any community means we must be able to construe the social constructions of that community. The question is, what *kinds* of "roles" are actually available to us? What happens when our own efforts to achieve a healthy and necessary sociality involve us in construing *social* constructions that perpetrate a kind of social *violence* against us?

In a "role relationship" (Kelly, 1963), the other person matters enough to us that we make the effort to see the world as she or he sees it. We may not always be very successful in this effort, but it matters that we try because this is the only way in which we can actually *engage* with the other person at the level of his or her own *process*. When we make the effort, it means that we do not see the other person as an *object* but as a person whose humanity is comparable to our own (Epting, 1984). The opposite of role relationships are relationships in which we do *not* make any attempt to construe what things look like to the other person, but instead relate to her or him as little more than a *thing* to be manipulated, exploited, violated, dismissed, or ignored. We do not feel obliged to actually *engage* with *this* person the way we might with some other people because, in our way of construing differences between people, this person does not merit making such an effort. We may be especially prone to this sort of behavior when the rules that govern how human differences are construed *socially* make the person in question appear very different from us, or when our sense of inclusion in the larger community seems to depend, because of our perception of what the *rules* are, on *not* seeing what things look like to the other person. Kelly's distinction between role relationships and their opposite, what I would call "objectifying" relationships, helps us to see where a certain kind of *violence* can enter into relations between people, simply based on how they construe each other.

344

Kelly's conception of role relationships (and their opposite) focuses primarily on how *individuals* construe one another. However, this construing takes place in a larger context of *social* meaning, in which certain kinds of people appear more accessible, more real, and more fully human to us than others because of how *humanness* and human worth are socially constructed within those communities. Next, I discuss in more detail what the philosopher Judith Butler (2004) describes as the terms of recognition by which humanness is conferred. What is important to understand here is simply that people are different from each other. Different people tend to occupy different positions in our society that confer upon them greater or lesser weight, voice, and value in the general concourse of human relationships, depending on how such differences are construed socially. This means that some of us have a "role" in society that helps other people establish role relationships with us, while others of us may find ourselves in a position where our "role" is to be more or less objectified (or at least in certain important contexts).

For those of us who occupy positions that are relatively privileged, this may be difficult to see, precisely because the privilege we are accorded is that of being seen and treated like a *person*, instead of like an object. The privilege we experience is that our point of view *matters* and that our lives are not considered disposable compared to the lives of others. Because we take this privilege as a matter of course (and have no particular reason not to), we may not see or really understand how other people come up against an almost *systemic* objectification, in which their point of view does *not* matter very much within the general concourse of human relationships, and their lives *are* more disposable, in terms of how society as a whole goes about its business.

All of us, by being social beings and belonging to a social world, enter into the existing *discourses* about human differences in which some people are construed as being more or less persons and others as being more or less objects. If sociality in relation to a larger community (or society) depends on construing the social constructions of that community, then sociality, at a psychological level, means engaging with the kind of violence that is implicit in the ongoing objectification of certain kinds of people. If the "other" is another person, then the *social* construction of our own personhood is, unfortunately, dependent on the objectification of this other person, and only some kind of social *reconstruction* can alter this relation. That is, we cannot simply maintain the status quo without maintaining the underlying violence that is a part of it. (Social construction, however, does not equal determination. Many people can and do challenge de-humanizing constructions of the other; and, in fact, it is part of our job as therapists to do exactly that.) If the "other" is ourselves, then we are forced to engage *psychologically* with the violence of being objectified. That is, we can construe the construction processes of others only by construing how they *objectify* us.

What we are construing, however, is not always the construction processes of *specific* other people, but the social constructions of our community. Such constructions are part of a larger context of social meanings that define the dominant perspectives (or discourses) of that community. These constructions become part of our own construction processes through our efforts to establish a psychological sense of *role* within that community (which is part and parcel of the *healthy* elaboration of our own personal constructs and personal processes in the actual world in which we find ourselves). When the dominant perspectives objectify us, then having a "role" can be a dangerous thing. Unfortunately, not having a "role" is also a dangerous thing because then we simply have no way of actually belonging to the community (or larger society) of which we are a part. Dominant discourses establish certain *rules* that tend to govern how we construe the constructions of whomever we encounter, so that we construe our *general* relation to others in accord with those rules. We then experience a kind of generalized violence against ourselves, even when we have significant relationships with people who are exceptions to the rule. The point is that they feel like exactly that—exceptions.

The great danger for those of us who experience this socially constructed objectification and violence is that we will get caught in a kind of double bind in which we either try to elaborate our own sense of "role" within the larger community by compartmentalizing, demeaning, silencing, or trying to erase the differences that mark us as "other," or we try to elaborate what makes us different from others by sacrificing the possibility of having a sustainable and *recognizably human* (Butler, 2004) role in that larger community. Put simply, we collude with the violence that is being committed against us or we reject the community and

346

become psychological outsiders. At different times and in different ways, we may try both of these solutions.

Collusion involves a process of construing against ourselves that in "minority" groups is often called something like "internalized homophobia" or "internalized racism," but is really just an unfortunate consequence of what is in many ways a healthy and necessary sociality. Being a psychological "outsider" may be associated with feelings of anger, rage, helplessness, hopelessness, self-destructiveness, and even violence. These feelings and behaviors, however, may well be the result of the one's efforts to hold onto some measure of personal integrity and wholeness in relation to other people, however inadequately, by rejecting the terms of a social contract in which one feels stripped of integrity and wholeness by the very nature of the "role" that has been given to one in the larger social world. In both cases, the double bind is that healthy feelings and intentions become the source of emotional struggle, pain, and relational problems because having a "role" in the social world means being objectified or dehumanized. Faced with this dehumanization, we can either give up our efforts to achieve a healthy, viable sociality (at great cost to ourselves) or we can continue to pursue a "role" in the social world by sacrificing our own ability to elaborate who we actually are or might be able to become.

This way of stating things puts into black and white a situation that, for many people, surely contains many grays and/or "exceptions to the rule." People often belong to multiple communities in which the "rules" differ substantially, so that differences that are often objectified in one community may be given ample room for elaboration in another. "Outsiders" often form their own "insider" communities and cultures (or subcultures), and people form personal bonds with each other over those very differences that have put them outside the dominant culture. Again, many people experience racism, sexism, homophobia or other kinds of de-humanizing social constructions more in the abstract than in their everyday relationships, so that the violence is buffered or experienced in a more distant way. They have ample opportunity to construe their way out of the aforementioned double binds. Some people are resilient and creative enough to approach this kind of systemic social violence as an opportunity to elaborate transformative constructions that can change relationships and humanize all involved. Ultimately, what many people

347

confront is a situation that is ambiguous, in which social violence is a regular part of the social reality in which they participate, but it does not characterize the whole of that reality nor define those relationships that are most important to them.

Nevertheless, we must be aware that belonging to categories of persons, or being "different" in ways that our culture tends to objectify and dehumanize, means that a person must at some level experience the violence that is inherent in these objectifying and dehumanizing constructions. Being *social* means engaging with this violence, so that a healthy and necessary sociality can become a source of real psychological (and interpersonal) difficulties. While some people may be more or less buffered from this kind of violence, others find themselves nakedly exposed. Either way, we must treat the violence that attends the social construction of race, ethnicity, class, gender, gender identity, sexual orientation, age, health, ability, religion (or spirituality), and other significant human differences as real clinical concerns. We must be aware that "symptoms" like anxiety, rage, self-destructive behavior, or a depression born of grief at the loss of a genuine and sustainable sociality or a belief in oneself are both perfectly *reasonable* (if not wholly *constructive*) responses to the experience of a *systemic* psychological violence. We should not be surprised that women, African-Americans, and gay people all suffer significantly higher rates of depression than white, heterosexual men (Solomon, 2000). It is just part of the territory, a territory that, as therapists, we ought to get to know, because it is the *world* that some of our clients live in, and it is the context in which their own personal constructions take shape.

THE JUNCTURE FROM WHICH CRITIQUE EMERGES

The idea of therapy as social critique puts a contextual perspective, a *situated* point of view, at the heart of Kelly's philosophy of "constructive alternativism." According to this philosophy,

> there are always some alternative constructions available to choose among in dealing with the world. No one needs to paint himself into a corner; no one needs to be completely hemmed in by circumstances; no one needs to be the victim of his biography. (Kelly, 1963, p. 15)

However, alternative constructions change not only ourselves, but also our relationships with others. When these relationships have been constituted on the basis of *social constructions* that objectify, dehumanize and, thus, do violence to one or more of the individuals involved, then what we need are *critical* constructions that open space for the kind of social *transformations* in which truly *constructive* alternatives can emerge.

Butler (2004) identifies the fundamental problem that we must be able to respond to in some sort of critical fashion. She says that

> the terms by which we are recognized as human are socially articulated and changeable. And sometimes the very terms that confer "humanness" on some individuals are those that deprive certain other individuals of the possibility of achieving that status, producing a differential between the human and the less-than-human. . . . The human is understood differently depending on its race, the legibility of that race, its morphology, the recognizability of that morphology, its sex, the perceptual verifiability of that sex, its ethnicity, the categorical understanding of that ethnicity. Certain humans are recognized as less than human, and that form of qualified recognition does not lead to a viable life. Certain humans are not recognized as human at all, and that leads to yet another order of unlivable life. (Butler, 2004, p. 2)

Black or white, male or female, recognizably male/female or transgendered, gay or straight, affluent or poor, young or old, able-bodied or disabled, tall or short, fat or thin, white-collar or blue-collar, mentally healthy or mentally disordered: all of these terms (and many others, of course) distinguish people from each other based on particular ways of construing *difference* that have a long history, and that serve to make one side of each pair more "recognizably human" (Butler, 2004)—more valued, more listened to, more understood, more respected, more socially powerful— than the other. The more we find ourselves on the less-than-human end of this differential, the more it constrains our relationships, restricts and distorts the elaboration of our own lives, and the less viable or even livable our lives become.

Butler's differential between the human and the less-than-human highlights the violence that is embedded in often-unquestioned ways of seeing people. If we are white, for instance, we do not see how the very *idea* of "race" gives us permission to see nonwhite people in terms of their *racial characteristics* while we see other people *like us* in terms of their *human* characteristics. The result is that, in our society, race is a category

349

that follows some people around like a ball and chain, while it leaves others with the illusion that race is something that has little or nothing to do with them. Those who are marked as *racial* beings find themselves struggling, whether they want to or not, in ways that can be very concrete, personal, and subjective, with this socially constructed distinction between their race and their (questioned) *humanity*.

The violence that is encoded in our ordinary, everyday ways of construing human differences becomes obvious when it is translated into the language of slurs and epithets. For some people, this is still the dominant language that is available for talking about certain kinds of differences. As transgender activist and author Riki Wilchins (2004) says,

> Tellingly there is not a single word for people who don't fit gender norms that is positive, affirming, and complimentary. There is not even a word that is neutral. Because all our language affords are strings of insults, it is impossible to talk about someone who is brave enough to rebel against gender stereotypes without ridiculing or humiliating them at the same time. Language works against you. It is meant to, because the language of gender is highly political. (p. 38)

However, slurs and insults, as well as outright physical attacks, are only the visible extreme of a violence that is part of how we, as a society, think about categories like "gender" in the first place. Wilchins (2004) sees the very language by which gender is divided into male or female as amounting to "a kind of crime—an assault of meaning that forces people to live as gendered impossibilities" (Wilchins, 2004, p. 38). When violence or the threat of violence serves to enforce categorical distinctions that include some people within the circle of the human while keeping others out, then the distinctions themselves represent "an assault of meaning" (Wilchins, 2004, p. 38) that some of us must reckon with as a matter of course.

Butler's (2004) differential gives us a core critical reference axis upon which we can chart the livability or unlivability of the different *relational* realities that people inhabit. If we think about this differential in socio-political terms, then we can use it to analyze how the institutional and other political arrangements that organize society serve to privilege certain kinds of people while oppressing others. But we can also think about this distinction between what and who is seen as recognizably human

350

(and what and who is seen as less-than-human) as setting up social and political *conditions of worth* that serve to construct different kinds of relationships between people. This is of great *psychological* importance. After all, what kind of person can we become (Rogers, 1961) if our status in the larger social world is always to be something less-than-human? What kind of room is there for the constructive elaboration of our own lives if the social world around us has little or no room for *us*, in terms of how *it* is constructed? How can we fully inhabit our own *process*, if we are perpetually subject to *social* conditionals that denigrate or deny our basic worth, or that make our worth contingent on *not* fully inhabiting our own process or constructively elaborating our own lives?

These are, at the very least, serious challenges for those of us who, more often than not, find ourselves on the less-than-human side of Butler's (2004) differential because of our class, race, ethnicity, religion (or spirituality), sex, sexual orientation, gender identity, looks, age, health, ability, educational status, or some other culturally salient distinction. Many of us find ourselves on both sides of this differential, depending on which distinction is most salient in a given context. What we must also understand is that Butler's (2004) differential is *conditional* on both sides. That is, being recognizably human is not the same thing as being *fully* human in the way that Rogers or other humanistic psychologists mean the term. Rather, it is a status that is defined by and dependent on its relationship to those who have *not* been accorded such a status in the larger social world. If there is a differential, then men, for instance, can occupy the status of the recognizably human only by making women something less than human and something more like objects. The same is true for whites versus non-whites, heterosexuals versus homosexuals, the affluent versus the less affluent, and so on. Otherwise, the differential itself disappears and with it, the privilege of *being human,* which is to say, of having one's point of view recognized as the standard of comparison, the perspective that *cannot* be dismissed or ignored. This means that we can easily feel pulled down to less-than-human status by having that privilege challenged, or we can stop feeling recognizably human if we fail to live up to the conditions and expectations that make that status privileged in the first place.

As a result, we may feel a real sense of *threat*—i.e. our *personal* constructions of our own *humanness* may be threatened

351

(Kelly, 1963)—if we are confronted with the consequences of our privilege for those on the less-than-human side of Butler's (2004) differential. We may feel compelled to protect our constructions of our own humanness by refusing to see what things look like to others. This is one reason why it is often so difficult for people who belong to some dominant majority or privileged group to really see or admit what the consequences of their dominance and privilege are for those on the other side of the equation. After all, one's very humanness becomes equated with being *inhuman* to others. Furthermore, if our own human worth *depends* on maintaining our share of the entitlements that go with social privilege, then any kind of challenge or perceived challenge to those entitlements may provoke us to one degree or another of *violence*, in order to remain recognizably human to *ourselves*. If we are not able to see ourselves in the accomplishments and successes of the privileged whose lives define what humanness looks like to us, then the fall from the ranks of the recognizably human may feel vertiginous indeed. It is, perhaps, no accident, that of the 60 gun deaths that occur every day in the United States among people over the age of twenty-five, according to the Centers for Disease Control and Prevention, 32 are suicides by white men (Marsh, 2007). In gun deaths among people age 40 and over, 25 out of 39 are suicides by white men (Marsh, 2007). This, too, is evidence of the violence embedded in the social construction of humanness in our society.

The problem, then, is a *social* problem that can have serious, if not grave, consequences at the level of personal process and interpersonal relationships. The problem is the very existence of "a differential between the human and the less-than-human" (Butler, 2004, p. 2) as an axis of social meaning that serves to construct very different positions for people to occupy in their relationships with each other and, hence, in their relationships with themselves. We do not, however, have to remain trapped within the terms of this differential. As Butler (2004) says, "the terms by which we are recognized as human are socially articulated and changeable" (p. 2). Alternative *social* constructions are always possible.

Even so, we cannot pursue alternative *personal* constructions outside the context of some kind of *social* recognizability, not without becoming unmoored from whatever *role* constructions we have that could guide us in our relationships with others (Kelly,

1963). Butler (2004) uses her own social constructionist language to talk about this same difficulty in terms of the "norms" that serve to constitute a recognizable sense of self for the individual:

> The "I" that I am finds itself at once constituted by norms and dependent on them . . . because the "I" becomes, to a certain extent, unknowable, threatened with unviability, with becoming undone altogether, when it no longer incorporates the norm in such a way that makes this "I' fully recognizable . . . I may feel that without some recognizability I cannot live. But I may also feel that the terms by which I am recognized make life unlivable. This is the juncture from which critique emerges . . . (p. 4)

To feel ourselves violating certain seemingly crucial norms brings home to us how those norms bind us to other people. It also makes clear the loss that such violations entail, even when the norms themselves are destructive and cruel. At the same time, certain norms—of class, race, ethnicity, gender, sexual orientation, etc.—may not be *livable*, either for us or for others. Norms of whiteness are not livable for non-whites; norms of maleness are not livable for women; norms of masculinity and femininity are not livable for gender non-conformists; norms of heterosexuality are not livable for lesbians, gays, and bisexuals; norms of the affluent are not livable for the poor and financially insecure. This is where any kind of *critique* must begin, with the recognition that we must be *recognizably human* in our *differences* from each other as well as our similarities, if our lives are going to be viable—psychologically, interpersonally, socially, and materially.

It is only when we have come to this critical juncture that we can begin to articulate alternative constructions that are, ultimately, reconstructions of what *humanness* means. It is through critique that we begin to *include* in the human those human differences that had previously been relegated to the status of the less-than-human. Such reconstructions must be *shareable*; they must be, as narrative therapists (Freedman & Combs, 1996) put it, *co-constructions* that change the meaning that is shared *between* people. They must help to make us *less* separate from and more connected to each other, so that sociality becomes a *strength* instead of a trap. This ought to be a basic goal in our work with any client. In order to achieve this goal, however, we must embrace the idea that therapeutic practice is also a form of critical practice.

353

It ought to be "a way of intervening into the social and political process by which the human is articulated" (Butler, 2004, p. 33).

LOOKING FOR THE CONTEXT IN THERAPY

- Hank is a white man in his early forties who comes to therapy because he is frequently verbally abusive to his wife and children. He and his wife, Ellen, previously tried couples counseling, but she decided (and he agreed) that this is his problem and he is the one who needs to change. Hank has struggled to find a sustainable career path and often talks about his unhappy childhood. He expects Ellen, as his wife, to be more nurturing towards him, as well as more sexually and emotionally available. When she seems distant or reserved, he often flies into a rage.

- Susan is a white woman in her late thirties, who has a teenage daughter and lives with her partner, Mike. She comes to therapy because Mike recently became enraged at her and her daughter. Consequently, Mike destroyed some of the furniture in their home. Susan talks about having been physically and sexually abused by both her father and her first husband. Mike knows about this history and has never previously been violent or abusive during their five years together. Susan says that she got together with Mike, in part, because he seemed to understand what she had been through. Now she is distraught, and says she feels like she's losing her mind. Her friends tell her to leave him, but he says he will never do it again and she does not know what to do.

- James is an African-American man in his late twenties, who has been married for seven years. He reports that he sometimes has sex with other men on the side, but insists that he is not gay. However, his wife has begun to suspect that he is having an affair with another woman, and he is afraid that she will eventually find out what is really going on. He has come to therapy because he wants to have a family and not lose his marriage. He is afraid that he will ruin his life by his behavior, if he has not done so already.

In all of these scenarios, *context* is very important. In terms of the therapeutic process, context means, above all, the context of *meaning* that orients people in their own personal processes of meaning-making. So, as therapists, we need to ask ourselves, what meanings (or social constructions) about being a man, being a white man, about success, and about normalcy, are in play in Hank's situation. Further, we need to consider how do these constructions prevent him from (1) seeing how his family experiences his behavior, and (2) having the kind of non-violent, loving relationship with his wife that he says he wants. We also need to ask ourselves how Susan's "symptoms" are connected to the violence—both physical and psychological—that she has experienced. We need to think about the double bind in which she finds herself. She feels she must either accept violence as a condition of being a woman and a partner, or reject violence by violently uprooting her own feelings of love and connection to Mike. As such, her core "role" in relation to Mike is being challenged. For James, we need to ask how stories within the larger culture and within the African-American and gay communities—about race, gender, religion, and homosexuality—have placed James in a position where he feels compelled to choose between, on the one hand, his own constructions of "role" and his communal/family relationships and, on the other, his feelings of love and attraction for members of his own sex.

Socio-political domains such as gender, race, age, sexual orientation, culture, and ethnicity organize both existential meaning and therapy in ways that confer privilege on some persons while marginalizing and disempowering others (Early, Nazario, & Steier, 1994). As therapists, we have an ethical obligation to engage in critical reflection not only about the influence of culture, power, privilege, and oppression in our clients' lives, but also about our own situatedness in these socio-political domains. We need to think about how our own "perceptions of and feelings toward our respective cultural backgrounds" (Hardy & Laszloffy,

1995, p. 227) both help and constrain our efforts to connect with and honor the experiences of our clients. The point is not only to create *awareness* of cultural differences, which is "primarily a cognitive function," but to promote a *sensitivity* to cultural differences and experiences of oppression, which involves "primarily an affective function" in which "an individual responds emotionally to stimuli with delicacy and respectfulness" (Hardy & Laszloffy, 1995, p. 227).

This sensitivity can be facilitated and increased by allowing ourselves to come face-to-face with the *violence* that is inherent in the social construction of each of these domains, a violence that some people have the privilege of not experiencing. Others are caught in the crossfire on a daily basis. What is more, this violence becomes embedded in both our clients' and our own personal constructions because we are all social beings, and accommodating such violence is presented as one of the terms of membership in the larger social world. This has the effect of putting all of us in a double bind of sorts, where being social means accepting or colluding with violence, and rejecting violence means rejecting, to one degree or another, our own psychological sense of "role" within the larger community (based on how we have construed the social constructions of our community.) Privilege, in this context, means that we experience this double bind only when we happen to think about it in relation to seemingly distant "others," while those "others" may experience it as one of the main psychological conditions of their being-in-the-world. What we need, then, are *critical* constructions that question the necessity and value of an often-taken-for-granted violence. Elaborating this kind of critique and forging these kinds of alternative constructions is, or ought to be, an important part of the therapeutic process for both clients and therapists.

Looking for the context in therapy means trying to construe the constructions of clients by also construing the constructions of the larger social world in which they find themselves. We try to think about the relevant "socio-political domains" (Early, Nazario, & Steier, 1994) in that world and then about the person in those domains. What is it like to be *this* person engaged with those meanings? We listen much more closely than we might otherwise for the ways in which the social world shows up in what our clients have to say, in their own personal construc-tions. Personal constructs are really just one side of an ongoing conversation in which the other side, the side we do not get to hear, is often much more demanding and much more powerful because it is *the world*. Even our most seemingly private thoughts take the form of inner conversations with other people, real or imagined (McNamee, 2004). So we listen for and ask our clients about what is being said on the *other* side of these conversations they are having. We explore together with them the effect of those social constructions (spoken or unspoken) that inform their own personal constructions of who they are, what other people expect of them, what life must be like, and what it is or is not possible for them to do in the world. How, and in what ways, are their personal constructions a response to what they hear being required of them by the world in which they live? Are these requirements *livable*, less than livable, or not livable at all? How are the problems that clients experience connected to or required by assumptions taken from the social world that function as constraints or as vehicles for perpetuating a kind of violence they do not know how to transcend or overcome?

Our job, ultimately, is to add our own voice to the other side of that conversion and to help clients articulate new and different responses. Therapy constitutes a social space in which we work together with clients to elaborate alternative *social* constructions that shift the balance away from voices that constrain and violate, and toward voices that do not preempt the possibility of hope, connectedness, and faith in oneself. There are many different possible alternative social constructions—it is a matter, in part, of finding or forging *relationships* where genuinely *constructive* alternatives can have real currency, and where standing up to violence is the beginning of sociality and not the end.

Early, Nazario, and Steier (1994) describe problems (or symptoms) as arising from *unsuccessful* attempts at *resistance* to oppression or, following my own argument, to the *violence* that is inflicted on people by the way human differences have been socially constructed. Symptoms are an expression of the unlivability of social terms that demand we do violence to ourselves or to our relationships with others. As such, they represent a form of resistance to those demands. Such resistance is a *healthy* impulse to be affirmed. We can, however, help to open up other, more constructive avenues of resistance (Early, Nazario, & Steier, 1994), by inviting clients to actively address the

357

constraints, violence, and oppression that have characterized their psychological, interpersonal, and social worlds. We can collaborate with clients in trying to make their resistance more hopeful, productive, and creative, so that resistance creates room to change how they are able to "go on together" (McNamee, 2004) with other people.

Sometimes, overtly political conceptions of therapy and therapeutic change begin to sound like versions of what the philosopher Karl Popper (1986) calls "utopian social engineering" (p. 67), which is to say, ways of using therapy to help make society over in the image of some political ideal. But therapy, as a process, is much more consistent with what Popper (1986) himself advocates, which is "piecemeal social engineering," (p.64), or change based on trying things out and seeing how they work. What we are doing is inviting our clients to experiment not only with their own personal constructions, but with their relationship to the larger social world, and with how *it* is constructed. Just as process discloses meaning, so a change in meaning can only be evaluated in terms of the kind of process— both personal and interpersonal—it does or does not help to bring about. We cannot know how things will turn out beforehand. However, therapy as a form of social critique helps to create room in clients' relational worlds for such experiments to take place by helping to clarify what the problem is, where it is coming from, and what alternatives might be possible. Critique allows us to extend Kelly's (1955/1991) basic idea of therapy as experimentation to the social world itself, and—perhaps most importantly—to the person's place within that world.

REFERENCES

Burr, V. (2003). *Social constructionism*. New York: Routledge.

Butler, J. (2004). *Undoing gender*. New York: Routledge.

Early, G., Nazario, A., & Steier, H. (1994, April). *Oppression-sensitive family therapy: A health-affirming model*. Paper presented at the meeting of the American Orthopsychiatric Association, Washington, DC.

Epting, F. R. (1984). *Personal construct counseling and psychotherapy*. Chichester, UK: John Wiley.

Freedman, J., & Combs, G. (1996). *Narrative therapy: The social construction of preferred realities*. New York: Norton.

Gergen, K. J. (1994). *Realities and relationships: Soundings in social construction.* Cambridge, MA: Harvard University Press.

Goodman, L. A, Liang, B., Helms, J. E., Latta, R. E., Sparks, E., & Weintraub, S. R. (2004). Training counseling psychologists as social justice agents: Feminist and multicultural principles in action. *The Counseling Psychologist, 32,* 793-837.

Hardy, K. V. & Laszloffy, T. A. (1995). The cultural genogram: Key to training culturally competent family therapists. *Journal of Marital and Family Therapy, 21,* 227-237.

Joxe, A. (2002). *Empire of disorder.* New York: Semiotext(e).

Kelly, G. A. (1963). *A theory of personality: The psychology of personal constructs.* New York: Norton.

Kelly, G. A. (1969). Ontological acceleration. In B. Maher (Ed.), *Clinical psychology and personality: The selected papers of George Kelly* (pp. 7-45). New York: John Wiley.

Kelly, G. A. (1991). *The psychology of personal constructs: Vol.2. Clinical diagnosis and psychotherapy.* London, UK: Routledge. (Original work published 1955)

Marsh, B. (2007, April 22). An accounting of daily gun deaths. *The New York Times,* Sec. 4, p.14.

McNamee, S. (2004). Relational bridges between constructionism and constructivism. In J. D. Raskin & S. K. Bridges (Eds.), *Studies in meaning 2: Bridging the personal and social in constructivist psychology* (pp. 37-50). New York: Pace University Press.

Paris, M. E. & Epting, F. (2004). Social and personal construction: Two sides of the same coin. In J. D. Raskin & S. K. Bridges (Eds.), *Studies in meaning 2: Bridging the personal and social in constructivist psychology* (pp. 3-36). New York: Pace University Press.

Popper, K. (1986). *The poverty of historicism.* London: Ark Paperbacks.

Rogers, C. R. (1961). *On becoming a person.* Boston: Houghton Mifflin.

Solomon, A. (2000). *The noonday demon: An atlas of depression.* New York: Scribner.

White, M. & Epston, D. (1990). *Narrative means to therapeutic ends.* New York: Norton.

Wilchins, R. (2004). *Queer theory, gender theory: An instant primer.* Los Angeles: Alyson Books.

William, P.J. (2006, August 28/September 4). The hydra of Jim Crow. *The Nation, 283*(6), 9

ABOUT THE EDITORS

Jonathan D. Raskin is a professor of psychology at the State University of New York at New Paltz. His scholarship focuses on constructivist psychology and psychotherapy. He has published many articles and book chapters on constructivism. He has also co-edited three books, including the first two *Studies in Meaning* volumes. Dr. Raskin serves as an associate editor for the *Journal of Constructivist Psychology*. He is also licensed as a psychologist in New York, where he maintains a small private practice. Dr. Raskin recently received the State University of New York Chancellor's Award for Excellence in Scholarship and Creative Activities, as well as the Carmi Harari Early Career Award for Inquiry from the American Psychological Association's Society of Humanistic Psychology.

Sara K. Bridges is an associate professor of counseling psychology at The University of Memphis. Her scholarship examines constructivism, sexuality, and depth focused approaches to psychotherapy. In addition to publishing extensively on constructivism, Dr. Bridges has co-edited both previous *Studies in Meaning* volumes. She is the current president of the Constructivist Psychology Network and is also active on the board of the American Psychological Association's Society of Humanistic Psychology, currently serving as treasurer. Dr. Bridges is licensed as a psychologist in New York.

About the Constructivist Psychology Network

Studies in Meaning is the official book series of The Constructivist Psychology Network (CPN). CPN is a network of persons interested in constructivist approaches to psychology, relationships, and human change processes. It is largely comprised of psychologists, but there are also members from related disciplines. Those interested in personal constructivism or related areas of constructivist, constructionist, narrative, or postmodern approaches to psychology are encouraged to join. CPN officially became a non-profit organization in July 2005. Up to date information about CPN is maintained on the organization's website: http://www.constructivistpsych.org.

CPN membership is open to anyone. An annual membership includes a subscription to the *Journal of Constructivist Psychology* (4 issues per year) and receipt of the CPN newsletter the *Constructivist Chronicle*. Members often receive discounted rates for the biennial CPN conference held in even numbered years. CPN membership rates for 2008 are as follows:

Professional memberships: $70
Student memberships: $40

This is an excellent deal, especially when you consider that the current non-CPN member price for the *Journal of Constructivist Psychology* alone is $213 US per year. Further, no matter where you live or what currency you use, you can pay your dues quickly and easily online using our secure online payments option.

How to Join CPN

The easiest way to join CPN is via our secure website using a credit card or PayPal account. Go to http://www.constructivistpsych.org and click the "Join" tab at the top of the page. Then follow the easy instructions.

Dues payments can also be made by check or money order (in US dollars made payable to CPN) and mailed to:

Sara K. Bridges, Ph.D.
Counseling Psychology
100 Ball Hall
The University of Memphis
Memphis, TN 38152   USA

Please include your name, affiliation, address, and e-mail for the membership database. Indicate whether you are a student or professional.

Index of Proper Names
[Numbers in *italics* refer to listings in reference sections.]

Abrams, D., 300, *321*
Acevedo, C. A., 266, *268*
Acton, T., 238, *252*
Adams-Webber, J. R., 130, 137, *142*, 240, 245, *247*
Adelman, R., vi, viii, xii, 183, 188, 190, 193, *199*
Adler, A., 148
Agnew, J., 236, *247*
Aguilar, T., 260, *269*
Ahrons, C. R., 222, *223*
Aksoy-Toska, G., v, viii
Albee, G., 313
Albert, C. J., 31-32, *53*
Alexander, P. C., 237, *247*, *249*
Allen, D., 240, *247*
Amato, P. R., 210, *223*
Anderson, A., 232, *249*
Anderson, H., 17, *27*, 150-151, 151-152, *163*, 307n, *321*
Anderson, W. T., 148, 205, *223*
Aristotle, 316
Arnold, W., 34, *53*
Arredondo, P., 277, *290*
Ashmore, M., 5, *27*
Axelson, J. A., 253, *268*

Bach, R., 95, *104*
Badesha, J., 135, *142*
Bandura, A., 148
Bannister, D., 130, 134, *142*, 183, *199*, 240, 245, *247*
Barlow, D. H., 312, *321*
Bartlett, F. C., 309n, *321*
Bateson, G., 148, 303, 315, *321*
Bateson, M. K., 304n
Baxter, V. A., 132, *143*

Beail, N., 236, *247*
Beck, A. T., 34, 44-45, *52*
Beckett, S., 98, *104*
Beels, C. C., 310-311, 311n, *321*
Beinfield, H., 295, *321*
Bell, R., 134, *142*, 230, *247*
Berg, I. K., 305, 308, *321*, *324*
Bergin, A. E., 276, *289*
Berlin, S. B., 204, *225*
Bernstein, R. J., 316
Bersonsky, M. D., 41-42, *52*
Bertrando, P., 309n
Beutler, L. E., 275, 276, *289*
Bhandari, S., 241, *251*, *252*
Bianco, J., 42, *52*
Bieri, J., 172, *179*
Bierman, R., 127, 132, 140, *144*
Biever, J. L., 16, *28*
Birdsall, M., 170, *181*
Black, E. L., 129, *142*
Bliss, H., 295n, 308
Blissett, J., 127, *142*
Bloodstein, O., 166-167, *179*
Bloom, H., 317, *321*
Bloom, L., 165, *179*
Boberg, E., 166, *179*
Bognarchuk, M., 132, *142*
Bohart, A. C., 229, *247*, 278, 279, 312, *321*
Boscolo, L., 308, 309, *321*, *327*
Boszormenyi-Nagy, I., 85n , *104*
Botella, L., 236, *247*
Bowen, M., 99
Bratton, S., 147, 148, 154, 160, 161, *163*
Bridges, S. K., v, viii, xi, xii, 4, *30*, 81, *84*, 173, *181*, 256, 257, *268*, 296, 316, *325*, *326*, 361, 363
Brown, E. M., 202, *223*
Brown, L., 278, 280
Bruner, J., 148
Brunsma, D. L., 267, *270*
Buber, M., 318, *321*

Buchanan, N. T., 266, *268*
Buckley, T. R., 260, 263, *268*
Buddha, 295, *321*
Bugental, J., 148
Burchfield, C., 276, *290*
Burr, V., 340, *358*
Bush, G. W., 90, 307n
Butler, J., 332, 345, 346, 349, 350-351, 352-353, 354, *358*
Butler, M., 284, *289*
Butt, T. W., 5, 27, 107, *122*, 257, 258, 267, *268*, 271
Button, E., 184, 197, *199*

Calkins, M. W., 148
Calver, P., 166, *179*
Caplan, F., 147, *163*
Caplan, T., 147, *163*
Carlson, J., 155-159, 160, *163*
Carter, R.T., 260, 263, *268*, *291*
Carver, C. S., 39, *54*
Casas, J. M., *291*
Catron, L. S., 201, *223*
Cauce, A. M., 260, *269*
Cecchin, G., 308, *327*
Celentana, M. A., 107, 108, 113, 118, *123*
Chasin, R., 308, *327*
Checkley, K. L., 129, *142*
Chiari, G., 4, 5, *27*
Chiriboga, D. A., 201, *223*
Clarfield, L. E., 24, *27*
Clayre, A., 306, *321*
Coddou, F., 87, 95, *105*
Colbert, S., 307n
Combs, G., 298, 307n, 311n, 314, *322*, *324*, 338, 353, *358*
Costa, P. T., 41, *53*
Coyne, J. C., 307, *321*
Craig, A., 166, 170, *179*, *180*
Craig-Bray, L., 255, 256, 267, *270*
Crocket, K., 14, 29, 309

Crockett, W. H., 172, *180*
Cruz-Janzen, M. I., 256, *269*
Culatta, R., 166, *180*
Cummings, J., 312, *326*
Cummings, N. A., 312, 314, *321*, *326*
Cummins, P., 131, *142*, 183, 188, 236, *248*

Daly, J. E., 129, *142*
Daniel, R. G., 255, *269*
Davison, G., 278, 281
Dawes, R. M., 93, *104*
de Shazer, S., 301, 304, 308, *321*
Dill-Standiford, T. J., 107, *123*
DiLollo, A., vi, vii, xii, 168, 170, 171, 172, 173, 174, 175, *180*, *181*
DiGiueseppe, R., 37, 49, *52*
Dingman, H. F., 133, *142*
Doherty, W. J., 276, *289*
Donovan, R. L., 211, *223*
Douthit, K., 312, *324*
Downing, J. N., 316, *321*
Draguns, J. G., 253, *270*
Drewery, W., 14, *27*
Dryden, W., 184, 188, *199*
Duffy, M., 20, *27*
Duncan, B. L., 93, *105*
Dunnett, G., 236, *248*
Durkin, J. E., 86, *104*
Durocher, L., 299
Dutton, D. G., 127, 131, 132, *142*, *144*

Eagle, M., 278, 281
Early, G., 355, 356, 357, *358*
Ecker, B., v, viii, xii, 3, 4, 9, 11, *27*, *30*, 57, 58, 59, 60, 60n, 61, 69, 79, 79n, 80n, 81, 82, *83*, *84*, 278, 304, 306n, *322*
Edwards, D., 5, *27*
Edwards, L. M., 259, 266, 267, *269*
Efran, J. S., v, viii, xii, 3, 24, *27*, 85, 91, 93, 99, 102, *104*, *104*, 296, 307, 312-313, *322*

Ellis, A., 37, 183, 184, 186-189, 190, 198, 199, 275, 289
Emerson, R. W, 318, 322
Emery, G., 44-45, 52
Empson, W., 307, 322
Epston, D., 3, 4, 12, 14, 29, 30, 151, 163, 173, 175, 180, 181, 304, 309, 310, 338, 359, 322
Epting, F. R., 4, 20, 22, 27, 236, 248, 329, 330, 344, 358, 359
Erhard, W., 95, 105, 297
Erickson, B. A., 311, 327
Erickson, M., 301, 304n, 305, 311, 312, 314, 322
Eron, J. B., 3, 14, 15, 27, 28, 307, 322
Escher, M. C., 316
Evesham, M., 169, 180

Faidley, A. J., v, viii, xii, 20, 34, 52, 107, 108, 109, 113, 114, 118, 123, 205, 224
Feixas, G., 230, 231, 248
Fernandez, C. A., 254, 255, 269
Fernandez-Alvarez, H., 42, 52
Fisch, R., 305, 327
Flaskas, C., 310, 322
Follette, V., 237, 247
Fonagy, P., 244, 250
Ford, D., 148
Forster, J. R., 236
Foster, H., 236, 248
Foster, R., 306n, 322
Fouad, N. A., 291
Fowers, B. J., 277, 289
Frankl, V., 148
Fransella, F., 130, 134, 142, 168, 169-170, 172-173, 180, 232, 245, 247, 248
Freedman, J., 307n, 311n, 338, 353, 358
Freeman, A., 278, 282
Freeman, J., 151, 160-161, 163
Freud, S., 317
Fried, I., 68

Friedman, S., 302n, 305
Frisbie, L. V., 133, 142
Frost, R., 319
Fuertes, J. N., 277, 290
Funderburg, L., 259, 261, 269

Gandhi, M., 89, 92, 92n
Gaines, A. D., 20, 28
Ganley, G. L., 127, 141, 142
Garcia, F., 42, 52
Garcia-Montes, J. M., 20, 29
Gardner, G. T., 16, 28
Garza, Y., vi, viii, xii, 148, 154, 160, 161, 163
Gaskins, P. F., 256, 269
Gergen, K. J., 3, 18, 20, 28, 29, 148, 205, 223, 296, 311n, 315, 317, 322, 323, 340, 341, 359
Gilbert, N., 238, 252
Gilchrist, E., 127, 142
Giles, S., 237, 248
Gillem, A. R., 254, 255, 269
Gillig, S. E., 20, 27
Gillman-Smith, I., 238, 239, 240, 248, 252
Giorigi, A., 277, 289
Gioscia, V., 95, 105
Gladwell, M., 299, 323
Glaser, B. G., 277, 283-284, 289
Glover, T., 214
Glover, V., 214, 223
Goin, M., 103, 105
Goldberg, L. R., 39, 52
Goldberg, S. A., 166, 180
Goldfried, M., 278, 280
Goncalves, O. F., 116, 122
Gondolf, E. W., 127, 129, 142
Gonzales, N., 260, 269
Gonzalez, R. C., 16, 28
Goodman, L. A, 333, 334, 338, 339, 359
Goolishian, H. A., 17, 27, 148, 307n, 321
Gordon, D., 237, 248

366

Gottman, J. M., 202, *223*
Gottwald, S. R., 177, *181*
Goulding, B., 298, 301, 304, *323*
Goulding, M., 301, 304, *323*
Gournay, K., 237, 238, *251, 252*
Granvold, D., vi, viii, xii, 33, 43, *52*, 148, 149, *163*, 202, 204, 206, 207, 208-210, 212, 214, 217, 221, *224, 225*
Greenberg, L. S., 232, *248*, 278
Greene, M. A., 93, *104*, 312-313, *323*
Gregson, D., 91
Griffin, B. L., 3, 4, *30*
Guidano, V. F., 148, 204, *224*
Guthrie, A. F., 107, 111, 117, *122, 123*
Gutsch. K. U., 31

Haken, H., 148
Haley, J., 305, 314, *323*
Halfond, M. M., 177, *181*
Hall, C. C. I., 253, *269*
Hallschmid, C. A., 129, 130, *142*
Hancock, K., 166, *180*
Hanson, C., 190, *199*
Harding, S., 148
Hardy, K. V., 332, 355-356, *359*
Harris, J. R., 93, *105*
Harrison, E., 166, 178, *180, 181*
Hart, S., 132, *142*
Harter, S., 237, *247, 249*
Haruki, Y., 148
Havens, L., 314, *323*
Hayek, F., 148
Hayes, S., 92, *105*
Heffner, K. P., *104, 104*
Held, B. S., 4, *28*, 316, *323*
Helms, J. E., 333, *359*
Henriksen, R. C., Jr., 267, *269*
Henry, R. M., 236, *250*
Hermans, H. J. M., 178, *180*
Hicks, G., 306n, *322*
Hill, T., 284, *289*

Hiller, T., 308, *328*
Hillman, J., 300, 313, *323*
Hinkle, D. N., 231, *248*
Hiraga, Y., 260, *269*
Hoffman, L., 298n, 311n, *323*
Holland, J. M., 244, *248*
Hollon, S., 278
Homans, G., 315
Honos-Webb, L., 20, *28*
Horley, J., vi, viii, xii, 130, 132, 133, 135, 139, *142, 143*
Horowitz, M. J., 306n, *323*
Houston, J., 130, *143*, 240, *248*
Hoyt, M. F., vii, viii, xii, 4, *28*, 149, 151, *163*, 295, 296, 298, 299, 301, 302, 302n, 303, 308, 311n, 313, 314, 317, 319, *323, 324, 327*
Hubble, M. A., 93, *105*
Hulley, L., v, viii, xii, 3, 4, 9, 11, *27*, 57, 58, 59, 60, 60n, 61, 79, 79n, 81, 82, *83*, 304, 306n, *322*

Ivey, A. E., 253, 257, 258, 267, *271, 291*

Jackson, B. L., 211, *223*, 236, *249*
Jackson, M. L., 253, *269*
Jackson, S., 236, *249*
James, W., 148, 300, *324*
Janis, I. L., 208, 210, *224*
Jensen, M., *291*
Jezer, M., 165, *180*
Jenkins, A., 278
Johnson, A., vi, viii, xii
Johnson, W., 165
Johnston, S. M., 212, *226*
Jones, S., 139, *143*
Joxe, A., 334, *359*

Kandel, E. R., 58, *83*
Keeney, B., 308, *324*
Keillor, G., 319

Keller, E. F., 148

Kelly, G. A., 3, 4, 6, 9, 21, *28*, 57, *83*, 102, *105*, 107, 108, 109, 110, *122*, 129-130, 132, 133, 134, 137, *143*, 148, 168, 175, 178, *180*, 184, 186, 187, 188, 197, *199*, 231, 232, 235, 236, 237, 238, 240, 241, 245, 246, *249*, 256, 266, *269*, 288, *289*, 297, 301, 303, *324*, 332, 339, 341, 342-343, 343-345, 348, 352, *358*, *359*

Kelly, J. B., 210, *226*

Kelly, T., 273, 276, *289*

Kerr, M. E., 99, *105*

Ketcham, K., 296, *324*

Kierkegaard, S., 317

King, E. W., 256, *269*

King, S., 297, *324*

Kitson, G. C., 211, *224*

Klein, R. E., 311, *327*

Knorr-Cetina, K., 148-149

Koch, C., 68

Korgen, K. O., 254, 255, 256, 266, *269*

Korngold, E., 295

Korzybski, A., 87, *105*

Kottman, T., 146, 147, 148, 153-159, 160, 161, *163*

Kreiman, G., 68, *83*

Kroll, J., 103, *105*

Kropp, R. , 132, *142*

Kuehlwein, K. T., 296, *326*

Kuhr, A., 166, 167, *180*

Kurtz, E., 296, *324*

LaFromboise, T., *291*

Lampropoulos, G. K., 7, *28*

Landfield, A. W., 109, 110, *122*, 234, 236, *249*

Landreth, G. L., 145, 145n, 146-147, 148, 152-153, 153-159, 160, 161, 162, *163*

Landridge, D., 107, *122*

Lane, L. G., 236, *249*

Laszloffy, T. A., 332, 355-356, *359*

Latta, R. E., 333, *359*

LeDoux, J. E., 58, *84*

Lee, J., v, viii

Lee, W. M. L., 260, *270*

Leitner, L. M., v, ix, xii, 20, *28*, 34, 35, *52*, 107, 108-109, 110, 113, 114, 116, 117, 118, *122*, 205, *224*, 229, 235, *247*, *249*, 312, *321*

Levitt, H. M., vi, ix, xii, 279, 283, 284, 287, *289*, *290*, *291*

Lewandowski, A. M., 20, 21, *30*, 205, *225*, 245, *250*

Lewin, K., 303

Liang, B., 333, *359*

Linscott, J., 37, 49, *52*

Llewellyn, S., 236, *248*

Lobovits, D., 151, *163*

Lonner, W. J., 253, *270*

Lorenzini, R., 184, *199*

Lukens, M. D., 3, *27*, 85, 102, *104*, 296, 307, *322*

Lukens, R. J., 3, *27*, 85, 102, *104*, 296, 307, *322*

Lund, T. W., 3, 14, 15, *27*, *28*, 307, *322*

Luterman, D.M., 166, *180*

Lutwyche, G., 241, *251*

Lyddon, W. J., 32, 33, 34, 39, 43, 44, 45, 48, 50, *52*, *53*

Machado, A., 298, 298n, *324*

Madanes, C., 305, *324*

Mahoney, M. J., xii, 3, 4, 24, *28*, 29, 31-32, 33, 34, 35, 36, 38, 39, 40-41, 42, 43, 44, 45, 51, *52*, *53*, 148, 149, *163*, 186, 204, 217, 221, *224*, 225, 295-296, 303, 313, *324*, *325*, *326*

Mancuso, J. C., xii

Manese, J. E., *291*

Maniacci, M., 155-159, 160, *163*

Mann, L., 208, 210, *224*

Manning, W. H., 167, 168, 169, 170, 172, 173, 175, *180, 181*
Marks, I. M., 133, *143*
Markus, H., 204, *225*
Marquis, A., 312, *324*
Marrow, A. J., 303-304, *325*
Marsh, B., 352, *359*
Marshall, M. L., 139, *143*
Martin, J., 16, *29*
Mascolo, M. F., 255, 256, 267, *270*
Mason, C., 260, *269*
Matthews, W. J., 316, *325*
Maturana, H. R., 3, *29*, 85, 87, 88, 95, 101, 103, *105*, 148
Mazzucco, A., 139, *143*
McCrae, R. R., 41, *53*
McGee, P., 190, *199*
McLain, D. L., 40, *53*
McLaughlin, M., 87, 87n
McNamee, S., 3, 4, 18, 20, *28, 29*, 206, *225*, 341, 343, 357, *358, 359*
McWilliams, S. A., 297, *325*
Mead, G. H., 315
Meichenbaum, D., 33, *53*
Mendez, C. L., 87, 95, *105*
Merluzzi, T.V., 236-237, *249*
Messer, S. B., 7, *29*
Metcalfe, C., 238, 241, 244, *249, 251, 252*
Miller, S. D., 93, *105*
Miller, W. R., 305, *325*
Milner, B., 58, *83*
Milosz, C., 318, *325*
Minuchin, S., 310, *325*
Monk, G., 14, *27, 29*, 173, *181*, 273, *290*, 309, *325*
Moore, M. K., 237, *247*
Morokoff, P., 254, 259, *270*
Morris, J. B., 236, *249*
Morton, R. J., 37, *53*
Mother Teresa, 90
Muran, C., 31, *53*

Murphy, C. M., 132, *143*

Nakashima, C. L., 259, *270*
Nakazawa, D. J., 256, *270*
Nath, S. R., 99, *105*
Nazario, A., Jr. , 236, *248*, 355, 356, 357, *358*
Neimeyer, G. J., v, ix, 9, *29*, 34, 37, 43, 44, *53*, 236-237, *249*, 311n, *325*
Neimeyer, R. A., vi, ix, xi, xii, 3, 4, 5, 20, 22, *29*, 32, 33, 34, 39, 44, 45, 46, 47, 48, 49, 50, 51, *53*, 81, *84*, 149, *163*, 168, 170, 173, 175, *180, 181*, 185, *200*, 202, 211, 215-216, 217, *225*, 232, 237, 241, 244, *247, 248, 250*, 255, 256, 267, *270*, 273, 274, 278, 283, 287, *290*, 296, 299, 302n, 303, 309n, 313n, 316, 317, *325, 326*
Nelson, M. C., 134, *143*
Nietzsche, F., 103, *105*
Nishimura, N., vi, ix, xii, 254, 255, 259, 260, 261-262, 266, 267, *270*
Norcross, J. C., 51, *53*
Nurius, P. S., 204, *225*
Nuzzo, M. L., xii, 4, 5, *27*

O'Donohue, W., 312, *326*
O'Hanlon, B., 8, 22, *29*, 301
O'Hara, M., 229, *247*, 312, *321*
Ogloff, J. P., 132, *142*
Oliver, M., 319, 320, *326*
Olson, D. L., 296, *326*
Onslow, M., 166, 178, *180, 181*
Ordonez, N., 260, *269*
Osgood, C. E., 133, *143*

Packman, A., 178, *181*
Paniagua, F. A., 253, *270*
Parham, T. A., 253, *270*
Paris, M. E., vii, ix, xii, 329, *359*
Parker, L., 307, *326*

Parker, S., 236, *247*
Parry, G., 243, *250*
Paymar, M., 127, *143*
Payne, M., 14, *29*, 175, *181*
Pedersen, P. B., 253, 257, 258, 267, *270*,
    271, 277, *290*
Pedrotti, J. T., 259, 266, 267, *269*
Pence, E., 127, *143*
Penn, W. I., 240, 245, *247*
Perez-Alvarez, M., 20, *29*
Perkins, W. H., 166, 167, *181*
Perlman, E., 307, *326*
Pfenninger, D. T., 108, 116, *123*
Phelps, E. A., 58, *84*
Phillip, D., v, ix
Phillips, K. A., 149, *164*
Phoenix, A., 255, 256, 260, 261, **271**
Piaget, J., 149
Pittman, F., 310
Plexico, L., 172, *181*
Poerksen, B., 3, *29*
Polkinghorne, D., 278, 283
Ponterotto, J. G., 277, *290*, *291*
Popper, K., *358*, *359*
Potter, J., 5, *27*
Power, R., 190, *199*
Power, T. G., 129, *142*
Prata, G., 308, *327*
Previti, D., 209
Priest, R., vi, ix, xii
Prochaska, J. O., 51, *53*
Procter, H. G., 240, *250*

Quaite, A., *252*
Quinsey, V. L., 133, 139, *143*

Radley, P. L., 240, 245, *247*
Raskin, J. D., v, ix, xi, xii, 3, 4, 5, 7, 20,
    21, *29*, *30*, 32, 48, 49, 51, *53*, 81, *84*,
    185, *200*, 202, 205, *225*, 245, *250*,
    296, 297, 302n, 303, 313n, *326*, 361

Ravenette, T., xii
Ray, D., 147, *163*
Rennie, D., 278, *289*, 290
Richardson, A., 243, *250*
Richardson, F. C., 277, *289*
Riley, T., 241, *251*, *252*
Rivers, P. C., 236, *249*
Roberts, A.C., 254, 259, *270*
Roberts-Clarke, I., 254, 259, *270*
Rocchi, M., 184, *199*
Rockquemore, K. A., 267, *270*
Roethke, T., 319, *326*
Rogers, C. R., 151, 274, 279, *290*, 331, 351,
    359
Rollnick, S., 305, *325*
Root, M. P. P., 254, 255, 259, *270*, *271*
Rosen, H., 296, *326*
Rosenthal, D., 276, *290*
Rossotti, N., 238, *251*
Roth, A., 244, *250*
Roth, S., 308, *327*
Roysircar, G., 277, *290*
Rubin, S., 97
Rush, J., 44-45, *52*
Rustin, L., 166, 167, *180*
Rychlak, J., 149
Ryle, G., 313

Saferstein, J., 34, *53*
Safran, J., 31, *53*
St. Augustine, 309n
Saleebey, D., 205, *225*
Salmon, P., xii
Sánchez, V., 230
Santoma, S., 42, *52*
Sarbin, T. R., xii
Sartorius, N. H., 133, *143*
Sartre, J. P., 101, *105*
Sassaroli, S., 184, *199*
Saunders, D. G., 127, 128, 132, *143*
Saúl, L. A., 230, 231, *248*

Sayama, M., 314, *321*
Scanzoni, J., 212, 219, *226*
Schaeffer, C., 147, *163*
Scheier, M. F., 39, *54*
Schwartz, R., 97, *104*, *105*
Seashore, C., 165
Seligman, M. E. P., 93, *105*
Selvini Palazzoli, M., 308, *327*
Semerari, A., 230, *250*
Sexton, T. L., 3, 4, *30*
Shakespeare, W., 311, 317
Shalif, Y., 307n, *327*
Shames, G. H., 166, *181*
Shaw, B., 44-45, *52*
Shaw, G. B., *104*, *105*
Sheehan, J., 166, *181*
Shelley, P. B., 319
Short, D., 311, 312, *327*
Shostrom, E., 274, 275, *290*
Silverman, F. H., 177, *181*
Simpkins, A. M., 304n, *327*
Simpkins, C. A., 304n, *327*
Sireling, L., 241, *251*, *252*
Sisemore, D. A., 31
Slater, P., 184, *200*
Slife, B. D., 276, *290*
Sluzki, C., 304n, *327*
Smith, A. F., 276, *290*
Smith, C., 150, 151, *163*
Smothermon, R., 89, 95, 96, 97, *105*
Soler-Baillo, J., v, ix, xii
Solomon, A., 348
Sommers-Flanagan, J., 34, *54*
Sommers-Flanagan, R., 34, *54*
Sparks, E., 333, *359*
Speight, S. L., 277, *291*
Spence, D., 278
Squire, L. R., 58, *83*
Stack, S., 212, *226*
Stanley, S., 209, *226*
Starkweather, C. W., 167, 177, *181*

Steier, H., 355, 356, 357, *358*
Stevens, C. D., 257, *271*
Stevens, W., 319, *327*
Stewart, T., 170, *181*
Stockton, L., 232, *249*
Stojnov, D., 257, 258, *271*
Strauss, A. L., 277, 283-284, *289*
Strupp, H. H., 276, *289*
Suci, G. J., 133, *143*
Sue, D., 253, 254, 255, 256, 259, 271, 273, 277, *291*
Sue, D. W., 253, 254, 255, 256, 257, 258, 259, 267, 271, 273, 277, *291*
Sugarman, J, 16, *29*
Suyemoto, K. L., 256, 262, *271*
Sweeney, D. S., 146, *164*

Tannenbaum, P., 133, *143*
Tarrant, R., 209, 210, *224*
Taylor, R., 101-102, *105*
Thelen, E., 149
Thompson, C. A., 254, 255, *269*
Thoreau, H. D., 307, *327*
Tinsley-Jones, H., 277, *291*
Tizard B., 255, 256, 260, 261, *271*
Tjeltveit, A. C., 276, *291*
Tolle, E., 317-318, *327*
Tomishima, S., 256, *271*
Toomey, B., 11, *27*, *30*, 57, 61, 69, 80n, 82, *83*, 84
Toporek, R. L., 277, *290*
Travis, L. E., 165
Trimble, J. E., 253, *270*
Trovato, F., 212, *226*
Truneckova, D., 236, *250*
Trusty, J., 267, *269*
Tschudi, F., 231, *250*
Tureern, R. M., 20, *27*
Tweed, R. G., 127, 131, *144*

Van Riper, C., 165, 166, *181*
Vanasek, F. J., 133, *142*
Varela, F. J., 3, *29*, 88, 93, 101, 103, *105*, 149
Vasco, A. B., 46, 47, 48, *54*
Vasquez-Nutall, E., *291*
Vera, E. M., 277, *291*
Viney, L. L., 3, 4, 22, *30*, 48, *54*, 170-171, *181*, 235, 236, 244, 245, *248*, *249*, *250*, *251*
von Foerster, H., 149
von Glaserfeld, E., 3, *30*, 149
Vygotsky, L., 315

Walker, B. M., 257, *271*
Walker, L. E. A., 127, 141, *144*
Wallerstein, J. S., 210, *226*
Wardle, F., 256, *269*
Watson, S., 46, 48, 49, *54*, 185, *200*, 230, 238, 239, 240, 241, 244, 246, *247*, *248*, *251*, *252*
Watts, A., 89, *105*
Watts, R. E., vi, ix, xii, 149, 155-159, 160, *164*
Watzlawick, P., 149, 295, 305, *327*
Weakland, J. H., 305, *327*
Wehrly, B., 254, 255, 262, *271*
Weimer, W., 149
Weintraub, S. R., 333, *359*
Weishaar, M. E., 34, 45, *52*
Weiss, R. S., 211, *226*
Wender, P., 308, *327*
Westbrook, M. T., 170-171, *181*
Whitaker, C., 301
White, M., 3, 4, 12, 14, *30*, 173, 175, *180*, *181*, 298, 301, 304, 305, 309, 310, 313, 314, *322*, *327*, 338, *359*
Whitman, W., 305, *328*
Wilchins, R., 350, *359*
Williams, D. C., vi, ix, xii, 279, 283, 287, *290*, *291*

Williams, P. J., 333-334, *359*
Williams, R., 168, *181*
Williams, R. L., 31
Williams, T., 300-301, *328*
Williams, T. K., 259, *271*
Winslade, J., 14, *27*, *29*, 173, *181*, 309
Winter, D. A., vi, ix, 3, 4, 9, 22, *30*, 46, 48, 49, *54*, 130, 131, 132, 141, *144*, 185, *200*, 230, 231, 232, 236, 237, 238, 240, 241, 244, 245, 246, *247*, *249*, *250*, *251*, *252*
Wittgenstein, L., 315
Wong, Y. J., 16, 18, *30*
Woolfus, B., 127, 132, 140, *144*

Yalom, I. D., 236, *252*
Ybarra, M. A., 20, *27*
Yeats, W. B., 316, *328*

Zeig, J. K., 312, *328*
Ziegler, P., 317, *324*, *328*
Zeiss, A. M., 212, *226*
Zeiss, R. A., 212, *226*
Zimmerman, J. L., 313, *327*

Subject Index

Adolescents, 183, 184, 185, 188, 189
    acting out, 189, 190, 198
    coping, 195
    defensiveness of, 196
    depression in, 195
    relationships with adults, 184, 185,
        189, 193
    resistance of, 191
    substance use in, 188, 189, 190, 191,
        193, 195, 196, 198
Agency, 204
Ambiguity, 40
Anger, 190, 196
Anti-symptom position, 59-60, 62, 81
Antirealism, 4-5
Assessment techniques, 230
Assimilative integration, 7
Attitudes
    therapists, 254, 258
Avoidance, 99-100

Behavior
    as related to construing, 21
    as related to change, 22, 23
Biological reductionism, 109
Body
    experience of personal meaning by,
        115-117
    illnesses and, 119
    invasions of, 113-114
    and meaning making, 111-112
    and psychopathology, 114
    and sex, 120-121
    touch and, 119-120
    vs. verbal reconstructions, 112
    view of, 113-114
Body invasions, 113-114
Body meanings, 118-119
Brief therapy, 230, 301, 302, 314

Case examples
    "A.C.," 137-140
    abandonment, 19, 20
    agoraphobia, 90-92, 237
    anxiety, 22, 118, 233, 242, 243
    assertiveness, 231
    attachment, 61-78, 80
    attention deficit hyperactivity
        disorder, 58, 59
    "Barry Potter," 233-235
    borderline personality disorder, 238,
        240
    childhood abuse, 8, 9
    coherence therapy, 61-77
    defensiveness, 196
    depression, 24, 25
    divorce, 217, 218, 219
    domestic violence, 137-140
    family communication, 193
    "Gloria," 274-276
    high blood pressure, 115-117
    indecision, 117
    marital problems, 8, 9, 12, 17, 18, 120
    multiracial client, 263-266
    obesity, 14, 15
    over eating, 61-78, 80
    parental/child relationship, 19, 20
    "Reiko Thompson," 263-266
    relationship problems, 10
    resistant adolescent, 191, 193
    sexual assault, 14, 15
    sexual issues, 232
    smoking, 96
    substance abuse, 137-140, 193, 195,
        196, 197, 199
    "Susan," 61-77, 77-81
    stuttering, 176, 177
    vocational issues, 19, 20, 22, 86, 88
    wedding ring ritual, 222

Challenging clients, 285, 288
Corrective vs. creative approach, 274-276,
  288-289
  by therapists, 285, 287, 288
  studies of, 271-282, 283-286
Change processes, 205, 223, 331
Changing Ways program, 128-129, 137, 141
Child centered play therapy
  assumptions, 145, 150
  and brief approaches, 160, 161
  and constructivist therapies, 148,
    149, 151-153, 162
  developmental perspective, 146, 161
  and diversity, 154
  esteem building, 157
  goals, 152, 153
  limit setting, 158, 159
  reflecting content, 156, 157
  reflecting feelings, 156
  returning responsibility, 157, 158
  research concerning, 147, 148
  role of parents and teachers, 159, 160
  role of play, 146-148
  role of therapist, 155
  therapeutic alliance, 147
  toys and materials, 153-155
  tracking behavior, 156
Circumspection-Preemption-Control Cycle,
  238, 239
Classism, 335
Clients
  coping, 195, 205, 214
  negative construing, 185, 186, 187
  resiliency, 205, 206, 217
  strengths, 205, 214, 217, 305
Cognitively oriented therapies, 32, 44, 45
  cognitions, 34
  goals, 45
  REBT, 34
  therapeutic practice, 34
  therapeutic relationship, 34

Cognitive behavioral therapy, 32, 45
  techniques, 47
Cognitive structure, 183, 184, 193, 198
Coherence empathy, 70
Coherence therapy, 9-11, 57-82
  anti-symptom position, 62, 81
  coherence empathy, 70
  as DOBT, 9
  as different from counteractive
    methods, 60, 80
  discovery, 61, 69, 70, 75, 76
  experiential, 9, 11, 61, 64, 67, 69, 80
  emotional truths, 9-11, 59, 66, 67, 70,
    71, 73
  and change, 60
  imaginal methods, 68
  and implicit knowledge, 11
  integration, 61, 67-69, 73, 75, 76, 79, 80
  and juxtaposition, 10, 11, 79, 82
  methodology of, 57-59, 61, 69, 70, 79,
    80-82
  and neuropsychology, 11, 57, 61, 68, 79
  principles, 57, 82
  pro-symptom position, 10, 59, 63-66,
    68, 70, 78, 79, 80, 82
  and reconsolidation, 11, 79
  reparative attachment, 69
  resolution, 77
  role of unconscious, 9, 60, 63, 72
  and symptoms, 10, 11, 57, 58, 59, 68,
    69, 72, 73, 77, 81
  symptom coherence, 59, 60
  symptom deprivation, 63, 64, 65
  therapist's role, 68, 69
  transformation, 61, 69
Collaborative empiricism, 188
Collaborative therapy, 13, 19, 185, 198,
  223, 234, 257, 301, 314, 316
Community, 344
Confrontation, 287
Construct systems, 7

Constructions, 34, 108-110, 130, 178, 205, 341
   personal, 6, 107, 109, 184, 205, 351,
     352, 357, 358
   social, 349, 352, 357
Constructive alternativism, 19, 129, 186-188,
     221, 232, 331, 332, 348, 352
Constructivist philosophy, 3-4
Constructivist Psychology Network, 362-363
Constructivist psychotherapy, 201, 206,
     215, 229, 253, 256, 257, 265, 266,
     268, 274, 297, 301, 302, 304, 305,
     307, 308, 310, 313, 314, 316, 317, 319
   as art, 26
   assessment, 230
   assumptions, 149
   as contrasted with medical model, 5
   clinical strategies, 4
   diversity, 4, 7
   divorce, 202, 216
   focus, 7
   goals, 7, 45, 150
   limitations of, 267
   and person centered therapies, 150, 151
   pathology, 205
   process, 34-36, 38, 45, 48
   relevance to practice, 4,
   ritual, 221
   role of symptoms, 24, 149
   techniques, 7, 25
   teleological approach, 35
   theory of human change, 24
   therapeutic relationship, 43
   time limited, 229, 230
Context
   defined, 86-88
   psychotherapy as, 88-89
Context-centered therapy, 85-104
   abstraction, 85, 86
   avoidance, 99, 103
   category mistake, 88
   content, 85

   context, 86-89, 97
   as differs from other theories, 86, 89, 91
   discovery, 100
   emotional contradiction, 87
   entitlement, 99
   goals, 88, 89, 91, 92, 102-104
   mastery, 99, 103
   meaning of life, 102
   mind, 85, 89-94, 96-99
   observation, 100
   process, 85, 86
   resolution, 88
   responsibility, 96, 97, 99, 100
   self, 85, 89, 90, 93, 94, 96
   structure determinism, 85
   therapeutic alliance, 93
   therapist assumptions, 101
Core construing, 109, 110-111, 112, 113,
     114, 116, 117, 118, 119, 185
Countertransference, 314
Creativity approaches, 274, 288, 319
Cultural competence, 253
Culture, 242, 254

Diagnosis, 20
   as socially constructed, 20-21
Diagnostic and Statistical Manual of Mental
    Disorders (DSM-IV TR), 20-21, 238
   constructivist criticism of, 21
Direction vs. discovery, 313-314
Discovery, 100
Diversity, 40, 41, 253
Divorce, 201, 202, 206, 207, 215
   as loss, 206, 211, 212, 214, 222
   cognitive process, 208
   constructivist treatment, 216
   crisis, 212,
   decision making, 206, 207, 208, 209,
     210
   recovery from, 213, 214
   stages of, 207

Domestic violence, 127
  and treatment approaches, 127, 128, 132
  and treatment research, 128-141

Embodiment, 107, 342, 343
Emotions, 39, 190, 197, 198, 199, 203, 216
  as change agents, 203, 216, 223
Empathy, 25, 70, 108, 256, 267, 274
Entitlement, 99-100
Epistemology, 31
  assessment, 37
  interventions, 44, 45, 46
  rationalist vs. constructivist, 33-51
  shifts in, 31, 32
  therapeutic practice, 32
Essentialism, 340
EST training, 297
Evidence based practice, 229, 243, 244, 312
Evolution of Psychotherapy, 298
Experiencing, 204, 332
Experience Cycle, 231
Experiential personal constructivism, 07
  awareness exercises, 115
  as based on sociality corollary, 108
  bodily sensations, 111, 112, 115, 116, 118, 119, 121
  role of the body, 113, 114, 116, 117, 122
  role of society, 111
ROLE relationships, 108, 110, 114, 116, 117, 120
Symptoms in, 108
  therapeutic implications, 115
  touch, 119, 120
  transference and, 121
  and trauma, 113
  and verbal psychology, 112
  verbal understandings, 112
Experiential realities, 5, 24
Experientially focusing methods, 51

Feminist counseling, 333, 335
Fixed role therapy, 6-9, 188, 232, 234, 235
  group, 236
Fundamental shift, 10, 13

Gap, 14-15
Gay men, 335
Genuineness, 274
Grief, 299
Grounded theory, 277, 283, 284
Group therapy, 235-237
  and PCT, 236, 237, 238, 239, 240
  PCT examples of, 237-240

Healing vs. treatment, 311-313
Hostility, 243
Homophobia, 334, 337, 347
Human nature, 32
Humanism, 317, 351
Humanness, 346, 347, 349, 351, 352, 353

Idiographic vs. nomothetic, 316-317
Implicit memory 11, 58-61, 64-66, 78, 79
Intra vs. inter, 315-316
Interpersonal Transaction Group, 236, 237

Joining vs. believing, 314-315
Journaling, 216, 217, 232

Knowing, 34, 41
  and coherence therapy, 57, 58, 66, 68, 70

Laddering, 231, 232, 233
Language, 32, 45, 149, 305, 310
  in child centered play therapy, 152, 161, 162
  in context centered therapy, 87, 93-95, 97, 98
Lesbian, 335, 336
Lived experience, 6

Marriage, 201, 202
Mastery, 99-100
Meaning, 20, 31
  in constructivist therapies, 149
  as construing, 4, 5, 6, 7, 110
  in context-centered therapy, 85, 88
  in experiential personal constructivism,
    108, 110-113, 119, 122
  as idiographic, 20, 24
  in personal construct psychology, 107
Meaning based practice, 5-6
Meaning making
  constructions of, 3, 9, 183, 186, 202,
    263, 296, 319, 329, 336, 337,
    338, 339, 340, 343
  context, 242, 267, 331, 333, 340, 355
  and embodiment, 107-122
  interpersonal, 316, 339, 343, 350
  personal, 183, 186, 202, 242, 263,
    296, 315, 316, 330, 335, 337-341,
    343, 348, 355
  social, 203, 242, 315, 330, 331, 335,
    337-341, 343, 345, 346, 348
  reconstruction, 211, 212, 299
Meaning systems, 25, 26, 32, 34
Metaphors, 31, 296
Memoing, 278
Mind, 89-99
  contrasted with self, 94
Multicultural counseling, 253, 254, 257,
    262, 264, 265, 333-336, 355
  theory of, 257-258
Multiculturalism, 273, 276-277
Multiracial clients, 253, 254, 255, 256, 259,
    262, 263, 268
  acceptance, 256, 260, 261
  counseling of, 253-268
  identity development, 260-262, 265
  influence of parents, 260-262, 264
  therapist attitudes towards, 258

Narrative constructivism, 303, 319
Narrative solutions therapy, 14
  narrative solutions, 14
  and preferred view of self, 14, 15
  techniques of, 14
Narrative therapy, 11, 32, 173, 175, 264,
    267, 303, 310, 338, 339, 353, 354
  dominant life narratives, 11, 13
  externalizing the problem, 12
  narratives/stories, 11, 12
  and problem-saturated stories, 12, 13
  and restorying, 12
  and reauthoring, 13
  techniques of, 12, 13, 14, 174
National Health Service, 229, 237, 240,
    241, 243, 244, 245
Natural givens, 340
Not-knowing approach, 15-18

Objectification, 259, 345-348
Oedipal conflict, 86
Objectivity, 34, 39
Observation, 100
Ontology, 33
Openness to experience, 41, 42
Oppression, 334, 337

Perception, 300, 310
Personal agency, 31
Personal constructs, 6, 10, 26, 57, 60, 107,
    129, 132, 135, 215, 331, 342, 346, 356
Personal construct psychology, 107-110,
    130, 229, 235, 240, 241, 243-246,
    257, 288, 301, 330, 332, 339, 340, 342
  choice corollary, 168
  constructive alternativism, 129
  repertory grid, 134-139
  self-characterization, 132
  and stuttering, 168, 169, 179
  theory of, 6, 129, 178
  view of domestic violence, 130-132

Personal construct psychotherapy, 6-9, 107-122, 229-247
Political, 242, 332-335, 350
   arguments, 336
   in therapy, 335, 336, 358
   place in counseling, 335
Politics
   and violence, 333-339
Postmodern psychotherapy, 203
Privilege, 299, 345, 349, 351, 352, 356
Pro-symptom position, 10, 59-61, 62-70, 72, 78-82
Problem identification, 240, 304, 305, 330
   personal, 330, 332, 333, 338, 339, 348, 355, 356
   social, 242, 331-333, 338, 348, 355, 356
Psychodynamic therapies, 32
Psychotherapists,
   research, 36-47
Public health, 229

Qualitative approaches, 277, 283, 284, 289

Race
   as a construct, 254
   classifications, 254
   definition, 255
   identity development, 254, 255, 260, 266
Racism, 267, 334, 337, 347, 349
Rational Emotive Therapy (RET), 275
Rational Emotive Behavior Therapy (REBT), 34, 183-185, 187-191, 193, 194, 196-198
   and constructivism, 185, 186, 188, 198
Rationalist therapy, 40, 43, 44
   vs. constructivist therapy, 33-36
Rationality, 18-20, 33, 49, 302-303, 319
   and constructions, 18, 26

Reality, 3, 9, 11, 24, 26, 33, 296, 297, 341, 350
   antirealism, 4-5
   as idealism, 5
   experiential reality, 5
Reframing, 305-308
Repertory grid technique, 134-135, 136-140, 169, 230, 233, 235-237, 245
Resistance, 287, 313
Right/wrong, 99-100
Rituals, 221
   unsent letter, 222
   wedding ring, 222
Role, 332, 343, 345-347, 352, 356
Role relationships, 108, 110, 116, 117, 213, 235, 343-345

Schizoaffective, 184
Schizophrenia, 183, 240, 245
Self, 93-98
   contrasted with mind, 94
Self awareness, 35, 38, 39
Self characterization, 232
Self harm, 240, 241, 244
Selfhood, 204
Semantic differential procedure, 133-135
Sex, 120-121
Sexism, 334, 337, 347
Sexual issues, 208, 215, 217, 232
Slot rattling, 238
Social constructionism, 15, 32, 298, 329, 330, 302, 303, 315, 317, 332, 338-341
   and language, 15-17
   method of, 16
   as opposed to diagnosis, 16
   and problem-saturated narratives, 16
   and role of society and culture, 16
   and social construction, 16
   as similar to multicultural and feminist therapies, 16
   as strength-based, 16

techniques of, 16
therapy as co-constructed, 17
Social constructionist therapy, 15-18, 32,
    302n, 313n
Social context, 329-333, 339, 352, 356
Social contract, 334-336, 347
Social justice, 277, 333, 334, 344, 351
Sociality, 332, 343-345, 347
Solution focused therapy, 8, 14, 302
Sparkling moments, 13, 173
Speech language pathology, 165, 166
    and research, 166
Strategic therapy, 14
Stuttering, 165-179
    behavioral approaches, 167, 178
    cognitive anxiety, 170, 171
    cognitive complexity, 172, 173
    constructivist approach, 166,168
    emotional response, 169
    and narrative therapy, 173, 175
    and reconstruction workbook, 175-177
    and relapse, 166, 177
    research, 169-173
    treatment approaches, 167
Stories, 296, 310
Substance abuse, 183-185, 191, 193, 195-197,
    199, 305
Suicide, 203, 212, 241
Superordinate constructs, 231
Symptom deprivation, 63
Systems therapy, 32

Technical eclecticism, 48, 49
Therapeutic relationship, 6, 12, 13, 16, 25, 26
    as collaborative, 13, 19, 185, 198, 223,
        234, 257, 301, 314, 316
Therapist
    attitudes, 254, 258
    personal style, 42
    practice, 32
    self awareness, 257, 258

and self-care, 51
    values, 276, 277, 279, 280
Therapist-client difference, 288
Therapy treatment manuals
    constructivist criticism of, 23-26
Threat, 351
Time limited therapy, 229, 230
Treatment manuals,
    criticism of, 23-25
Truth, 295, 341
Two-chair technique, 232

Unconditional positive regard, 274
Unsent letter technique, 222-223

Value conversion, 276
Values, 273, 276, 279
    of clients, 276, 279, 280, 287
    influencing therapy, 279, 281-284
    of therapists, 208, 276, 277, 279, 280
Violence, 331-333, 337, 344, 346, 348, 349
    as oppression, 337, 338, 344, 346,
        349, 350
    interplay between social and
        personal, 338, 344, 346, 350
    social, 337, 338, 341, 345-348, 350, 356

Printed in the United States
201036BV00003B/1-18/A